Instruments and Related Concepts at the Syntax-Semantics Interface

Koen Van Hooste

d|u|p

Hana Filip, Peter Indefrey, Laura Kallmeyer, Sebastian Löbner,
Gerhard Schurz & Robert D. Van Valin, Jr. (eds.)

Dissertations in Language and Cognition

5

Koen Van Hooste

2018

Instruments and Related Concepts at the Syntax-Semantics Interface

d|u|p

**Bibliografische Information
der Deutschen Nationalbibliothek**
Die Deutsche Nationalbibliothek verzeichnet diese
Publikation in der Deutschen Nationalbibliografie;
detaillierte bibliografische Daten sind im Internet
über http://dnb.dnb.de abrufbar.

D 61

© düsseldorf university press, Düsseldorf 2018
http://www.dupress.de
Einbandgestaltung: Doris Gerland, Christian Horn, Albert Ortmann
Einbandgrafik: Koen Van Hooste
Satz: Thomas Gamerschlag, Koen Van Hooste
Herstellung: Docupoint GmbH, Barleben

Gesetzt aus der Linux Libertine
ISBN 978-3-95758-059-7

To Heinz Thomas, he will be sorely missed

Acknowledgments

I would like to express my gratitude to the Sonderforschungsbereich 991 "The Structure of Representations in Language, Cognition, and Science" (supported by the German Science Foundation – DFG) for funding and supporting me throughout my dissertation project. I would like to thank Robert D. Van Valin, Jr. for his supervision these past four years. Our conversations greatly inspired me with confidence regarding my scientific creativity and abilities. When I declared my intention to merge Force Dynamics with RRG, he enthusiastically supported the undertaking despite the daunting challenges it posed and still poses. Thomas Gamerschlag has been the post-doc supervisor since the beginning of my project. I would like to thank him for our conversations and the comments he provided. Conversations with him always managed to uplift my sprits whenever they needed uplifting.

Ruben van de Vijver has also played an important role these past few years. He provided an external point of view. That is, the perspective of a non-syntactician. His comments have been very detailed and covered every possible angle. He made it clear to me that it is important to keep an eye on the non-syntacticians and to write in such a way that the content is accessible to *all* linguists. This thesis has benefited greatly from his input. Furthermore, I would like to thank him for guiding me through the more difficult phases of my project.

I also wish to express gratitude to Laura Kallmeyer who joined the supervision team at a later stage. I would like to thank her for her helpful suggestions. The conversations I had with Leon Stassen proved very useful for my handling of the typological material and for this I thank him. Jens Fleischhauer has played a very important role in my development as a linguist. We shared an office for quite a while and I could always rely on him to discuss ideas. He taught me to think not one but two steps further. I thank Jens for asking me the right questions at the right times. I extend my thanks to all colleagues who discussed parts of this thesis with me or were in helpful in other ways: Rainer Osswald, Sebastian Löbner, Lea Kawaletz, Adrian Czardybon, Jean-Pierre Koenig, Vasiliki Tsouni, Samuel Taylor and Felix Knuth.

I would like to thank Lea Kawaletz and Jasmin Pfeifer for extensively proofreading the manuscript, which greatly improved the quality of the text. I am immensely grateful to my friends and my parents, Rita Stevens and Marc Van Hooste, for being the unwavering support by my side.

Although he was not connected to my project or to the Heinrich-Heine-University, I wish to thank Johan van der Auwera for inspiring me to pursue a PhD in linguistics with his interesting lectures.

Finally, I would like to thank my language informants: Jens Fleischhauer (German), Thomas Gamerschlag (German) Alexandra Redmann (German), Lea Kawaletz (German), Jasmin Pfeifer (German), Adrian Czardybon (German, Polish), Frauke Albersmeier (German), Robert D. Van Valin, Jr. (English), Elizabeth Nizzi (English), Samuel Taylor (English), Peter Sutton (English), Kurt Erbach (English), Rita Stevens (Dutch), Marc Van Hooste (Dutch), Ruben van de Vijver (Dutch), Pia-Mareen van de Kerkhof (Dutch), Tim Robeers (Dutch), Amandine Dumont (French), Simon Petitjean (French), Heimir Viðarsson (Icelandic), Audronė Šolienė (Lithuanian), Adri Breed (Afrikaans), Brian Nolan (Irish), Nikolai Skorolupov (Russian, Estonian), Dejan Matić (Serbian), Vasiliki Tsouni (Greek), Marios Andreou (Greek), Alex Tillas (Greek), Adina Dragomirescu (Romanian), Borja Ariztimuño Lopez (Basque), Thomas Brochhagen (Spanish), Hugo Cardoso (Portuguese), Sena Ceylan (Turkish), Ana Kolkhidashvili (Georgian), Keti Chilaia (Georgian), Ana Ogorodnikova (Russian), Zoltán Magyar (Hungarian), Shinichi Iguchi (Japanese) and several others who requested to remain anonymous.

Contents

1	**Introduction**	**1**
	1.1 Instruments, instrumentals & comitatives: phenomena and problems	1
	1.2 Methodology	7
	1.3 Glossing in this thesis	7
	1.4 Structure of this thesis	9
2	**Role and Reference Grammar**	**11**
	2.1 Introduction	11
	2.2 Fundamentals	11
	2.3 Overall organization of Role and Reference Grammar	14
	2.3.1 Constituent Projection	15
	2.3.2 Operator Projection	22
	2.4 The Semantic architecture of Role and Reference Grammar	26
	2.4.1 Aktionsarten	26
	2.4.2 Logical structures	35
	2.5 Linking semantics to syntax	37
	2.5.1 The Actor-Undergoer Hierarchy and the macroroles	37
	2.5.2 Privileged Syntactic Argument	42
	2.5.3 The Linking Algorithm	44
	2.6 Conclusion	49
3	**Instruments at the syntax-semantics interface**	**51**
	3.1 Thematic relations as an interface component	52
	3.1.1 Finite-primitive approaches	55
	3.1.2 Lexical decomposition	58
	3.1.3 Causality-driven approaches	60
	3.1.4 Generalized Semantic Roles	61
	3.1.5 Instrument as a thematic relation	64

3.2	Role and Reference Grammar		65
	3.2.1	Thematic relations	65
	3.2.2	The effector role: agents	69
	3.2.3	The effector role: forces vs. instruments	75
3.3	Case Grammar		80
	3.3.1	Overview	80
	3.3.2	Instruments	83
3.4	Causality-driven approaches		85
	3.4.1	Thematic relations	87
	3.4.2	Instruments	88
3.5	Lexical-Functional Grammar		90
	3.5.1	A-Structure and mapping to grammatical functions	90
	3.5.2	Instruments	93
3.6	Conceptual Semantics		95
	3.6.1	Overview	96
	3.6.2	Thematic relations	97
	3.6.3	Instruments	99
3.7	Instruments as subjects		102
	3.7.1	The general approach	104
		3.7.1.1 Naturalness conditions	105
		3.7.1.2 Deliberation & mediation constraint	108
		3.7.1.3 Conjunction test & do-test	110
		3.7.1.4 Instruments as members of the agent class	111
	3.7.2	The subtype approach	118
		3.7.2.1 Intermediary & facilitating instruments	118
		3.7.2.2 Instruments & implements	124
		3.7.2.3 Webb's Causal Force	128
	3.7.3	Summary of instruments as subjects	131
3.8	Conclusion: properties of thematic relations and instruments		133

4 Semantic range of instruments, agents & forces — 137
- 4.1 Degrees of animacy & autonomy — 138
  - 4.1.1 Animacy — 139
  - 4.1.2 Autonomy — 145
  - 4.1.3 The actionality scale — 155
  - 4.1.4 Pseudo-agents — 157
  - 4.1.5 Inherent vs. induced features — 165
- 4.2 The prevalence of instruments and implements with respect to verb classes — 169
- 4.3 Integrating the actionality scale with logical structures — 179
- 4.4 The three problems revisited — 182
- 4.5 A different approach to the semantic range — 187

5 Instruments and causation: A Force Dynamic view — 191
- 5.1 Fundamentals of Force Dynamics — 193
  - 5.1.1 Further patterns — 197
  - 5.1.2 Instruments in relation to causation — 200
  - 5.1.3 Integrating Force Dynamics with logical structures — 203
  - 5.1.4 Force Dynamics: More than causation — 205
  - 5.1.5 Configurations of volition and Holisky's principle — 207
- 5.2 Implements as facilitating instruments — 217
  - 5.2.1 Helping as weaker causality — 217
  - 5.2.2 Identifying implement and instruments: a new diagnostic — 220
- 5.3 A proposal for enriched causation — 225
  - 5.3.1 Relevant dimensions for neutralization — 226
  - 5.3.2 Neutralization of causation — 231
  - 5.3.3 Enriched causation in the logical structures — 237
- 5.4 Conclusion — 238

6 The Instrument-Subject Alternation and subtypes of instruments — 239
- 6.1 Delineating instruments in subject position from other inanimates in subject position — 239
- 6.2 Mechanics & purpose — 241
- 6.3 A new naturalness condition as a prerequisite for ISA — 243

6.4	Actionality constraint		247
6.5	Ability readings vs. ISA		249
6.6	General statements vs. ISA		257
6.7	Subtypes of instruments		259
	6.7.1	Free instruments & blocked instruments	260
	6.7.2	Conjoined instruments & conjoined implements	260
6.8	Conclusion		267

7 Delimiting instruments from instrument-like participants 269

7.1	Causees		270
	7.1.1	Causees taking instruments	281
	7.1.2	Expanding the effector role	285
7.2	Comitatives		287
	7.2.1	True comitatives	288
	7.2.2	Undergoer & NMR comitatives	290
	7.2.3	Comitatives with inanimate components	291
	7.2.4	Inanimate comitatives	297
	7.2.5	False inanimate comitatives	301
7.3	Proper parts as instruments		303
7.4	Potential instruments, implements & comitatives		306
7.5	Problematic cases of instruments		310
7.6	Conclusion		311

8 Linking semantics to syntax 313

8.1	Three classes of prepositions		314
8.2	Argument linking in Role and Reference Grammar		315
	8.2.1	Instrument and implement marking	317
	8.2.2	Causee marking	321
	8.2.3	Comitative marking	330
	8.2.4	Inanimate comitatives	334
	8.2.5	Marking of proper part-implements	335
	8.2.6	Marking of potential instruments, implements and comitatives	337
	8.2.7	Extending predicative with and without	342
8.3	Passive construction with an instrument		344
8.4	Passive ISA construction		346

8.5	Instrument unaccusative construction	347
8.6	Middle construction with an instrument	350
8.7	Impossible structures	352
8.8	Conclusion	354

9 Conclusion: A semantic-syntactic landscape for instruments and related concepts — 357

9.1	Summary of instrument-like concepts	359
9.2	Summary of expanded causation	361
9.3	Overview of tests	362
9.4	Future research	364

Appendix: Figures — 367

References — 371

List of Figures

1	General organization of RRG	12
2	Constituent projection of a simple English sentence	15
3	Constituent projection including the periphery	16
4	Dutch sentence with a PrCS	17
5	English sentence with an LDP	17
6	Dutch sentence with an RDP and a resumptive pronoun in the core	18
7	A non-exhaustive list of Dutch syntactic templates in the syntactic inventory	19
8	The layered structure of a Reference Phrase	21
9	A non-predicative and a predicative PP in English	22
10	Constituent and operator projections of an English sentence	24
11	Constituent and operator projections of a Dutch RP	25
12	The Actor-Undergoer Hierarchy (AUH)	39
13	General overview and summary of the RRG linking system	48
14	Semantics-to-syntax linking in its successive steps	49
15	General organization of Role and Reference Grammar (final)	50
16	Overview of thematic relation approaches discussed in this dissertation	54
17	Causal chain representation of *Fred ate the banana*	61
18	Neutralization of semantic contrasts	63
19	Thematic relations in terms of argument positions on the Actor-Undergoer Hierarchy	68
20	Top section of the saliency scale proposed by Van Valin & Wilkins	368
21	Basic causal chain	86
22	Chain representation of *Fred ate the banana*	87
23	Causal chain representation of *John broke the window with the hammer*	88

24	The relation between lexical semantics, a- and f-structure	91
25	Lexical entry for *go into* (conceptual semantics)	97
26	Thematic tier and action tier	98
27	Jackendoff's analysis of an instrument construction (pre-1990)	100
28	Jackendoff's reformulated analysis of an instrument construction (1990)	101
29	Grimm's agency lattice	369
30	The combined agency-animacy lattice	370
31	Overview of Alexiadou & Schäfer's instrument classification	120
32	LCS of *John opened the door with the key*	128
33	LCS of *John ate pasta with a fork*	128
34	ISA in Webb's LFG-approach	129
35	The actionality scale with example referents	156
36	Semantic space of pseudo-agents	163
37	Range of instruments, forces, agents, pseudo-agents and causes within the actionality scale	164
38	Preliminary Multiple Inheritance Hierarchy analysis of the actionality scale	189
39	An overview of a force dynamic configuration	195
40	Primary steady-state oppositions	196
41	Example configuration with disengaging antagonist and two-state resultant	198
42	Structure of a basic causative event with an instrument	202
43	Force dynamic configurations in a standard instrument construction	204
44	Force dynamic configurations in a standard instrument construction (II)	205
45	Standard instrument construction with micro- and macro-configurations	207
46	Micro-FD configurations for an implement construction	218
47	Micro- and macro-configurations for an implement construction	220
48	Feature neutralizations	229
49	Force dynamic configurations underlying the four principle causal operators	231

50	Neutralization of conceptual causation to generalized causative relations	233
51	Causal operators ordered along strength of causation	234
52	Split between free & blocked instruments and implements	259
53	Partial causal chain	263
54	Linking to syntax of a clause containing an instrument	318
55	Linking to syntax of a clause containing an implement	321
56	Syntactic structure of a French sentence expressing permissive causation	323
57	Syntactic structure of a French sentence expressing direct causation	323
58	Causee under the scope of direct causation taking an instrument	327
59	Causee under the scope of indirect causation taking an instrument	328
60	Linking to syntax for *Todd destroyed the ship with Michael*	331
61	Linking to syntax for *Edward ran to the hospital with the hammer*	335
62	Linking to syntax for *Evie ate the soup without a spoon*	340
63	Linking to syntax for *Caroline ran to the store without Elena*	342

List of Tables

1	Semantic units underlying the syntactic units of the Layered Structure of the Clause	13
2	Summary of operators in the LSC	23
3	Operators in the layered structure of the RP	25
4	Feature matrix for the base aktionsart classes as recognized by RRG	27
5	Aktionsart tests and the values for the respective aktionsart classes	33
6	Summary of aktionsart tests with tested properties and caveats	34
7	Lexical representations for aktionsart classes	37
8	Transitivity in Role and Reference Grammar	42
9	PSA-assignment overview	44
10	Definition of thematic relations in terms of argument positions in the logical structure	67
11	Comparison of thematic relation properties between varieties of Case Grammar	85
12	(Simplified) overview of approaches and ISA-problems	132
13	Overview of treatment of intermediary and facilitating instruments	133
14	Overview of approaches to thematic relations and instruments	134
15	Feature matrix for the principal levels of autonomy	153
16	Tests for distinguishing instruments from forces	158
17	Verb classes and the prevalence of instruments and implements	179
18	Performance matrix	200
19	Summary of diagnostics for instruments and implements	225
20	Matrix of proposed types of causation and their operators	230

21	Constructional schema for the *instrument-subject alternation* (preliminary)	242
22	Constructional schema for the *instrument-subject alternation* (complete)	247
23	The German ability construction	257
24	Constructional schema for English General Property construction	259
25	Summary of intermediate effector classes	281
26	Summary of proposed effector subtypes	286
27	Constructional schema for French causee construction with an instrument	330
28	English passive construction	345
29	English passive instrument as actor construction	347
30	Overview of concepts explored in this dissertation	361
31	Matrix table of causation types	362

List of Abbreviations

1	First person	ERG	Ergative
2	Second person	F	Figure or Feminine
3	Third person	FD	Force Dynamic(s)
A	Actor	G	Ground
ABIL	Ability	GCR	Generalized Causative Relation
ABS	Absolutive		
AC	Actionality Constraint	GEN	Generic
ACC	Accusative	GPSG	Generalized Phrase Structure Grammar
ADE	Adessive		
ADJ	Adjective	GSR	Generalized Semantic Role
ADV	Adverb(ial)		
Ago	Agonist	I	Instrument
Ant	Antagonist	IF	Illocutionary Force
AOR	Aorist	IND	Indirect Causation
AP	Adpositional Phrase	INDEF	Indefinite
AT	Actor of a transitive verb	INF	Infinitive
AUH	Actor-Undergoer Hierarchy	INGR	Ingressive
AUX	Auxiliary	INS	Instrumental
BEN	Beneficiary	ISA	Instrument-Subject Alternation
CAUS	Causative		
CF	Causal Force	LCS	Lexical Conceptual Structure
CL	Clause/Clausal		
CNJ	Conjunction	LDG	Lexical Decomposition Grammar
COM	Comitative		
CRC	Collaborative Research Center	LDP	Left-Detached Position
DAT	Dative	LFG	Lexical-Functional Grammar
DEF	Definite		
DEM	Demonstrative	LGR	Leipzig Glossing Rules
DET	Determiner	LOC	Location
DIST	Distal	LS	Logical Structure
d-S	Derived Subject	LSC	Layered Structure of the Clause
E/e	Event		

M	Masculine	REL	Relative pronoun or Relative clause marker
MOD	Modal/Modality		
MR	Macrorole	REFL	Reflexive
MSE	Multi-purpose Syntactic Element	RP	Reference Phrase
		RPFP	RP-final position
M-	Macrorole transitivity	RPIP	RP-initial position
N	Noun or Neuter	RRG	Role & Reference Grammar
NMR	Non-Macrorole Argument		
NOM	Nominative	S	Subject
NP	Noun Phrase	SAE	Standard Average European
NUC	Nucleus		
NUM	Numeral/Number	SEML	Semelfactive
NV	Neutral Version	SG	Singular
O	Objective	S_n	Situation
OBJ	Object	STA	Status
P	Preposition	S-	Syntactic transitivity
PART	Partitive	SUBJ	Subject
PERF	Perfective	TNS	Tense
PL	Plural	U	Undergoer
PoCS	Post-Core Slot	V	Verb
POSS	Possessive	VOL	Volitional causation
PP	Prepositional Phrase	VP	Verb Phrase
PR	Preverb	VPR	Verb Prefix or Verb Particle
PrCS	Pre-Core Slot		
PRED	Predicate		
PREP	Preposition		
PROX	Proximate		
PRS	Present		
PSA	Privileged Syntactic Argument		
PST	Past		
PTCP	Past Participle		
QNT	Quantification/Quantifier		
R	Restricted		
RDP	Right-Detached Position		

1 Introduction

In this dissertation I explore the status of instruments and related concepts at the Syntax-Semantics Interface. I look into these concepts from the point of view of Role and Reference Grammar (or: *RRG*), using a core set of languages (primarily languages belonging to the Standard Average European group) for illustration. I pursue three main goals: 1) To explore the status of instruments in linguistic theory and provide answers to problems connected to instruments, 2) to deepen the RRG approach to these concepts and 3) to contribute to the further development of RRG as a theory. The central question of my investigation is: *What is instrumentality and how does instrumentality link to syntax?*

1.1 Instruments, instrumentals & comitatives: phenomena and problems

Instruments are usually treated in terms of thematic relations in the relevant literature. Such treatments are often problematic for several reasons: 1) There are many theoretical problems concerning thematic relations in general and treatments of instruments usually suffer from the same flaws, 2) the instrument relation is usually treated only peripherally, 3) there is an alternation in many languages where the instrument appears as the subject and this is often not captured sufficiently or not at all, 4) only the standard, prototypical occurrence of instruments (such as in (1a)) is explored whereas there are several other constructions with instruments and 5) instrumental marking is cross-linguistically very multifunctional.

The status of instruments is fully dependent on the general conception of thematic relations in the framework under investigation. As there is a wide range of conceptions of them, there is an equally diverse landscape of approaches to the instrument role. For instance, for Dowty (1991), instruments are participants that have an equal amount of proto-agent and proto-patient properties. This captures the fact that instruments are both acted upon by a manipulator and act on another participant themselves. An example of this is given in (1a): *Lumberjack* acts on the *chainsaw* and in turn, it acts on the *tree* with the result that the tree is cut down. Instruments, like other thematic relations, are treated as primitive notions by many linguists and linguistic traditions (e.g. Lexical-Functional Grammar). A treatment in terms of primitive, unanalyzable relations is highly problematic in itself, but especially problematic for instruments. The example in (1a) reveals that instruments have a dual role: they are simultaneously agentive and patientive. Treating them in isolation thus seems questionable.

With respect to 3), there is an important difference between instruments, implements and instrumentals. Based on the morphosyntactic behavior of instruments, some linguists distinguish between two different classes of instruments. Even though the motivation for positing two different classes can vary, it is usually based on roughly the same observation. I refer to this alternation as the *Instrument-Subject Alternation* (or: *ISA*). Consider the difference between (1a–1b) and (1c–1d):

(1)   a.   *The lumberjack cut down the tree with the chainsaw.*
        b.   *The chainsaw cut down the tree.*
        c.   *The lumberjack cut down the tree with the axe.*
        d.   **The axe cut down the tree.*

The inability of *axe* to occur as the subject, compared to the ability of *chainsaw* to undergo precisely that alternation has led some linguists to assume two distinct classes of instruments. RRG (Van Valin & LaPolla 1997, Van Valin 2005) labels the former *implements* and the latter *instruments*. With respect to this alternation, there is a great deal of cross-linguistic variation. Dutch is less permissive than English, for example. German disprefers ISA as well, clearly preferring an ability reading. Consider the example in (2).

(2) Dieses   Messer schneid-et   das Brot.
    DEM.PROX knife   cut-PRS.3SG DEF bread
    'This knife cuts the bread.'

In (2), the referent in subject position, *Messer* (*knife*), is described as having the ability to cut another referent (in this case, *bread*) rather than describing a situation as it unfolds. The ability-reading in Dutch is also less common and generally requires a modal auxiliary. Slavic, on the other hand, strongly disprefers instruments in subject position altogether. There are further problems with this alternation, which will be explored in chapter 3. Most theories can handle one of these issues, but not all. I will propose an approach that can capture the behavior of this construction in all its facets.

I reserve the term *instrumental* for the morphological and syntactic marking of the semantic concepts (either implement or instrument). *Instrumental* covers both adpositional marking and case marking. Examples of this are given in (3). Irish (Celtic) uses a preposition, but Hungarian (Uralic) uses a case marker.

(3) a. Ghearr   Sean an   t-arán le   scian.
       Cut.PST John DET bread with knife
       'John cut the bread with a knife.' (Irish)
    b. János   egy   kés-sel   felvágta   a
       John.NOM INDEF knife-INS up_cut.3SG DEF
       kenyer-et.
       bread-ACC
       'John cut the bread with a knife.' (Hungarian)

Apart from differences like those between Irish and Hungarian, many languages mark comitatives – roughly the expression of accompaniment – and instruments with the same means. Consider the differences between French (Romance) and Finnish (Uralic) in (4).

(4) a. *Jean a   coupé   le pain avec*
       Jean AUX.3SG cut.PTCP DEF bread with
       un   couteau.
       INDEF knife
       'Jean cut the bread with a knife.' (French)
    b. *Jean travaille   ensemble avec Marie.*
       Jean work.PRS.3SG together with Marie.
       'Jean works together with Marie.'
    c. *Hän kirjoitta   kynä-llä.*
       3SG write.PRS.3SG pen-ADE
       'He writes/is writing with a pen.'
       (Finnish, Karlsson 2004: 135, glossing mine)
    d. *Läsnä   ol-i   Veikko Väätäinen*
       Present be-PST.3SG   Veikko Väätäinen
       vaimo-ine-en.
       wife-COM-POSS
       'Veikko Väätäinen was there with his wife.'
       (Karlsson 2004: 145, glossing mine)

French uses the same marker for accompaniment as for the instrument ((4a–4b)): *Marie* and *couteau* express the former and the latter, respectively, and are both marked by *avec*. In Finnish, by contrast, accompaniment is expressed by the comitative case marker *-ine* ((4d)), whereas the instrument ((4c)) is marked with the adessive case *-llä*. The prototypical use of this case is to express a form of static location, but it also encodes instrumentality.

In addition to the standard occurrence of instruments and ISA, such as in (1a), there are also other types of examples that feature instruments (examples in (5)). These occurrences cover passives containing an instrument ((5a)), passive versions of ISA ((5b)), unaccusative constructions with an instrument ((5c)), middle constructions with an instrument ((5d)) and the like. Because such occurrences are only sporadically examined in the literature, I will provide a discussion of them and propose an analysis based on the standard treatment of instruments.

1.1 Instruments, instrumentals & comitatives: phenomena and problems

(5) a. *The tree was cut down with the axe.*
b. *The bread was cut by the knife.*
c. *The door opened (with the key).*
d. *This glass breaks easily with a hammer.*

The examples in (4) illustrated that French uses typical instrumental marking for more than just instruments. English, Dutch and German, too, use this marking for a wide range of functions. The multifunctional nature of the preposition *with* in English and its counterparts in, for example, Dutch and German is a particular challenge. Consider (adapted from McKercher 2003) the various uses of *with* in (6).

(6) a. *Kim ate pizza with a fork.*   Instrument
b. *Kim ate pizza with her friend.*   Comitative
c. *Kim ate pizza with enthusiasm.*   Manner
d. *Kim ate pizza with pesto sauce.*   Attribute
e. *Her argues with Sandy about that issue.* Opposition
f. *Kim needed help with that problem.*   Reference
g. *Kim left her keys with her wallet.*   Proximity
h. *Kim was paralyzed with fear.*   Cause
i. *The garden swarms with bees.*   Locatum

Dutch and German would use *met* and *mit*, respectively, for all of these, except for (6g–6i). In this dissertation, I do not discuss all of these functions as the focus of this dissertation lies on instrumentality. Nevertheless, many of the functions of *with* can be accounted for with the approach that I develop in this dissertation.

Apart from instruments and comitatives, there are other, seemingly related notions. Causees, for instance, are often implicitly treated as a type of instrument. I argue in favor of distinguishing instruments from causees, partly over the strength of causation that each is under the scope of. In addition to causation, animacy differences between the referents is central in the distinction between causees and instruments. It is to this end that Force Dynamics will be integrated with RRG's *logical structures*. Force Dynamics (Talmy 2000) is a production model of causation in that the precise type causation is the sum of the interaction of the components in a configuration. Using the combinatorial possibilities of force dynamic configurations, Talmy proposes a wide range of causation types. I propose an integration of Force Dynamics with RRG as a theoretical contribution and I argue that my account deepens the latter's approach to causation.

Furthermore, there are other non-canonical, instrument-like notions. The arguments marked by *with* in the examples in (7) superficially look like instruments or comitatives but they are, in fact, neither. For example, in (7a) *hammer* is not wielded by the *lumberjack* to arrive at a certain result, nor does it perform the action of running as a companion of the aforementioned lumberjack. In (7b), the *book* is not wielded and it is not interpreted as accompanying the running individual. Rather, it conveys the meaning of an attribute: The *woman* seems to be (at least partly) defined over her possession of a book. In (7c), the use of an instrument in the coming about of a result state is explicitly denied. However, as it is present in the morphosyntactic structure, it must somehow be present in the semantic representation as well. Finally, in (7d), the accompaniment is explicitly denied. From a semantic point of view, it would be questionable to simply negate a normal expression of accompaniment (i.e. comitative) as comitatives are often defined over the observation that two entities perform an action simultaneously. Adopting such an approach would be overly simplistic and present problems for the linking to syntax.

(7) a. *The lumberjack ran to the store with the hammer.*
    b. *The woman with the book ran to the store.*
    c. *John broke the window without a hammer.*
    d. *Bill went home without Eric.*

In this dissertation, I present an RRG-based analysis of the concepts superficially related to instruments. In addition to ISA and the phenomena in (7), I will explore the occurrence of other inanimate referents in subject position and how they are related to the more canonical instances of instruments.

1.2 Methodology

This dissertation is primarily an investigation of the syntax-semantics interface based on a small sample of languages. It is not a typological study in the strictest sense of the word, even though typological data are certainly used at times to illustrate a point. This study primarily uses English (West-Germanic), Dutch (West-Germanic), German (West-Germanic) and French (Gallo-Romance) as main data points. The following languages are also referenced to or used to varying degrees: Afrikaans (West-Germanic), Russian (East-Slavic), Croatian (South-Slavic), Serbian (South-Slavic), Bulgarian (South-Slavic), Georgian (Kartvelian), Finnish (Balto-Finnic), Estonian (Balto-Finnic), Hungarian (Ugric), Icelandic (North-Germanic), Basque (Isolate), Portuguese (Ibero-Romance), Spanish (Ibero-Romance), Romanian (Eastern Romance), Lithuanian (Baltic), Irish (Celtic), Persian (Indo-Iranian), Greek (Hellenic), Quechua (Quechua), Malayalam (Dravidian), Japanese (Isolate) and Jingulu (Jingulu) and several others. All examples that were not drawn from the literature, including those from my own native language (Dutch), were supplied and validated by native speakers. I employed questionnaires with example sentences in a lingua franca that the native speakers were most familiar with, i.e. there are 4 base questionnaires (one in Dutch, one in German, one in English and one in French). Many of the examples do not concern strict grammaticality vs. ungrammaticality. Rather, they are a matter of acceptability and degrees thereof. If more consultants accepted an example than not, I included the example as acceptable. Beyond the questionnaires, further interviews conducted with consultants constitute the bulk of the data used in this dissertation. Finally, the RRG-trees were generated with Praat (Boersma & Weenink 2016).

1.3 Glossing in this thesis

I loosely follow the Leipzig Glossing Rules (or: *LGR*, Comrie 2008). There are, however, several exceptions. I do not apply the same level of glossing in every example. The level of detail depends on the purpose the example serves and the morphological complexity of the language. For instance, Georgian and Basque are always glossed in extensive detail with an extra top line provided for the sake of clarity. Another exception to the standard LGR concerns the marking of morphophonological changes. In addition to the backslash, the locus of change is marked in boldface. As German and Dutch employ such a marking strategy quite productively to mark past tense, it will be found throughout this dissertation. An example of this is given in (8).

(8) Lena l**ie**f   in-s   Haus.
     Lena run\PST.3SG in-DEF house
     'Lena ran into the house.'

Another exception to the LGR concerns the marking of personal pronouns. Rather than including long sequences like *PERS.PRN.DAT.3SG* I have opted to simply use *3SG*. Case information for German has mostly been omitted, unless directly relevant for the matter at hand or if leaving it out would create confusion. The relevant preposition marking the instrument in German is *mit* and it always takes dative case. As Dutch does not have a case system any more than English does, the fact that the preposition *met* takes oblique marking (in the rare cases where there is overt marking) is hardly relevant.

I have also opted to use several labels that are not in the LGR-inventory. Both German and Dutch exhibit a phenomenon where a prefixed verb is split into the base verb and a postposed prefix or particle. Instances of this are labeled *VPR* (Verb particle/verb prefix). Dutch also has a syntactic element (*er*) with a wide array of uses, such as that of a placeholder pronoun or that of a locative pronoun. This element is an ongoing topic in Dutch (and general) linguistics and I do not wish to go into its details. As it is very frequent, it will appear throughout the Dutch examples. I will label it as *Multi-purpose Syntactic Element* (*MSE*). Examples of these phenomena are given in (9a) and (9b–9c), respectively.

(9) a. *Jan schl**u**g   das Fenster ein.*
         Jan break\PST.3SG DEF window VPR
         'Jan broke the window.' (German)

b   Ik   ben   er   goed   aan<ge>komen.
    1SG AUX.1SG MSE good arrive<PTCP>arrive
    'I arrived there well.' (Dutch)
c. Jan heef-t   er   drie.
    Jan have-PRS.3SG MSE three
    'Jan has three.'

The glossing of English taken from the literature has been maintained, unless explicitly indicated. The glossing of languages other than Dutch, English, French and German was validated by the native speakers of the respective languages. The Dutch examples are from Standard Belgian Dutch. These will be simply indicated as 'Dutch'.

1.4 Structure of this thesis

Chapter 1 has been a brief introduction to several basic phenomena that are the central object of study: Instruments, implements, causees and others that are either semantically or superficially related to them. I will employ the Role and Reference Grammar framework and therefore, chapter 2 supplies a detailed introduction to the theory. Chapter 3 provides an overview of the relevant literature regarding thematic relations, the types of semantics they employ and of instruments and related phenomena. Chapter 4 presents the first major pillar of my own approach: A proposal to revise the concept of animacy and to merge it with another concept which I call *autonomy*. Chapter 4 also includes a brief excursion into a different type of analysis, using a multiple inheritance hierarchy. This type of hierarchy can be used as a starting point to translate parts of my research into Barsalou's frame semantic approach as developed in the CRC 991 at the Heinrich-Heine-Universität Düsseldorf (cf. Löbner 2014, 2015, Petersen 2007/2015, Kallmeyer & Osswald 2013). Chapter 5 presents the second major theoretical pillar. I provide an analysis of the causal relations that instruments occur with using *Force Dynamics* and I argue in favor of merging Force Dynamics with logical structures, a central component of RRG's theory of linking. In doing this, I explore a weaker type of causation (*helping*) that will constitute the core of my analysis of a specific type of instrument-related class, the *implement*. Chapter 6 is an approach to ISA, drawing from RRG's approach to constructional schemas. ISA presents special challenges for handling the notion of context and the cross-linguistic validity of theories of instruments. The main problems concerning ISA that are often not addressed in the relevant literature will be discussed in detail and a solution for each of them will be proposed. The principle topic of chapter 7 is how to distinguish instruments from phenomena that are (superficially) related. These include comitatives and causees but also phenomena like the ones that the examples in (7) illustrated. Chapter 8 concerns the linking of the semantics of instruments, causees and comitatives (in various forms) to the syntactic representation. As RRG is a non-derivational theory of syntax, the semantic analysis of these notions will prove crucial to account for their marking and surface behavior. I primarily explore marking and linking in English, Dutch, French and German. Chapter 9 is a summary of the most relevant semantic analyses and morphosyntactic tests.

2 Role and Reference Grammar

2.1 Introduction

Role and Reference Grammar (Foley & Valin 1984, Van Valin & LaPolla 1997, Van Valin 2005) is a functionalist grammatical framework which is monostratal in nature. Its ongoing development is driven by two major questions (Foley & Van Valin 1984, Van Valin 2005: 1): 1) What would a theory of language look like if it were not based on the analysis of English but rather on the analysis of typologically diverse languages such as Lakhota, Tagalog and Dyirbal? and 2) How can the interaction of the syntax, semantics and pragmatics in different languages with differing systems best be captured and explained?

The main focus of work in RRG lies on syntax-semantics interface and pragmatics (Van Valin & LaPolla 1997, Van Valin 2005), although advances are being made in the area of morphology (e.g. Martín Arista 2008, 2009, 2011, 2012 and Nolan 2010, 2011). Most RRG work is synchronic in nature (including this dissertation), although there is some diachronic work available (e.g. Matasović 2004, Martín Arista 2011). This chapter is intended to serve as an overview of RRG in its present-day conception.

2.2 Fundamentals

Apart from the research questions above, RRG holds a number of fundamental insights that make it quite distinct from other theories. Van Valin (2005: 3) points out that any theory of clause structure must meet two fundamental requirements, as displayed in (1).

(1) a. A theory of clause structure should capture all of the universal features of clauses without imposing features on languages in which there is no evidence or them.
 b. A theory should always represent comparable structures in different languages in comparable ways.

In addition to these requirements, RRG rejects any kind of underlying deep structure syntactic representation or transformation commonly found in the generative tradition, Relational Grammar and certain varieties of Case Grammar. RRG's structures can be considered to be flat and the syntactic representation of a given clause reflects its actually occurring form very closely (Van Valin 2005: 3-4).

In general, RRG posits a semantic base which is linked into the syntax using a system known as the *linking algorithm* (Van Valin 2005: 1-2). Discourse pragmatics – or information structure - influences the whole system and can be described as 'mediating' the linking (Van Valin 2005: 1-2). Information structure operates in all aspects of the grammar. Each of the components of RRG has its own representation. These will be discussed in more depth in the following sections. The organization of RRG is visualized in the figure below (Van Valin 2005: 2):

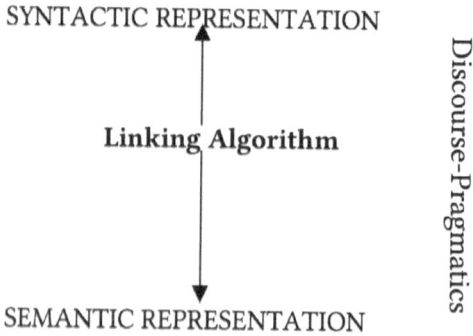

Figure 1: General organization of RRG.

Central to RRG's conception of non-relational clause structure is the *Layered Structure of the Clause* or LSC (Van Valin 2005: 3-4). It is based on two distinctions; one is made between the predicate and elements that do not predicate. Another (within the class of non-predicating elements) is made between arguments and non-arguments. These distinctions result in units that are defined semantically rather than syntactically (Van Valin 2005: 5). Each of the semantic units has a syntactic equivalent, for which they are the motivating elements:

Semantic Element(s)	Syntactic Unit
Predicate	Nucleus
Argument in semantic representation of predicate	Core argument
Non-arguments	Periphery
Predicate + Arguments	Core
Predicate + Arguments + Non-arguments	Clause (=Core + Periphery)

Table 1: Semantic units underlying the syntactic units of the Layered Structure of the Clause (Van Valin 2005: 5).

It stands out that contrary to other theories, there is no syntactic unit called *verb phrase*. RRG treats VPs in languages that have them as grammaticalized focus structure patterns (Van Valin 2005: 8 & 80–81). This means that from the RRG perspective, VP is not a universal constituent and thus it is not listed as a syntactic unit.

Contrary to other theories, Role and Reference Grammar is represented through three different structures or 'projections': a *constituent projection* (representing the syntactic structure), an *operator projection* and an *information structure projection*. Not all of these projections need to be construed in every analysis or visualization. Indeed, representing all three simultaneously comes with certain difficulties as the result is a three-dimensional figure[1]. As the information structure projection is not relevant for the topic of this thesis, it is not discussed in this chapter. The operator and constituent projections will be discussed in the

---

[1] See Van Valin (2005: 80) for an example of such a figure.

following sections. For more background on information structure and its projection, see Van Valin (2005).

It is important to point out that Van Valin (2008) argued for replacing the concept of the *noun phrase* with the concept of *reference phrase* or RP. Van Valin points out that language is used to refer and predicate (Van Valin 2005: 1). Calling an 'NP' a reference phrase is a logical consequence of this point of view, as RPs are indeed referring expressions (Van Valin 2005: 28) and as such refer to real world participants. They are also categorically varied. That is to say, just like predicates need not be verbs (although they canonically are), RPs are usually headed by nouns but do not need to be (Van Valin 2005: 28). Consider (Van Valin 2008: 167) the German nominative phrase *Der Lange* ('The tall one') in *Der Lange ist eingeschlafen* ('The tall one has fallen asleep'). In German, it is undeniably headed by an adjective, whereas the English equivalent has the nominal 'one' as a head. RP has become the standard unit in RRG in post 2008-work. Consequently, in this thesis *RP* is used in all RRG-analyses. In the discussion of other frameworks, the labels and terminology of the respective approach will be respected.

2.3 Overall organization of Role and Reference Grammar

Role and Reference Grammar can be described as a semantically driven syntactic theory. RRG assumes that every verb belongs to a certain aktionsart class. These classes are largely drawn from Vendler's classes (1957, 1967) but there are also several non-Vendlerian aktionsart classes in RRG. Each class is paired with a so-called *logical structure*, which reflects the syntactically relevant elements. These logical structures are based on Dowty's (1979) system of lexical decomposition. A logical structure (or: *LS*) is thus a decomposition of certain predicate (including argument slots). Such decompositions constitute the basis for the linking algorithm. The logical structures are not usually depicted together with any of the projections. An exception is when the workings of the linking algorithm are graphically illustrated (see section 2.5.3 and chapter 8).

2.3 Overall organization of Role and Reference Grammar

The logical structures are stored in the mental lexicon (Van Valin 2005: 47 & 130ff.). Parallel to the mental lexicon, the *syntactic inventory* is a syntactic equivalent in that it stores the syntactic structures available in a given language (Van Valin 2005: 13–15). As the logical structures (and aktionsarten) play a vital role in the workings of RRG, they are the principle topic of section 2.4. The following sections will focus on the projections and their respective components, explore the semantic basis of RRG (which will play a pivotal role in this dissertation) and finally discuss the linking algorithm. As RRG is an elaborate theory, not all aspects of it will or can be discussed in this chapter.

2.3.1 Constituent Projection

The constituent projection is the representation of the syntactic structure in RRG. The concept of the Layered Structure of the Clause is crucial here. The units posited by Van Valin (2005: 4–5) are directly reflected in the constituent projection and form the backbone of syntactic representation: The nucleus is the syntactic unit that contains the predicate (Van Valin 2005: 4–5). The core consists of the nucleus and the arguments of the predicate. Consider the following example from English.

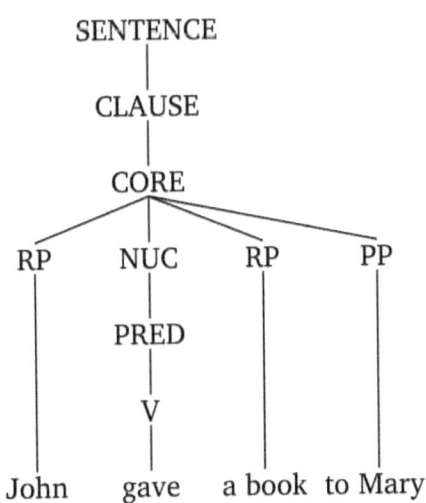

Figure 2: Constituent projection of a simple English sentence.

2 Role and Reference Grammar

The clause is the core and periphery (which contains non-arguments) combined. The highest level in the LSC is the sentence:

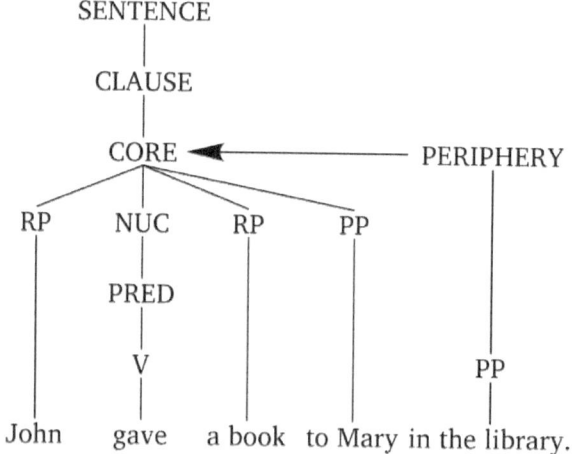

Figure 3: Constituent projection including the periphery.

In addition to these semantically motivated units, there are also pragmatically motivated units. Languages can have an extra-core slot (*pre- or postcore slot*) and a detached position (*left- or a right-detached position*). The former contains fronted elements and question words in languages where they do not appear in situ (Van Valin 2005: 5). In the Dutch sentence *BIER drinkt hij niet graag*[2] ('BEER he doesn't like to drink'), the fronted object-RP is located in the precore slot (PrCS).

---

[2] 'The Dutch adverbial *graag* roughly translates as *gladly* or *happily*. In English, this is expressed by the verb *like*.

2.3 Overall organization of Role and Reference Grammar

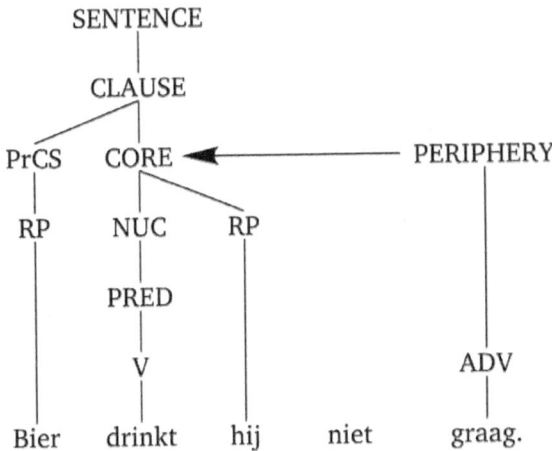

Figure 4: Dutch sentence with a PrCS.

The detached positions (LDP and RDP) are often the location of adverbials that are set off from the rest of the sentence by an intonation break (Van Valin 2005: 5–6). Consider the following example.

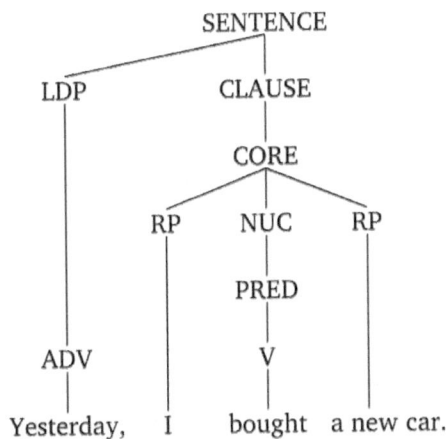

Figure 5: English sentence with an LDP
(adapted from Van Valin 2005: 6).

2 Role and Reference Grammar

Van Valin (2005: 8) points out that the pragmatically motivated units (the detached positions and extracore slots) are not universal, whereas the other syntactic units are universal. This means that not all languages will have an extracore slot, whereas others will have both and still others will only have one. Van Valin (2005: 17) stresses that the extracore slots cannot contain more than one RP or PP at a time and that there can never be more than one such slot in the clause. It is possible in some languages to have a semantic argument of the predicate in a detached position. If this is the case, a resumptive pronoun will be present in the core (Van Valin 2005: 6). Van Valin offers an example from English, but the situation in Dutch is similar: *Ik ken hem, je broer* ('I know him, your brother') or *Ik zie het, dat onweer* ('I see it, that thunderstorm'). Consider:

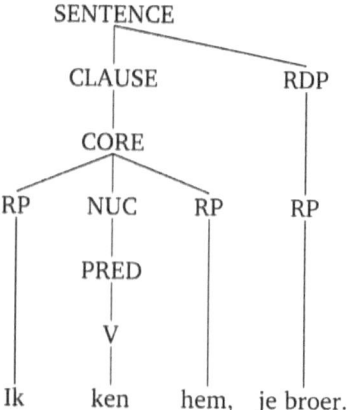

Figure 6: Dutch sentence with an RDP and a resumptive pronoun in the core.

RRG assumes that the syntactic structures are stored as templates in the syntactic inventory rather than being derived by any kind of phrase structure rule (Van Valin 2005: 13). As different languages show different configurations in the constituent projection, the templates in the syntactic inventory are not universal but subject to considerable cross-linguistic variation. In short, the content of the syntactic inventory is language specific. Judging from the Dutch examples in figures 4 and 6,

2.3 Overall organization of Role and Reference Grammar

we can theorize that Dutch has (at least!) a right detached position-template, a precore slot-template and two different core templates. Within the process of linking semantics to syntax, the correct templates are selected and merged to form the complete structure that is depicted in the constituent projection. This non-exhaustive Dutch inventory is given in figure 7.

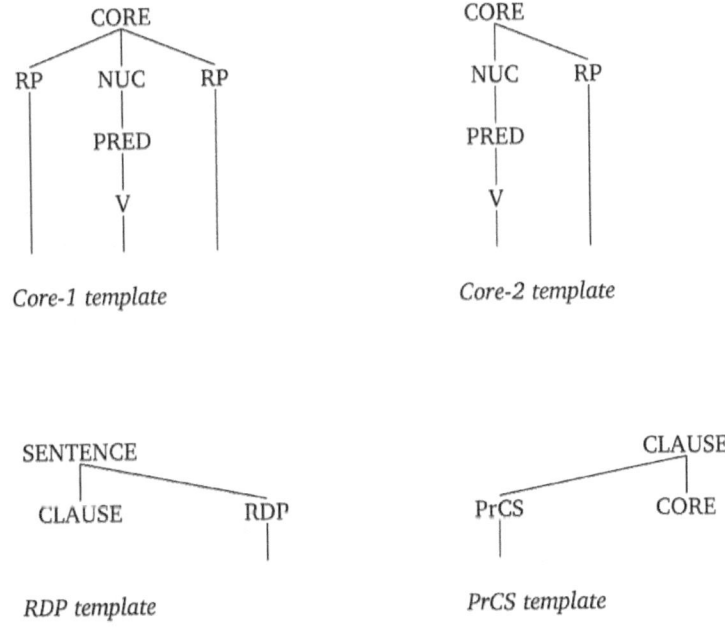

Figure 7: A non-exhaustive list of Dutch syntactic templates in the syntactic inventory.

It has been previously explained that the periphery contains the non-arguments, the adjuncts. Van Valin (2005: 19) distinguishes between phrasal and non-phrasal adjuncts. PPs are an example of the former, adverbs an example of the latter. An element of the periphery, depending on its precise content, can modify any layer of the LSC. Van Valin (2005: 19) posits that temporal or locational PPs (such as in figure 3) modify the events encoded by the elements of the core. Consequently, the periphery that contains them modifies the core level. Adverbs may modify all three layers of the LSC, depending on their nature. For example, a manner adverb like *carefully* modifies the core, but an aspectual adverb like *completely* modifies the nucleus.

Generally speaking, the structure of phrases is similar to that of clauses (Van Valin 2008, Van Valin 2005: 24): both have a layered structure, both have a set of operators modifying this structure and a (potential) periphery for each level. The phrase level is equivalent to the clause and sentence levels in the LSC. Parallel to the LSC, there is a nucleus and a core[3]. The nucleus in an RP is usually filled by a noun but is not restricted just to nouns. Similar to the nucleus in the LSC, other categories such as verbs and adjectives can function as filler (Van Valin 2008, Van Valin 2005: 28). 'Core arguments' can occur in certain complex RPs. Adjectives are treated as modifiers in the nucleus$_R$ periphery. Similarly to adverbs in the clause, they are constrained by iconicity: Adjectives must occur closer to the nucleus than other modifiers and operators (Van Valin 2005: 26).

Phrases can also have a unit which functions like an extracore slot and a detached position (Van Valin 2005: 26). Similar to both units in the LSC, this 'RP-slot' can be phrase initial or phrase final, depending on the language. They are therefore termed the *RP-initial position* (RPIP) and *RP-final position* (RPFP) respectively. All of these units are also stored as templates in the syntactic inventory (Van Valin 2005: 24). An example for the structure of an RP is given below. The Dutch example reads 'big bridges' and is adapted from Van Valin (2005: 25).

---

[3] In the projections, a subscript R identifies a given unit as belonging to a reference phrase. Thus CORE$_R$ is the nominal core.

2.3 Overall organization of Role and Reference Grammar

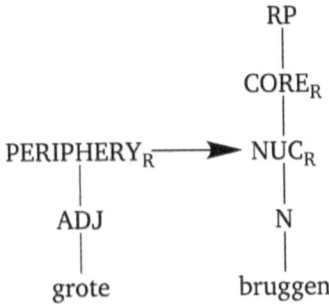

Figure 8: The layered structure of a Reference Phrase.

The account presented above applies to phrase structure in general. There is however an important addition to be made concerning the nature of prepositional phrases. Van Valin (2005: 21-23) points out that from the RRG-perspective, PPs[4] can be predicative or non-predicative. Non-predicative PPs are characterized by a flat structure. They are – as the name suggests – licensed by the predicate and do not predicate anything themselves. They are, in other words, core arguments and the preposition is considered to be a type of case marker, an insight also shared by, for example, Fillmore (1968, 1977a). In the sentence *John gave a book to Mary*, the PP *to Mary* is a non-predicative PP functioning as a core argument[5].

A predicative PP is a PP where the adposition itself licenses an argument, contributing semantic information. Such PPs are usually found in the core periphery. A locational PP, such as the one in figure 3, is a good example. The location coded by the phrase is licensed by the adposition. Figure 9 shows both types of PPs (adapted from Van Valin 2005: 23).

---

[4] It would probably be more precise to use the term AP (adpositional phrase) as this distinction also applies to postpositional phrases in language where they occur.
[5] A core argument marked by a preposition is termed *Oblique Core Argument* in RRG. Core arguments not marked thus are *Direct Core Arguments* (Van Valin 2005: 7).

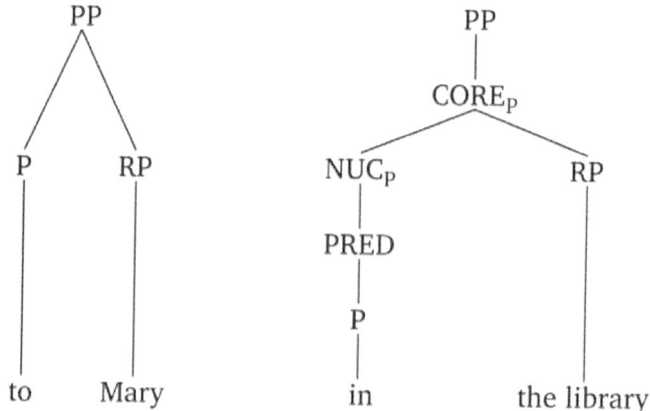

Figure 9: A non-predicative and a predicative PP in English.

2.3.2 Operator Projection

RRG treats grammatical categories such as tense and aspect as operators modifying different layers of the clause (Van Valin 2005: 8). Some operators can only modify one layer (e.g. aspect), whereas negation is the only operator that can occur on all three levels[6] (Van Valin 2005: 9). Van Valin crucially points out that operators are largely language-specific; only negation and illocutionary force are universal. Even though operators modify the different layers of the LSC they are separate from them (Van Valin 2005: 11). Therefore, they warrant a separate projection; the operator projection. A list of operators is given in the table below (Van Valin 2005: 9).

---

[6] It is to be remarked, however, that there are still important differences between negation on the different levels. This is a complex matter, which I will not go into here.

2.3 Overall organization of Role and Reference Grammar

Operators in the LSC		
Nuclear	**Core**	**Clausal**
Aspect	Directionals[7]	Status[8]
Negation	Event quantification	Tense
Directionals[9]	Modality[10]	Evidentials
	Internal (narrow scope) negation	Illocutionary Force

Table 2: Summary of operators in the LSC.

The operator projection is treated as the mirror image of the constituent projection. The morphological expression of an operator is connected with a dashed line to the respective layer it modifies. It is crucial to point out that an iconic *Universal Scope Constraint* applies in RRG in various ways (Van Valin 2005: 11, 12 and 21). This principle dictates that the morphemes expressing nuclear operators occur closer to the verb (stem) than morphemes expressing core operators. In turn, morphemes expressing clausal operators must occur outside of those expressing core operators. According to Van Valin (2005: 11), no counter-examples to this ordering principle have been found to date. The sentence from figure 3 is repeated in figure 10, this time with the matching operator projection.

Adverbs interact quite intensely with operators and they are iconically constrained by the operator projection and the scope of different operators. That is to say, adverbs related to inner operators must be closer to the predicate than adverbs related to (more) outer operators (Van Valin 2005: 20). 'Outer' operators are to be understood as operators operating on a higher level of the LSC. Ergo, nuclear adverbs must occur closer to the predicate than core adverbs. In turn, core adverbs must occur closer to the predicate than clausal adverbs (Van Valin 2005: 21).

---

[7] Only those expressing the orientation or motion of one participant with reference to another participant or to the speaker.
[8] Epistemic modals, external negation.
[9] Only those modifying orientation of action or event without reference to participants.
[10] Root modals, e.g. ability, permission, obligation.

2 Role and Reference Grammar

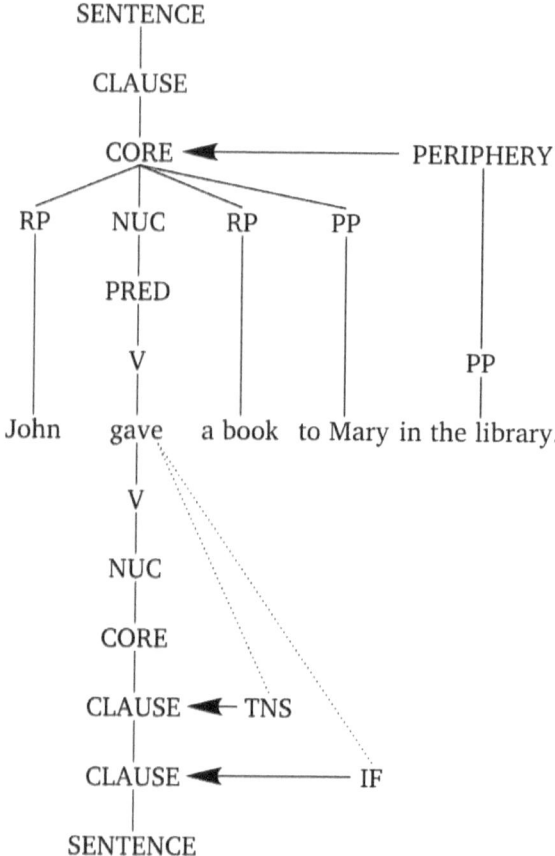

Figure 10: Constituent and operator projections of an English sentence.

Similar to the LSC, phrases have their proper set of operators and an operator projection. These operators have scope over different levels, as is the case with the LSC. For example, definiteness is an RP-level operator whereas quantification is a core level operator. A list of RP-operators is provided below (Van Valin 2005: 24).

2.3 Overall organization of Role and Reference Grammar

Operators in the layered structure of the RP		
Nuclear$_R$	**Core$_R$**	**RP**
Nominal aspect[11]	Number	Definiteness
	Quantification (quantifiers)	Deixis
	Negation	

Table 3: Operators in the layered structure of the RP.

The example of the RP in the previous section only had a constituent projection. Expanding the phrase from figure 8 to *de drie grote bruggen* ('the three big bridges') involves including operators. The expanded phrase is given below, this time with the operator projection included.

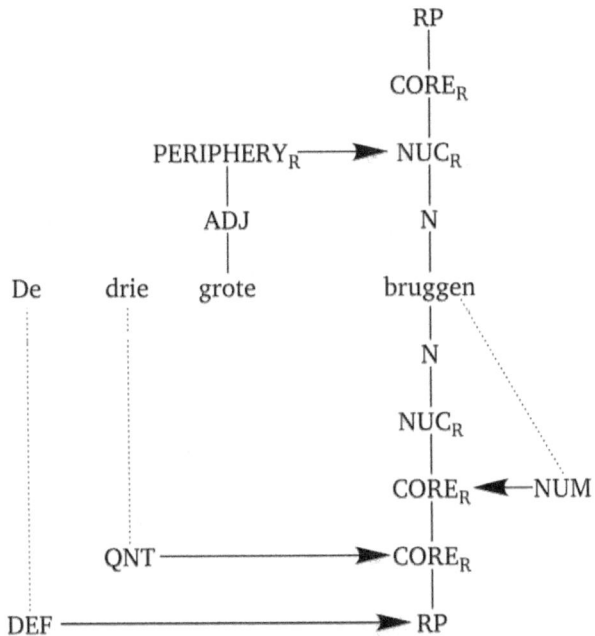

Figure 11: Constituent and operator projections of a Dutch RP.

---

[11] Count-mass distinction, classifiers in classifier languages.

It is crucial to point out that the operator projection is just that, a projection. Operators can be included in the logical structure of a sentence (or can be omitted for the sake of clarity) to represent the scope of each within this structure.

2.4 The Semantic Architecture of Role and Reference Grammar

2.4.1 Aktionsarten

RRG is a semantically driven syntactic theory. The semantic representation of sentences is directly based on the semantic representation of the predicating element (usually the verb). It is crucial to describe and capture the semantic relationships that hold between a predicate and its arguments. As the most typical predicate is a verb, a systematic theory of verb classes is at the heart of Role and Reference Grammar. RRG assumes that verbs can be classified according to their aktionsarten (Vendler 1957, 1967). It recognizes the Vendlerian aktionsart classes but also includes non-Vendlerian classes. Each class can be defined over a set of features, summarized in a feature matrix. Van Valin (2005: 32) points out that there is great cross-linguistic validity to the proposed verb classes. Hence, it is not unreasonable to assume that these distinctions are universal to human language.

Four features characterize the aktionsart classes: [±static], [±dynamic], [±telic] and [±punctual]. I provide a short description of each of them, followed by an overview of tests that help determine the precise aktionsart class.

Van Valin points out that [+static] verbs code a 'non-happening', whereas [-static] refers to a 'happening' (Van Valin 2005: 33). A fairly rudimentary way to test this is to ask the question 'what is happening?'. If the sentence that is to be tested could be a possible answer, then the verb is [-static]. For example, *John is running* could be an answer to that question but *John knows Mary* is not. Hence, *run* is [-static] and *know* is [+static].

2.4 The Semantic Architecture of Role and Reference Grammar

The feature [±dynamic] is related to whether or not the situation coded by the verb involves action. [+dynamic] verbs can be modified by so-called dynamic adverbs such as *violently* amongst others. This also constitutes the test for this feature (see below).

The feature [±telic] refers to whether or not the situation coded by the verb has an endpoint. [+telic] verbs do, [-telic] verbs do not have an inherent endpoint. In a sentence like *John knows Mary* the verb (a state) does not have an inherent endpoint, making it [-telic]. This can be contrasted with *the ice melted* where the point in time where the ice has completely turned to water is the inherent endpoint.

The feature [±punctual] refers to whether or not the situation coded by the verb has internal duration. In a sentence like *the window shattered*, the event coded by the verb is a punctual change-of-state. The change-of-state occurs instantaneously. As such, it is considered [+punctual]. The feature matrix for all classes is given in table 4 (Van Valin 2005: 33).

Class	Features			
State	[+static]	[-dynamic]	[-telic]	[-punctual]
Activity	[-static]	[+dynamic]	[-telic]	[-punctual]
Achievement	[-static]	[-dynamic]	[+telic]	[+punctual]
Semelfactive	[-static]	[±dynamic]	[-telic]	[+punctual]
Accomplishment	[-static]	[-dynamic]	[+telic]	[-punctual]
Active accomplishment	[-static]	[+dynamic]	[+telic]	[-punctual]

Table 4: Feature matrix for the base aktionsart classes as recognized by RRG.

Two of these classes, however, warrant a closer look: semelfactives and active accomplishments. Semelfactives are pure, punctual events without a change of state. Examples include sentences like *the light flashed* (Van Valin 2005: 32), where the state of the light after the event is identical to the state of the light before the flashing took place. In other words, there is no result state. There is one further important point to make with respect to semelfactives. In the feature matrix they are listed as either

[+dynamic] or [-dynamic]. This simply reflects the fact that some semelfactives are indeed dynamic in nature, a fact which is represented by a **do´** in the logical structure (see below). Consider (adapted from Van Valin 2005: 31ff.):

(2) a. *The light flashed (*violently).*
    b. *John coughed (violently).*

The acceptability of the adverb in (2b) and the unacceptability of that adverb in (2a) show that semelfactives do come in two flavors. This has to be borne in mind when applying the aktionsart tests.

The most important non-Vendlerian aktionsart is the active accomplishment. Active accomplishments can be considered as telically used activity predicates (Van Valin 2005: 32). They are derived from activity predicates, a fact that becomes very clear in the logical structure of both classes: the LS of an active accomplishment is a subset of the LS of an activity predicate (see below for further details). Consider the following examples (adapted from Van Valin 2005: 33):

(3) a. *I ran.*   = activity
    b. *I ran to the park.*   = active accomplishment
    c. *Dana ate fish.*   = activity
    d. *Dana ate the fish.*   = active accomplishment

All of these aktionsart classes have causative counterparts. These classes will be discussed in more detail in the following sections.

Drawing from the work of different linguists, RRG provides a set of tests with which the precise patterning of a given verb in a given language can be determined. It is, however, crucial to realize that these tests come with numerous caveats. First, the tests have to be adapted to fit the language under investigation (Van Valin 2005: 35). For example, tests 4 and 5 use the format [Prep + unit of time]. In Van Valin (2005) and in this chapter, the tests appear in an English-specific format (*in an hour* vs. *for an hour*). In the case of the for/in-alternation, it has to be determined how the language in question expresses *for* and *in* in their temporal senses (Van Valin 205: 37). Second, these tests have their limitations with respect to individual verbs. For example, the verb *bleed* is an activity but

2.4 The Semantic Architecture of Role and Reference Grammar

is not compatible with dynamic adverbs and thus fails test 2 (Jens Fleischhauer, p.c.). Despite these limitations, the tests are a powerful tool to determine the aktionart class of a given predicate. The account presented below is the one presented in Van Valin (2005) and represents the standard RRG-account.

Test 1 involves the use of the progressive and identifies a verb as an actvity, an accomplishment or an active accomplishment if it is compatible with the progressive. With the other classes, the progressive is less (or not at all) compatible. Consider for example the questionable grammaticality of sentences like *The glass was shattering or *I was seeing the painting. Most states disallow the progressive altogether, whereas achievements seem to allow it with plural subjects only. Semelfactives can occur with the progressive, but only in an iterative reading (Van Valin 2005: 35–36). In both cases, the verb patterns like an activity verb and no longer like an achievement or a semelfactive, respectively (Van Valin 2005: 36). Causative states are particularly interesting in this regard. Causative states allow the progressive more easily when the state of affairs described by the sentence is more actional in nature. Consider (Van Valin 2005: 39) the sentence *your attitude upsets/?is upsetting me* as compared to *your boorish behavior upsets/is upsetting me*. There are two important caveats with this test: 1) it is only useful if the language in question has progressive aspect and 2) it does not isolate a singular property. Rather, it sets three classes apart from the others (Van Valin 2005: 35). I have therefore listed the property tested by test 1 as 'multiple*' in table 6.

Test 2 involves the use of dynamic adverbs and isolates [±dynamic]. The compatibility of the verb under investigation with an adverb encoding a dynamic action reveals a positive value for dynamicity. An important restriction for this test is that no dynamic adverb be used that requires a controlling subject (Van Valin 2005: 36). Doing so would mean mixing the properties [±dynamic] and [±controlling] which could yield wrong or distorted results. Incompatibility might then be due to the agentive reading of the adverb conflicting with semantic properties of the verb. Consider (Van Valin 2005: 36) the examples in (4).

2 Role and Reference Grammar

(4) a. *The dog shivered.*   Activity ([+dynamic])
     b. *The dog shivered violently.*   Activity ([+dynamic])
     c. **The dog shivered deliberately.*   Activity ([+dynamic])

With test 2, causative states again present an interesting, additional complication: The more actional the state of affairs described by the sentence is, the more acceptable dynamic adverbs will be, e.g. (Van Valin 2005: 40) *The clown actively amused the children.*

Test 3 isolates [±punctual] and involves using pace adverbs (e.g.: *quickly, rapidly, slowly* etc.). In other words, test 3 tests whether or not a verb has temporal duration. If the pace adverb and the verb are compatible, the verb has temporal duration and thus is [-punctual]. For example: *The ice melted slowly* (melt = accomplishment, [-punctual]) as opposed to **The window shattered slowly* (shatter= achievement, [+punctual]). This test is not linked through any kind of redundancy with test 2. These pace adverbs are compatible with [-punctual] irrespective of the dynamicity of the verb. For example (after Van Valin 2005: 36): *The ice melted slowly* as opposed to **The ice melted violently.* The main caveat with test 3 is that adverbs denoting very short units of time distort the test results. Using such adverbs could lead the user to wrongly rate [+punctual] predicates, such as achievements and semelfactives, as [-punctual]. Consider for example (Van Valin 2005: 36–37) the sentence *the bomb exploded instantly/*gradually* (achievement, [+punctual]). Semelfactives, again, seem to allow for an iterative reading[12], making them pattern like activities (see above). It is thus important to use adverbs denoting an adequately long temporal interval.

Test 4 involves adding (in English) a *for*-PP with a temporal meaning. As such, this test focusses on whether a verb has temporal duration or not. Consider the sentence (Van Valin 2005: 37) *he read the book for an hour.* The PP specifies that the event denoted by the verb went on for a certain amount of time. No reference to any endpoint is given. All classes except achievements and semelfactives are compatible with *for*-PPs and thus have duration in time. Semelfactives are only compatible with

---

[12] To counteract any iterative reading, *once* (or a similar adverb) can be added (Van Valin 2005: 36–37).

2.4 The Semantic Architecture of Role and Reference Grammar

for-PPs denoting very short time spans. An important caveat with this test is that states denoting inherent properties do not take *for*-PPs (Van Valin 2005: 37) as in for example *?John was intelligent for an hour*. One last remark needs to be made. Accomplishments and active accomplishments can co-occur with *for*-PPs. Van Valin (2005: 37–38) points out that this follows from their [-punctual] nature (as determined by test 3). Van Valin (2005: 37–38) considers the occurrence of *for*-PPs with these classes irrelevant and they are therefore marked as such in table 5.

Test 5 is often used in conjunction with test 4 and uses an *in*-PP with a temporal meaning. This test focuses on terminal points (Van Valin 2005: 37). In the sentence *he read the book in an hour*, the act of reading is complete. The reading took one hour and the book has been finished. A caveat with test 5 is that even though achievements have an endpoint (i.e. [+telic]) they are incompatible with most *in*-PPs due to their [+punctual] nature. Only PPs denoting very short time segments are possible (e.g. *in a fraction of a second*). Practically speaking, accomplishments, active accomplishments and their causative counterparts take *in*-PPs. Tests 4 and 5 are often collectively known as the *for/in*-alternation and are used to distinguish the [+telic] classes from the [-telic] classes. Van Valin points out that both tests should be used with 'temporal expressions of substantial duration' (Van Valin 2005: 37).

Both semelfactives and achievements are [+punctual] and test 6 is used to distinguish them. The verb is used as a stative modifier. Consider (after Van Valin 2005: 38):

(5) a. *The window shattered* → *The shattered window*.
     b. *The light flashed.* → **The flashed light*.

As semelfactives are pure events without a result state, they cannot be used as a stative modifier.

Test 7 makes use of a paraphrase to ascertain whether the verb is causative or not. It is however crucial that the number of arguments remain constant: All the arguments of the original sentence have to feature in the paraphrase. Consider the examples (Van Valin 2005: 38) in (6).

(6) a. *The cat popped the balloon.*
The cat caused the balloon to pop.
b. *The hot water melted the ice.*
The hot water caused the ice to melt.
c. *Leslie runs.*
*Leslie causes to run./*Leslie causes herself to run.

It is important to stress that this test cannot be applied to single-argument verbs as using a cause-paraphrase with only one argument is not possible (6c). Causativity always includes (at least) two participants. Values with caveats are marked with an asterisk in the table. Table 5 is a summary of the aktionsart tests and their result when applied to the individual classes including the causative versions of each (Van Valin 2005: 39). Table 6 is a summary of the aktionsart tests, the properties that they test and possible caveats. Note that the question-answer pairing has been included as test 1'. It is not featured in Van Valin (2005) as a test in its own right, but due to its usefulness it should be included here. The causative classes are derived from the non-causatives ones, a fact which is represented in the table. The tests were applied to all example sentences in this book.

2.4 The Semantic Architecture of Role and Reference Grammar

Class	T1	T2	T3	T4	T5	T6	T7
State	No*	No	No	Yes*	No	Yes	No
Achievement	No*	No	No*	No*	No*	Yes	No
Semelfactive	No*	No*	No*	Yes*	No*	No	No
Accomplishment	Yes	No	Yes	Irrelevant*	Yes	Yes	No
Activity	Yes	Yes	Yes	Yes	No	No	No
Active accomplishment	Yes	Yes	Yes	Irrelevant*	Yes	Yes	No
Causative state	Yes*	Yes*	No	Yes	No	Yes	Yes
Causautive achievement	No	Yes*	No*	No	No*	Yes	Yes
Causative semelfactive	No*	Yes*	No*	No*	No*	No	Yes
Causative accomplishment	Yes	Yes*	Yes	Irrelevant*	Yes	Yes	Yes
Causative activity	Yes	Yes	Yes	Yes	No	Yes	Yes
Caus. active accomplishment	Yes	Yes	Yes	Irrelevant*	Yes	Yes	Yes

Table 5: Aktionsart tests and the values for the respective aktionsart classes.

2 Role and Reference Grammar

Test	Format	Property tested	Caveat
1	Progressive	Multiple*	Only in languages with progressive aspect
2	Dynamic adverb	[±dynamic]	Avoid adverbs with controlling subject
3	Pace adverb	[±punctual]	Avoid time units that are very short
4	*For*-PP	Temporal duration	(1) Semelfactives only with PPs denoting very short intervals (2) Not with state predicates denoting inherent properties
5	*In*-PP	Terminal point	Achievements only possible with PPs denoting very short intervals
6	Stative modifier	Result state with [+punctual] verb	
7	Causative paraphrase	Causativity	Maintain number of arguments!
1'	Question-answer	[±static]	

Table 6: Summary of aktionsart tests with tested properties and caveats.

2.4.2 Logical structures

Each aktionsart class is represented by a certain logical structure. In RRG, the system of lexical decomposition proposed by Dowty (1979) in a modified form is used as the basis for the logical structures. RRG assumes that the LSs of the aktionsart classes are all derived from either an activity or a state predicate. States are represented as bare predicates whereas activities are characterized by the predicate **do´** in their logical structure. In other words, activities and states are basic and all others are derived from them (Van Valin 2005: 42). Achievements are characterized by the presence of the operator INGR (ingressive), accomplishments by the presence of BECOME. Semelfactives are characterized by the presence of the SEML-operator and causatives are characterized by the CAUSE-operator. It is to be borne in mind that causative predicates have a more complex logical structure following the pattern α CAUSE β, where α and β are logical structures of any type (Van Valin 2005: 45).

In the LS, each of the aktionsart classes is represented as an operator or combination of operators. Bold face indicates a predicate and the variables x, y and z represent the argument slots. A list of sentences with their corresponding logical structures (adapted from Van Valin 2005: 42ff.) is given in (7).

(7) a. *John knows Pat.*   State
  know´ (John, Pat)
 b. *Carl ate pizza.*   Activity
  do´ (Carl, [**eat´** (Carl, pizza)])
 c. *The window shattered.*   Achievement
  INGR **shattered´** (window)
 d. *The ice melted.*   Accomplishment
  BECOME **melted´** (ice)
 e. *Dana glimpsed the picture.*   Semelfactive (stative)
  SEML **glimpse´** (Dana, picture)
 f. *Mary coughed.*   Semelfactive (dynamic)
  SEML **do´** (Mary, [**cough´** (Mary)])
 g. *Chris ran to the park.*   Active accomplishment
  do´ (Chris, [**run´** (Chris)]) & INGR **be-at´** (park, Chris)

h. *The dog scared the boy.* Causative state
[**do**′ (dog, Ø)] CAUSE [**feel**′ (boy, [**afraid**′])]
i. *The girl walked the dog.* Causative activity
[**do**′ (girl, Ø)] CAUSE [**do**′ (dog, [**walk**′ (dog)])]
j. *The cat popped the balloon.* Causative achievement
[**do**′ (cat, Ø)] CAUSE [INGR **popped**′ (balloon)]
k. *The hot water melted the ice.* Causative accomplishment
[**do**′ (hot water, Ø)] CAUSE [BECOME **melted**′ (ice)]
l. *The soldier flashed the light.* Causative semelfactive
[**do**′ (soldier, Ø)] CAUSE [SEML **do**′ (light, [**flash**′ (light)])]
m. *The Praetor marched the soldiers to the fort.*
Causative active accomplishment
[**do**′ (Praetor, Ø)] CAUSE [**do**′ (soldiers, [**march**′ (soldier)]) & INGR **be-at**′ (fort, soldiers)]

A small note on causation has to be made at this point. Van Valin (2005: 42) distinguishes between three kinds of causation: *direct, indirect* and *permissive* causation. The former two are represented by CAUSE in the logical structure, the latter is represented by LET. However, in the logical structures the (potential) distinctions are generalized over for practical reasons (Van Valin, p.c.). This means that the three types of causation are amalgamated – as far as the LS is concerned – into CAUSE. Table 7 is a summary of possible LS-configurations.

Aktionsart Class	Logical Structure
STATE	**predicate'** (x) or (x, y)
ACTIVITY	**do'** (x, [**predicate'** (x) or (x, y)])
ACHIEVEMENT	INGR **predicate'** (x) or (x, y) or INGR **do'** (x, [**predicate'** (x) or (x, y)])
SEMELFACTIVE	SEML **predicate'** (x) or (x, y) or SEML **do'** (x, [**predicate'** (x) or (x, y)])
ACCOMPLISHMENT	BECOME **predicate'** (x), (x, y) or BECOME **do'** (x, [**predicate'** (x) or (x, y)])
ACTIVE ACCOMPLISHMENT	**do'** (x, [**predicate1'** (x, (y))]) & INGR **predicate2'** (z, x) or (y)
CAUSATIVE	α CAUSE β, where α, β are logical structure of any type

Table 7: Lexical representations for aktionsart classes (Van Valin 2005: 45).

2.5 Linking semantics to syntax

In the previous sections, I have introduced the basics of the syntactic representation and the semantics of the theory. In the following sections, the mechanisms relating semantics to syntax will be discussed.

2.5.1 The Actor-Undergoer Hierarchy and the Macroroles

In the linking of the semantic base into the syntax, RRG employs two crucial tools: the macroroles (*actor* and *undergoer*) and the *actor-undergoer hierarchy* (AUH). Macroroles (Van Valin 2005: 60, Van Valin & LaPolla 1997, Van Valin 1977, 1999 and 2004, Foley & Van Valin 1984) are generalized semantic roles or GSRs.

GSRs have been proposed by various scholars in recent decades, in various incarnations (see Levin & Rappaport Hovav 2005: 51ff.). Dowty, for example, posits semantic proto-roles as cluster concepts rather than as discrete semantic roles. Van Valin (1999: 373) points out that GSRs have important functions in monostratal theories of syntax as they are employed to capture important generalizations that are handled in terms of deep subjects and objects (and similar devices) in the various versions of transformational grammar. The main motivation behind GSRs is that there is a fundamental opposition between the two cardinal arguments of a transitive predication (Van Valin 1999: 373, 2005: 60-61). Van Valin points out that many syntactic phenomena are tied to these two cardinal arguments. RRG's macroroles are similar to Dowty's proto-roles in that both are derived concepts with no invariant semantic entailments (Levin & Rappaport Hovav 2005: 68), but they differ with respect to their importance for linking mechanisms (Ibid.) In RRG, they occupy a prominent position in many aspects of the system. It is crucial to stress that GSRs are not thematic relations. Rather, Van Valin distinguishes (1999: 373) between three levels of semantic relationships: verb-specific semantic roles, thematic relations as generalizations across verb-specific roles and, finally, GSRs as generalizations *across* thematic relations. The first type does not really play any role in RRG, the second can play a role in interpretation and differences therein. For linking, the GSRs are by far the most important ones. GSRs are partly motivated by similar considerations that inspired the concept of thematic relations (e.g. active vs. passive sentences). GSRs are, however, an attempt to address the inherent shortcomings of standard thematic relations (Dowty 1991). Due to their generalized nature, they are much more robust and adequate to capture the behavior of a grammatical system. Most approaches using GSRs have two such roles, although some linguists posit three roles (e.g. Primus 1999). Van Valin (1999) provides arguments against three macroroles, defending the dual nature of RRG's GSR-conception. First, some languages disprefer or even completely prohibit three arguments in a single core (Van Valin 2004: 74ff). Therefore, a hypothetical third macrorole can never be universal. As such, it would not be adequate to use as a cornerstone of syntactic theory. Second, morphosyntactic coding of actor and undergoer is fairly consistent cross-linguistically, contrary to the coding of the third argument in a ditransitive predication (Ibid.), which is typologically not consistent at all.

RRG's macroroles are semantic notions that play a crucial role in the syntax (Van Valin 2004: 64). As was explained above, actor and undergoer are distinct from both thematic relations and syntactic relations such as subject and direct object. RRG does not use these latter two concepts because they are deemed to be non-universal (Van Valin 2005: 89ff.). Rather, actor and undergoer are the pivotal linking concepts in RRG. Put simply, the actor is the most agent-like argument and the undergoer is (usually) the most patient-like argument. Altough the notions have no place in RRG, actor and undergoer can be (more or less) equated to 'logical subject' and 'logical object'. The third argument of ditransitive verbs is treated as a *non-macrorole argument* (NMR). This means that the argument in question simply does not receive a macrorole. Single-argument verbs have either the actor or the undergoer macrorole, correlating with the respective presence or absence of **do´** in the logical structure (Van Valin 2005: 63). Throughout the linking process, reference is made to the macroroles and, to a lesser extent, the NMR (for example in the domain of case assignment – Van Valin 2009a and Van Valin 2005: 108–110).

Because the base semantics in RRG are dealt with in terms of logical structures, the assignment of macroroles to arguments of the predicate can be described in terms of the argument positions relative to each other. The more 'agent'-like arguments will be to the left (in the LS) of the more 'patient'-like arguments. It is therefore possible to capture the relation between macroroles and the arguments in the LS in terms of a hierarchy, the Actor-Undergoer Hierarchy (Van Valin 2005: 61 & 126):

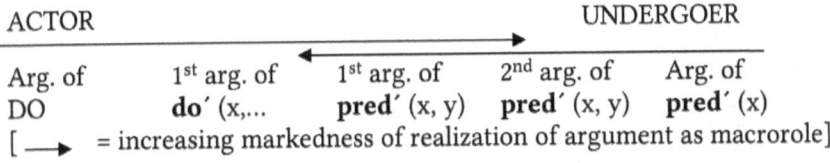

ACTOR				UNDERGOER
Arg. of	1ˢᵗ arg. of	1ˢᵗ arg. of	2ⁿᵈ arg. of	Arg. of
DO	**do´** (x,...	**pred´** (x, y)	**pred´** (x, y)	**pred´** (x)

[⟶ = increasing markedness of realization of argument as macrorole]

Figure 12: The Actor-Undergoer Hierarchy (AUH).

The argument in the LS that ranks highest on the AUH is selected as actor, the argument that ranks lowest is selected as undergoer. If there is a third argument, it is neither the highest nor the lowest and therefore becomes the non-macrorole argument (NMR). Actor assignment is not

2 Role and Reference Grammar

variable. Undergoer assignment is variable, although there is a default. Variable undergoer selection is possible in certain languages, such as English and Dutch. RRG analyzes the 'dative shift' phenomenon in the languages (and verbs) that allow it in terms of variable undergoer selection (Van Valin 2005: 61ff, Foley & Van Valin 1985). Consider the following examples of macrorole assignment (adapted from Van Valin 2005: 46ff. & 61). Example (8d) is the dative-shifted version of (8c):

(8)   a.   The ice melted.
           BECOME **melted**′ (ice)
                             U
     b.   Sara melted the ice.
           [**do**′ (Sara, Ø)] CAUSE [BECOME **melted**′ (ice)]
            A   U
     c.   Pat gave the book to Chris.
           [**do**′ (Pat, Ø)] CAUSE [BECOME **have**′ (Chris, book)]
            A   NMR   U
     d.   Pat gave Chris the book.
           [**do**′ (Pat, Ø)] CAUSE [BECOME **have**′ (Chris, book)]
            A   U   NMR

Macrorolehood and NMR-hood have important implications for the workings of the theory. The selection of the *Privileged Syntactic Argument* (PSA) – the closest RRG-equivalent to the notion of the traditional subject – is selected on the basis of the macrorole-status of the arguments in the logical structure. The macrorole assignment principles are summarized below (Van Valin 2005: 63).

(9)   Default Macrorole Assignment Principles
     a.   Number: the number of macroroles a verb takes is less than or equal to the number of arguments in its logical structure.
           1. If a verb has two or more arguments in its logical structure, it will take two macroroles;
           2. If a verb has one argument in its logical structure, it will take one macrorole.

b. Nature: for verbs which take one macrorole,
   1. If the verb has an activity predicate in its logical structure, the macrorole is actor.
   2. If the verb has no activity predicate in its logical structure, the macrorole is undergoer.

RRG distinguishes between syntactic transitivity (S-transitivity) and macrorole transitivity (M-transitivity). As macroroles have such a pivotal position within the theory, the concept of M-transitivity is the more important of the two. S-transitivity is an indication of the number of direct core arguments, whereas M-transitivity is an indication of the number of macroroles a verb takes (Van Valin 2005: 63–64). The importance of macroroles for the workings of RRG cannot be underestimated. Case marking and preposition assignment (Van Valin 2005: 107ff.), for instance, are tied to the macrorole-status of the argument in question. Dative case (in languages with a case system) is treated as the default case for NMRs, for example. Atypical case assignment is dealt with in terms of exceptional M-transitivity (Dahm-Draksic 1997, Van Valin 1991, Van Valin 2005). Semantic valence refers to the number of arguments in the logical structure. A table (adapted from Van Valin 2005: 64) comparing M-transitivity and semantic valence is given in table 8. Transitivity is always understood as M-transitivity in this book, unless otherwise specified.

Semantic valence	Macrorole number	M-transitivity	Example verb
0	0	Atransitive	rain, snow
1	1	Intransitive	die
1 or 2	1	Intransitive	drink (activity)[13]
2	2	Transitive	drink (active accomplishment)
2	2	Transitive	kill
3	2	Transitive	set
3	2	Transitive	send

Table 8: Transitivity in Role and Reference Grammar.

2.5.2 Privileged Syntactic Argument

Partly as a reaction to the problematic handling of ergative languages in terms of grammatical relations, RRG posits the so-called *privileged syntactic argument of a construction* (or: PSA). Van Valin points out that in all languages there are restrictions on the RPs and PPs that can feature in syntactic constructions. These restrictions are said to define a privileged syntagmatic function with respect to the construction (Van Valin 2005: 94). It is crucial to make clear that one cannot speak of 'the PSA in Dutch' or 'the PSA in English'. PSAs are constructionally defined (Van Valin 2005: 99). Therefore, there is no single PSA for a given language. Rather, English or Dutch have many PSAs, one per construction. All PSAs in one and the same language can be quite similar, however. It would be erroneous to treat the PSA as a notational variant of the term subject. 'Subject' is treated as a non-universal concept in RRG. The so-called *S-function* is considered to be a (restricted) neutralization of the actor and the undergoer of an intransitive verb. Simply put, if a language treats the actor-argument and the undergoer-argument of an intransitive verb the same way, then the language has an S-function. To illustrate: If a language treats *John* in *John ran* and in *John died* the same way, it has

---

[13] If the second argument of activity verbs is non-referential, it does not take a macrorole. If it is referential, a second macrorole is assigned (Van Valin 2005: 64, also see Van Valin & LaPolla 1997).

an S-function. Languages like English, German and Dutch have such an S-function, but others, such as Acehnese, do not (Van Valin 2005: 96). In languages like Dutch and English the S, the actor of the transitive verb (A$_T$) and the 'derived subject'[14] (d-S) are treated alike as PSA; they are 'restrictively neutralized'. In Acehnese, there is no such neutralization: Actor-PSAs are treated differently from undergoer-PSAs. Van Valin points out that besides the aforementioned S-function, languages are often very consistent in their treatment of PSAs across constructions. This high level of consistency in a given language can allow for positing a 'subject' as a kind of generalized PSA if most (or even all) of the major constructions in a language have the same pattern of restricted neutralization (Van Valin 2005: 99).

After the macroroles have been assigned to arguments in the logical structure by the application of the AUH, the PSA has to be assigned. The assignment of the PSA can be captured in terms of an accessibility hierarchy, which, in essence, is the actor half of the AUH (Van Valin 2005: 100):

(10)   Arg. of DO > 1st arg. of **do**′ > 1st arg. of **pred**′ (x, y) > 2nd arg. of **pred**′ (x, y) > arg. of **pred**′ (x)

In accusatively-aligned languages, the highest-ranking direct core argument (in terms of (10)) becomes PSA. In ergatively-aligned languages, the lowest-ranking direct core argument becomes PSA. The hierarchy – and the markedness of the choices – is thus inverse for ergatively-aligned languages. Principles for the default and marked assignment of the PSA can be now drawn up (Van Valin 2005: 100). These are given in table 9.

---

[14]   Crudely speaking, the subject of a passive.

Syntactic system	Default choice for PSA	Choice for PSA requiring special construction
Accusative	Actor	Undergoer [Passive]
Ergative	Undergoer	Actor [Antipassive]

Table 9: PSA-assignment overview.

There is considerable cross-linguistic variation with respect to the PSA along three dimensions. First, there are languages that have variable PSAs. This means that not only the default choice for PSA is allowed, but also a marked choice (e.g. English and Dutch). Other languages (e.g. Lakhota) have fixed or invariable PSAs: they only have the default choice available to them. Roughly speaking, such languages do not have a passive (or antipassive in the case of ergative systems). Second, languages vary with respect to the required macrorole status for the PSA. Some languages only allow macrorole arguments as PSAs, whereas others also allow non-macrorole direct core arguments to function as PSA. German is an example of the former, Icelandic of the latter (Van Valin 2005: 100). However, oblique core arguments becoming PSA seem to be crosslinguistically strongly dispreferred (Van Valin 2005: 136, Van Valin 2009b). Third, some languages have case-sensitive PSAs (e.g. English and German). Others have case-insensitive PSAs (e.g. Belhare). Examples of PSA-assignment are given in (11).

(11) a. *Pat gave the book to Chris.* Default assignment
[do´ (Pat, Ø)] CAUSE [BECOME have´ (Chris, book)]
A+PSA   NMR   U
b. *The book was given to Chris by Pat.* Marked assignment
[do´ (Pat, Ø)] CAUSE [BECOME have´ (Chris, book)]
A+ Peripheral PP   NMR   U+PSA

2.5.3 The Linking Algorithm

All of the aforementioned systemic devices come together in the linking algorithm, the centerpiece of RRG. The linking algorithm can be considered as a set of ordered rules that relate the semantics to the syntax, with discourse pragmatics playing an influential role (figure 1). The linking algorithm is considered bidirectional. It not only links semantics to syntax, but also maps a syntactic structure onto a semantic base through use of a parser. This 'reversed' linking occurs when language material is processed by the hearer. In other words, one direction captures language production, the other captures language comprehension (Van Valin 2005: 129). The RRG linking system is regulated by a general, overarching constraint, called the *completeness constraint*. It is given in (12).

(12) **Completeness constraint** (Van Valin 2005: 129–130)

All of the arguments explicitly specified in the semantic representation of a sentence must be realized syntactically in the sentence, and all of the referring expressions in the syntactic representation of a sentence must be linked to an argument position in a logical structure in the semantic representation of the sentence.

One can summarize the linking system as follows: The predicate comes with a certain logical structure. The semantic representation is built up out of these components in the lexicon. The semantic representation and the information therein determine the choice of syntactic templates (stored in the syntactic inventory). The *syntactic template selection principle* states that the number of arguments a verb takes must be equal to the number of positions that arguments can appear in (in the core). This can be considered a logical consequence of the completeness constraint. The syntactic template selection principle can be complemented by language-specific requirements, however. The syntactic template selection principle and language-specific qualifications (Van Valin 2005: 130) are given in (13).

(13) **Syntactic template selection principle**

The number of syntactic slots for arguments and argument-adjuncts within the core is equal to the number of distinct specified argument positions in the semantic representation of the core.

Language-specific qualifications

1. All cores in the language have a minimum syntactic valence of 1.
2. Argument-modulation voice constructions reduce the number of core slots by 1.
3. The occurrence of a syntactic argument in the pre/post-core slot reduces the number of core slots by 1 (may override 1. above).

Now that the main components of RRG's linking system have been introduced, the tenets of the theory presented in this chapter can be summarized as in figure 13.

Because the linking algorithm is bidirectional, two possible linking procedures can be spelled out. For my purposes, the semantics-to-syntax linking is by far the most important aspect. Therefore, only this direction of the algorithm is represented in (14) (adapted from Van Valin 2005: 123). It is important to stress that all the steps in the algorithm show cross-linguistic variation (for instance, variable undergoer selection or pragmatically influenced PSAs).

(14) **Linking algorithm: semantics-to-syntax**

1. Construct the semantic representation of the sentence, based on the logical structure of the predicator.
2. Determine the actor and undergoer assignments, following the actor-undergoer hierarchy in figure 12.
3. Determine the morphosyntactic coding of the arguments
   a. Select the privileged syntactic argument, based on the privileged syntactic argument selection hierarchy and respective principles.
   b. Assign the arguments the appropriate case markers and/or adpositions.
   c. Assign the agreement marking to the main or auxiliary verb, as appropriate.

2.5 Linking semantics to syntax

4. Select the syntactic template(s) for the sentence following the appropriate principles.
5. Assign arguments to positions in the syntactic representation of the sentence.
   a. Assign the [-WH] argument(s) to the appropriate positions in the clause.
   b. If there is a [+WH] argument of a logical structure,
      1. assign it to the normal position of a non-WH-argument with the samefunction, or
      2. assign it to the precore or postcore slot, or
      3. assign it to a position within the potential focus domain of the clause (default = the unmarked focus position).
   c. A non-WH argument may be assigned to the precore or postcore slot, subject to focus structure restrictions (optional).
   d. Assign the [-WH] argument(s) of logical structure(s) other than that of the predicator in the nucleus to
      1. a periphery (default), or
      2. the precore or postcore slot, or
      3. the left- or right-detached position.

It is crucial to bear in mind that everything discussed so far applies to simple sentences. Even though matters are obviously more complicated in complex sentences, the same basic principles apply. It is possible to graphically represent the linking in its various stages. The representation of figure 2 is given in figure 14, including the logical structure and the various stages of linking from semantics to syntax.

2 Role and Reference Grammar

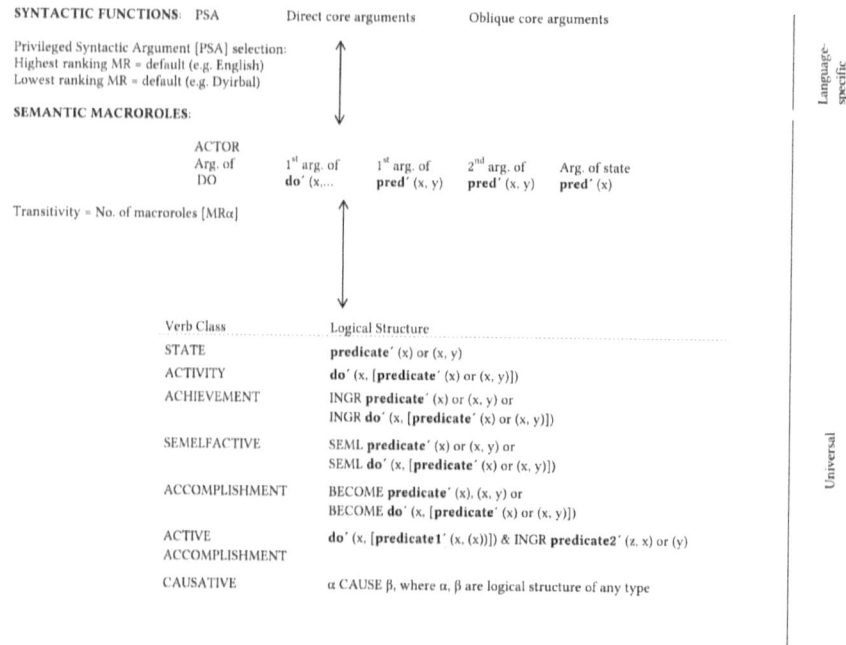

Figure 13: General overview and summary of the RRG linking system (Van Valin 2005: 129).

Figure 14 is a visualization of the linking algorithm using the sentence from figure 2 as an example (adapted from Van Valin 2005: 140). The steps in the linking are indicated in the circles and correspond to the phases of linking described in (14).

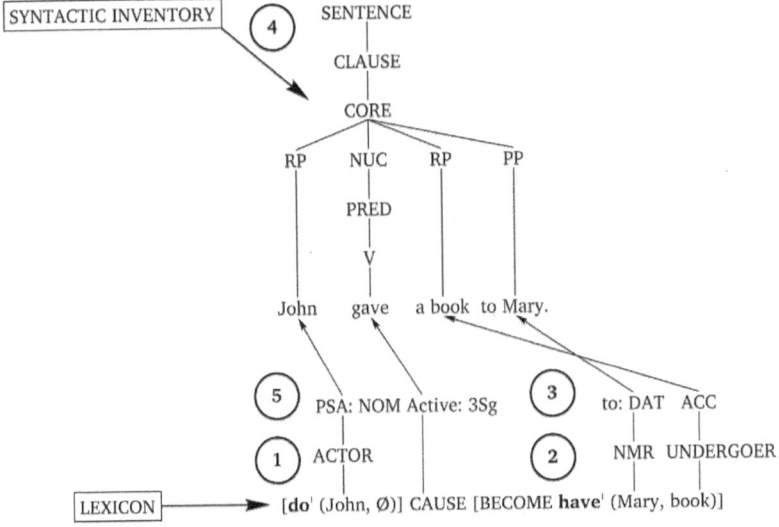

Figure 14: Semantics-to-syntax linking in its successive steps.

2.6 Conclusion

In this chapter, I have introduced the basic tenets and principles of Role and Reference Grammar. I have discussed the fundamentals of the theory, its general organization and single components. We have seen that the Layered Structure of the Clause and its phrase-level equivalent are versatile concepts capable of capturing a wide range of language phenomena without resorting to transformations, movement or similar devices. RRG makes extensive use of its GSRs actor and undergoer. PSA-assignment and case assignment (Van Valin 2009b and 2005: 107ff.) are tied to them, for example. This brief exploration of RRG applies primarily to simple sentences. With the information presented in this chapter, it is possible to refine the organizational figure in 1 into the one in 15 (Van Valin 2005: 134) by adding several important mechanisms that were discussed in this chapter.

2 Role and Reference Grammar

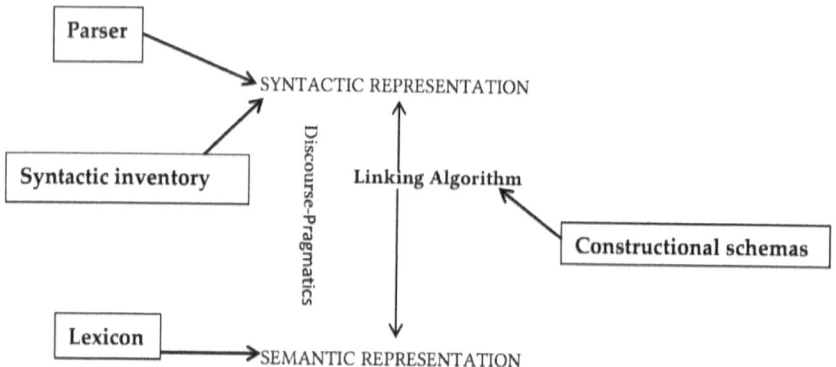

Figure 15: General organization of Role and Reference Grammar (final).

Case and preposition assignment in RRG were not discussed in this chapter. They are, however, very relevant for the topic of this dissertation. They will be introduced in chapter 8 where the linking of instruments to the morphosyntax is explored.

3 Instruments at the syntax-semantics interface

In most approaches and formal frameworks thematic relations are the usual way to handle instruments and related concepts. Theories that use them usually have the instrument as one of the more prominent members in their inventory. Yet, despite the instrument's ubiquitous presence in frameworks and loose approaches alike, they are often not coherently defined, nor are they in the center of attention when it comes to developing a view of thematic relations. They are 'peripherally present' if you will. It does, however, seem to be the case that the instrument is generally treated as a dependent relation that plays some causal, intermediate role. It is often dependent on the presence or existence of other relations, such as the agent. This chapter aims to provide an overview of thematic relations in a number of topic-relevant theories, placing them in the broader field of lexical semantics, while focusing specifically on instruments and related concepts. Some of these approaches are looked at in more detail in following sections: Case Grammar, Lexical-Functional Grammar, Jackendoff's Conceptual Semantics and Role and Reference Grammar. They will become relevant for the discussion of instrument-related alternations explored in later sections and chapters. Therefore, a general introduction to thematic relations and to each of the aforementioned frameworks is warranted. The overviews are, however, limited to only those mechanisms which are required to gain a deeper understanding of instruments.

3 Instruments at the syntax-semantics interface

3.1 Thematic relations as an interface component

Language describes events, canonically expressed by a predicate and its arguments (and its adjuncts). A thematic relation R can be defined as the relation of a participant x in an event e relative to the event as a whole (after Davis 2011: 400). Put somewhat informally, a thematic relation is the relation between an event and a participant. Semantically, they can be defined as partial functions (Dowty 1989: 80, Chierchia 1984: 326-327, Carlson 1984 and Davis 2011: 401):

(1) A θ-role θ is a partial function from the set of events into the set of individuals such that for any event k, if θ(k) is defined, then θ(k) ∈ k.

In linguistics, thematic relations are a central explanatory tool in accounting for the linking from semantics to syntax (Davis 2011: 399ff.). They are essentially theoretical constructs to account for empirical facts concerning syntactic behavior and they are often argued to be an *intermediary* in the mapping from semantics to syntax (Bierwisch 2006: 89-90 & Carlson 1984: 259, 270). This is often referred to as the *interface character*. Thematic relations are usually nested inside a more general theory of event conceptualization, in the broader endeavour of argument realization (Levin & Rappaport Hovav 2005: 2).

Bierwisch (2006: 89) points out that approaches to thematic relations are essentially driven by two principles: 1) *parsimony*, which requires the stipulations to be as minimal as possible and 2) *adequacy*, which requires that all relevant empirical facts be covered. With respect to instruments, adequacy is hardly ever reached and parsimony is often not satisfied due to the attempts to attain adequacy (e.g. Alexiadou & Schäfer 2006, Schlesinger 1989). There are several possibilities to classify theories of thematic relations. One very general classification involves dividing such approaches into *instrinsic* and *extrinsic* ones (Bierwisch 2006: 98ff.). *Intrinsic approaches* assume that thematic relations and relevant ordering and mapping mechanisms arise from the semantic representation of the event. Typically, but not exclusively (Bierwisch 2006: 120), such approaches are decompositional in nature. Wunderlich's Lexical Decomposition Grammar, for example, assumes that thematic roles can simply be extracted from SF (semantic form) by virtue of argument positions relative to the predicate they are arguments of (1997: 43). On the *extrinsic view*, thematic relations are defined independently from any kind of semantic representation, as are mapping mechanisms, well-formedness constraints and the like. Thematic relations are, under this view, self-contained organizing elements that are separate from the semantic base they function in (Bierwisch 2006: 105 & 109). Even though Bierwisch (Ibid.) assumes many theories have problems meeting the two conditions, he points out that especially the extrinsic approaches have problems in this respect.

Ideally, thematic relations[1] serve to capture linguistic generalizations *across* and *within* languages. Therein lies the appeal of such a type of relations: The syntax can vary, the thematic relations between predicate and argument will remain the same. This enables linguists to build salient grammatical descriptions around these concepts and to use them as the corner stones for a descriptive framework. Yet, despite their appeal, they are faced with a myriad of problems of both a practical and a theoretical nature. Carlson (1984: 259-260) argues that despite their weaknesses, thematic relations prove so useful that we should work with them nonetheless. It is important to stress that thematic relations in their traditional, primitive form are only one of several forms they can take. As thematic relations are usually seen in connection to a governing verb, theories intending to be complete should also propose a more general theory of event conceptualization as a backdrop against which thematic relations function (Levin & Rappaport Hovav 2005: 4ff.). Understanding what thematic relations really *are* in a given theory depends on understanding how the theory conceptualizes events. Event conceptualization

---

[1] In modern linguistics, thematic relations are known under a plethora of names: semantic roles, semantic relations, thematic roles, deep cases, thematic relations, θ-roles, thematic role types etc. In this dissertation the more general term *thematic relations* is employed. The terminology used by the original author may vary. In addition, the same label may be used with a different content depending on the author. This is a general problem with respect to the thematic relations literature (Levin & Rappaport Hovav 2005: 48).

3 Instruments at the syntax-semantics interface

often takes the form of a variety of lexical decomposition, but this need not be the case. Several approaches include lexical decompositions with variables embedded in hierarchal structures to account for 'thematic structure' and linking preferences (e.g. Dowty, RRG) whereas others combine a more conceptual approach with the decompositional approach (e.g. Jackendoff) and even others analyze thematic structure with causality as a central driving component (e.g. Croft). As these approaches can be vastly different, the nature, number and properties of thematic relations will vary dramatically. For instance, J. Anderson's Case Grammar recognizes only four roles, whereas Ostler (1979) recognizes 48 roles. A non-exhaustive overview of several important schools of thought is given in figure 16.

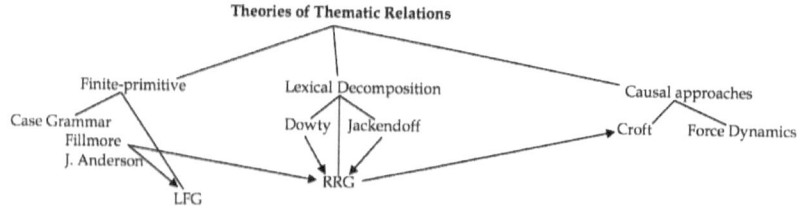

Figure 16: Overview of thematic relation approaches discussed in this dissertation.[2]

Generally, theories of thematic relations share five theoretical pillars (Croft 2015: 104-105 & Davis 2011): 1) a conception of event structure, 2) 'participant' roles, 3) a ranking for thematic relations (or: *thematic hierarchy*), 4) a special status role designation (e.g. RRG's macroroles) and 5) mapping rules relating thematic roles to grammatical roles and concepts.[3] In addition to these five features, most theories on thematic relations come with some version of thematic relation uniqueness (Carlson 1984: 271, Davis 2011: 403-404), stipulating that there may only be one

---

[2] A straight line indicates a subtype of the superordinate. An arrow denotes an influence from one on the other.
[3] This includes stipulations of well-formedness or completeness and the like (Levin & Rappaport Hovav 2005: 7). These are intended to make sure that there is close mapping from the semantic base to the syntax.

thematic relation of a kind in each sentence. Especially extrinsic approaches to thematic relations are in need of such an independent stipulation, as the structure itself does not provide any meaningful information of this kind (Bierwisch 2006: 107). Despite extrinsic approaches' necessity to have some form of this stipulation, the idea has been subject to criticism for not being compatible with certain linguistic observations. As the instrument is usually present in proposed role inventories and the status of the role varies across proposals, the status of the instrument role likewise varies.

It is possible to carve up the theoretical space concerning in thematic relations in several ways. For instance, the graph in figure 16 shows the development of theories, roughly ordered along the type of semantics they employ. It is also possible to divide them on the basis of the nature of their thematic relations (*primitive* vs. *derived*, Davis 2011). These notions will be discussed further in this chapter. For the purposes of this overview, I have grouped together relevant theories based on their most salient characteristics: 1) finite-primitive theories, 2) decompositional theories and 3) causality-driven theories. Many linguists acknowledge explicitly or implicitly that thematic relations are, in fact, not primitive. However, apart from briefly stating this fact, no attention is devoted to the subject (Levin & Rappaport Hovav 2005: 9). In such cases, I treat such approaches as assuming primitive thematic relations.

3.1.1 Finite-primitive approaches

The modern notion of thematic relations developed out of Fillmore's early proposal and is largely conceptual in nature. Levin & Rappaport Hovav (2005: 4, 35) term these *semantic role lists*. Essentially, in their simplest forms, that is exactly what they are: Lists of thematic relations with an unanalyzed semantic grounding. They contain labels identifying the role that each participant plays in the event as denoted by the verb. This type of approach is the most widely adopted one, but is wrought with enormous problems (Ibid.: 4). As a solution to these problems, some linguists have argued in favor of a highly diversified set of relations, whereas others have rejected thematic relations in their traditional form altogether (e.g. Dowty). Some linguists, such as DeLancey (1991), have also criticized the objectivist nature of thematic relation-approaches: Rather than grounding them in objective truth about an event, they should rather be modeled on the mental conceptualization of the event (e.g. Jackendoff).

It is important to distinguish the verb-specific relations from the more general thematic relations. The thematic structure of an expression is a partial representation of its meaning which consists minimally of a semantic relation and its arguments (Wechsler 2006: 645–646): The verb *bake* thus expresses a bake-relation between two participants, the baking entity (the 'baker') and the baked entity (the 'bakee'). Such relations are verb-specific and thus only apply to a specific event or predicate type (Davis 2011: 401). Verb-specific relations (thematic roles in Dowty's terminology; Dowty 1989 & 1991) are relations such as 'see-er', 'seen', 'runner', 'giver', 'given' etc. (Van Valin 2001: 28–29, Van Valin 2005: 53–55); they are specific to the semantics of the individual verb. Although one might contend this gives such roles a high degree of specificity, it also makes generalizing across different verbs very difficult, if not impossible. It is indeed pointless (and somewhat absurd) to refer both to the doer of 'run' and to the doer of 'give' with 'giver'. Furthermore, using verb-specific roles would nullify the positive, practical effects of semantic generalizations (Dowty 1991: 551), which leads many linguists to reject them (e.g. Dowty, Van Valin). The verb-specific roles can be semantically *neutralized* to thematic relations (Van Valin 2001: 30), which implies a neutralization of semantic contrasts between them so as to arrive at relations that are generalized across individual verbs. It is this, neutralized, level of semantics that finite-primitive approaches place their semantic roles on. Contrary to thematic relations and verb-specific roles, *participant* roles are not linguistic entities and are thus not part of natural-language semantics (Van Valin & LaPolla 1997: 113).

Finite-primitive theories assume that thematic relations are semantically unanalyzable units that 1) are finite in number (Croft 1991: 156, Engelberg 2011a: 368), 2) are defined independently of the verb's meaning (Levin & Rappaport Hovav 2005: 35) and 3) are independent from each other (Davis 2011: 407). In other words, finite-primitive approaches all assume a simple, atomic predicate, with equally atomic relations. The logical representations (adapted from Davis 2011: 401 and Bierwisch 2006: 106) for *kill* and *break* are given in (2a–2e) and in (2f–2j), respectively. The governing predicate is the most basic primitive element available. In other words, predicates do not conceal a more complex structure made up of smaller semantic components.

(2) a. **kill′** (x, y)
     b. Agent(**kill′**) = x
     c. x(**kill′**) = agent
     d. Patient(**kill′**) = y
     e. y(**kill′**) = patient
     f. **break′** (x, y)
     g. Agent(**break′**) = x
     h. x(**break′**) = agent
     i. Patient(**break′**) = y
     j. y(**break′**) = patient

Theories operating under such assumptions rely quite heavily on independently motivated thematic hierarchies to provide some form of ranking as the structures themselves provide no hierarchical information relevant for linking (Bierwisch 2006: 107) nor is any causal or aspectual information entailed, contrary to the lexical decomposition approaches.

There are several important problems with finite-primitive approaches. These problems can be clustered as follows: 1) The exact number of semantic roles is a hotly debated topic and little consensus has been reached (Van Valin 2001: 23, Dowty 1991: 548, Bierwisch 2006: 110), 2) it is difficult to delineate roles from one another with respect to their content (Dowty 1991: 553–554, Carlson 1984: 259, Bierwisch 2006: 110), 3) there are very often lacking or wrongful motivations for positing certain semantic roles (Dowty 1991: 556–557), 4) further analyzability (Croft 1991: 163), 5) the proposals lack the power to adequately capture the complexity of the linguistic expression of human experience (Croft 1991: 163), 6) there is a lack of reliable diagnostics (Wechsler 2006: 648, Levin & Rappaport Hovav 2005: 38), 7) there are no rigorous definitions available (Davis 2011: 404), 8) there are often no limits on the number of roles per verb even though linguistic evidence suggests those are required

(Levin & Rappaport Hovav 2005: 43) and 9) as a consequence of the above, there is an inflationary fragmentation of thematic relations (Levin & Rappaport Hovav 2005: 40).

The shortcomings of finite-primitive approaches have inspired many different alternative solutions: Augmenting them with two generalized roles (RRG, Dowty), considering them to be readings of structural configurations (Jackendoff, RRG), treating them as the result of the interaction of semantic features (Dowty, Rozwadowska 1988), or combinations thereof. Primitive-finite approaches represent the simpler systems of thematic relations and they are standard components of several frameworks (such as LFG). The nature and the properties of these relations are commonly left unexplored by those who do not explicitly deal with them; they are simply 'there'. If thematic relations are not primitive, then they are *derived*. There are two subtypes of derived thematic relations (Davis 2011: 411): *structural* (configurational) and *featural*.

3.1.2 Lexical decomposition

Theories of lexical decomposition started out with Generative Semantics challenging certain widely held views within generative grammar (Engelberg 2011a: 359). To cope with the shortcomings of Generative Semantics, linguists like Jackendoff and Dowty proposed new, but still decompositionally grounded approaches. For Dowty, state predicates are the smallest component and there will be no decomposition beyond that.[4] These will combine with a set of operators to build complete decompositional structures. Dowty's system has since inspired many different linguists and frameworks such as LDG (Wunderlich 1997) and RRG (Foley & Van Valin 1984, Van Valin & LaPolla 1997, Van Valin 2005). RRG, for instance, assumes that verb meaning is decomposable into state predicates with several constant logical operators (such as DO,

---

[4] From a Montague-perspective, if one assumes such a system, thematic relations become superfluous entities (Carlson 1984: 260). They would become epiphenomena without theoretical implications (Ibid.).

CAUSE, BECOME etc.) and a set of connectives.[5] All decompositional theories share the same central assumption: Word meaning is complex and can be broken up (or: *decomposed*) into smaller, more basic components (Engelberg 2011b: 124, Wechsler 2006: 648). However, any such system requires a means of preventing infinite regression into smaller and smaller components. Jackendoff (2002: 336f.) and Van Valin & Wilkins (1993: 503–504), amongst others, acknowledge this issue.

Consider the thematic structure analysis of the sentence *John sold the book to Mary* in a finite-primitive approach (3a, early Fillmorean case) and two decompositional approaches (Wechsler 2006: 648, after Jackendoff 1991: 191) and RRG, respectively:

(3)   a.   [___O + D + A]

     b. Cause ⎯ {John, [Go$_{Poss}$ (book, [from(John) to (Mary)]), Go$_{Poss}$ (δ, [from(John) to (Mary)])]}

     c.   [**do**′ (John, Ø)] CAUSE [BECOME **have**′ (Mary, book)]

The representation of thematic structure in (3a) simply lists the semantic roles that have to be realized in the surface syntax. There is no further analysis of verb meaning, which is taken to be atomic (to be inserted on the line). In (3b)[6] and (3c), verb meaning is broken up into several smaller components, which allows for the inclusion of more specific information. For instance, in (3b), the direction of the transaction is explicitly represented with 'GO'. The same is true in the RRG-representation: There, the entire section CAUSE [BECOME **have**′ (Mary, book)] represents the direction of transaction. (3b) and (3c) nicely illustrate *derived* thematic relations. The position an argument occupies relative to the

---

[5]   It is crucial to point out that theories that use decomposition do not necessarily accord it the same place and importance within the wider theory (Engelberg 2011b: 125, 132ff.).

[6]   The variable δ stands for the price of the transaction. For the clarity of the example, it has been left unspecified.

3 Instruments at the syntax-semantics interface

whole structure makes up the thematic relation. *Mary* is considered the recipient in (3c) because the Mary-argument is the first argument of BECOME **have´** (x, y). This structurally derived notion of thematic relations was originally proposed by Gruber (1965) and further developed by Jackendoff (1972, 1987). Jackendoff (1987: 379–380 & 1990: 48) points out that a configurational approach to thematic roles transcends primitive-finite approaches in that the roles can be precisely and – most importantly – independently defined by constraints that are generated by the units in the decomposed structure itself. Under a featural view, the coalescence or the interaction of features (whatever they might be) makes up for the thematic relation. Even though Dowty's (1991: 572) proto-agent and proto-patient and their properties are located on a higher level of neutralization (generalized semantic roles), they are nonetheless a prime example of the featural, derived approach. Despite the theoretical nature of lexical decomposition, there is psycholinguistic (Piñango 2006) evidence in favor of thematic relations derived from such decompositional structures.

3.1.3 Causality-driven approaches

Theories of the third type start out from causality-inspired representations of event structure. Rather than introducing causality as an operator the way the decompositional theories do, the causality-driven theories posit a chain of events. Croft (1991), for instance, posits causal chains which not only represent verb meaning, but rather the complete event as it occurs in the outside world. This means it does not succumb to the problem of 'objectivism' as DeLancey put it. Subsections of the larger chain are usually selected as the representation of verb meaning. Thematic relations are entities in relation to their position in the chain. Consider an example from Croft (1991: 173) in figure 17.

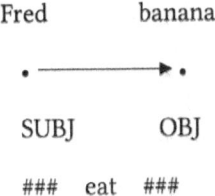

Figure 17: Causal chain representation of *Fred ate the banana*.

In figure 17, *Fred* is an agent and *banana* is a patient due to their position in the causal chain. Causality-driven approaches are quite diverse amongst themselves and each must be discussed individually.

3.1.4 Generalized Semantic Roles

It was established above that one can consider thematic relations as a type of relations holding between a predicate and its arguments (Van Valin 2001: 23). Such relations can be considered neutralizations of verb-specific roles. Neutralization of semantic contrasts always occurs with increasing generalization (Van Valin 2001: 30–31). It is possible to generalize even further, to Generalized Semantic Roles (GSRs). RRG's macroroles actor and undergoer introduced in chapter 2 are the original GSRs and they have no exact equivalent in other theories (Van Valin 2005: 60ff.). GSRs were introduced by some linguists as a means of remedying certain problems of the finite-primitive approaches (Levin & Rappaport Hovav 2005: 51), especially the problem of associating thematic relations with certain grammatical functions (Ibid.: 52). Influential in the development of GSR-theories was the observation that languages tend to cluster grammar around two diametrically opposed semantic prototypes (Bossong 2006: 237). GSR-proposals can differ widely, however. Some have proposed them as stand-alone solutions, whereas others combine them with an extensive system of lexical decomposition. Dowty considers his proto-agent and proto-patient not to be discrete roles, contrary to RRG, where the macroroles are entities that grammatical rules can refer to. Rather, Dowty (1991) posits semantic proto-roles as cluster

concepts or prototypes rather than as discrete semantic roles. They are
given in (4–5) (adapted from Dowty 1991: 572).

(4) Contributing properties of proto-agent:
   a. Volitional involvement in the event or state.
   b. Sentience (and/or perception).
   c. Causing an event or change of state in another participant.
   d. Movement (relative to the position of another participant).
   (e. Exists independently of the event named by the verb.)

(5) Contributing properties of proto-patient:
   a. Undergoes a change of state.
   b. Incremental theme.
   c. Causally affected by another participant.
   d. Stationary relative to movement of another participant.
   (e. Does not exist independently of the event, or not at all.)

These features are to be understood as lexical entailments recurring cluster-wise (Levin & Rappaport Hovav 2005: 53). For Dowty (1991: 576), subject selection follows from the simple principle that the participant with the largest number of proto-agent properties becomes the subject. Conversely, the participant with the largest number of proto-patient properties will become the direct object. This shows that GSRs have important functions in monostratal theories of syntax as they are employed to capture important generalizations that – in the various incarnations of transformational grammar – are handled in terms of deep subjects, objects and similar devices (Van Valin 1999: 373). Even though Dowty's approach may be very appealing, there are some problems with it. For instance, Wechsler (2006: 650) points out that there is no unifying semantic dimension behind these lists, nor is there any attempt to come up with one. It is also not clear how linking to obliques would be handled (Levin & Rappaport Hovav 2005: 60). Partly because of these issues, Primus proposes a third proto-role (Ibid.). Van Valin (1999: 386) also criticizes Dowty for simply stating generalizations about the properties of a verb's subject and object. Dowty's proto-roles were not proposed in the

3.1 Thematic relations as an interface component

context of a linking algorithm and due to their cluster-like nature, it is unclear how he sees them in practical linking.

It is crucial to stress that GSRs are not thematic relations. Rather, Van Valin distinguishes (1999: 373) between three levels of semantic relationships: verb-specific roles, thematic relations as generalizations across verb-specific roles and, finally, GSRs as generalizations *across* thematic relations. The first type does not play any meaningful role in RRG, the second can play a role in interpretation. The neutralization patterns are given in figure 18.

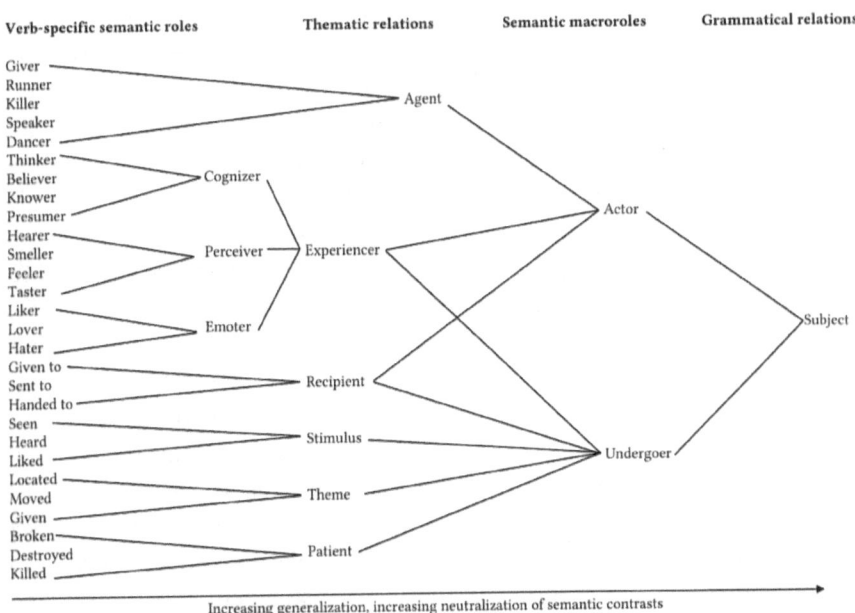

Figure 18: Neutralization of semantic contrasts (Van Valin 2005: 54).

The main motivation behind macroroles (and GSRs in general) is that there is a fundamental opposition between the two cardinal arguments of a transitive predication (Van Valin 1999: 373, 2005: 60–61). Van Valin points out that many syntactic phenomena are tied to these two cardinal arguments. Due to their generalized nature, they are much more robust and adequate to capture grammatical behavior. Most approaches using

GSRs have two roles, although some linguists posit three (also see section 2.5.1).

3.1.5 Instrument as a thematic relation

Instruments appear in many grammatical frameworks and different approaches to language. However, of all the traditional thematic relations, the instrument is only studied peripherally. Agents and patients (or equivalents) are in the focus of research, as their relevance for linking is obvious. Instruments, on the other hand, are often assumed to be simply 'there'. Sometimes, they are employed as concepts without even having been introduced in the theory at all. Generally speaking, the thematic relation of the instrument has several fundamental characteristics (Jackendoff 1990: 142) that shine through in most approaches, explicitly or implicitly: 1) the instrument plays a role in the means by which the agent/actor carries out a certain action, 2) the agent/actor acts on the instrument and as a consequence, 3) the instrument acts on the patient/undergoer and 4) agents and instruments have some semantic similarities (Levin & Rappaport Hovav 2005: 45). The instrument role has been faced with the same problems that generally thematic relations have been faced with. For instance, Nilsen (1973) assumes that the instrument is actually a grouping of four more specific roles. As instruments are an integral part of the array of thematic relations, the status of 'the' instrument cannot simply be generalized over in one section. With respect to instruments, many frameworks fail to achieve what Bierwisch (2006: 89) labels adequacy. Several commonplace phenomena are not accounted for in the theories, such as the instrument functioning as a subject or the nature and the corresponding syntactic behavior of more complex 'tools' (e.g. computer programs). In the following sections, I will discuss the instrument relation after having introduced the necessary information on the respective frameworks or approaches. I will then illustrate that many theories and approaches to instruments do not achieve adequacy, for various differing reasons.

3.2 Role and Reference Grammar

In chapter 2, RRG was extensively introduced. Yet, the theoretical component that is so commonplace in other frameworks – thematic relations – was not introduced as the macroroles are the primary tools for linking. In this section, I will discuss thematic relations as they exist in RRG.

3.2.1 Thematic relations

The Actor-Undergoer Hierarchy captures the relationships between the thematic relations themselves in relation to the macroroles. This was introduced in figure 12. RRG has an intrinsic conception of thematic relations, that is, they arise from the decompositional structure itself. RRG assumes that thematic relations are *functions of argument positions* in the logical structure (Foley & Van Valin 1984: 34, 47ff., Van Valin 2005: 53, 59 & 126, Van Valin & LaPolla 1997: 114). In other words, they are – similar to Jackendoff's proposals – structural configurations and belong to the *derived* class. They can thus be considered readings of argument positions in relation to the governing predicate: A participant is read as an experiencer because it is the 1st argument of the **pred´** (x, y) where **pred´** is a predicate of internal experience. This means that thematic relations are entirely dependent on the logical structures and do not have a meaningful existence independent of them. Logical structures, in turn, can be motivated with independent criteria (i.e. aktionsart-tests). This ensures that thematic relations are not arbitrarily assigned to a predicate (Van Valin & LaPolla 1997: 116). It is therefore adequate to posit thematic relations as labels or shorthand for expressions of the type '1st argument of a two-place predicate of internal experience'. An overview of thematic relations, defined over argument positions, is given below (Van Valin 2005: 55) in table 10.

3 *Instruments at the syntax-semantics interface*

I STATE VERBS
A. Single argument
1. State or condition **broken'** (x)   x = patient
2. Existence   **exist'** (x)   x = entity

B. Two arguments
1. Pure location   **be-LOC'** (x, y)   x = location
                                                y = theme
2. Perception   **hear'** (x, y)   x = perceiver
                                                y = stimulus
3. Cognition   **know'** (x, y)   x = cognizer
                                                y = content
4. Desire   **want'** (x, y)   x = wanter
                                                y = desire
5. Propositional attitude **consider'** (x, y) x = judger
                                                y = judgment
6. Possession   **have'** (x, y)   x = possessor
                                                y = possessed
7. Internal experience **feel'** (x, y)   x = experience
                                                y = sensation
8. Emotion   **love'** (x, y)   x = emoter
                                                y = target
9. Attributive   **be'** (x, [**pred'**]) x = attributant
                                                y = attribute
10. Identificational   **be'** (x, [**pred'**]) x = identified
                                                y = identity
11. specificational   **be'** (x, y)   x = variable
                                                y = value
12. Equational   **equate'** (x, y)   x, y = referent

II ACTIVITY VERBS
  A. Single argument

1. Unspecified action	**do′** (x, Ø)	x = effector
2. Motion	**do′** (x, [**walk′** (x)])	x = mover
3. Static motion	**do′** (x, [**spin′** (x)])	x = ST-mover
4. Light emission	**do′** (x, [**shine′** (x)])	x = L-emitter
5. Sound emission	**do′** (x, [**gurgle′** (x)])	x = S-emitter

  B. One or two arguments

1. Performance	**do′** (x, [**sing′** (x, (y))])	x = performer
		y = performance
2. Consumption	**do′** (x, [**eat′** (x, (y))])	x = consumer
		y = consumed
3. Creation	**do′** (x, [**write′** (x, (y))])	x = creator
		y = creation
4. Directed perception	**do′** (x, [**hear′** (x, (y))])	x = observer
		y = stimulus
5. Use	**do′** (x [**use′** (x, y)])	x = user
		y = implement

Table 10: Definition of thematic relations in terms of argument positions in the logical structure.

Examples of logical structures and their thematic relations are given below:

(6)   a.   *John killed Barry.* (adapted from Van Valin 2005: 56)
        [**do′** (John, Ø)] CAUSE [BECOME **dead′** (Barry)]
        (Agent-)Effector   Patient
    b.   *The snow melted.* (Van Valin 2005: 47)
        BECOME **melted′** (snow)
                     Patient
    c.   *Dana saw the picture.* (Van Valin 2005: 46)
        see′ (Dana, picture)
            Perceiver   Stimulus

3 Instruments at the syntax-semantics interface

Table 10 might imply that RRG posits a vast number of thematic relations, but Van Valin (2005: 57) points out that there are only five relevant distinctions, namely those distinctions that directly correspond to the five possible argument positions in the logical structures. Thematic relations can thus be lumped into five groups on a continuum with the strongly affected participants on the right end of the scale and the strongly *affecting*, controlling and willful participants on the left end. RRG's conception of derived thematic relations comes from merging the Gruber-Jackendoff notion of structurally determined relations with a Dowty-inspired semantically decompositional structure (Van Valin & Wilkins 1993: 503). Each of the five groups of thematic relations illustrated below thus corresponds to one of the five distinctions on the actor-undergoer hierarchy.

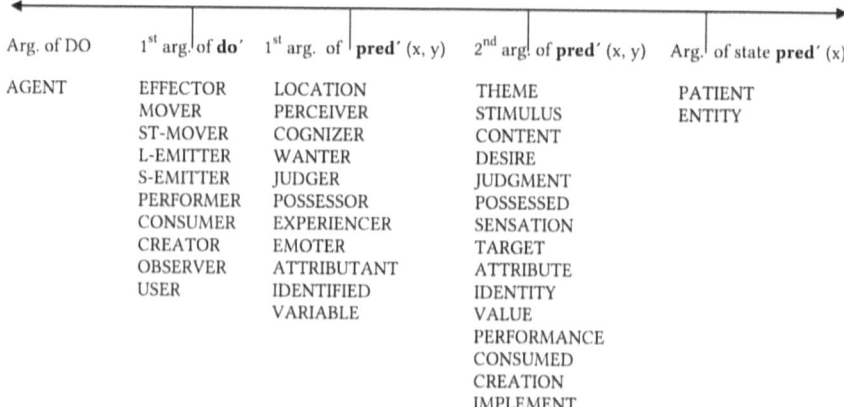

Figure 19: Thematic relations in terms of argument positions on the Actor-Undergoer Hierarchy (Van Valin 2005: 58).

Certain thematic relations that are present in most other theories, like recipient or goal are absent from the list above. There are three ways to expand a base logical structure: 1) Adding an implement (see section 3.7.2.2), 2) to specify a source, goal or path with the respective predicates or 3) to specify a full causal chain (Van Valin 2005: 59). With transfer predications, for example, a logical structure of the form INGR/BECOME

have' (x, y) is expanded into a more complex logical structure of the form [**do'** (x, Ø)] CAUSE [BECOME **have'** (x, y)]. The thematic relation of recipient can be defined as the x-argument of this predicate expansion and a notion like *source* can be defined as the possessor or location argument in INGR/BECOME NOT **have'** (x, y) or in INGR/BECOME NOT **be-at'** (x, y), respectively. In contrast to other theories, no list of thematic relations is stored in the mental lexicon, only the logical structures.

RRG also has a quite distinct conception of agency (Van Valin & Wilkins 1996), where instrument, with several others, is treated as a reading of a more basic thematic relation called 'effector'. This is the topic of the following sections.

3.2.2 The effector role: agents

RRG posits a basic thematic relation called *effector* (Foley & Van Valin 1984: 51ff., Van Valin & Wilkins 1996, Van Valin & LaPolla 1997 & Van Valin 2005) which underlies the *agent*, *instrument* and *force* thematic relations. Explicit agentivity is less basic than non-agentivity, an insight also shared by Talmy (2000: 421). RRG's view of agency is thus that of an implicature, contrary to (for example) Jackendoff (1990: 129) for whom agency corresponds to a set of different action tier configurations. Because *instrument* is only one reading of effector, it is crucial to discuss *agents* and *forces* as well.

An effector is considered to be the dynamic participant in an event (Van Valin & Wilkins 1996: 289). In terms of the logical structures (Van Valin & LaPolla 1997: 118), the effector can be defined as the 1st argument of **do'** (x, Ø). However, there is no implication of it performing the action in question intentionally or willfully (Van Valin & LaPolla 1997: 118). By contrast, an *agent* is defined as an effector performing an action willfully, rationally and intentionally (Van Valin & Wilkins 1996: 313 & 316). *Intentional* is treated as distinct from *volitional*: volitional[7] acts are defined as non-conscious, basic acts of will. *Rational* means that the

---

[7] Some authors use *volitional* as a synonym to *intentional* or as a component or prerequisite of intention. Dowty, for example, uses *volitional* in his work where RRG would employ *intentional*. If this is the case, I will point it out at the relevant moment.

entity is aware of the consequence of their actions, whereas *intentional* is considered to be the ability to plan an action and that one is conscious of one's will to perform the action. Van Valin (2005: 57) adds *instigating* as a prerequisite for agenthood. However, not all instigators have to be agents. An instigator can be defined as the effector of the first CAUSE (Van Valin & Wilkins 1996: 318). Forces are by definition also instigators. An instigator is thus the *initial effector* in the LS.

Several factors influence and determine whether an effector is read as an agent or as a force. These factors include pragmatics, properties of the predicate, grammatical constructions and the referent's properties. A human instigator is read as an agent, unless if there is evidence to the contrary. This is the core of Holisky's pragmatic principle which states that agency arises from pragmatics rather than being lexically inherent to the predicate (Van Valin & Wilkins 1996: 309). Consider (Holisky 1987: 119, Van Valin & Wilkins 1996: 309):

(7) **Pragmatic Principle**: You may interpret effectors and effector-themes which are human as agents (in the absence of information to the contrary).

This raises the question of what can serve as information or evidence to the contrary. Certain adverbs cancel agency, such as *accidentally* (after Van Valin & Wilkins 1996: 309):

(8) a. *Larry killed the deer.*
   b. *Larry killed the deer accidentally.*
   c. *Larry killed the deer intentionally.*

Holisky's principle predicts that *Larry* in (8a) is read as an agent. The sentence in (8b) contains an agency-canceling adverb and thus blocks the agent reading. The agency-signaling adverb in (8c) simply confirms an interpretation that is predicted by Holisky's principle. *Intention* is a central component: An agent is a human effector that intentionally does something. This observation in itself is not new. Talmy (2000: 521), for instance, also considers agent to be a composite of the *author* of a certain event and the *intender* of that event. The addition of these two concepts yields an agentive reading. This approach, however, is of a more conceptual nature and it is unclear how it can deal with agency-ambiguous sentences such as *Larry killed the deer*.

Inanimate effectors cannot be agents (Van Valin & Wilkins 1996: 319): The unacceptability of (9b) results from the presence of an agency-signaling adverb (adapted from Van Valin & Wilkins 1996: 309–310).

(9) a. *The explosion killed the deer.*
    b. **The explosion intentionally killed the deer.*

From an RRG-perspective, *intention* is a property that can only belong to humans. There are cases where agency is lexicalized into the verb's semantics, thereby obligatorily requiring an agent. Adding an agency-cancelling adverb ((10c)) yields a contradiction, illustrating the lexicalization of agency with *murder* (Van Valin & LaPolla 1997: 120). The occurrence of inanimate instigators with such verbs is not possible as the ungrammaticality of (10b) proves (adapted from Van Valin & Wilkins 1996: 310).

(10) a. *Larry murdered the lumberjack.*
     b. **The explosion murdered the lumberjack.*
     c. **Larry murdered the lumberjack accidentally.*

Lexicalized agency is expressed with the operator DO ('big' DO) in the logical structure (Van Valin 2005: 56, Van Valin & LaPolla 1997: 119). Big DO can be considered a semantic property of the verb. Big DO always co-occurs with little **do′** in the logical structure because both of them have arguments that do something (Van Valin 2005: 57).

(11) a. *Larry killed the lumberjack.*
        [**do′** (Larry, Ø)] CAUSE [BECOME **dead′** (lumberjack)]
     b. *Larry murdered the lumberjack.*
        DO (Larry, [[**do′** (Larry, Ø)] CAUSE [BECOME **dead′** (lumberjack)]])

Lexicalized agency varies across languages: English has very few such verbs, while Japanese *kill* and *break* encode agency (Van Valin & Wilkins 1996: 310, Hasagawa 1996: 60). As the sentence (10b) illustrates, the x-argument for the verb in question cannot be inanimate. This restriction can be annotated in terms of qualia with the relevant argument position in the logical structure of the verb (Van Valin 2005: 50–51 & 52).

Agency can also be coerced by a construction; grammatical constructions can impose a certain reading or interpretation on an argument. In the case of, for instance, purposive constructions, the subject-argument intends for something to happen or come about, which forces an agency reading on the initial effector argument (Van Valin & Wilkins 1996: 311):

(12) a. *John rolled down the hill.*
b. *John rolled down the hill in order to get to the road before the bikers got there.*
c. *Mary slid from her chair.* (own data)
d. *Mary slid from her chair in order to dodge flying debris.* (own data)

In (12a) and (12c), the argument in question (*John* and *Mary*, respectively) is ambiguous with respect to agency. In both cases, the referents could have performed the action described accidentally or on purpose. When a purposive clause is added, only the agentive reading remains a possibility as adding an agency-canceling adverb proves:

(13) a. **John accidentally rolled down the hill in order to get to the road before the bikers got there.*
b. **Mary accidentally slid from her chair in order to dodge flying debris.*

Van Valin and Wilkins (1996: 312–313) posit that purposive clauses can be strong enough to even overrule normal implications of the lexical meanings of verbs:

(14) *Jesus died to save us from our sins.*

The single argument of *die* is a patient but the purposive clause forces an agent-reading on this typically patient-taking verb. The authors note that this is cross-linguistically not uncommon in the context of religious martyrdom (Van Valin & Wilkins 1996: 312). Outside of religious contexts or contexts of great personal sacrifice, this is not admissible:

(15) a. *John died to save his sister.*
b. **John died to make us clean up the room.*
c. **John died to save Sarah's bike.*

Even though certain constructions force an agentive reading, certain RPs cannot have an agentive reading due to their inherent properties (adapted from Van Valin & Wilkins 1996: 311ff.):

(16) a. *The ball rolled down the hill.*
b. **The ball rolled down the hill in order to bounce into the lake.*
c. **The ball intentionally rolled down the hill.*
d. *The baby broke the window.*
e. **/?The baby intentionally broke the window.*
f. *The looter broke the window.*

The ungrammaticality of (16b) and (16c) shows that the referent's properties also determine grammaticality: The examples in (16a–16e) show that an agency-signaling adverb is compatible with a human referent but is incompatible with an inanimate referent as these cannot intentionally or willfully do something. Another argument against positing [±human] as a property that automatically correlates with agency is illustrated in (16d–16e). The semantic properties of *looter* in (16f) make an agentive interpretation plausible, if not, likely. By contrast, *baby* is considered as an entity too young and dependent on others to intentionally perform an act. This again shows that the referent's properties have a tangible impact on the grammaticality of certain sentences. In next chapter 4, I will propose an expansion of this principle and its incorporation into RRG.

Van Valin and Wilkins (1996: 314–315) propose to capture the relation between agency and the referent's properties with two interrelated, yet distinct hierarchies (Van Valin and Wilkins 1996: 313 & 316): 1) a *saliency hierarchy* which ranks entities according to the likelihood of them being interpreted as agent when placed in an actional event and 2) an *animacy hierarchy* with various degrees of animate entities (with prototypical animates near one end of the scale). Due to the large size of the graph, figure 20 has been included in the appendix.

The operational range of Holisky's principle can be mapped onto the graph: it is active in the right top (everything branching to the right of [+human]). There are, however, some issues with this scale: 1) Certain types of referents are not included, such as AI-driven referents and 2) the ranking is only relevant for capturing agentive readings. In chapter 4, I will propose a different scale that not only captures the occurrence of agentivity, but also accurately captures the morphosyntactic behavior of instruments, forces and those referents that occupy the grey area between them.

Apart from the referent's properties and constructions, the logical structures themselves also play a role in agentive readings: The LS correlates with the likelihood of the occurrence of an agentive interpretation. If a verb has the activity predicate **do'** (x, Ø) in its LS, it is (quite obviously) more likely to have an agent argument. As logical structures are the manifestation of aktionsarten, it is possible to posit a hierarchy of aktionsart-classes in terms of their agent-admitting probability (Van Valin & Wilkins 1996: 313):

(17)   activity/accomplishment > achievement > state[8]

Summarizing, the origins of agent-readings can be summarized in two groups: 1) coerced agency and 2) non-coerced agency. Coerced agency is either forced by a construction or lexicalized agency. In these cases, an agent-reading is imposed on the relevant argument, irrespective of other considerations. Non-coerced agency is more complicated. The combination and interaction of several factors determines whether agency is present or not: the referent's properties (figure 20), the predicate's properties (the ranking in (17)) and, finally, pragmatic considerations as captured by Holisky's principle.

---

[8]   The hierarchy in (17) is based on the pre-1997 decomposition system.

3.2.3 The effector role: forces vs. instruments

Contrary to many other accounts, instruments are not treated as a thematic relation in their own right. They are considered as an allorole of effector (Van Valin & Wilkins 1996: 289ff. & 319). Both instruments and forces are distinguished from agents by animacy: instruments and forces are [-animate].

These two readings are both inanimate, but are essentially distinguished over argument positions: Instruments are always under control of another effector. They are manipulated entities in a causal chain. In the structure in (18), an effector x performs an action which causes another effector (y) to cause another action in turn (adapted from Van Valin & Wilkins 1996: 317). The y-argument is thus manipulated by x to arrive at some result which is specified after the second causal operator.

(18) [[**do**′ (x, Ø)] CAUSE [**do**′ (y, [...])] CAUSE [BECOME **pred**′ (z)]]

The y-argument in this schema is the canonical slot for the (manipulated) instrumental entity in RRG. Forces cannot, by their very nature, occupy this argument slot as they are always at the top of a causal chain. In other words, forces are instigators and instruments are always under the scope of an instigator. Consider the inanimate effectors in the following examples from English, German, Dutch and French (own data and after Van Valin & Wilkins 1996: 318):

(19) a. *John broke the window with a rock.*
[**do**′ (John, Ø)] CAUSE [[**do**′ (rock, Ø)] CAUSE [INGR **broken**′ (window)]]
b. *Mary cut the sausage with a knife.*
[**do**′ (Mary, Ø)] CAUSE [[**do**′ (knife, Ø)] CAUSE [BECOME **cut**′ (sausage)]]
c. *The terrorists destroyed the car with a bomb.*
[**do**′ (terrorists, Ø)] CAUSE [[**do**′ (bomb, Ø)] CAUSE [INGR **destroyed**′ (car)]]

3 Instruments at the syntax-semantics interface

    d. *Maria hat   den Baum mit der Axt*
       Maria AUX.3SG DEF tree   with DEF axe
       ge-fäll-t.
       PTCP-cut down-PTCP
       [**do**′ (Maria, Ø)] CAUSE [[**do**′ (Axt, Ø)] CAUSE [BECOME
       cut down′ (Baum)]]
       'Maria cut down the tree with an axe.'
    e. *Jan heeft   de winkel met sten-en verniel-d.*
       Jan AUX.3SG DEF store with rock-PL destroy- PTCP
       [**do**′ (Jan, Ø)] CAUSE [[**do**′ (stenen, Ø)] CAUSE [INGR
       destroyed′ (winkel)]]
       'Jan destroyed the store with rocks.'
    f. *Sophie a   coupé   le pain avec le   couteau.*
       Sophie AUX.PST cut.PTCP DEF bread with DEF knife
       [**do**′ (Sophie, Ø)] CAUSE [[**do**′ (couteau, Ø)] CAUSE
       [BECOME **cut**′ (pain)]]
       Sophie cut the bread with the knife.'

In each of these examples, an entity expressed by the x-argument performs some manipulation of another entity (expressed by the y-argument), which leads to a specific change of state of third entity (expressed by the z-argument). In all of these, the instigator is human. Forces, however, can also take instruments due to the fact that they occupy the same position (see below).

Following the proposal in Van Valin and LaPolla (1997: 121), the full logical structure for instruments should be represented with a **use**′ included into it as the second argument of the first **do**′ and the main predicate repeated as the second argument of the intermediate **do**′:

(20)   [**do**′ (Mary, [**use**′ (Mary, knife)])] CAUSE [[**do**′ (knife, [**cut**′ (knife, sausage)])] CAUSE [BECOME **cut**′ (sausage)]]

This logical structure is thus more specific in that it includes **use**′ (x, y). The rationale for including **use**′ (apart from attaining a higher degree of specificity) is that in wielding the knife to perform the cutting action, *Mary* manipulates the *knife* throughout the macro-event to arrive at a state of affairs where the *sausage* is cut. This manipulation is represented by **use´**. As such manipulation is logically implied by the rest of the structure, it can be left out. Likewise, the intermediate **cut´** predicate can be left out. This can be treated the same way: It is more accurate to include it, as what the knife is caused to do is indeed a cutting action. Therefore, the LS in (21a) can be represented in a reduced form (21b) (adapted from Van Valin & Wilkins 1996: 318). I use the reduced logical structures by default, unless it is relevant to use the full structure. I am, of course, aware that the full structure is the complete one.

(21) a. [**do´** (John, [**use´** (John, rock)])] CAUSE [**do´** (rock, [**hit´** (rock, window)])] CAUSE [INGR **broken´** (window)]]
 b. [**do´** (John, Ø)] CAUSE [[**do´** (rock, Ø)] CAUSE [INGR **broken´** (window)]]

Contrary to instruments, forces are capable of independent motion ([+motive]) and action and are never under control of another effector. Typical forces are meteorological or astronomical phenomena. Consider the following examples:

(22) a. The hail storm destroyed the barn.
 [**do´** (hail storm, Ø)] CAUSE [[**do´** (Ø, Ø)] CAUSE [BECOME **destroyed´** (barn)]]
 b. The meteorite shattered the window.
 [**do´** (meteorite, Ø)] CAUSE [[**do´** (Ø, Ø)] CAUSE [BECOME **shattered´** (window)]]
 c. The typhoon destroyed the village.
 [**do´** (typhoon, Ø)] CAUSE [[**do´** (Ø, Ø)] CAUSE [BECOME **destroyed´** (village)]]

In the logical structures above, a second **do´** sequence is included and its two argument positions are left open because 1) forces can take instruments (like agents) and one wants to indicate this ability explicitly in the logical structure, 2) to indicate that forces are at the top of causal chains (like agents) and 3) to differentiate such logical structures from those where metonymic clipping has occurred, which will be discussed in section 3.7.2.2. With human effectors the second **do´** sequence is not included, because those are expected to be at the top of the causal chain anyway due to their semantic properties.

Forces are thus not under control of other effectors and can instigate a causal chain (Van Valin & Wilkins 1996: 317–319). In a sentence like *The typhoon destroyed the village with its storm surge*, the structure in (22c) would include the phrase *its storm surge* as the x-argument of the second **do′** in the chain. This is given in (23a), together with a second example.

(23) a. [**do′** (typhoon, Ø)] CAUSE [[**do′** (its storm surge, Ø)] CAUSE [BECOME **destroyed′** (village)]]

b. The storm destroyed the house with the storm surge.
[**do′** (storm, Ø)] CAUSE [[**do′** (storm surge, Ø)] CAUSE [BECOME **destroyed′** (house)]]

This observation also immediately provides a test to distinguish forces from instruments. If the referent occupies the instigator position, then it must be able to take an instrument. If the referent is an instrument, then it cannot take an instrument itself. Ergo, by adding an instrument one can be distinguished from the other. The unacceptability of (24b) identifies *knife* as an instrument. Conversely, the acceptability of (24a) identifies *storm* as a force.

(24) a. The storm destroyed house with the storm surge.
b. *The knife cut the bread with the blade.

This may seem to provide a clear-cut distinction between forces and instruments. However, there are referents that pass both sides of the test. They can function as an instrument, yet take instruments themselves as well. Consider the following examples from Dutch and English:

(25) a. *Mara vernietig-de   de   mainframe met*
Mara destroy-PST.3SG DEF mainframe with
het   computer programma.
DEF computer program
'Mara destroyed the mainframe with the computer program.'

b. *Het computer programma vernietig-de de*
DEF computer program destroy-PST.3SG DEF
mainframe met het stuk code.
mainframe with DEF piece of code
'The computer program destroyed the mainframe with the piece of code.'
c. *John destroyed the barn with the crane.*
d. *The crane destroyed the barn with the large boulder.*

It is unclear how standard RRG would account for the referents in (25a–25d). It is conceivable that there is a semantic grey area, where referents can be conceptualized as an instigator and a non-instigator. This will be explored in chapter 4.

A force argument can be defined as the [-animate], [+motive] effector of the first CAUSE in the causal sequence (Van Valin and Wilkins 1996: 318–319). The authors point out that the logical consequence of this definition is that, in their analysis, effectors that meet force-criteria are only forces in causal sequences (Van Valin & Wilkins 1996: 319). Thus, in the examples in (22), the effectors are forces, contrary to (26), where it is a plain effector (after Van Valin & Wilkins 1996: 319).

(26) *The wind is blowing briskly.*
[**briskly'** (**do'** (wind, [**blow'** (wind)])))]

Irrespective of whether the instigator is a force or an agent, the instrument (if present) is always an intermediate effector manipulated by a higher-ranking effector. To sum up, formal definitions (adapted from Van Valin & Wilkins 1996: 319 and Van Valin & LaPolla 1997: 122) of agent, force and instrument are given in (27).

(27) a. *Agent*: animate (usually human) x-argument of initial **do'**.
b. *Force*: inanimate x-argument of initial **do'**.
c. *Instrument (Full LS)*: Implement y-argument in LS configuration [**do'** (x, [...])] CAUSE [[... **do'** (y, [...])] CAUSE [BECOME/INGR **pred'** (...)]]
d. *Instrument (reduced LS)*: x-argument of intermediate **do'**.

The definition of instrument in (27c) is a definition in relation to the full logical structure. Because usually reduced logical structures are used, the definition must be rewritten. It is given in (27d). The definition in (27c) also highlights another important point: *Implement* is the basic class of 'tools' in RRG. They are defined as the y-argument of a **use'** predicate. Only if this predicate is incorporated into the causal chain, does an implement become an instrument. To avoid confusion I will always refer to causally embedded 'tools' as *instruments* and to those that are not as *implements*. This latter class will be discussed in section 3.7.2.2.

3.3 Case Grammar

3.3.1 Overview

Case grammar refers to an array of approaches to grammatical theory originally inspired by Fillmore's influential 1968 paper *The Case for Case* and subsequent work (1971a, 1971b, 1971c, 1972, 1977a, 1977b). All of these varieties of case grammar share the same assumption that semantic functions are basic and that many aspects of the syntax are derivative of them or driven by them (J. Anderson 2006: 220). Fillmore's original proposal has greatly influenced the way linguists think about semantic functions and traces of Fillmore's case grammar can be found in many other grammatical frameworks.

Fillmore (1968) posits semantic functions that are linked to language-specific surface encoding. These functions are called case relations (Fillmore 1965 [1969], 1968) or simply cases (J. Anderson 2006: 220). This is the first modern formulation of thematic relations and their interface character. From a contemporary perspective, the use of *case* seems in need of an explanation. Anderson points out that the term was used because of the frequent observation that in many languages – like Old English, Russian or Latin – nominal inflection marks semantic relations. However, two remarks must be made: 1) in many instances nominal cases mark grammatical relations rather than pure semantic functions and 2) many languages mark grammatical or semantic relations with other strategies such as word order (J. Anderson 2006: 220). It is crucial to point that, usually, case relations do not have a one-to-one relation with a certain marking strategy (J. Anderson 2006: 221). This is a fundamental principle that can be found in all approaches using thematic relations. Somewhat similar to RRG, grammatical relations are considered neutralizations of case relations (Ibid.)

Fillmore assumes that cases "comprise a set of universal, presumably innate, concepts, which identify certain types of judgments human beings are capable of making about the events that are going on around them, judgments about such matters as who did it, who it happened to, and what got changed" (Fillmore 1968: 45–46). This is often an intuitive way of defining thematic relations (Chierchia 1984: 323, Jackendoff 2002: 260). It is possible to treat case relations in Fillmore's earliest conception as linguistically relevant translations of cognitively salient concepts. Put differently, case relations are a speaker's *conceptualized intuitions* which are employed in the grammar. Cases are seen as basic in grammar, contrary to grammatical relations like subject and direct object (J. Anderson 2006: 223). In his 1968 paper, Fillmore proposes a non-exhaustive list of case relations but he often revised it and added more cases in later work. For instance, in his (1971b: 376) paper, he proposes the so-called *counter-agent* and proposes to split the dative into several others (also see J. Anderson 2006: 228). In Fillmore's other work, the counter-agent is not (or no longer) present. For the purpose of this dissertation, Fillmore's (1968: 46) original list suffices:

(28) **Agentive (A)**: The case of the typically animate perceived instigator of the action identified by the verb.
Instrumental (I): The case of the inanimate force or object causally involved in the action or state identified by the verb.
Dative (D): The case of the animate being affected by the state or action identified by the verb.
Factitive (F): The case of the object or being resulting from the action or state identified by the verb, or understood as a part of the meaning of the verb.
Locative (L): The case which identifies the location or spatial orientation of the state or action identified by the verb.

Objective (O):[9] The semantically most neutral case, the case of anything representable by a noun whose role in the action or state identified by the verb is identified by the semantic interpret tation of the verb itself; conceivably the concept should be limited to things which are affected by the action or state identified by the verb. The term is not to be confused with the notion of direct object, nor with the name of the surface case synonymous with accusative.

One major problem with Fillmore's characterization of instrumental is the conflation of force and instrument: Forces can take instruments themselves, but instruments cannot take other instruments. Fillmore's characterization does not capture this. Each predicate comes with a certain set of cases, summarized in the case frame. Consider the sentences below and their respective case frames:

(29) a. *John ran.* [___A]
b. *John gave Mary a book.* [___O + D + A]
c. *John murdered Pat.* [___D + A]

For example, the verb *run* has +[___A] as a case frame. The verbs *give* and *murder* have the case frames +[___O D A] and +[___D A], respectively. Optional case roles are indicated with round brackets. The overlapping brackets in (30) mean that either of the two must be present (or both).

(30)   +[___D (I ⟨A)]

The sentence in (29b) determines that and O, D and A are involved in the action, producing this case frame. The verb that is to be inserted must have a case frame with matching cases. However, this mechanism needs to be complemented by restrictions on the lexical material bearing cases. Without such restrictions, *any* noun is eligible for *any* case role. For example, inanimates cannot bear agentive case (Fillmore 1968: 48).

---

[9] This case is termed *neutral* by Anderson and others (J. Anderson 2006: 220ff).

As far as the mapping to syntax is concerned, Fillmore introduced a simple principle: a subject selection hierarchy (cf. Wechsler 2006: 647), thereby fulfilling three out of five of Croft's (2015: 104–105) theoretical pillars: The hierarchy is a ranking of roles (3), it simultaneously constitutes a method for designating a certain case as preferable in the linking (4) and generally provides mapping rules from thematic roles to syntactic units (5). Fillmore distinguishes between an unmarked subject choice and a marked subject choice. Consider Fillmore's *unmarked subject selection rule* (Fillmore 1968: 55), which is essentially a hierarchy (J. Anderson 2006: 222) in (31).

(31) If there is an A, it becomes the subject; otherwise, if there is an I, it becomes the subject; otherwise, the subject is the O.

In later work, Fillmore (1977a: 75) made the syntactic level more prominent again – following Stephen Anderson's criticism (1971) – leading to the concept of nuclear elements (subject and direct object) directly interacting with subject selection. Fillmore (1977a: 79–80) also introduces foregrounding: Of all the participants one can identify only a few are brought into perspective (or 'foregrounded'). A saliency hierarchy determines which elements are foregrounded, after which the foregrounded elements are subjected to the hierarchy in (31).

3.3.2 Instruments

In Fillmore's earlier variety of case grammar, the instrument is treated as a distinct case role (1968: 46 & 1971b: 376). He characterizes the instrument as an inanimate force or object causally involved in the action or state identified by the verb (Fillmore 1968: 46). A different wording, but with the same underlying idea, is found in Fillmore 1971b where the instrument is considered as *the stimulus or immediate physical cause of an event* (Fillmore 1971b: 376). Consider (J. Anderson 2006: 229):

(32) Emma killed Albert with the poison.

In his 1968 and 1971b work, he treats the instrument as a discrete, finite-primitve case relation. In his 1977a paper however, Fillmore entertains the possibility of treating instrument as a derived notion, which is dependent on a very specific causal relationship of the instrument to its wielder. Consider (Fillmore 1977a: 77):

(33) a. *I broke the vase with the hammer.*
b. *I broke the hammer on the vase.*

In (33a), the *hammer* is a manipulated entity causing a change of state in a third entity as the result of being wielded by the instigator. In (33b), *hammer* undergoes the change of state. Now consider a paraphrase like (34).

(34) *I used the hammer to break the vase.*

In (33a), the *with*-PP is the canonical expression of the instrument. Drawing on paraphrases like (34) for justification, Fillmore (1977a: 77–78) posits that an instrument is any patient that is not included in the sentence nucleus due to the higher salience of a competing patient. As the entity undergoing the change of state is included in the perspective, the manipulated entity is removed from the set of nuclear grammatical relations (Fillmore 1977a: 77). The less salient of the two competing patients is realized with (in English) a preposition outside the nucleus. The more salient patient is realized as the direct object. Thus, contrary to his 1968 (and 1971b) opinion, Fillmore assumes that instrument is not a case relation in its own right, rather a syntactic operation driven by the patient's lower salience. Contrary to many other approaches, Fillmore's derived instrument hints at multiple linking strategies for that concept, the oblique being the preferred one. One problem with Fillmore's derived instrument is that he considers it to be a patient. It is not clear what implications this would have for his subject selection hierarchy. Does that mean the instrument is removed from the hierarchy and subsumed under patient? If so, the intermediate position of the instrument disappears and the natural way of dealing with instruments in subject position is lost. Similar to Fillmore (1977a), John Anderson assumes that the instrument is derivative of another case relation, the absolutive. An instrument-PP is the result of displacement from object position (J. Anderson 1977: 124).

Whereas in John Anderson's approach the combination of two features in a feature matrix makes up a semantic role (instruments are handled differently), Fillmore uses primitive thematic relations. Anderson treats the instrument as the result of a displaced absolutive case, similar to later Fillmore's displaced patient. I shall refer to this treatment of instruments as *displacement*. A summary is given in table 11 below.

	Role Type	Instrument type
Fillmore 1968	Primitive	Primitive
Fillmore 1977a	Primitive	Displacement
J. Anderson	Featural	Displacement

Table 11: Comparison of thematic relation properties between varieties of Case Grammar.

3.4 Causality-driven approaches

Croft rejects the primitive, reductionist notion of thematic relations. Instead, Croft (1991: 159) argues in favor of defining thematic relations on the basis of verb semantics, which he primarily analyzes in terms of causal structure. From Croft's point of view, causality and thematic relations cannot be viewed separately. Therefore, I will begin by introducing Croft's approach to causality.

Croft rejects the independence of thematic relations from their governing predicate. Rather, he (1991: 159) assumes that regularities in verbal semantics correlate with regularities in thematic relations. Croft (1991: 161–162) proposes an approach to causation that is distinct from both the Davidsonian and the proposition-argument approach. He argues for a third approach, which is supposedly better suited to capture linguistic generalizations. He argues that his proposal has two advantages over the others: 1) causally related events share participants (e.g. the participant at the endpoint of an event is the initiator of the next) and 2) the causal chain approach will impose an ordering of participants and thus constitutes a thematic hierarchy without having to stipulate one independently. Croft's claim that the second advantage is

3 Instruments at the syntax-semantics interface

absent from the other approaches is a tenuous one. Where this may be true for the Davidsonian approach, RRG's logical structures or LDG's *Semantic Form* clearly impose an ordering on participants. As was pointed before, RRG recognizes different ways to expand a base logical structure, one of which is the expansion into a full causal chain. It is this ordering that provides the basis for actor and undergoer assignment and it is also central for instruments by virtue of being a *causally embedded* effector. Croft's first advantage is also false with respect to RRG. Certain participants can occur several times in the logical structure, thereby allowing different segments of the structure to share participants.

Croft (1991) proposes to analyze causation as individuals acting on individuals, rather than events acting on events, as is the case with Davidsonian-style treatments. In later work, he identifies this as a major flaw (2015: 105). In his 1991 work, Croft proposes an analysis of event structure in terms of causal chains. A basic causal chain is given in figure 21 (Croft 1991: 163).

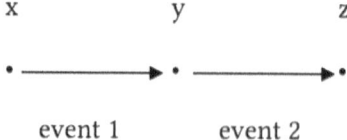

event 1   event 2

Figure 21: Basic causal chain.

The nodes in the chain represent the participants and the arrows in between mark the transmission of force. Croft (1991: 172) points out that full causal structure is incredibly complex and must therefore be simplified to a predicate-argument structure, which will include thematic relations. For Croft, the link between event structure (the causal chain) and the clause expressing it is characterized by a verb denoting a *segment* of the causal chain (the *verbal segment*). Each verbal segment is delimited by ###. For example (Croft 1991: 173) in (35).[10]

---

[10] Croft (2015: 106–109) points out that the earlier representations (1991) suffer from serious flaws: 1) the arrow notation is too coarse (as it cannot capture a non-causal

(35) Fred ate the banana.

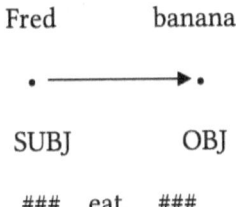

Figure 22: Chain representation of *Fred ate the banana*.

3.4.1 Thematic relations

Croft (1991: 176ff., 2015: 105) defines the points in the causal chain as thematic relations. The causally prior end of the chain is the *initiator* and the causally posterior end is the *endpoint*. Croft distinguishes between *oblique* thematic relations and *direct* thematic relations. The direct thematic relations can be considered as different subtypes or readings of initiator and endpoint, depending on the type of causation they are involved in. Croft considers these relations primary (or: *direct*) because they have a priority in subject and object choice. It is typically initiator and endpoint (regardless of their thematic role) that are selected as subject and object. As a rule, the participant in the chain that becomes subject must be antecedent to the object (Croft 2015: 108). Croft's emphasis on initiator and endpoint can be placed in the tradition of logical subject and logical object. The direct thematic roles are given in (36) (adapted from Croft 1991: 176):

(36) **Agent:** Initiator of an act of volitional causation.
Stimulus: Initiator of an act of affective causation.
Experiencer: Endpoint of an act of affective causation.
Patient: Endpoint of an act of physical causation.

---

relation), 2) only states and processes are distinguished and 3) it only shows participants acting on participants.

3.4.2 Instruments

Oblique thematic relations are defined in terms of the ordering of participants in the causal chain, relative to the choice of object and subject (Croft 1991: 176). In other words, they are only secondary to the direct thematic relations. A selection of oblique thematic relations (Croft 1991: 178–179) is given in (37).

(37) **Comitative:** An entity that participates in a causal chain at the same point and in the same role as the subject of the main verb.
Instrument: An entity that is intermediate in a causal chain between the subject (initiator) and the direct object (final affected entity).
Manner: A property holding of some or all of the verbal causal segment.

Consider the following example (adapted from Croft 1991: 177). The RRG equivalent is given in (39):

(38) *John broke the window with the hammer.*[11]

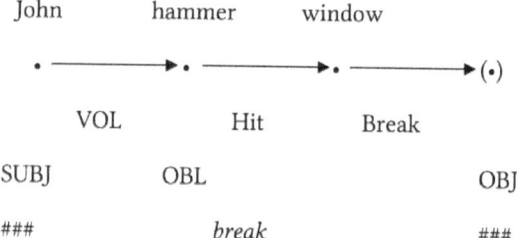

Figure 23: Causal chain representation of *John broke the window with the hammer.*

(39) [**do**′ (John, Ø)] CAUSE [[**do**′ (hammer, Ø)] CAUSE [BECOME **broken**′ (window)]]

---

[11] 'VOL' stands for *volitional causation*. It is one of four types of causation recognized by Croft.

The chain approach to event structure certainly has advantages as far as the ordering of events is concerned. However, the lexical decomposition approach is also capable of imposing order on events, which the logical structure in (39) clearly shows.

Croft's approach fails to capture three instrument-related phenomena: 1) instrument-subject alternation, 2) instruments that cannot undergo ISA and 3) the fact that ISA varies across languages.

As far as 1) is concerned, the approach falls short: It cannot account for sentences such as *The knife cut the bread*, because instruments are defined as oblique roles. Because oblique roles depend on subject and object selection, instruments (amongst others) cannot become subject themselves. This is problematic as this would amount to defining a thematic role relative to itself. One might of course posit that the 'instrument' is an agent in such cases. This is prohibited by Croft's definition of agent, however. Croft points out that instruments cannot be the initiator of an arc of volitional causation. Therefore, they cannot be agents, either.

Secondly, certain instruments cannot undergo ISA. For example, *The spoon ate the soup* is not grammatical, whereas *The knife cut the bread* is. This distinction leads some approaches to distinguish between two types of instruments (see section 3.7). For Croft (1991), there is only one type of instrument and thus this point remains unaddressed.

Thirdly, causal chains are reflections of conceptual structure and aspire to be universal in nature. Yet, there are unmistakably language-specific concerns with respect to ISA. *The knife cut the bread* is perfectly acceptable in English, but is highly ungrammatical in Russian. It is hard to explain any kind of language-specific status of the instrument-role in Croft's framework, as it would contravene the very idea of universal causal structures.

I have illustrated that Croft characterizes thematic relations as participants in a causal chains. Furthermore, he subdivides them in two separates classes, making one class dependent on the other. The instrument is dependent on the primary class of relations and thus on subject and object selection.

3.5 Lexical-Functional Grammar

Lexical-Functional Grammar (Bresnan 2001, Falk 2001, Dalrymple 2001 & 2006, Asudeh & Toivonen 2012) is a theory of syntax that places heavy emphasis on the lexicon (Dalrymple 2006: 82) rather than on the syntax proper (Van Valin & Wilkins 1993: 500–501). In this regard, LFG is on one end of a spectrum, with frameworks such as Relational Grammar or Generalized Phrase Structure Grammar (GPSG) occupying the other end (Van Valin & Wilkins 1993: 500–501). Similar to RRG, LGF rejects the idea of abstract underlying syntactic representations and transformations of any kind (Asudeh & Toivonen 2012: 2ff.). Rather, it makes extensive use of constraints and is thus considered a constraint-satisfaction theory (Asudeh & Toivonen 2012: 10f.). Grammatical functions like subject and object are considered primitives of the theory rather than being defined by phrase structure or syntactic configurations (Dalrymple 2006: 82). LFG's emphasis on the lexicon entails the risk of turning that lexicon into a list of ad-hoc list rules and facts that would otherwise be treated systematically, thereby losing the power to generalize (Van Valin & Wilkins 1993: 501).

3.5.1 A-structure and mapping to grammatical functions

Bresnan (2001: 302–303) argues that the argument structures (*a-structures*) project skeletal functional-structures (*f-structures*). A-structure is conceptualized as an interface (see *interface character* in section 3.1) between the semantics and syntax of predicates and 'houses' the thematic relations themselves. The LFG-view of this interface can be summarized as in figure 24 (adapted from Bresnan 2001: 306).

3.5 Lexical-Functional Grammar

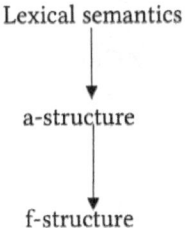

Figure 24: The relation between lexical semantics, a- and f-structure.

Classical LFG (Bresnan & Zaenen 1990) posits a linking theory based on a hierarchy of thematic relations (Bresnan & Kanerva 1989, Butt et al. 1997: 3) as illustrated in (40).

(40) AGENT > BEN[12]> EXP/GOAL > INST > PATIENT/THEME > LOCATIVE

The linking hierarchy essentially assists in mapping the thematic role-bearing arguments to grammatical functions. The highest thematic relation will be given priority in mapping to functions. The semantic roles play a crucial role in determining the grammatical function that the argument is linked to (Bresnan 2001: 309). The principle is simple: Each thematic relation in an argument structure intrinsically has a specific [± restricted] or [±objective] value that is relevant for the mapping to the grammatical functions (which are decomposed in terms of these features, see *Lexical Mapping Theory*). Agents, for example, are intrinsically [-objective] (Dalrymple 2006: 90). In addition, there are so-called 'default values', determined by the relative position of the arguments in the hierarchy (Dalrymple 2006: 90). The highest argument is, in addition to its intrinsic value, assigned [-restricted].[13] In the example below (Dalrymple

---

[12] Beneficiary
[13] There is some theory-internal variation with respect to this aspect of mapping. Butt (1997: 6ff.) proposes to work with numbers assigned to the thematic relations relative to the thematic hierarchy. A similar approach underlies Webb's characterization of instruments in standard LFG (see section 3.5.2).

2006: 90), the agent-argument's combined features yield a linking to subject.

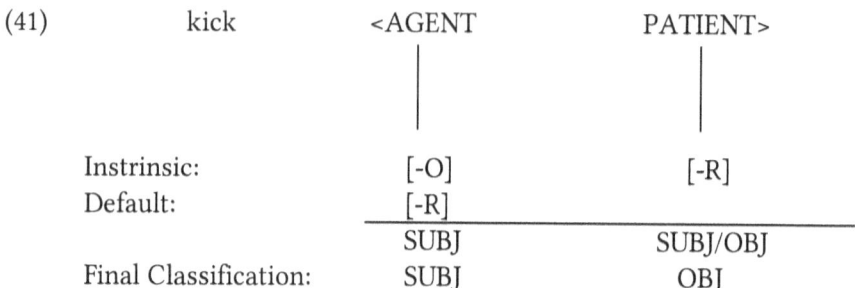

(41)   kick   <AGENT   PATIENT>

Instrinsic:	[-O]	[-R]
Default:	[-R]	
	SUBJ	SUBJ/OBJ
Final Classification:	SUBJ	OBJ

This does not, however, answer the question what thematic relations *are*. Bresnan (2001: 304) points out that a-structure captures the core participants of events designated by a predicate. The main problem here is that of grounding: Where are these roles located in theoretical space (cf. Engelberg 2011a, 2011b)? The early definitions (2001: 11) point in the direction of conceptually-grounded roles, but the presence of an elaborate semantic structure (s-structure) could point to a more formal semantic grounding. In short, this is unclear and thus quite problematic. Bresnan does present brief definitions of selected thematic relations that indeed point to a more conceptual grounding (2001: 11). For example, agent is defined as the participant in an event that essentially controls or causes the action, whereas the patient is the participant that undergoes the effect of the action (after Bresnan 2001: 11). Such an approach is not unlike Fillmore's early formulations where he assumes that speakers are able to conceptually identify "who does what to whom". Assuming the LFG-roles are conceptually grounded, the definitions suffer from the same theoretical flaws pointed out in section 3.1: Roles are poorly defined, there is no fixed amount of roles, diagnostics for testing are absent, delineating one from the other seems problematic etc. Bresnan, however, acknowledges that there are several different conceptions of a-structure in the LFG-community, including using Dowty's proto-roles (Bresnan 2001: 304 & 320). Mainstream LFG, however, still uses the semantically primitive thematic roles as described by Bresnan (2001).

3.5.2 Instruments

Instruments in LFG are considered to be primitives like all other thematic relations. Instruments occupy an intermediate position on the thematic hierarchy given in (40), a commonly held idea in the linguistic community. Consider a standard LFG-analysis of a sentence containing an instrument. The example is taken and adapted from Webb (2008: 24):

(42)
	Jack opened	the door with	the key.
Thematic relation:	Agent	Theme	Instrument
Feature:	[-o]	[-r]	[-o]
Thematic Hierarchy rank:	1	5	4
Mapped to:	SUBJ	OBJ	OBL$_\theta$

This example illustrates the purpose of the thematic hierarchy nicely. The features of Agent and Instrument are the same, creating a potential conflict. Due to the higher rank of the agent in terms of the hierarchy, it and not the instrument is mapped to the SUBJ-function. The theme-argument is mapped to object because of its [-r] feature. The instrument is mapped to OBL due to the fact that the other function it is eligible for (SUBJ) is already filled (Webb 2008: 24). This is somewhat reminiscent of RRG's assignment of the non-macrorole argument.

Standard LFG has problems handling the instrument in subject position phenomenon (Webb 2008: 25). The sentences in (1.1) would be handled the same way in LFG. Yet, due to the different syntactic behavior of the instruments, this is untenable. This leads Webb to redesign LFG's a-structure to a two-tier system with proto-roles in the tradition of Dowty. Webb (2008: 25) also argues that 1) the causal relation between the agent and the instrument is not captured by standard LFG and 2) that there is no principle difference between instrument and other roles (say, experiencer). To remedy these issues, Webb proposes several innovations: 1) a second tier in a-structure, 2) the use of Dowty's proto-roles in a-structure and 3) Croft's causal chains that feed conceptual event information into a-structure (Webb 2008: 38). Webb justifies a second tier in a-structure with what he calls the optionality of the instrument-NP. He argues that instruments are argument-adjuncts because they are

3 Instruments at the syntax-semantics interface

optional (like adjuncts) but cannot be increased in number (like arguments). To account for this, he considers instruments proto-agents on the second tier. A skeletal reformed a-structure is given in (43) (Webb 2008: 26):

(43) VERB 1st tier <α β>
           2nd tier <γ>

Webb recognizes the similarity between instruments and agents in that they both share two proto-agent properties: 1) causing an event or a change of state in another participant and 2) movement (relative to the position of another participant). The similarities would justify according the role of *proto-agent* to the instrument and the agent. Webb does, contrary to Dowty's original proposal, use the proto-roles in a more discrete way that makes them linking-concepts, a widely acknowledged problem with Dowty's proposal (see section 3.1). In a single-tier system, the very essence of having only two, opposed proto-roles would be violated. In Webb's system, it is possible as the two proto-agents will be on different tiers (Webb 2008: 28ff.). Due to the alleged optionality of the instrument, it is placed in the 2nd tier. Arguments on the 1st tier take precedence in the mapping process (Webb 2008: 40). Consider Webb's analysis of *Jack opened the door with the key* in (44).

(44)

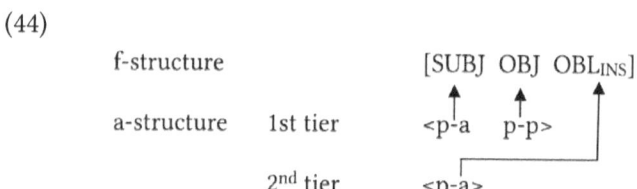

In other words, a more principled linking pattern emerges (Webb 2008: 41):

(45) 1st tier proto-agent   > SUBJ
      1st tier proto-patient > OBJ
      2nd tier proto-agent   > OBL$_{INS}$

Webb's system remedies some of the issues faced by classical LFG: Thematic relations are largely dispensed with and replaced with a non-primitive system. A solution to analyzing ISA follows naturally. This will be discussed in section 3.7. The major problem with Webb's system is that it is not clear how the third argument in ditransitives can be handled. In a traditional Dowty-based approach, recipients would be poor candidates for either proto-agent or proto-patient. By virtue of not being either, they can be 'linked' into an oblique. Standard LFG can deal with ditransitives by virtue of a recipient thematic relation, even though there is no adequate definition. Webb's approach seems to hinge on the fact that there can only be two elements on 1st tier. A recipient argument would have to be placed on the 2nd tier, but that would mean it is optional. This is clearly not the case:

(46) a. *John gave Mary a book.*
 b. **John gave Mary.*

To conclude; LFG is a theory that is primarily concerned with providing a computationally plausible system of grammar. Thematic relations generally are not in the focus of LFG-research, and that includes the instrument. Webb's proposal is the most extensive LFG-based analysis of the instrument role in its various occurrences to date. Webb's views will feature prominently in section 3.7.

3.6 Conceptual Semantics

Jackendoff's conceptual semantics (1983, 1987, 1990, 1991, 2002, 2011) can be seen as an elaboration of Gruber's (1965) original proposal (Van Valin & Wilkins 1993: 503, Jackendoff 2014: 2). The essence of Conceptual Semantics is that meanings are considered to be conceptual entities (Engelberg 2011a: 368), located in the minds of the speakers and in the speaker's conceptualization of the world (Jackendoff 2011: 688). Semantics, therefore, is considered to be the organization of those thoughts that can be expressed by language (Jackendoff 2002: 123). Jackendoff uses abstract motion and location predicates in his decompositions, making his theory localist in nature (Engelberg 2011a: 370): Local and spatial relations are taken to be basic.

3.6.1 Overview

The centerpiece of Jackendoff's system is an autonomous level called *conceptual structure* where meanings are represented. He considers this level to be the universal model of the human mind's construal of the world (Jackendoff 1983: 57ff., 1991: 10 & 12, Engelberg 2011a: 396) and as such universal to all languages. The strict division that some theories make between semantic meaning and world knowledge is not present in Conceptual Semantics (Jackendoff 2002: 267ff., Engelberg 2011a: 369, Jackendoff 2011: 689). Therefore, it does not suffer from what DeLancey calls 'objectivism'. Jackendoff's (2011: 688) theory is decompositional in nature, although these decompositions are very different from those employed by Dowty or RRG. The basic building blocks need not be words in themselves, for instance (Engelberg 2011a: 370). Conceptual primitives belong to several major conceptual categories such as *Event, Thing, Path, Place* etc. (Jackendoff 1991: 13). These are the arguments of functions, such as *CAUSE, TO* or *GO*. The sentence in (47a) corresponds to the structure in (47b) (Jackendoff 1991: 13). The RRG representation of (47a) is given in (47c):

(47) a. *Bill went into the house.*
 b. [Event GO ([Thing BILL], [Path TO ([Place IN ([Thing HOUSE])])])]
 c. [**do´** (Bill, Ø)] CAUSE [BECOME **be-in´** (house, Bill)]

Square brackets mark a conceptual constituent (Jackendoff 1991: 13). Lexical entries are construed according to the same logic (figure 25, Engelberg 2011a: 369). Similar to RRG, lexical entries contain a skeletal decomposed structure with open argument slots.

$$\begin{bmatrix} \text{go into} \\ \text{V} \\ \_\_ <\text{NP}_j> \\ [_{\text{Event}} \text{GO} ([_{\text{Thing}}] \ i), [_{\text{Path}} \text{TO} ([_{\text{Place}} \text{IN} ([_{\text{Thing}}] \ j)])]) \end{bmatrix}$$

Figure 25: Lexical entry for *go into* (conceptual semantics).

The top line in the lexical entry in figure 25 represents phonological structure, the second and third lines represent syntactic structure and the bottom line is conceptual structure.

3.6.2 Thematic relations

Thematic relations are a crucial tool in Conceptual Semantics for the mapping to syntax (Jackendoff 1987: 372, Engelberg 2011a: 371). Essentially, thematic relations are simply structural configurations in the conceptual structure (Jackendoff 1972, 1987: 378, 1990: 47). Jackendoff (1987: 372 & 1990: 46), unlike other generative linguists, places them in the semantics and not in the syntax. For instance, in (47b) the first argument of GO is the *theme*. This places Conceptual Semantics' thematic relations clearly in the 'derived' class. This line of reasoning was the inspiration for RRG's conception of thematic relations, which are structurally determined readings as well (Van Valin, p.c.). For Jackendoff, conceptual structure consists of a *thematic* tier (hosting relations related to motion and location) and an *action tier*. The latter was introduced as a proposed solution to some of the shortcomings having only one tier (Levin & Rappaport 2005: 47f.). The action tier bears some similarity to the generalized semantic roles found in RRG or in Dowty's work. Even though Jackendoff's *actor* and *patient/undergoer*[14] cannot be directly equated to RRG's actor and undergoer, Jackendoff's motivation for them follows

---

[14] Patient and Beneficiary are considered to be subtypes of undergoer (Nikanne 1995: 2). Yet, in the literature on conceptual semantics, patient and undergoer are often used interchangeably.

3 Instruments at the syntax-semantics interface

similar lines: The action tier and its components are intended to capture how (and which) participants are 'affected'. For Jackendoff, the action tier is the primary level involved in the linking to morphosyntax while the thematic tier plays a secondary role at best.[15] Arguments bearing action tier-roles are prioritized in linking; arguments bearing thematic tier-roles follow the action-tier roles in linking (Nikanne 1995: 2). Consider the following example (The car hit the tree) (adapted from Jackendoff 1990: 126–127):

$$\begin{bmatrix} \text{INCH [BE ([CAR], [AT [TREE]])]} \\ \text{Event} \quad \text{AFF ([CAR], [TREE])} \end{bmatrix}$$

Figure 26: Thematic tier and action tier.

The top level in figure 26 is the thematic tier and the lower level is the action tier. The structural configuration means that *car* is a theme on the thematic tier and an actor on the action tier, whereas *tree* is a goal on the thematic tier and a *patient* on the action tier. An ordering of thematic relations is provided by a thematic hierarchy. This hierarchy is mapped onto a *syntactic hierarchy* to account for linking (Jackendoff 1990: 258ff, Engelberg 2011a: 372). Consider Jackendoff's *Thematic Hierarchy* and its structural 'translation' (Jackendoff 1990: 258) in (48). Asterisks indicate the relevant constituents:

(48) a. Order the A-marked arguments in the action tier from left to right, followed by the A-marked arguments in the main conceptual clause of the thematic tier, from least embedded to most deeply embedded.

---

[15] This is very reminiscent of RRG's extensive use of the GSRs actor and undergoer. The more basic-level thematic relations sometimes play a role, but similar to Jackendoff's thematic tier, only secondarily so.

b. [AFF (X*, <Y>)]   (Actor)
    [AFF (<X>, Y*)]   (Patient (AFF⁻) or
                                    Beneficiary (AFF+))
    [_Event/State_ F (X*, <Y>)]   (Theme)
    [_Path/Place_ F (X*)]   (Location, Source, Goal)

In later work, Jackendoff (2011: 695) revises the tier-system and subdivides conceptual structure into *propositional structure* on the one hand and *information structure* on the other. Despite the revisions, the basic idea remains the same.

3.6.3 Instruments

As the thematic hierarchy in (48) shows, there is no instrument role. Rather, instrument is an interaction of actor and patient. To capture this, Jackendoff (1987: 398ff.) proposes to augment the thematic and action tiers with a *temporal tier*. The temporal tier operates with two primitives: P (point in time) and R (region in time). Jackendoff describes, for example, an achievement as the combination $R\ P$. A region in time is bounded by a point in time (these annotations are always to be read from left to right). Individual Ps and Rs can be expanded into sequences of smaller Ps and Rs: P can be decomposed into R P R and R can be decomposed into P R P.

Instruments are nothing more than entities that are acted on and that act on another entity themselves. This double role can be simultaneous or it can be sequential. The former implies a continuous manipulation on the part of the instigator, whereas the latter does not. Each of these options is associated with a different temporal tier configuration, (P P) and (P R P) respectively. Associations are indicated with association lines, dashed lines indicate potential associations. The system of association lines permits the conceptualization of the event as one where there is constant manipulation on the part of the instigator or where there is only initial contact manipulation. In terms of the decomposition, an 'instrument' is a theme argument of a predication (in the example below of

3 Instruments at the syntax-semantics interface

GO) that is demoted[16] in the sense that it does not feature in the action tier (Jackendoff 1987: 400–401), contrary to – for example – the car in the car hit the tree. Rather, it appears on the temporal tier twice, as a goal in the first section of the tier and as a theme in the second section of the tier. An overview of this for *Sue hit Fred with the stick* is given in the decomposition in figure 27:[17]

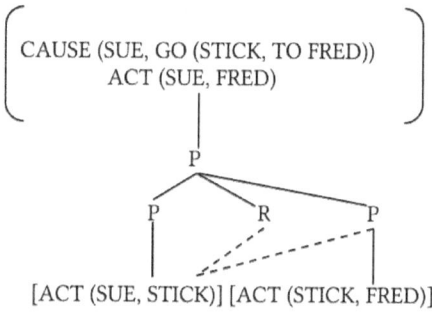

Figure 27: Jackendoff's analysis of an instrument construction (pre-1990).

Jackendoff (1990: 142–145) revises his analysis of instruments in his later work, although the basic assumption remains the same: Instrument is an entity that is acted upon and in turn acts on another. However, Jackendoff (1990) no longer resorts to a temporal tier. Rather, he treats the instrument as an entity embedded in a *means expression* (expressed with *by* in the decomposition). The BY-function turns events into *means modifiers* (Jackendoff 1990: 142). Here, too, the instrument can be defined structurally (Jackendoff 1990: 142–143): It is a conceptual entity embedded in an event which acts as a modifier of a superordinate event. Consider (Jackendoff 1990: 143) the 1990 analysis of *Sue hit Fred with a stick* in figure 28.

---

[16] The analysis in Foley & Valin (1984: 54) is similar: Instruments are considered to be effector-themes.
[17] This graph was taken from Jackendoff (1987: 401). The notation used there on the thematic and action tiers is the pre-1990 notation.

3.6 Conceptual Semantics

$$\begin{bmatrix} \text{CS}^+ \text{ ([SUE], [INCH [BE}_\text{c} \text{ ([STICK], [AT}_\text{c} \text{ [FRED]])])} \\ \text{AFF}^- \text{ ([SUE], [FRED])} \\ \text{[BY} \begin{bmatrix} \text{CS}^+ \text{ ([SUE], [AFF}^- \text{ ([STICK], [FRED])])} \\ \text{AFF}^- \text{ ([SUE], [STICK])} \end{bmatrix} \text{]} \end{bmatrix}$$

Figure 28: Jackendoff's reformulated analysis of an instrument construction (1990).

The structures proposed by Jackendoff for instruments are quite complex. When compared to RRG or to the finite-primitive approaches, it is doubtful whether *parsimony* is met. Jackendoff assumes that instrumental subjects are instances of inanimate instigators rather than instruments (Jackendoff 1990: 295), but he does not explore this matter any further. Positing *key* in (49a) as an instigator is implausible as (49b) illustrates. Because the key cannot take an instrument itself, it cannot be an inanimate instigator. This means that is fundamentally different from *storm* in (49c). There is a further issue with Jackendoff's system: Some instruments cannot undergo ISA, yet this point remains unaddressed.

(49) a. The key opened the door.
 b. *The key opened the door with the stick.
 c. The storm destroyed the village with its strong winds.

There does not seem to be any straightforward way in Jackendoff's system to account for ISA itself and the fact that some instruments cannot undergo it whereas others can. Instruments depend on the presence of agent and patient and seem too circumstantial here to account for ISA. Second, in the 1990 representation, the more extensive temporal-causal information from the pre-1990 representation is gone. Yet, it is important in order to account for ISA, as will become clear in section 3.7.

3 Instruments at the syntax-semantics interface

3.7 Instruments as subjects

Many, if not most, linguists who acknowledge the category of instrument do not distinguish within this class any further. However, there are good empirical reasons to assume that there are subtypes of instruments, motivated by diverging morphosyntactic behavior of some instruments when compared to others. In the introduction, the instrument-subject alternation (ISA) was briefly introduced. It has been observed that some instruments can occur as subjects, whereas others cannot (e.g. Marantz 1981: 285–286, Wojcik 1976: 165). I denote instruments that can undergo ISA as *intermediary instruments* and those that cannot as *facilitating instruments*. The use of this terminology is borrowed from Marantz (1981). I use these terms for the sake of theoretical neutrality. The former's conceptual ability to act 'independently' is often cited as an explanation for ISA (see Kamp & Rossdeutscher and Alexiadou & Schäfer below). Fillmore acknowledged the existence of ISA as a natural consequence of the subject selection hierarchy A > I > O (Schlesinger 1989: 189–190). Fillmore can account for the alternations in (50a–50b) by positing that they refer to the same scene. The second sentence's case frame simply lacks an A and thus, the I becomes the subject. Yet, difficulties emerge for this kind of approach when confronted with (50c–50d), which should, following the same logic, be possible. It is difficult in many approaches to account for this alternation because all instruments are treated as one monolithic class. Croft's account has difficulties capturing this alternation because instruments always occupy an intermediate position in the causal chain (Webb 2008: 32). Although numerous explanations to capture ISA have been suggested (Kamp & Rossdeutscher 1994, Alexiadou & Schäfer 2006, Webb 2008, Grimm 2013, RRG), most theories, however, are silent on the subject. Generally speaking, ISA is a phenomenon where participants of an event that are conceptualized as instruments are 'moved' to subject position. Consider:

(50) a. *John picked up the container with the crane.*
 b. *The crane picked up the container.*
 c. *Larry picked up the potato with the fork.*
 d. **The fork picked up the potato.*

e. *Jan sneed   het   brood door   met   het   mes.*
   Jan cut\PST.3SG DEF bread through with DEF knife
   'Jan cut the bread with a knife.' (Dutch)
f. **Het mes   sneed   het   brood door.*
   DEF knife cut\PST.3SG DEF bread through
   'The knife cut the bread.'
g. *Jean a   coupé   le   pain   avec le   couteau.*
   Jean AUX.3SG cut.PTCP DEF bread with DEF knife
   'Jean cut the bread with the knife.' (French)
h. **Le couteau a   coupé   le   pain.*
   DEF knife   AUX.3SG cut.PTCP DEF bread
   'The knife cut the bread.'
i. *Jan schnitt   das   Brot   mit   dem   Messer.*
   Jan cut\PST.3SG DEF bread with DEF knife
   'Jan cut the bread with the knife.' (German)
j. *?/*Das Messer schnitt   das Brot.*
   DEF   knife cut\PST.3SG DEF bread
   'The knife cut the bread.'
k. *Jovan je   sekao   hleb   nožem.*
   Jovan AUX.3SG cut.PTCP bread(ACC) knife.INS
   'John cut the bread with a knife.' (Serbian)
l. **Nož je   sekao   hleb.*
   knife AUX.3SG cut.PTCP bread(ACC)
   'The knife cut the bread.'
m. *John killed the man with a silver bullet.*
n. *A bullet to the heart killed the man.*
o. *John murdered the man with a silver bullet.*
p. **A bullet to the heart murdered the man.*

These examples reveal that there are three main issues that need to be addressed: 1) There are different classes of instruments (50a–50d), 2) predicates vary (50m–50p) and 3) languages vary (50a–50l). Not every approach has an answer to each of these issues. In fact, many do not even recognize 3) at all, focusing exclusively on English. Even though examples (50e–50l) illustrate that this phenomenon is language-specific. For instance, Dutch, French and Serbian do not allow for this alternation at all here, whereas in German the sentence in (50j) comes with an ability reading only: The knife was capable, at one point in the past, of cutting bread. The past tense indicates that it has since lost the ability to do so.

Variation with respect to ISA generally comes in two flavors: (a) variation *within* languages and (b) variation *across* languages. Even though (b) is hardly ever investigated, it is sometimes acknowledged (e.g. Webb (2008) and Schlesinger (1989)).

Generally, two approaches can be discerned: 1) Approaches that assume that instruments in subject position are nothing more than agents, albeit less prototypical ones; 2) approaches that use ISA to justify a diversification of the instrument participant into several subtypes. The former usually uses features or traits to capture the similarities between instruments and more prototypical agents (i.e. humans). For instance, some linguists assume that agent and instrument crucially share a feature like *causal change* or the like (Levin & Rappaport Hovav 2005: 46). Due to the crucial presence of a certain feature, instruments can occur as subjects. The latter assumes that ISA is a type of construction. The second class of approaches does not treat all inanimates in subject position as instruments, whereas the first class of approaches does (at least tacitly). The former runs the risk of diluting the notion of the 'instrument' into a non-relation because the boundary between instigator and intermediate is blurred (or even lost). The latter has a clear definition of what an instrument is, yet it must find a principled way to distinguish cases of ISA from mere inanimate subjects.

3.7.1 The general approach

For Schlesinger and DeLancey (1984), instruments in subject position are best analyzed as inanimate agents, rather than instruments that are constructionally highlighted. DeLancey (1991: 348) assumes that *key* in *the key opened the lock* must be an agent because as it is a perfectly normal transitive clause, there is no reason to assume another agent. Being identified as a causally involved argument is sufficient to be agent (DeLancey 1991: 349). He claims that even though there might be an ultimate cause (i.e. agent), it is not necessary to include it in the event representation. In other words, only the proximate cause is included in the semantics and it is a normal agent. If they were normal agents then there is no reason why they could not take instruments. This is, however, impossible, calling their agent status into question.

Schlesinger (1989: 193) proposes that the agent-category is not a discrete but a graded category, with different degrees of membership. Inanimate tools are usually instruments, but can be read as agents if the referent's membership in the agent-category is high enough. This approach not only accounts for typical instruments (e.g. *fork lift*) but for all inanimates in subject position. Schlesinger (1989: 193 & 197) also points out that mechanisms are 'better agents' than simple inanimate objects and more complex mechanisms are better agents than less complex ones. Alexiadou & Schäfer (2006: 43) and Grimm make similar observations. However, Schlesinger does not explore this further. Schlesinger proposes two *naturalness conditions* and a set of *constraints* to account for ISA. Only if certain conditions are met, can an inanimate become the subject of a sentence. For example, Schlesinger (1989: 189–190) argues that the sentence (51b) is unusual because the *stick*'s membership in the agent-category is not high enough for it to be considered agent and, consequently, to be accepted as the subject of the sentence.

(51) a. Carol hit the horse with the stick.
     b. ?The stick hit the horse.

3.7.1.1 Naturalness conditions

Schlesinger (1989) proposes two naturalness conditions. Consider *naturalness condition 1* (Schlesinger 1989: 190):

(52) **Naturalness condition 1:** When the event is not instigated by a human agent, or when the agent is unknown or no longer on the scene, the instrument by means of which the action is performed or which is involved in the event may be naturally expressed as the subject.

This condition, in combination with Schlesinger's examples, implies that there is always a manipulating entity with every inanimate in subject position. Consider the very conceivable interpretation for (51b) that a falling stick impacts a horse (say, when the stick falls from the tree by natural-physical causes such as the wind or, even more basic, gravity). In such a reading, a speaker would not readily conceptualize the wind or gravity as an instigator or as a manipulating entity, even though it would certainly be one in the realm of physics. A similar concern is valid for (53a–53b), given by Schlesinger (1989: 190) as illustrations of naturalness condition 1.

(53) a. *The rust has eaten away at the lock.*
      b. *The clock was ticking so loudly that it woke the baby.*
      c. *The rust has eaten away at the lock by means of its oxidizing processes.*
      d. **John broke the metal box with the rust.*
      e. **The knife cut the box with the blade.*

It is problematic to consider *rust* as instrument, as there is no realistic instigator. Furthermore, *rust* cannot be instrument, because it can take instruments (53c) and, more importantly, it cannot be under manipulation of an instigator (53d). Natural forces cannot conceivably have an agent governing them, as DeLancey points out (1991: 347). I thus follow DeLancey (1991: 347) and Grimm (2013: 2–3) when they argue that they are simply not instruments. Schlesinger, however, claims that forces and instruments are essentially the same and that naturalness condition 1 applies to both. This is doubtful because forces and instruments CAN be distinguished quite easily. Forces can take instruments themselves and cannot be instruments of another instigator ((53c) and (53d)), whereas instruments can never take other instruments ((53e)). Schlesinger's examples given in (54) are even more problematic:

(54) a. *A fence barred his access.*
      b. *A pile of rubble barred his access.*

In (54), there is not even a change of state, as *bar* tests as a state. There is no activity predicate, and consequently, there is no instigator. Therefore, assigning forcehood to *fence* and *pile of rubble* is highly doubtful.

Another problem is the example (Schlesinger 1989: 190) *the letter of introduction opened all doors to him*. The *letter of introduction* does not literally open doors. It is an idiomatic expression and should be disqualified as an example. A similar concern applies to Schlesinger's (1989: 192) use of Shakespeare to illustrate his point, which uses poetic language. A fourth problem is '*no longer on the scene*'. Although one can claim that the instigator is no longer present or unknown in e.g. *The computer virus crippled John's computer*, this is not true for *the knife cut the bread*, as the knife requires continuous manipulation. An additional problem is Schlesinger's (1989: 190) illustration in (55a).

(55) a. *The World War II mine wounded him when he stepped on it.*
b. *The World War II mine wounded him with shrapnel when he stepped on it.*

However, the *mine* is not an instrument in (55a): It takes other instruments ((55b)), but more importantly, there is no event link between the stricken individual[18] and the instigator of the mine's planting. Consider:

(56) a. *???The WW II-soldier killed the civilian in 2015 with a landmine.*
b. *The soldier killed the civilian with the landmine.*
c. *The landmine killed the civilian.*

There are two events involved in (56a): The planting of the mine in World War II and the mine killing a civilian in 2015. It is strange to claim that a soldier planting a mine some 70 years ago is directly responsible for a civilian in 2015 dying, as (56a) illustrates. The *mine*-examples do reveal two interesting facts, though: 1) some referents can be conceptualized as both instrument and a type of force (55b) and 2) for ISA to be acceptable, there has to be some kind of event link between the 'standard' sentence (e.g. (56b)) and the shifted sentence ((56c)). Schlesinger (1989: 191) also proposes a second naturalness condition, shown in (57).

---

[18] I assume that *him* refers to a person in the here and now. If it referred to a person in the World War II-era, the use of the RP 'The World War II mine' would be very strange.

(57) **Naturalness Condition 2**: To the extent that attention is drawn to the instrument by means of which an action is performed and away from the instigator of the action, the former will be naturally expressed as the sentence subject.

Criticism is in order here as well. Consider (adapted from Schlesinger 1989: 191) the examples in (58).

(58) a. *The pencil draws lines.*
b. *John draws lines with the pencil.*
c. [**do´** (John, Ø)] CAUSE [[**do´** (pencil, Ø)] CAUSE [BECOME **drawn´** (lines)]]
d. *John draws lines with the pencil today.*
e. *?The pencil draws lines today.*
f. *John cut the bread with a knife today.*
g. *The knife cut the bread today.*

The sentence in (58b) corresponds with the LS in (58c). One can paraphrase (58b) as *The pencil is a/the cause of the lines being drawn*. This stands to reason: Without the pencil, John would have been unable to draw lines. However, I reject the idea that (58a) is the ISA-version of (58b). Rather, I believe it has an ability reading. Contrary to (58f–58g), adding a temporal adverbial makes (58e) less acceptable.

3.7.1.2 Deliberation constraint & mediation constraint

Apart from the naturalness conditions, Schlesinger proposes two constraints. These can be used as tests to determine how similar the instrument in question is to the prototypical agent. The first constraint Schlesinger (1989: 195) proposes is the *deliberation constraint*. Essentially, the more the task requires deliberation, the less likely the inanimate will be realized in subject position. Consider (59) (Schlesinger 1989: 195):

(59) a. *The baton is jerking nervously above the conductor's head.*
b. **The baton is conducting Tchaikovsky's fifth Symphony.*

The sentence in (59a) is said to be fine because little or no deliberation is needed on the part of the instrument. This is problematic, because there is no instrument in (59a): *Baton* is not causally involved in any way. It does not cause anything in turn. Rather, *baton* in (59a) is an inanimate x-argument of the LS: SEML **do**′ (baton, [**jerk**′ (baton)]). However, if the deliberation constraint is stripped of its instrument-related aspects, then it can be useful to account for the appearance of at least some inanimates in initial x-argument position. Consider (Schlesinger 1989: 195):

(60) a. *The black king moves to H4.*
      b. **The chess pieces play a short game.*

Schlesinger posits that if too much deliberation is entailed in the verb's meaning, agentivization is 'blocked'. I believe one should turn this perspective around: Verbs with higher deliberation in their meaning will require a more prototypically agentive subject-referent. Verbs like *murder* and *beat* are said to have a great deal of deliberation in their meaning, only allowing humans as subjects (Schlesinger 1989: 196). There are two problems with this: 1) The concept of *deliberation* is ill-defined and 2) due to Schlesinger's refusal to posit *deliberation* as an annotation in the mental lexicon, it is unclear how it would function technically. Schlesinger (1989: 196–197) states that the deliberation constraint can be overridden if one of the naturalness conditions is satisfied, thereby explaining (61).

(61) *The musical box played the madrigal.*

Positing overrides to constraints considerably complicates matters and fails to achieve *parsimony*. The second constraint that Schlesinger (1989: 197) proposes is the *mediation constraint*: An inanimate object can only be an agent if it cannot take instruments, contrary to prototypical agents. Schlesinger claims that the mediation constraint explains why (62a) is ungrammatical. Yet, this sentence is grammatical.

(62) a. *The wind broke the window with a twig.*
      b. *The storm destroyed the village with huge tidal wives.*
      c. *The computer virus crippled Mary's computer with a batch of junk files.*
      d. *The assembly robot cut the steel in half with a saw.*

The mediation constraint does predict the unacceptability of instruments taking instruments: As soon as an instrument is added to an ISA-sentence, it becomes ungrammatical ((53e)). However, the mediation constraint overgeneralizes: It would correctly filter out the ungrammatical sentence in (53e) but it would wrongly rate the examples in (62a–62d) as ungrammatical. Schlesinger (1989: 199–200) proposes an override here as well. If the instrument is a proper part of or 'otherwise intimately associated with the agent', then the inanimate agent can take instruments. Consider (Schlesinger 1989: 200) the examples in (63).

(63) a. *The new apparatus bores holes with a laser beam.*
b. *The piper plane exterminated the insects with a special spray.*

Even though this override seemingly captures (63a–63b), it does not explain cases where the instrument is not necessarily closely associated with the agent (e.g. *saw* in (62d)). Needless to say, the subject referents above are mechanisms and thus rank high on the Van Valin-Wilkins scale (1996). An additional problem with the mediation constraint is that Schlesinger cannot adequately draw a line between those instruments where it holds and those where it does not hold (Schlesinger 1989: 200). For instance, he claims that it does not hold in (64) and therefore these sentences are grammatical. Why the constraint does not apply here is not explained.

(64) a. *The cruiser bombarded the coast with heavy shells.*
b. *The locomotive cleared the track with a snow plow.*

3.7.1.3 Conjunction test & do-test
Fillmore (1968) sought evidence for his cases in the fact that it appears that entities bearing different cases cannot be conjoined (1968: 43). Consider (Schlesinger 1989: 201, after Quirk et al. 1972):

(65) a. **Carol and the stick hit the horse.*
b. **John and the key opened the door.*

For Fillmore, *Carol* and *John* are agents (A) and *stick* and *key* are instruments (I). Schlesinger concedes that this might pose problems for his analysis, because *stick* and *key* can be read as agents. If they are agents, then (65a–65b) should be grammatical. Schlesinger believes that even if two referents have the same case, they still require a degree of agentivity that is similar. Because *Carol* and *stick* are too dissimilar, they cannot be conjoined. In RRG, *John* and *the key* would occupy the same argument position in the logical structure as a conjoined RP of the form (John ∧ key). As the two referents are not co-agents, the sentence is ungrammatical. I will revisit this in chapter 7.

Schlesinger argues that the permissibility of highly agentive instruments as the subject of *do* affirms their agent-like status. From an RRG-perspective, a *do*-test only detects that the referent is under the scope of a **do´**, nothing more. Furthermore, such a test is not cross-linguistically valid for two reasons: 1) Not all languages have a general *do* verb and 2) even languages that have such a verb often do not allow for such a test. Consider Schlesinger's (1989: 202) illustrations with their Dutch equivalents:

(66) a. What did the bullet do?
　　 b. *Wat deed　　 de　 kogel?
　　　　What do\PST.3SG DEF bullet
　　 c. Bob showed Dick what the new type of chisel can do.
　　 d. *Bob toon-de　　　 Dick wat het nieuwe type
　　　　Bob show-PST.3SG Dick REL DEF new　　 type
　　　　beitel kan doen.
　　　　chisel can do.INF

3.7.1.4 Instruments as members of the agent class

Schlesinger (1989) and Grimm (2013) assume that the more agentive an inanimate is, the more likely it can be a subject. Schlesinger and Grimm argue that the agentivity of referents is largely (but not exclusively) determined by properties inherent to the referents. Schlesinger proposes a set of features to capture this, whereas Grimm proposes a network.

Schlesinger's features
Schlesinger considers agentivity as a graded concept: There are more prototypical agents (e.g. *John*) and less prototypical ones (e.g. *knife*). The ability to appear in subject position depends (amongst others) on the degree of membership in the agent class. Schlesinger (1989: 207) posits that instruments that can become subject crucially share features like [+cause] or [+control] with prototypical agents. Schlesinger emphasizes that the constraints and conditions he stipulates cannot be transformed into features and must therefore remain a separate part of the apparatus. This is mainly due to the fact that the constraints depend on context or on the interaction between agent and instrument, rather than on a referent's inherent properties. Constraints are thus *context-sensitive* and features are *context-insensitive*. The main problems with this account is that the features are not defined properly and that they are used in a fairly ad hoc-fashion. There are no independent criteria for assigning [+cause] to a referent. Yet, the idea that 'agency' is a cluster concept is very intriguing. This idea is also present in the Van Valin-Wilkins hierarchy: Traits and features are ranked hierarchically and interact with other factors such as constructions.

Grimm's lattice(s)
Grimm (2013) proposes to capture the limits of *subjecthood* with the interplay of two hierarchically structured lattices. Referents are placed on the lattice according to the features that make up the lattice's architecture. Rather than positing constraints and conditions, Grimm assumes that argument slots can access certain sections of the lattice, whereas they cannot access other portions of it. In a nutshell, inanimates must be in a portion of the lattice that the argument slot can access for them to become subject. Canonical subjects such as humans are near the top of the lattice. The main difference between Schlesinger's and Grimm's approaches lies in the consistency with which the lattice is built: A set of well-defined features is chosen and made subject to entailment relations. This puts Grimm in the 'general approach': A system is set up to deal with inanimates in subject position (including ISA). Grimm argues that there is no equivalence between normal instrument constructions and ISA (Grimm 2013: 1–2) as not all instruments can appear in subject

3.7 Instruments as subjects

position, an observation that leads others to assume subtypes of instruments (RRG, Alexiadou & Schäfer). Grimm concludes that instruments in subject position are simply inanimate referents in subject position and are governed by general linking principles. Contrary to Schlesinger, Grimm distinguishes forces from instruments, stating that the former do not appear in a *with*-PP or, generally, exhibit the syntactic behavior of instruments (Grimm 2013: 2). This is only partly true, as instruments exist that are 'agentive' enough to be realized as an instrument *or* an instigator (e.g. *assembly robot*).

Grimm (2005 & 2013) proposes two related lattices: A more basic *agency lattice* and an *agency-animacy lattice*, the latter being a combination of the former with a typical animacy hierarchy. The agency lattice is compiled from the features *instigation, motion, sentience, volition* and *persistence*, some of which are inspired by Dowty's proto-role properties (Grimm 2005: 20). Grimm considers his features to be event-based properties. Hence, the agency lattice is intended to capture event structure.

Some of these features are problematic however. For example, the feature *persistence* supposedly tracks how a participant is affected over time (Grimm 2005: 21–22). The *apple* in *John ate the apple* would be ranked as *existential persistence (end)* as the referent ceases to exist. Grimm subdivides *persistence* by introducing the distinction between *existential* and *qualitative persistence* and including *beginning/end* as values. The main problem is that the features are not adequately defined or delineated. For instance, in the sentence *he was thinking about his dream last night* the referent *dream* no longer exists; it ended the moment the person woke up. Yet, it is possible to speak of the dream as if it still existed. The vagueness and overcomplexity of *persistence* makes it a very confusing feature.

Grimm (2005: 21) follows Rozwadowska (1988) in defining *sentience* as "conscious involvement in the action or state", making it an event-based property. I strongly disagree with their use of the term *sentience*. In this thesis, I define *sentience* as "the ability to judge intentions in others and/or the ability to make independent decisions. I consider *sentience* as an inherent feature, that is, a feature inherent to the referent.

3 Instruments at the syntax-semantics interface

Motion is defined (Grimm 2005: 21) as a requirement of being in motion during the event, which is evident with predicates like throw. For instance, in the stick hit the horse the subject position imposes the requirement on its filler that it moves. Therefore, whatever fills this slot must be capable of moving or being moved, which is captured with the NP-related feature [±mobile]. As stick can be moved, it possesses the feature [+mobile] and is thus compatible with throw's requirements (Grimm 2013: 8). Volition is defined as a feature characterizing an entity that consciously plans to bring about a specific result. In RRG, *volition* is defined as a basic act of will. What Grimm calls volition is termed *intention(al)* in RRG. Despite the differences between the two concepts, they are not necessarily discrete categories. Determining whether something is intention or volition is tricky and it may be advantageous to leave it underspecified. In this dissertation, *volition* is used as a label for such an underspecification. *Sentience* and *motion* illustrate that there are good reasons to assume a distinction between *inherent properties* and *induced properties*. Grimm's agency lattice is given in figure 29 (see appendix).

Grimm's treatment of agentivity and patientivity as two different axes is contradictory. This theoretically allows for referents to be simultaneously highly patientive and agentive. In RRG, the deeper a referent is embedded in an LS, the more 'patientive' it will be and vice versa. The event-related features that Grimm introduces are captured naturally with the Actor-Undergoer Hierarchy. Interesting, however, are the notions of *upward-closed* and *downward-closed*. Grimm states that if a referent with a position x on the hierarchy is treated as a patient relative to its verbal predicate, then every referent that ranks lower would also also treated as such (e.g. downward-closed). The same applies to agents and upward-closed. This gives rise to the idea (Grimm 2013: 5) that potential agents and patients form *regions* in structured semantic space. I agree with this reasoning and it will feature prominently in my own approach (see chapter 4).

Grimm combines the agency lattice with an *animacy hierarchy*, yielding the combined *agency-animacy lattice*. For the construction of the animacy hierarchy, Grimm again proposes a combination of features, compiled into a lattice-like structure (Grimm 2013: 5–6). He proposes four features that are subject to entailment relations: *human, sentient, mobile* and *potent*. *Human* is self-explanatory, but *sentience* is not. Grimm treats sentience as a feature referring to a referent's ability to perceive stimuli. For him, [-sentient] equals inanimate and [+sentient] equals animate. This crucially assumes that there is a binary opposition between them. Such oppositions make it difficult to characterize referents like *Artificial Intelligence*. *Mobile* are those referents that can be moved; *non-mobile* are those that cannot be moved, such as houses or trees. This feature is distinct from the event-related *motion* that was described above. The event-related motion feature refers to whether something is in motion in the event, the NP-mobile describes an inherent quality of the referent. *Mobile* is less straightforward than it would appear, however. Consider:

(67) a. *Mara saw the house.*
      b. *Mara saw the parked car.*
      c. *Mara saw the car.*

In (67a), *house* is inherently unable to move, whereas the car in (67b) is only induced immobile. It has the inherent ability to move, but context (here in the form of an adnominal modifier) dictates that it is immobile. In other words, in (67b) the immobility of *car* is owed to context, whereas in (67a) it is an essential feature of the referent. Whereas Grimm's approach can capture the immobility of referents like *house*, it is unclear how he would capture the induced immobility of (67b). Barring the fact that Grimm's labeling is unfortunate and confusing, I believe the mobility of referents can be captured in a more natural way. If movement is relevant in the event described by the predicate, it will be encoded as such in the logical structure. Nevertheless, the inherent (in)ability to move or be moved is an important distinction that will appear in my own approach in chapter 4. Last, *potent* is considered to be true of inanimates that have their own internal power or are considered to have it, a concept often found in the literature. Here, Grimm (2013: 7) follows Chafe (1970: 109). This feature is used to distinguish inanimates capable of semi-autonomous activity ([+potent]) from those that are not ([-potent]).

3 Instruments at the syntax-semantics interface

These features are related to each other through entailment relations, similar to the event-related features. *Sentient* entails *potent* and *mobile*. *Human* entails *sentient*, thereby also entailing *potent* and *mobile* (Grimm 2013: 7):

(68) inanimate < mobile inanimate, potent inanimate < mobile and potent inanimate (e.g. natural force, autonomous machine) < animate < human

Grimm believes that this approach can also account for autonomously acting machines and natural forces: They possess *potent* and *mobile*. There are two problems with this assumption: 1) Natural forces and autonomous machines behave differently syntactically and 2) there is gradation within the class of 'autonomous machines' illustrated by diverging syntactic behavior.

Grimm's combined lattice is given in figure 30 (see appendix). The combined lattice raises important questions: How is this combination accounted for? What principles are followed in connecting nodes with each other? Grimm points out (2013: 7) that 'one is inserted into the other', thus taking their Cartesian product. However, this is not made explicit any further.

Grimm wants to use this combined lattice for the broader purpose of argument linking. As much of these event-based properties are handled in the logical structures in RRG, I see no need for Grimm's agency lattice. Rather, the combination of this lattice with an animacy hierarchy complicates his account considerably. Despite the philosophical merit such a combined lattice might have, it is highly impractical for linking purposes. Grimm also states (2013: 7) that the higher in the lattice, the fewer entities there are to meet the requirements. As can be seen quite clearly in the Van Valin-Wilkins hierarchy, the amount of potential referents for a given 'lattice-position' does not become smaller with an ascending position, rather, the referents become more specific. For instance, the referent expressed by the personal pronoun *I* is higher than the referent *John*.

The key to Grimm's account for instrumental subject follows naturally from his general approach to argument linking: A predicate imposes

3.7 Instruments as subjects

certain semantic restrictions on its argument slots. These can be expressed as regions in the lattice. A referent filling the argument slot must occupy a position within the lattice-region imposed on the slot by the predicate. If a referent that would typically be realized as an instrument (e.g. in a *with*-PP) is inside the semantic region imposed by the predicate, then they, too, can become subject. For example (Grimm 2013: 8):

(69) a. The worker moved the dirt with the shovel/crane.
     b. The crane/*shovel moved the dirt.

Shovel possesses, similar to *stick*, only the feature [+mobile] and therefore does not meet the predicate's requirements for that slot. *Crane*, on the other hand, also possesses *potent*, which places the referent within the correct portion of semantic space. Therefore, it is eligible as subject whereas *shovel* is not. Grimm (2013: 10–11) explains the ungrammaticality of (70a–70b) with the same principle.

(70) a. Carl ate the spaghetti with a fork.
     b. *The fork ate the spaghetti.

Grimm claims that the position of *fork* in the lattice is essentially the same as that of *shovel*. *Eat* requires its subject slot to possess sentience, a property *fork* cannot possible have. Grimm ignores the causal distinction that exists between the fork- and the crane-example. *Crane* is directly causally involved. Without the crane, there is no moving of the dirt, whereas without the fork, there is an eating event. I share RRG's assumption that the causal difference is more important than the micro-semantics of individual verbs. The strengths of Grimm's approach are clear: Predicate variation and, more importantly, language variation can be accounted for. Even though Grimm does not even mention this himself, it can be theorized that languages (even with similar predicates) will impose different requirements on their slots. Predicate variation is solved in according stronger requirements to the subject slot filler of *murder* than to that of *kill*. While *kill* requires the referent to be *potent*[19],

---

[19] *Bullet* is considered *potent* because it is conceptualized as having a form of kinetic energy (Grimm 2013: 9 & Kearns 2000: 241). Alexiadou & Schäfer (2006: 43),

murder requires its filler to be sentient in addition. This is a requirement that the referent bullet cannot possibly meet. I believe it is possible to treat 'lexicalized agency' as a form of shorthand for predicates that only allow actors from an extremely small section of semantic space, usually coinciding with humans. Consider, for example, the sentences in (71):

(71)   a.   *The lumberjack murdered the engineer.*
       b.   **The robot murdered the engineer.*

The sentence in (71a) is grammatical; meaning that its referent possesses some form of sentience that allows it to act intentionally. The example in (71b), on the other hand, is ungrammatical, as the referent does not meet the correct criteria (i.e. is not in the correct portion of semantic space).

3.7.2 The subtype approach

The observation that some instruments can undergo ISA whereas others cannot leads many linguists to assume two subtypes of instruments. Intermediary instruments seem to be more intimately associated with the event, whereas facilitating instruments appear to be only auxiliary to the event (Webb 2008: 5ff.). The motivation for the distinction between intermediary and facilitating instruments varies, however. RRG posits causal embedding as the defining criterion, whereas Alexiadou & Schäfer assume a combination of causality and referent properties. Webb introduces a single feature which he terms *causal force*. Even though these approaches are all different, causality is component common to all of them (to some extent).

3.7.2.1   Intermediary instruments & facilitating instruments

Kamp & Rossdeutscher (1994) assume that intermediary instruments possess a form of causal independence (or near-independence). That is to say, the referent needs only to be initiated by an instigator. The rest of the action is a separate causal process that is carried out autonomously;

---

following DeLancey (1984), also entertain the possibility of referents acquiring some form of kinetic energy that allows them to be in subject position. Cruse (1973: 16, 19) makes a similar claim. This is an assumption I also share, be it in a slightly different way. This is explored in chapter 4.

3.7 Instruments as subjects

the referent is conceived to be acting on its own (Kamp & Rossdeutscher 1994: 144–145). In (72), the drug is administered by an instigator (the doctor), but continues to do the healing autonomously.

(72) a. *Der Arzt heil-te den Patienten mit der*
 DEF doctor cure-PST.3SG DEF patient with DEF
 Kamille.
 camomile
 'The doctor cured the patient with the camomile.' (German)
 b. *Die Kamille heil-te den Patienten.*
 DEF chamomile cure-PST.3SG DEF patient
 'The camomile cured the patient.'

This type of instrument is considered to have some form of causal power in bringing about the result state. Kamp & Rossdeutscher (1994) call this subtype *Instrument-causers*. The sentences in (73) illustrate the other subtype:

(73) a. *Der Arzt heil-te den Patienten mit dem*
 DEF doctor cure-PST.3SG DEF patient with DEF
 Skalpell.
 scalpel
 'The doctor cured the patient with the scalpel.' (German)
 b. **Das Skalpell heil-te den Patienten.*
 DEF scalpel cure-PST.3SG DEF patient
 'The scalpel cured the patient.'

The authors theorize that ISA is impossible because of the fact that the referent needs to be manipulated throughout the event. Kamp & Rossdeutscher (1994: 145) therefore assume that such instruments are strictly auxiliary to the event and do not have causal power. This subtype is termed *instruments*, later rebranded as *pure instruments* by Alexiadou & Schäfer (2006). This approach seems intuitive enough, but is faced with a rather stringent issue: There are pure instruments that can nevertheless undergo ISA (see also Alexiadou & Schäfer 2006: 44) as ((74)) illustrates.

(74) a. *John cut the bread with the knife.*
b. *The knife cut the bread.*

Such observations lead Alexiadou & Schäfer (2006) to make a further distinction in the class of intermediary instruments (or, to use Kamp & Rossdeutscher's terminology, instrument-causers). Alexiadou & Schäfer argue that intermediary instruments can undergo ISA for either of two reasons: (a) They are causally (quasi-)independent (following Kamp & Rossdeutscher 1994) or (b) the referent in question has a so-called *grounding property*. In effect, this categorization gives rise to a further subclassification. I have summarized this in figure 31:

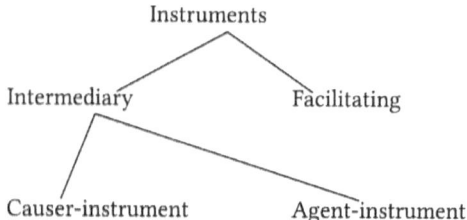

Figure 31: Overview of Alexiadou & Schäfer's (2006) instrument classification.

The further distinction that Alexiadou & Schäfer make is in line with the observation made by Gruber (amongst others) that there is a fundamental distinction between causers and agents (Alexiadou & Schäfer 2006: 40–41). They transport this dichotomy into the class of instruments. Alexiadou & Schäfer (2006: 42–43) posit that causer-instruments are causers by virtue of their involvement in an event and due to the fact that they do not need to be controlled (permanently) by a human agent. Thus, the motivation behind causer-instruments seems to be one of *causal independence*. They believe Schlesinger's *crane/fork*-example can be accounted for with causal independence: Because *crane* has a higher degree of causal independence than *fork*, it is the better subject for the event. In this respect they follow Kamp & Rossdeutscher's (1994) line of thought. This is then also the motivation behind acceptability of (72b) and the unacceptability of (73b).

Alexiadou & Schäfer (2006: 42–43) argue that this level of causal independence is similar to that of natural forces. It might be tempting to equate forces with this kind of instruments, motivated by a superficial similarity in causal independence, but this is problematic: I wish to stress that forces behave differently from instruments in that the former can take instruments whereas the latter cannot.

The other class of instruments, the *agent-instruments*, can undergo ISA by virtue of having a *grounded property*. Rather than possessing causal independence or eventivity like the causer-instruments, these instruments have an internal property that is crucial in the coming about of the event (Alexiadou & Schäfer 2006: 45–46). For instance, a *knife* has a blade which has the property that it is sharp. It can therefore perform a cutting action on the object. For Alexiadou & Schäfer it therefore constitutes a non-trivial relation with the event as a whole. Consider (Alexiadou & Schäfer 2006: 44):

(74) a. *Ashley cut the melon with a knife.*
b. *Casey opened the door with the key.*

Both *key* and *knife* are crucial for the result: The melon being cut and the door being opened. Therefore, ISA is possible. In standard RRG, however, one explanation covers both such cases and the causer-instruments. Both are analyzed as being embedded in a causal chain, i.e. under the scope of the CAUSE-operator, contrary to implements. Despite the fact that native speakers judgments have confirmed that (74a–74b) can undergo ISA, Alexiadou & Schäfer's (2006: 44) proposed ISA-variants in (75) are problematic:

(75) a. *This knife cuts the melon easily.*
b. *This key opened that door.*

In addition to the ability adverbial in (75a), the use of the demonstrative actually weakens the argument for ISA. The use of the demonstrative is rather indicative of an ability reading. In German, (76a) is ungrammatical and the sentence in (76b) can only have an ability reading, as was confirmed by informants.

3 Instruments at the syntax-semantics interface

(76) a. *Das Messer schneid-et die Melone leicht.
DEF knife cut-PRS.3SG DEF melon easily
'The knife cuts the melon easily.'
b. Dieses Messer schneid-et die Melone leicht.
DEM knife cut-PRS.3SG DEF melon easily
'This knife cuts the melon easily.'

In Dutch, the ability reading must always be expressed by a form of the verb *can*:

(77) a. *Dit mes snijd-t het brood makkelijk.
DEM knife cut-PRS.3SG DEF bread easily
'This knife cuts the melon easily.'
b. Dit mes kan het brood makkelijk snijd-en.
DEM knife can DEF bread easily cut-INF
'This knife can cut the bread.'

Alexiadou & Schäfer claim, following DeLancey (1984), that the use of demonstratives puts contrastive focus on the instrument in subject position, thereby making it more acceptable. My informants have confirmed that there is nothing unacceptable about *the key opened the door*, contrary to DeLancey's and Alexiadou & Schäfer's claim. Be that as it may, I believe the use of the demonstrative illustrates the ability reading: The use of the proximate demonstrative contrasts it with other knives that do not have this ability. Therefore, the acceptability of such constructions is higher when a present tense is used. In English, the acceptability of (75a) changes drastically when other tenses are used (78a–78b):

(78) a. ???This knife had been cutting the melon easily.
b. ???This knife was cutting the melon easily.
c. The knife had been cutting the melon (easily).
d. The knife was cutting the melon (easily).

By contrast, using a definite article is perfectly acceptable in tenses other than the present (78c–78d). This shows that an ability reading is more natural with proximate demonstratives and present tenses, whereas ISA is not constrained in this fashion. Alexiadou & Schäfer (2006: 45) assume that focusing on the instrument (e.g. with demonstratives) highlights the non-trivial relation that some instruments have with their VPs (i.e. the grounded property). However, the authors do not consider the existence of an ability reading. Second, there is no precise definition of *grounded property*, as Webb (2008: 14) points out. One could claim that *spoon* is a grounded property in *John ate the scolding-hot soup with the spoon* because without the spoon the eating event could not have taken place due the high temperature of the soup. Yet, ISA is impossible:

(79)   *The spoon ate the scolding-hot soup.*

The lack of proper definition of *grounded property* constitutes a fundamental weakness in their approach.

Alexiadou & Schäfer (2006: 45) assume that machines are designed for a specific task. Therefore, their ability to undergo ISA can be motivated by either causal independence *or* a grounded property. The examples they offer are questionable though (Alexiadou & Schäfer 2006: 46):

(80)   a.   *Sheila extracted the square root of 1369 with the pocket calculator.*
       b.   *The pocket calculator extracted the root of 1369.*

One might posit that a standard function of pocket calculator is the extraction of roots. However, the function of *computer* described below is not and yet ISA is possible:

(81)   a.   *Sheila calculated how much time was left with the computer.*
       b.   *The computer calculated how much time was left.*

From an RRG-perspective, the answer is simple: *Pocket calculator* and *computer* are causally embedded in both these example sets. Alexiadou & Schäfer could, of course, still account for (81b) with the property of causal independence. They argue that RRG's view of an underspecified thematic role cannot explain language-variation with respect to ISA, a point of criticism I agree with. Alexiadou & Schäfer's and approach covers a case of ISA that Kamp & Rossdeutscher's would find difficult to explain: Causally dependent instruments that undergo ISA. Language variation with respect to ISA would also be very difficult to handle in Kamp & Rossdeutscher's approach.

3.7.2.2 Instruments & implements

RRG recognizes that ISA is a phenomenon that certain instruments can undergo. In essence, the first effector in the causal chain is left unspecified. This is a process described by Van Valin & Wilkins (1996) as *metonymic clipping*. Due to the fact that the instrument is the highest explicit effector in the chain, it takes the actor macrorole. In turn, it is selected as the PSA in active sentences. Consider (adapted from Van Valin & Wilkins 1996: 318):

(82) a. *The terrorists destroyed the car with the bomb.*
 b. [**do´** (terrorists, Ø)] CAUSE [[**do´** (bomb, Ø)] CAUSE [BECOME **destroyed´** (car)]]
 c. *The bomb destroyed the car.*
 d. [**do´** (Ø, Ø)] CAUSE [[**do´** (bomb, Ø)] CAUSE [BECOME **destroyed´** (car)]]

In (82d), the x-argument of the initial **do´** predicate is left unspecified. Actor is then assigned to the highest available candidate, in line with RRG's linking algorithm. RRG however recognizes cases where ISA cannot take place (Van Valin & LaPolla 1997: 121, Van Valin 2005: 59):

(83) a. *Abdul ate the cereal with a spoon.*
 b. **The spoon ate the cereal.*
 c. *Tanisha looked at the comet with a telescope.*
 d. **The telescope looked at the comet.*
 e. *Chris ate the soup with a spoon.*
 f. **The spoon ate the soup.*

Van Valin & LaPolla assume that this is due to the fact that the instruments used in (83a), (83c) and (83e) are not included in a causal chain. As it not part of the causing process leading to a result state, it cannot be a part of the causal chain. *Cereal* and *soup* can be eaten without a *spoon* and a *comet* can be seen without a *telescope*. These events are, at best, facilitated by these items rather than being dependent on them. This distinction is captured in RRG by treating the instrument as the y-argument of an unembedded **use′** predicate. Contrary to the full logical structures[20] for instrument clauses (which embed the **use′** predicate as the y-argument of the first do'), the use' predicate here is attached to the main logical structure by means of a connective. The y-argument of use' is called an implement. The representations for (83a), (83c) and (83e) are given below:

(84) a. **do′** (Abdul, [**eat′** (Abdul, cereal) ∧ **use′** (Abdul, spoon)]) & INGR **consumed′** (cereal)
b. **do′** (Tanisha, [**see′** (Tanisha, comet) ∧ **use′** (Tanisha, telescope)])
c. **do′** (Chris, [**eat′** (Chris, soup) ∧ **use′** (Chris, spoon)]) & INGR **consumed′** (soup)

Van Valin & LaPolla (1997: 121) posit that such structures can be identified by using a gerund-based paraphrase (in English at least):

(85) a. *Abdul ate the cereal, using a spoon.*
b. *Tanisha looked at the comet, using a telescope.*
c. *Chris ate the soup, using a spoon.*

These paraphrases seem to identify a tool that is used in the action. However, this paraphrase would also – but wrongly – predict that clear examples of instruments ((86a–86d)) are implements:

(86) a. *Mara cut the bread with the knife.*
b. *Mara cut the bread, using the knife.*
c. *Ragnar broke the window with the rock.*
d. *Ragnar broke the window, using the rock.*

One might contend that the example in (86a–86b) does show a difference because the using-paraphrase is somewhat of a tautology, whereas in (86c–86d) above, genuinely new information is added. However, in

---

[20] Recall that the shorter logical structures are primarily used in this dissertation (and in general RRG-literature) for the sake of clarity.

(86c-86d), no tautological reading appears, yet *rock* is an instrument. I therefore reject this diagnostic as a tool to identify implements.

The major diagnostic in RRG to distinguish instruments from implements is ISA itself. The very occurrence of ISA led Van Valin & LaPolla (1997) and Van Valin & Wilkins (1996) to posit the distinction in the first place. If one wants to know whether something is an instrument or an implement, simply apply ISA to it. If it can undergo ISA, then it is an instrument and is embedded in a causal chain. If it cannot, it is an implement and is not embedded in a causal chain. This approach suffers from the first and the third problems indicated at the beginning of this section: Instruments are not the same as instruments and language-variation is hard to explain. With respect to the first problem, the referent's properties clearly play a role in the grammaticality judgment ((87a-87d)).

(87)   a.   *John picked the container with a crane.*
        b.   *The crane picked up the container.*
        c.   *John picked up the potato with a fork.*
        d.   **The fork picked up the potato.*

It is hard to see how RRG can deal with this in terms of logical structures. Claiming that *fork* is an implement in (87c-87d) but *crane* is an instrument in (87a-87b) is an untenable solution, for two reasons: 1) Conceptually, the states of affairs expressed are essentially the same. This means that it is rather unlikely that there are two separate logical structures, just because of a different referent and, 2) if one were to pursue such an explanation, one would have to resort to the referent's properties anyway. Grimm would solve this by assigning different positions to the two referents in his lattice. I will pursue a similar solution in chapter 4. RRG can, however, provide annotations to logical structure positions in terms of qualia. Qualia can capture the difference between a *fork* and a *crane*, for instance. This allows for annotation of a certain argument position (see Van Valin 2005 & 2013), thereby restricting its filler to arguments whose referents meet those exact criteria. This constitutes a type of hard constraint. Like Grimm, I propose regions of semantic space as *soft* constraints. An argument's referent would not exactly need to meet the criteria. Rather, it would need to be in the same general area of semantic space. If an argument slot can be filled by several arguments with different properties, multiple qualia annotations would be required, whereas in the region-approach, a more global area can be defined. Exceptions to this area could, in turn, be handled in terms of qualia. This issue will be explored further in chapter 4.

Problem three is a very fundamental problem for the logical structure approach. Take the Dutch equivalents in (50e) and (50f). This verb expresses the same content as English *cut*, yet ISA is not possible in Dutch. If one were to follow standard RRG, the Dutch logical structure would look very different (...∧ **use**´) from the English one (causal embedding) even though the predicates express the same propositional content. This, again, is problematic for two reasons: 1) It is an ad hoc solution and 2) it calls the fundamental principle of the (near-)universality of the logical structures into question.

Ono (1992) makes a very similar proposal in a Conceptual Semantics framework, but diverges noticeably from Jackendoff. Similar to RRG, Ono (1992: 202) assumes that intermediary instruments can undergo ISA because there is a causal chain with the instrument contained in one of the subevents: An initiating cause contains the instrument-subevent and this in turn brings about the caused event (Ibid.). Consider the following examples of an intermediary and a facilitating instrument, respectively (Ono 1992: 202–203):

(88) a. *John opened the door with the key.*
 b. *John ate pasta with a fork.*

The sentence in (88a) can undergo ISA, but the one in (88b) cannot. Ono assumes that the instrument in (88b) is contained in a modifying subevent clause under the scope of the function USE. As this clause is not part of the main causal chain, ISA cannot occur. This is reminiscent of RRG's addition of the **use**´-predicate. The LCSs for (88a–88b) are given in figures 32 and 33, respectively.

3 Instruments at the syntax-semantics interface

$$\begin{bmatrix} \text{CAUSE ([JOHN]} \begin{bmatrix} \text{CAUSE([KEY], [INCH(BE([DOOR],)} \\ \text{[OPEN])]) AFF ([KEY], [DOOR])} \end{bmatrix} \\ \text{AFF ([JOHN], [DOOR])} \end{bmatrix}$$

Figure 32: LCS of *John opened the door with the key* (Ono 1992: 202).

$$\begin{bmatrix} \text{CAUSE ([JOHN], [GO ([PASTA], [TO [IN [MOUTH OF} \\ \text{[JOHN]]]])]) [BY [USE ([JOHN], [FORK])]]} \end{bmatrix}$$

Figure 33: LCS of *John ate pasta with a fork* (Ono 1992: 203).

Ono's approach suffers from the same issues as standard RRG (see above): 1) It is difficult to account for the influence of the referent's properties (see (87)) and 2) as the LCSs are intended to be universal (Ono 1992: 214), it is hard to capture cross-linguistic variation (see (50e–50f)) without canceling the universal validity that is claimed for the LCSs.

3.7.2.3 Webb's Causal Force

In section 3.5.2, I presented Webb's approach to instruments and thematic relations compared to classical, standard LFG. Webb's approach can account for ISA in a more natural way, using the shortcomings of Alexiadou & Schäfer's account. This shows that Webb's approach has a clear advantage over standard LFG. Webb (2008: 65–66) assumes that ISA involves an operation where the 1st tier proto-agent[21] is deleted from a-structure. Semantically, however, the agent is still implied. This is parallel to RRG's account of the unspecified instigator. The 2nd tier proto-agent (the instrument) is promoted to first tier, where it can then access the SUBJ-function. This process, together with an example (Webb 2008: 66–67)[22] is given in figure 34.

---

[21] Recall that the first tier proto-agent is located there by virtue of being the initial causer in the chain (Webb 2008: 66).
[22] The shading indicates the target for deletion and that which has been deleted, respectively. The process is represented from top to bottom.

Open 1st <p-a₁ p-p>
2nd <p-a₂>

Open 1st <p-a₁ p-a₂ p-p>
2nd < >

Open 1st < p-a₂ p-p>
2nd < >

The key opened the door.

F-structure   [SUBJ OBJ]
                                  ↑   ↑
A-structure   1st tier   <...   p-p>
                                ↑
               2nd tier   <p-a>

Figure 34: ISA in Webb's LFG-approach.

Two notes are in order (Webb 2008: 66–67): 1) It is crucial to promote the 2nd proto-agent to the 1st tier, because otherwise, it would be optional and could be left out. Leaving it out would result in ungrammaticality and 2) the 1st proto-agent is deleted and not demoted to 2nd tier. If it were only demoted to 2nd tier, sentences like *the key opened the door by Jack* would be grammatical.

Because the verb's semantics encodes a causal relation that is inherited from the underlying causal chain, a 1st tier proto-agent with the feature *causal force* (CF) is required. Causal force is Webb's translation (2008: 34) of one of Dowty's (1991: 572) proto-agent properties: A participant possesses causal force if it brings about another event or a change of state in another participant. If a participant possesses this entailment, it will be marked with 'CF' in the causal chain representation. Only those referents with CF satisfy the requirement set by the verb's semantics (Webb 2008: 39). The referents *knife* and *camomile* in (72) possess CF and therefore allow ISA. By contrast, *spoon* in (83a) does not. Webb also makes a connection to the type of causation. Webb (2008: 35) combines Croft's causal chain approach with Talmy's (1988) distinction between

3 Instruments at the syntax-semantics interface

onset causation and *extended causation*. Roughly speaking, onset causation can be equated to Kamp & Rossdeutscher's causal independence. To account for the observation that causal independence seems to be a good indicator of the acceptability of ISA, Webb (2008: 51–52) posits that onset causation automatically licenses causal force to the instrument, whereas instruments under the scope of extended causation only sometimes get CF licensed. For instance, in the sentence *the doctor cured the patient with the scalpel* the instrument is under scope of extended causation. As ISA is impossible here, Webb concludes that it does not have the CF feature. This implies that the scalpel does not cause a change of state in the other participant involved. Yet, this is questionable as it passes a causal paraphrase:

(89)   *The scalpel acted upon the patient, causing him/her to be healed.*

From an ontological point of view, a scalpel *can* be the direct cause of someone's healing. This can be the case if the scalpel removes a spot of, say, skin cancer. In this respect it would be rather similar to *knife* in (74). Webb (2008: 68) argues that *X wrote the letter with the pen*, cannot undergo ISA despite the instrument possessing CF. He theorizes that some verbs will put highly specific constraints on the SUBJ-function, in this case the requirement that the filler of SUBJ be [+animate]. Such constraints will override CF, if present. However, the verb *write* essentially has two meanings: 1) The creation of meaningful content and 2) the creation of symbols on a medium. ISA is impossible with the first meaning, but is – depending on the speaker – more acceptable[23] with the second meaning. Evidence for the 'two-verb' theory is found in the fact that with the first meaning a wide range of instruments is acceptable, including pens and computers. With the second meaning, only pens and the like are generally accepted. In terms of Grimm's approach, it could be stated that the argument positions of both meanings are open to different portions of semantic space, the subject slot of the second meaning being open to a larger portion of semantic space.

---

[23] Native speakers of English that I have consulted accept ISA with the second meaning, even if it still not as natural as *the knife cut the bread*. I will assume, following Alexiadou & Schäfer (2006: 42), that such judgments are often a matter of gradation.

A further problem for Webb's approach is that it seems hard to handle language-variation. The *knife*-example is said to allow ISA because of the CF that can be traced back to the causal chain describing the event underlying the utterance. Yet, in Dutch, this alternation is not possible. Does this then mean that, contrary to an English-speaker, in a Dutch speaker's causal chain representation the instrument does not possess CF? This seems questionable: Event representations (of whatever type) are supposed to be (near-)universal. This is a major problem in Webb's approach that also exists in standard RRG's conception of instruments and implements and in Ono's conception of the two classes. Webb (2008: 107) himself concedes that analyses of multiple languages are desirable and necessary.

3.7.3 Summary of instruments as subjects

Schlesinger can be criticized for treating the 'instruments' as normal agents. In RRG terms, this would be tantamount to treating two different structural positions the same. However, there are good reasons to assume that these positions are quite distinct. A more general issue with the approaches discussed here is that they do not adequately define the degrees of membership or the features they posit: Some use features like *causing*, *intentional* or *grounding* without defining them properly or without explaining how they relate to each other. Schlesinger's strength is the other approaches' weakness: Schlesinger gives reasons *why* one would use ISA. If one wishes to focus on the instrument instead of the instigator or if one wants to leave the instigator unspecified. RRG, Grimm, Ono, Kamp & Rossdeutscher and Alexiadou & Schäfer, however provide an account of the limits and the mechanics of ISA but they do not go into its communicative purpose. A (simplified) overview of which approaches provide an account for which of the three problems is given in table 12.

3 *Instruments at the syntax-semantics interface*

	Instrument variation (1)	Predicate variation (2)	Language variation (3)
Schlesinger	Yes	No	No
Grimm	Yes	Yes	(Yes)
Kamp & Rossdeutscher	Yes	No	No
Alexiadou & Schäfer	Yes	No	No
RRG	Partially	Yes	No
Ono	No	Yes	No
Webb	Yes	Yes	No

Table 12: (Simplified) overview of approaches and ISA-problems.

Table 13 provides an overview of how the different frameworks and approaches that were discussed in this chapter treat the distinction between intermediary and facilitating instruments. Motivations for distinctions are given as a number in brackets:

(1) Causal independence
(2) No causal independence
(3) Grounding property
(4) Either causal independence or grounding property
(5) Neither causal independence nor grounding property
(6) Close enough to agentive prototype
(7) Not close enough to agentive prototype
(8) Causal Force
(9) No Causal Force
(10) Causal embedding
(11) No causal embedding

	Intermediary	Facilitating
Fillmore	Instrument	
J. Anderson	Instrument	
Dowty	Instrument	
Conceptual semantics	Instrument	
Croft	Instrument	
Standard LFG	Instrument	
Kamp & Rossdeutscher	Instrument-causers (1)	(Pure) instruments (2)
Alexiadou & Schäfer	Intermediary (4) Causer-like (1) Agent-like (3)	Facilitating (5)
Schlesinger	ISA-instrument (6)	Non ISA-instrument (7)
Grimm	ISA-instrument (6)	Non ISA-instrument (7)
Webb (LFG)	CF-instrument (8)	Non CF-instrument (9)
RRG	Instrument (10)	Implement (11)
Ono	Intermediate (10)	Facilitating (11)

Table 13: Overview of treatment of intermediary and facilitating instruments.

3.8 Conclusion: properties of thematic relations and instruments

In this chapter, I presented a selection of theories and framework and, more specifically, how they capture thematic relations. As instruments are an integral part of thematic relations, it was necessary to introduce the general approach to thematic relations. To understand the instrument in a given framework, one must understand its general conception of thematic relations.

In general, theories of instruments are faced with several issues: 1) Instruments are often only treated peripherally (e.g. LFG), 2) ISA is rarely captured in a principled way (e.g. Croft), 3) if ISA is captured by the theory, then language variation, predicate variation and referent variation are not captured fully, thereby failing to meet *adequacy* and 4) many of these theories only draw from English data rather than embracing a cross-linguistic perspective.

I have summarized the approaches to thematic relations and instruments discussed in this chapter in table 14.

	Role Type	Inventory	Instrument type
Fillmore 1968	Primitive	Medium	Primitive
Fillmore 1977a	Primitive	Medium	Displacement
J. Anderson's CG	Featural	4	Displacement
RRG	Configurational	Irrelevant	Reading
LFG	Primitive	± 8	Primitive
Webb-LFG	Featural	2	Featural
Conceptual Semantics	Configurational	Irrelevant	Combined configurational
Dowty	Featural	2	Featural
Croft	Causal	Medium	Causal participant

Table 14: Overview of approaches to thematic relations and instruments.

I distinguish between several types of thematic relations: 1) primitive, 2) causal, 3) featural, 4) configurational. The latter two are often termed derived thematic relations in the literature. The reason for recognizing a causal type of thematic relations is due to the fact that causality is the defining component behind them. As it is unclear whether Croft's approach is decompositional or not, I chose not to consider his thematic relations as configurational (or featural for that matter). As they depend on the type of causation, it would not be adequate to treat them as primitives either. The inventory part of table 14 contains the number of roles posited by the respective approaches. In many cases though, it is

3.8 Conclusion: properties of thematic relations and instruments

difficult to come up with a fixed number of relations, hence entries like *medium*. It seems intuitive to assume that the type of instrument a theory has is the same as its general type of thematic relations. Yet, in some theories, instruments are not thematic relations of the same order. They are, for instance, readings of a patient argument, brought about by a syntactic operation (*displacement*). For Jackendoff, it is a relation of a secondary level as well. For him, it is a combination of configurations rather than a unique configuration as is the case with, say, *agent*. I used the term *reading* if the instrument is a reading of a specific position (e.g. RRG), rather than a combination of configurations. Granted, some theories of instrument defy a simple classification.

In the following chapters, I will present my own approach to instruments and related concepts, using RRG's theory of thematic relations as a basis. I will draw from the work discussed in this chapter, Talmy's Force Dynamics and cross-linguistic data to arrive at an approach that captures ISA and ISA-variation with respect to language, referent and predicate.

4 Semantic range of instruments, agents & forces

In this chapter I will propose solutions to some of the instrument-related problems raised in the previous chapter, such as ISA and the restrictions that it occurs with.

The most pressing question is what an instrument really is. It has been argued that instruments are a subtype of the more basic effector in RRG: Instruments are intermediary effectors (x-argument of **do'** (x, Ø)) in a causal chain. Instruments that are not causally embedded are implements. In chapter 5, I will formally introduce an alternative way to distinguish instruments from implements. Until then, all examples will feature instruments unless indicated otherwise. It is important to realize that instruments (and implements) are components of the logical structures. Most (English) examples in this dissertation use the *with*-PP format, which is the most common linking strategy for instruments and implements. Consider:

(1) a. *Seymour sliced the salami with a knife. (Lakoff 1968: 6–7)*
    b. *Adewalé opened the locked box with a key.*

Other linking strategies will be explored in chapter 8. The full LSs for the sentences in (1a–1b) are given in (2a–2b). As I pointed out in chapter 3, in the 'usual' logical structures employed in RRG, the **use'** predicate[1] is often left out because it is clearly implied by the rest of the structure. The same is true for the embedded predicate functioning as the second argument of intermediate **do'**. Leaving them out is a matter of clarity. The 'full' LSs corresponding to (1) are given in (2).

---

[1] The intermediate **cut'** predicate is also usually left out, for the very same reasons. For the sake of clarity, I prefer to use the reduced LSs in this dissertation.

(2) a. [**do′** (Seymour, [**use′** (Seymour, knife)])] CAUSE [[**do′** (knife, [**cut′** (knife, salami)])] CAUSE [BECOME **cut′** (salami)]]
b. [**do′** (Adewalé, [**use′** (Adewalé, knife)])] CAUSE [[**do′** (key, [**open′** (key, door)])] CAUSE [BECOME **open′** (door)]]

This full representation is rarely used and this is true for this dissertation as well. The 'simple' version of (2b) is given below in (3).

(3) [**do′** (Adewalé, ∅)] CAUSE [[**do′** (key, ∅)] CAUSE [BECOME **open′** (door)]]

This chapter focuses on how the semantic space of instruments can be characterized. I will also go into concepts that are seemingly related to instruments, such as implements and forces including the less canonical ones. Consider:

(4) a. *John destroyed the barn with the crane.*
b. *The crane destroyed the barn with a load of cinder blocks.*
c. *The storm destroyed the levee with huge tidal waves.*

The cases above are challenging for standard explanations of instruments for various reasons. For example, in (4a) and (4b) the same inanimate referent occurs as an instrument and as a participant taking an instrument, and in (4c) the force argument takes an instrument itself. To capture the distinctions between such referents, I will argue in favor of a revised and expanded animacy hierarchy.

4.1 Degrees of animacy & autonomy

In the following sections, I will explore the semantic space that agents, forces and instruments occupy, together with several problematic borderline cases. How can that semantic space be characterized? The Van Valin-Wilkins hierarchy (1996) was intended to capture *if* and *when* effectors are read as agents. Animacy is a central component of this hierarchy. Animacy also features prominently in Grimm's (2005, 2013) approach. As a part of mapping semantic space I will explore the role of animacy further and argue in favor of an additional, interrelated concept called *autonomy*.

4.1.1 Animacy

Animacy is a category that often stays in the background and is taken for granted, despite its pervasive role in grammar and despite substantial evidence in favor of including it as a central component in a theory of language (Dahl & Fraurud 1996: 47). Animacy manifests itself in language mainly in two ways: 1) It influences grammatical rules (case assignment and word order, for example) and the choice of expression (Aissen 2003) and 2) statistical regularities can be observed (Dahl 2008: 141). Yamamoto (1999: 41–70) provides evidence for the cross-linguistic influence of animacy on case marking, word order, subject selection and topicality. Consider the following examples from Malayalam:

(5) a. *Avan kuṭṭi-ye aticcu.*
 3SG.M child-ACC beat.PST
 'He beat the child.' (Fauconnier 2011: 533–534)
 b. *Avan oru paʃu-vine vanni.*
 3SG.M INDEF cow-ACC buy.PST
 'He bought a cow.' (de Swart et al. 2008: 132)
 c. *Avan pustakam vaayiccu.*
 3SG.M book read.PST
 'He read the book.' (Fauconnier 2011: 533–534)

In Malayalam, the direct object receives accusative case only if the referent is animate. Fauconnier (2011: 533, 541–542) theorizes that *unexpectedness* plays a crucial role in such an assignment: Statistically, most direct objects are inanimates [2] (89% in Swedish for example; Dahl

---

[2] Grewe et al. (2006) provide psycholinguistic evidence for the importance of animacy. They manipulated the animacy of certain referents, thereby violating the principle that animates come before inanimates ('animates first'). They found that such violations activate the same brain areas that are activated when syntactic principles are violated. There is also evidence of knowledge pertaining to animates being sep-

2008: 142). One strategy to deal with this 'unexpected object' is to assign a different case marker to it (or in the case of Malayalam, a marker). In the same vein (and following Silverstein 1976), Fauconnier (2011: 541ff.) theorizes that languages generally prefer to avoid inanimate subjects, or, if they are allowed, they are treated differently from animate subjects. Japanese (Kuno 1973: 31), for example, strongly disprefers inanimate subjects, instead requiring (at least) higher animals as subjects.

(6) a. *Taihuu ga mado o kawasita.
 Typhoon SUBJ window OBJ break.PST
 'The typhoon broke the window.' (Kuno 1973: 31)
 b. Sono otoko ga mado o kawasita.
 DEF man SUBJ window OBJ break.PST
 'The man broke the window.' (own data)

The Australian language Jingulu assigns instrumental marking to inanimate subjects, whereas animate subjects receive ergative marking (Pensalfini 2003: 178, 189):

(7) a. Babi-rni ikiya-rnarnu-nu ibilkini.
 Older brother-ERG wet-3SG>1SG-PST water
 'My brother wet me.'
 b. Darrangku-warndi maya-ngarnu-nu.
 Tree-INS hit-3SG>1SG-PST
 'A tree hit me.'

But also in languages with less extensive morphology like English or Dutch, animacy can have a profound influence on grammatical rules: Rosenbach (2008) theorizes that the animacy of the referents in possessive constructions influences whether an s-genitive or an *of*-genitive is selected in English. Similarly, Bresnan & Hay (2008: 250) argue that English dative shift is partly dependent[3] on animacy: Animate recipient

---

arately stored from knowledge related to inanimates in the brain (cf. Rosenbach 2008: 157).

[3] Bresnan & Hay (2008: 246) provide evidence that this animacy effect is also dependent on the variety of English. New Zealand English is more sensitive to animacy considerations than US English.

arguments are likely to be expressed in a double object construction whereas inanimate recipients have a preference for the prepositional dative. In Dutch, for instance, animates are more likely to be pronominalized than inanimates (Vogels et al. 2014: 116).

The examples discussed above illustrate that animacy can have a substantive influence on the grammar of many languages and should – more generally – be included in theories of language (cf. Bresnan et al. 2001). In what follows, I will argue in favor of a revised animacy scale, mainly drawing from Van Valin & Wilkins (1996), Grimm (2005, 2013), Schlesinger (1989) and Yamamoto (1999).

In the previous chapter, I pointed out that it is possible to make the logical structures explicit with a matching paraphrase, thereby revealing whether there is causal embedding or not. In some cases, the instrument is causally embedded, but ISA is nevertheless impossible. In the examples in (3.50), ISA was shown to be ungrammatical in Dutch but acceptable in English despite the instrument being causally embedded in both languages. Furthermore, some instruments allow ISA whereas others do not, even if the predicate remains the same. I will argue that animacy is directly relevant for instruments, and more specifically, for the acceptability of ISA *within* and *across* languages. Roughly speaking, I will argue that the argument positions in a given logical structure are open to a specific portion of semantic space (cf. Grimm 2005, 2013). In short, I will make a case for animacy as one of the drivers of ISA. This is in line with Yamamoto's claim (1999: 67) that more animate entities will occupy more salient positions in clauses and discourse. Zaenen et al. (2004: 118) argue that positions on the animacy hierarchy correlate with the accessibility of the referents for the morphosyntax. My approach to ISA can be seen as an extension of both these claims. In languages that allow ISA, the instrument-referent's properties relative to the predicate's requirements will determine whether ISA can take place. The referent must be high enough on a revised animacy scale, relative to the requirements of the predicate. One problem, however, is that animacy is often used in a somewhat undefined way, similar to many linguists' use of thematic relations. I thus agree with Rosenbach (2008) and Grewe et al. (2006: 1397), amongst others, in treating animacy as an important, genuine factor in grammatical behavior, rather than an epiphenomenon.

Most animacy hierarchies in the literature are roughly based on the one proposed by Silverstein (1976, 1981). Silverstein's original hierarchy is a very fine-grained one. However, in the general literature on animacy, it is usually drastically simplified to a coarse three-way distinction, between humans, other animates/animals and inanimates. This distinction is motivated as a hierarchical scale (Dahl 2008: 141, Yamamoto 1999: 1, 9, Foley & Van Valin 1985: 288). It is ultimately an assumed cognitive distinction between animates and non-animates and (by analogy) between humans and non-humans (Yamamoto 1999: 9).

(8)   human > other animate > inanimate

Whatever form such a hierarchy may take, I largely follow Dahl (2008), Yamamoto (1999) and Comrie (1981: 178) with respect to the general properties of animacy: 1) The borders between the different 'steps' are fuzzy and membership in the categories can be fluid (Yamamoto 1999: 9), 2) the (human) self is the model for other humans and other animates, which are in turn models for lower-ranking entities (cf. a ranking of 'sameness' to one's self), 3) personhood appears to be a core trait of prototypical animacy (anthropocentric human cognition, see below), 4) animacy is cognitively deeply rooted in humans due to it being a central component ('sameness') in the organization of social life, 5) animacy is a property of a referent (Comrie 1981: 56, 179), 6) linguistic animacy is distinct from biological animacy (being 'alive', cf. Yamamoto 1999: 1ff.) and 7) animacy is a universal category that exists independently of its language-particular realization (Comrie 1981: 179). Animacy thus refers to the cognitive and ontological status of an entity (Yamamoto 1999: 36) and the distinction is considered to be fundamental and universal to human cognition (Boas 1911: 67).

The hierarchy in (8) is quite primitive and there is an abundance of explicit (and implicit) proposals to be found in the literature to refine it. Yamamoto (1999: 2) considers this hierarchy as the core component of any animacy hierarchy; it constitutes what she calls the *General Animacy Hierarchy* (Yamamoto 1999: 2) or *animacy per se*. Yamamoto (1999: 1) considers the General Animacy Hierarchy as a basic cognitive scale, which interacts with several others that further refine the basic scale's echelons. The most important one in this respect is the Hierarchy of Persons, which effectively provides an ordering *within* the human echelon (Yamamoto 1999: 3, 6).

Van Valin & Wilkins (1996: 316) argue that, for example, 1st person pronouns rank higher than 2nd or 3rd person pronouns, because one can be sure of one's own intentions, but not of those of others. Langacker (1991: 306–307) arrives at a similar conclusion, focusing on the notion of empathy: One shows more empathy for the self than for the individual one is speaking to and even more than for a third party. Both these points of view lead the respective authors to treating 1st persons as occupying a higher position on the hierarchy than second persons and so on. This does not mean that second persons are considered to be less animate than first persons, however. The Hierarchy of Persons simply provides a further refinement of the human section of the hierarchy, all its members being equally animate. This line of thought reveals that animacy hierarchies are both *anthropocentric* and *egocentric* (cf. Yamamoto 1999: 9f., 37). The speaker is at the center of the world and all other entities are judged and considered from that perspective (Langacker 1991: 307). Humans (and particularly the self) are seen as the 'supreme representatives of all animate beings' (Yamamoto 1999: 9) and imbue other entities (even those that are inherently inanimate) with degrees of animacy. Due to the speakers investing different degrees of animacy to different referents, certain entities will be considered more animate than others. For instance, Yamamoto (1999: 2–3) argues that cats will be considered more animate than amoebae, even though from a biological point of view both are equally alive.

Some linguists also attempt to refine the other echelons. For instance, Zaenen et al. (2004: 121) and Øvrelid (2006: 53) propose to further subdivide the 'other animates'-category by not only recognizing animals as subtypes but also organizations, intelligent machines and vehicles. Likewise, the inanimate category is enriched with concepts such as concrete inanimate, non-concrete inanimate, place and time. The reason to provide further divisions is to be able to handle the grey, 'fuzzy' area that exists between referents. Such borderline cases include machines, especially those that have human traits like intelligence (Yamamoto 1999: 18) or a decision-making ability that is commonly found in various types of Artificial Intelligence. Furthermore, Yamamoto points out that machines that have an internal power source are often seen as more animate than those that receive their power from an external source.

Often however, such proposed categories are not ranked respective to each other, whereas examples in chapter 3 illustrated that more complex machines are better ISA-candidates than less complex ones. This means that some form of internal ranking should be imposed on the finer categories.

I propose the animacy hierarchy in (9). In my proposal, I do not propose all or nothing parameters for animate beings. I agree with Yamamoto (1999) and others that animacy is a gradient, fluid notion. I therefore consider the superordinate labels *animate* and *inanimate* as vaguely delineated portions of the hierarchy rather than discrete categories.

(9)   Non-entity < abstract entity < concrete entity (immobile) < concrete entity < animate entity < (pseudo-)sentient entity < anthropomorphic entity < 3rd person < 2nd person < 1st person

Animate entity is defined the same way that [+animate] is defined in the Van Valin- Wilkins Hierarchy (1996: 314): an entity that feels, responds and moves. This does not imply sentience, however. By way of clarification, I have repeated the scale's steps below with types of referents and example referents (the three highest echelons are self-explanatory and have not been repeated). (Pseudo-)sentient entities are those that are assumed to have the ability to judge intentions in others[4] and/or the ability to make independent decisions. This includes computers and other forms of Artificial Intelligence. I do not sharply delineate between these two features as I assume them to be somewhat interdependent.

Anthropomorphic refers to the prototypical nature of human beings, i.e. the entity talks, walks, has limbs, potentially even has emotions (cf.

---

[4]   This was inspired by Miller and Johnson-Laird (1976: 92ff., 100ff.) and Tomasello (2003). The concept of intention reading features prominently throughout Tomasello's work.

Zaenen et al. 2004: 121). My proposed category also includes entities that are only superficially human in appearance. For instance, in Zaenen et al.'s (2004: 122) experiment, the fictitious Vulcan race was consistently ranked as human by all participants. I theorize that this extends to supernatural or fictitious entities like ghosts, vampires and wookies. Bresnan & Hay (2008: 249) also argue in favor of grouping such beings under human. Because of this, I prefer the label *anthropomorphic* to *human*. Furthermore, animals are also often anthropomorphized and referred to as if they were human (Yamamoto 1999: 13). In this case, they would be ranked as anthropomorphic in my approach.

(10) a. Non-entity: events, properties (birth, death, tall, short)
 b. Abstract entity: ideas, notions (federalism, revolution)
 c. Concrete entity (immobile): places, landmarks (city, island, mountain)
 d. Concrete entity: objects, artifacts (spear, chainsaw, axe)
 e. Animate entity: animals (ant, dog, eagle), plants
 f. (Pseudo-)sentient entity: higher animals, infants, Artificial Intelligence (chimpanzee, Deep Blue)
 g. Anthropomorphic entity: entities human in appearance and groups thereof (humans, Poseidon)

4.1.2 Autonomy

The scales that aim to refine the General Animacy Scale are typically lumped together on a single axis, thereby greatly expanding it. This often leads to problems that require questionable solutions. For example, groups of people do not all pattern alike:

(11) a. *???The mob carefully planned the assault.*
 b. *The army brigade carefully planned the assault.*

The example in (11b) is more acceptable than the one in (11a).[5] The traditional approach would be to consider army brigade more animate than

---

[5] I agree with Zaenen et al. (2004: 119) when they point out that as far as animacy differences are concerned, acceptability of a sentence is a more apt concept than

mob. Therefore, so the argument goes, army brigade is more natural to use in conjunction with adverbs like carefully and verbs like plan. I do not agree with the idea that mob is less animate. In fact, as argument could be made that army brigade is 'less animate' because formal organizations can be considered dehumanized (cf. Yamamoto 1999: 20). I reject the idea that either of these is less animate than the other. What we have here – in both cases – are groups of people that are conceptualized as a collective. The crucial difference between them is that mob is inherently without internal organization, whereas armies and their constituent units are highly organized along formal lines.[6] I believe it is more fitting to use the level of organization within a collective of people as a feature. This is a subsection of a hierarchy I call the Autonomy Hierarchy. It is necessary to introduce this hierarchy as an extra axis due to the shortcomings of the Silverstein hierarchy: Fauconnier (2011: 544), for example, stresses that the Silverstein hierarchy has difficulties capturing the semantic distinction between dependently and independently acting inanimates.[7] Furthermore, the distinction between groups of animates is hard to capture with the hierarchy, as the mob and army brigade example illustrates. As far as typology is concerned, Dahl (2008: 142) points out that grammatical restrictions are often proposed in terms of cut-off points on a hierarchy. However, many phenomena are not reducible to a well-behaved hierarchy. Therefore, a system with two axes would allow for cut-off regions thereby greatly enhancing the explanatory power of animacy (in the broadest sense of the word).

Essentially, the autonomy hierarchy describes the referent's ability to perform an action independently. The higher a referent is located on the autonomy hierarchy, the less external manipulation it requires to perform the action in question. For instance, a *knife* requires more external manipulation to cut a loaf of bread to pieces than an *electric knife*. Therefore, *knife* will rank lower on the autonomy hierarchy than its more

---

grammaticality of sentences. That is to say, instead of categorical *Yes* vs. *No* judgments, the acceptability in this domain is very gradient.

[6] A vaguely related distinction (*collective voice/purpose*) is used by Zaenen et al. (2004) as a tagging tool.

[7] This distinction will prove to be crucial to capture the behavior of instruments and ISA.

sophisticated counterpart. Placing actional independence on an axis of its own solves the problem of ranking these referents relative to each other in terms of animacy. This equally solves the dilemma of trying to distinguish a loose group of humans from a formally organized collective in terms of animacy (cf. Bresnan & Hay 2008: 250). In my approach, both are equally animate but not equally autonomous.

Lakoff (1987) advocates an approach of radial categorization, whereby humans sit at the center and all other entities are at a distance. The more peripheral entities are located further away from the core, more human-like ones are closer to the center. Unclear, however, is why – for example – supernatural beings are considered to be equally distant from the center as organizations like corporations. In my approach, a supernatural being like *Poseidon* would be considered as animate (i.e. anthropomorphic) like a normal human (e.g. *Joe*), but *Poseidon* would rank higher on the autonomy hierarchy. Important in Lakoff's (1987) approach, however, is the recognition of human-like machines. In the previous chapter, it was pointed out that more complex machines are better subjects than less complex ones. Also recall that internally powered machines are considered more animate than those with external power (Yamamoto 1999: 18). Rather than placing the explanation for this entirely on the animacy axis, I propose to use the autonomy hierarchy as a central explanatory tool. More complex machines or those with an internal power source are not more animate, but more autonomous.

Mechanisms are usually better candidates for 'agenthood', to use Schlesinger's (1989: 193) terminology, and, within the class of mechanisms, more complex and self-sufficient ones are 'better agents' than less complex and less self-sufficient ones (Schlesinger 1989: 197, 206–207). This seems to be true across languages (Alexiadou & Schäfer 2006: 43–44 and own data):

(12) a. *Der   Kran   hob   die   Kiste hoch.*
        DEF.NOM crane lift\PST.3G DEF.ACC crate up
        'The crane picked up the crate.' (German)
     b. *?Die   Gabel   hob   die   Kartoffel hoch.*
        DEF.NOM fork   lift\PST.3SG DEF.ACC potato   up
        'The fork picked up the potato.' (own data)

c. O geranos sikose to kivotio.
   DEF.NOM crane picked up DEF.ACC crate
   'The crane picked up the crate.' (Modern Greek)
d. *To piruni sikose tin patata.
   DEF.NOM fork picked up DEF.ACC potato
   'The fork picked up the potato.' (own data)
e. De kraan til-de de kist op.
   DEF crane pick-PST.3SG DEF crate up
   'The crane picked up the crate.' (Dutch)
f. ?De vork til-de de aardappel op.
   DEF fork pick-PST.3SG DEF potato up
   'The fork picked up the potato.'
g. Sarah disabled Bill's computer with the hammer/the virus.
h. */?The hammer disabled the computer.
i. The virus disabled the computer.
j. Sarah sneed het brood in stukk-en
   Sarah cut\PST.3SG DEF bread to piece-PL
   met het mes.
   with DEF knife
   'Sarah cut the bread to pieces with the knife.'(Dutch)
k. *Het mes sneed het brood in stukk-en.
   DEF knife cut\PST.3SG DEF bread to piece-PL
   'The knife cut the bread to pieces.'
l. Sarah sneed het brood in stukk-en
   Sarah cut\PST.3SG DEF bread to piece-PL
   met het elektrisch mes.
   with DEF electrical knife
   'Sarah cut the bread to pieces with the electrical knife.'
m. Het elektrisch mes sneed het brood in
   DEF electrical knife cut\PST.3SG DEF bread to
   in stukk-en.
   to piece-PL
   'The electrical knife cut the bread to pieces.'

4.1 Degrees of animacy & autonomy

To put this in line with my proposed approach: More complex mechanisms or appliances (e.g. those with electronic circuitry) rank higher on the autonomy hierarchy than simple inanimate objects like sticks or knives. Because of this, they are generally more acceptable in ISA. Mechanical machines occupy a middle position, as can be seen from the degree of acceptability:

(13) a. *Sarah beschadig-de de computer met de*
Sarah damage-PST.3SG DEF computer with DEF
drilboor.
pneumatic drill
'Sarah damaged the computer with the pneumatic drill.'
(Dutch)

b. *?De drilboor beschadig-de de computer.*
DEF pneumatic drill damage-PST.3SG DEF computer
'The pneumatic drill damaged the computer.'

c. *Het computervirus beschadig-de de computer.*
DEF computer virus damage-PST.3SG DEF computer
'The computer virus damaged the computer.'

d. **De hamer beschadig-de de computer.*
DEF hammer damage-PST.3SG DEF computer
'The hammer damaged the computer.'

e. The lumberjack cut down the tree with the axe.

f. *The axe cut down the tree.

g. The lumberjack cut down the tree with the chainsaw.

h. ?The chainsaw cut down the tree.

i. *O ksilokopos ekopse to dentro*
DEF.NOM lumberjack cut down DEF.ACC tree
me to tsekuri.
with DEF.ACC axe
'The lumberjack cut down the tree with the axe.'
(Modern Greek, own data)

j. **To tsekuri ekopse to dentro.*
DEF.NOM axe cut down DEF.ACC tree
'The axe cut down the tree.'

k. O   ksilokopos ekopse   to   dentro
    DEF.NOM lumberjack cut down DEF.ACC tree
    me   to   alisopriono.
    with DEF.ACC chainsaw
    'The lumberjack cut down the tree with the axe.'
l. ?To   alisopriono ekopse   to   dentro.
    DEF.NOM chainsaw   cut down DEF.ACC tree
    'The chainsaw cut down the tree.'

Not only mechanisms produce varying levels of acceptability, simpler objects do to. The examples in (14) all feature instruments that are not mechanical in nature.

(14) a. The assassin killed the man with the knife.
     b. *The knife killed the man.
     c. The assassin killed the man with the spear.
     d. The spear killed the man.
     e. The lumberjack cut down the tree with a saw.
     f. The lumberjack cut down the tree with an axe.
     g. ?De houthakker vel-de   de   boom met
        DEF lumberjack cut down-PST.3SG DEF boom with
        een   zaag.
        INDEF saw
        'The lumberjack cut down the tree with a saw.' (Dutch)
     h. De   houthakker vel-de   de   boom met
        DEF lumberjack cut down-PST.3SG DEF tree with
        een   bijl.
        INDEF axe
        'The lumberjack cut down the tree with an axe.'

It stands out that *spear* is a better candidate for ISA than *knife*. Contrary to a *knife*, a *spear* is specifically designed to kill. By contrast, knives have a wider array of functions such as cutting open boxes, applying butter to bread etc. Because of the spear's specific purpose, it ranks higher on the autonomy scale than *knife*. Likewise, the sentences in (14e) and (14g) are more marked than the ones in (14f) and (14h) because the referent *axe* is more compatible with *cut down*. This does not mean that (14e) and (14g) are ungrammatical, they are simply more marked.

I have illustrated that referents can intuitively be ranked on the autonomy hierarchy. How can this be formally captured? A gradual increase in autonomy correlates with an equally gradual increase in acceptability. Ergo, different levels of autonomy have to be distinguished. However, it would not suffice to posit *mechanical* vs. *electronic* vs. *simple* as dichotomies in the hierarchy. The reason for this is simple: It has been illustrated that there are acceptability differences *within* these categories as well, not only between them.

As far as mechanisms and self-motive entities are concerned, I propose a bifeatural analysis. The two features I propose are [±independent] and [±controllable]. They are defined as follows:

(15) a. A referent ranks as [+independent] iff the referent is potentially capable of independent action, i.e. action not immediately governed by another entity.
b. A referent ranks as [+controllable] iff the referent can be under control of another referent.[8]

Referents that are [-independent] are entities not capable of independent action. They are therefore always initiated or governed by another entity (i.e. [+controllable]). Examples of this category include cranes, printers, DVD-players and the like. They typically carry out relatively simple, direct orders given by a governing entity (such as a crane operator). Orders typically look like: "Move mechanical arm in direction of joystick's motion", "Print page 1", or "Play movie". The manipulation involved is less direct than with simple artifacts. For example, a *chainsaw* needs to be activated and held by a wielder, but the cutting motion is carried out by the machine itself. I will label this feature combination and referents fitting the description as *semi-autonomous*. I not only recognize mechanisms as being semi-autonomous or higher, but also chemicals or medication. These have to be administered or deployed by a

---

[8] What is controllable is judged from the perspective of humans (i.e. anthropocentric).

4 *Semantic range of instruments, agents & forces*

manipulator, but then function according to the purpose they were designed for (curing a headache, for instance). Consider:

(16) a. *The acid ate away at the lock.*
  b. *The aspirin cured his headache.*

Referents that are [+independent] and [+controllable] are entities that can act on their own, but within the framework of carrying out instructions. These instructions are typically more complex and require (at some stages in the process) independent decision making on the part of the governed entity. An excellent example here is any object that has some degree of AI. A computer virus is intended and initiated by a governing entity to wreak havoc on a target. In the process of wreaking havoc (of whatever nature), the program will have to make *independent decisions* on how to progress without the governing entity being able to intervene. I will call this combination of features *autonomous*. It is clear to me that there are huge differences within the field of AI as far as the degrees of autonomy are concerned. Yet, I do not think these are relevant to the average speaker's conceptualization of AI. In fact, AI's decision making abilities often cause it to pattern with humans, despite clearly being inanimate. Dabrowska (1998: 124) points out that nouns from this domain tend to be assigned more human traits than typical inanimate tools. They are considered to be capable of malice, amongst others (Rosenbach 2008: 155). Consider the following sentences that have been uttered to me in the context of videogames:

(17) a. *De AI deed dat met opzet!*[9]
    DEF AI do\PST.3SG DEM.OBJ on purpose
    'The Artificial Intelligence unit did that on purpose!'
    (Dutch)
  b. *De AI heef-t blijkbaar een plan.*
    DEF AI have-PRS.3SG apparently INDEF.OBJ plan.
    'Apparently, the AI unit has a plan.'

---

[9] In Dutch, in contrast to English, *AI* can refer to a single unit of artificial intelligence. To make the English translation more sensical, I have opted to translate *AI* as *AI unit*.

Both sentences in (17) attribute human or quasi-human traits to an inanimate but intelligent program. Doing something *on purpose* is certainly the product of intention (and in this case also malice) and *having a plan* is a sign of decision making abilities. Despite the inanimate nature of the referents, both examples are grammatical and acceptable. Humans are also considered to be autonomous. They do rank higher than instances of AI because humans are more mobile due to their having limbs that can interact with the real world. By contrast, most entities endowed with a form of artificial intelligence are confined to storage facilities of some sort.

A referent that is [+independent] and [-controllable] is a typical force-effector, such as a *storm* or a *meteor shower*. These referents act independently and cannot be controlled by another entity. This is evidenced by the unacceptability of the sentences in (18).

(18) a. *John wrecked his neighbor's yard with a meteor shower.
      b. *Eric used the storm to cut down the tree.

I propose to label this combination of features as *para-autonomous*. Despite what the terminological background might suggest, referents that are [-independent] and [-controllable] do exist. They cannot act independently, but cannot be controlled either. These are usually parts of an interconnected system beyond conscious human control, such as organs. They are, as it were, *interdependent*. As such referents cannot be consciously controlled, they can never be instruments and are therefore not relevant for the current discussion (they are marked accordingly in the table). I have summarized this in table 15:

	[+controllable]	[-controllable]
[+independent]	Autonomous	Para-autonomous
[-independent]	Semi-autonomous	*Irrelevant*

Table 15: Feature matrix for the principal levels of autonomy.

More importantly, it is possible to visualize these distinctions in a scalar way: para-autonomous ranks highest, semi-autonomous ranks lowest and autonomous ranks in the middle. This fits the intuition that entities that sometimes need control rank lowest, referents that do not have be to controlled rank above those, and entities that *cannot* be controlled rank highest.

The distinctions above do not apply to those referents that must be controlled directly or continuously by a wielder due to their inherent properties. Simple artifacts like *knife* and *axe* do not carry out instructions like semi-autonomous referents. Rather, they are continuously and directly manipulated by the wielder. In other words, they do not fall into this schema. It would be erroneous to assume that *knife* also ranks as [+controllable]. [+controllable] means that a referent *can* be controlled, but does not have to continuously or directly. With simple artifacts, however, a manipulator *must* exercise a form of control directly and continuously. For example, the difference between a knife and an electrical knife is that the latter does the cutting action by itself as the blade moves by itself. The manipulator guides it in the process. By contrast, a simple knife requires the user to move it and make the cutting motion in order for it to cut. I consider such referents as ranking beneath semi-autonomous. I term all referents below semi-autonomous as *non-autonomous*.

It is possible to make a distinction within this class. Here my account is vaguely inspired by Alexiadou & Schäfer's (2006) concept of 'grounded property'. They do not define this feature, nor do they treat it consistently (see chapter 3). I do believe, however, that there is some relevance to it. Consider:

(19) a. *John unlocked the door with the key.*
b. *John unlocked the door with the stick.*
c. *Pierre spliced open the boulder with a knife.*
d. *Pierre spliced open the boulder with a pick-axe.*

Even though all sentences are grammatical, (19a) and (19d) are more acceptable and more natural. This is because in those two examples the instrument is specifically designed for the action described by the verb. I therefore propose to rank *specifically tailored* referents above *plain artifacts*. This also fits the idea of manipulation as the inverse of autonomy.

Cutting a cake with a stick will require more lengthy manipulation on the part of the instigator than with a knife, as the latter was specifically designed for the cutting activity, requiring less total effort.

The borders between the echelons of the autonomy axis are not always clear. Similarly to animacy (cf. Yamamoto 1999), I propose to treat these categories as fluid and gradient. For example, *knives* are very multifunctional. Therefore, it is not always clear whether they are to be considered as a higher-level plain artifact or as a specifically tailored object.

The complete autonomy hierarchy is given below in (20). Autonomy can be considered the inverse of manipulation: The lowest levels must be manipulated by a manipulator. The higher a referent is located, the less manipulation it requires, until a level is raeched where the referent cannot be manipulated. Echelons (1–2) taken together are considered *nonautonomous* and echelons (4–7) are considered to be *autonomous*.

(20) plain artifact (1) < specifically tailored (2) < semi-autonomous (3) < autonomous (proper) (4) < group (5) < organization (6) < hive/individual human (7) < para-autonomous (8)

In the previous section, levels of organization and groups were discussed in relation to the autonomy hierarchy. Since humans and groups of humans rank as autonomous, I have introduced the relevant distinctions in the *autonomous* class.

4.1.3 The actionality scale

Similar to proposals found in the literature, the animacy hierarchy that I proposed is egocentric and anthropocentric. The autonomy hierarchy, on the other hand, is not anthropocentric (even though the terminology might be): Humans are not the highest level. This allows for a very natural ranking of referents such as *meteor shower* or *storm*: They are more autonomous than humans but not animate. This 2-dimensional characterization does the inherent features of referents more credit than the traditional, one-dimensional animacy hierarchies.

The combination of the animacy hierarchy and the autonomy hierarchy yields an axis-system. An axis-system allows for a cluster-wise identification of (groups of) referents, rather than forcing them on a

4 Semantic range of instruments, agents & forces

one-dimensional line. Forces, for instance, pattern in a very specific portion of the axis system (figure 35). This 2-dimensional clustering provides the benefit of identifying specific zones, similar to Grimm's lattice system. If the referent is within the portion of semantic space as required by the verb (logical structure), it will be able to occupy that LS-position. The animacy axis was loosely inspired by Van Valin & Wilkins (1996).[10]

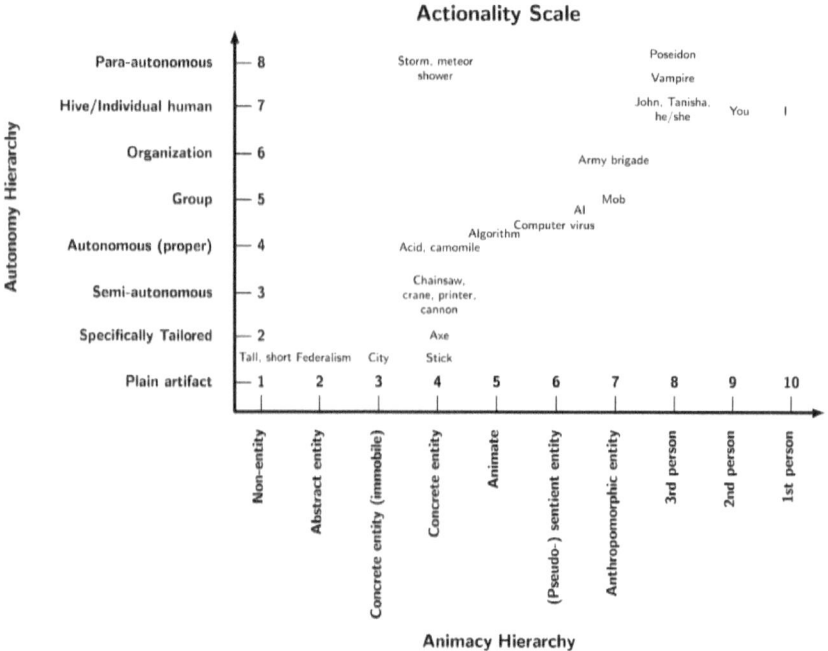

Figure 35: The actionality scale with example referents.

The graph in figure 35 represents the actionality scale with several examples. Do note that this graph is mainly intended for illustration purposes. Due to limitations on graphical representation, the referents' position should be treated as approximate and not as absolute.

---

[10] For instance, the notion of *non-entity* was adopted from Van Valin & Wilkins (1996).

RRG's AUH-approach illustrates that structurally higher positions tend to be occupied by more animate entities (de Swart et al. 2008: 134). The actionality scale can be seen as a more elaborate version of this idea: Certain regions in the scale tend to correlate with certain argument positions.

4.1.4 Pseudo-agents

In the previous sections, it has become clear that the traditional concepts of instrument, force and agent correlate with certain areas on the actionality scale. The gradience of the scale suggests that there might be referents that can be conceptualized as both instruments and instigators in their own right. Consider:

(21) a. *John sprayed the fields with the piper plane.* (after Schlesinger 1989: 193)
 b. *The piper plane sprayed the fields.* (Schlesinger 1989: 193)
 c. *The piper plane sprayed the fields with the wing-mounted spray guns.*
 d. *John picked up the crate with the crane.*
 e. *The crane picked up the crate.* (adapted from Schlesinger 1989: 193)
 f. *The crane destroyed the house with a big boulder.*
 g. *The hacker disabled John's computer with a computer virus.*
 h. *The computer virus disabled John's computer by means of an algorithm.*
 i. *Mara destroyed the village with the tank.*
 j. *The tank destroyed the village with one artillery shell.*

I assume that referents have to be within the correct portion of space in figure 35 for them to be realized as an instigator or an instrument. For instance, the referent *knife* does not occupy the correct area on the scale to allow a realization as an instigator. As the referents in question are inanimate, an obvious step in a classification is to distinguish forces from instruments by testing. To do this, I propose two sets of tests. The first involves isolating the referent's ability to occupy certain LS-positions: (1) Use the referent as an instigator using another instrument

4 Semantic range of instruments, agents & forces

and (2) use the referent as an instrument. These tests correspond to positions in the logical structure. Hence, 'use as an instrument' means that the referent is inserted into an intermediate effector position. Consider the examples in (22).

(22) a. *John destroyed the barn with the sledgehammer.*
b. **The sledgehammer destroyed the barn with the boulder.*
c. *The storm destroyed the barn with its strong winds.*
d. **John destroyed the barn with the storm.*

Sledgehammer fails test (1) but passes test (2), making it an instrument. *Storm* passes test (1) but fails test (2) making it a force. I have summarized the tests proposed by Van Valin & Wilkins (1996) in the table below.[11]

	Use as instigator (1)	Use as instrument (2)
Force	Yes	No
Instrument	No	Yes

Table 16: Tests to distinguish instruments from forces.

The previous sections have illustrated, however, that animacy and autonomy are gradient notions. This predicts the existence of referents that pass both these tests and thus belong to what Yamamoto (1999: 18) calls 'borderline cases'. As was pointed out before, typical instances include intelligent machines. Consider (23).

---

[11] These tests obviously have to be adapted to the fit language under investigation. Japanese, for instance, does not allow any inanimates in subject position (Kuno 1973: 31), thereby making test (1) unusable.

(23) a. *Mara breached the firewall with the cleverly constructed computer virus.*
b. *Het computer virus doorboor-de   de firewall*
DEF computer virus breach-PST.3SG DEF firewall
met   afvalbestand-en.
with junk file-PL
'The computer virus breached the firewall with junkfiles.'
(Dutch)
c. *Peter assembled the car by means of the assembly robot.*
d. *The assembly robot assembled the car with a screwdriver.*

In the examples in (23), the referents pass both tests. It follows therefore, that these borderline referents can be instruments or instigators. Generally, there are two subtypes of instigating effectors, forces and agents. Forces themselves can be distinguished from agents by the fact that the former are inanimate. The second diagnostic is intended to see how a referent patterns and to determine what type of instigator they are most similar to: a force or an agent. To do this, I propose a test that isolates the para-autonomous feature that uniquely defines forces (the *control-test*). That is to say, they are conceptually uncontrollable. Humans (the most prototypical agents) rank as autonomous because they can be controlled. If a referent tests as controllable, then it is more like an agent. If it is uncontrollable, it patterns with forces. Verbs like *command* or *order* or causative auxiliaries entail a form of control on the part of the controller with respect to the controllee. Consider the following examples with their Dutch[12], German and French equivalents:

(24) a. *Mara commanded the computer virus to attack the mainframe.*
b. *Mara made the computer virus attack the mainframe.*

---

[12] The Dutch examples in (24h) and (24j) use a form of the verb *doen*. This is typical of Belgian Dutch (Heine & Kuteva 2006: 60. Also see Taeldeman (1978: 60), in contrast to Netherlandic Dutch, which prefers to use *laten* (*let*) to express all types of causation (also see chapter 5). Belgian Dutch has two causative verbs (*doen* and *laten*) expressing different types of causation. In this respect, Belgian Dutch is more similar to French and Netherlandic Dutch is more similar to German. All Dutch examples in this thesis are from Belgian Dutch, unless explicitly indicated.

4 *Semantic range of instruments, agents & forces*

c. *Mara commanded Bill to attack Pat.*
d. *Mara made Bill attack Pat.*
e. *??Mara commanded the storm to back down.*
f. *??Mara made the storm back down.*
g. *Mara beval   de   AI de   mainframe*
   Mara order\PST.3SG DEF AI DEF mainframe
   aan te vallen
   to   attack.INF   (Dutch)
h. *Mara deed   de   AI de   mainframe aanvallen.*
   Mara do\PST.3SG DEF AI DEF mainframe attack.INF
i. *??Mara beval   de   storm te gaan   liggen.*
   Mara   order\PST.3SG DEF storm to go.INF lie.INF
j. *??Mara deed   de   storm gaan   liggen.*
   Mara   do\PST.3SG DEF storm go.INF lie.INF
k. *Mara befahl   der   KI den   Mainframe anzugreifen.*
   Mara order\PST.3SG DEF AI DEF mainframe attack
   (German)
l. *Mara ließ   die KI den   Mainframe angreifen.*
   Mara let\PST.3SG DEF AI DEF mainframe attack.INF
m. *??Mara befahl   dem Sturm sich zu legen.*
   Mara   order\PST.3SG DEF storm REFL to lie.INF
n. *??Mara ließ   den Sturm sich legen.*
   Mara   let\PST.3SG DEF storm REFL lie.INF
o. *Mara a   commandé au   virus d'attaquer*
   Mara AUX.3SG order.PTCP to.the virus to=attack
   l'unité central.
   DEF=mainframe (French)
p. *Mara a   fait   attaquer l'unité central*
   Mara AUX.3SG do.PTCP attack.INF DEF=mainframe
   par le   virus.
   by DEF virus

q. ??Mara a   commandé à la   tempête
    Mara   AUX.3SG   order.PTCP to DEF storm
    de   reculer.
    to   recede.INF
r. ??Mara a   fait   reculer la   tempête.
    Mara   AUX.3SG   do.PTCP   recede.INF DEF storm

The examples in (24a–24f), (24g–24j), (24k–24n) and (24o–24r) show that the borderline cases pattern with agents rather than with forces. This confirms the provisional ranking of referents in figure 35 where they are closer to humans than to forces.

I will term these borderline referents *pseudo-agents* because they can be conceptualized by speakers as either instigators or instruments. One might wonder why I do not simply label them 'agents'. There is a principled reason for this: Despite being closer to agents than to forces, there are still some differences between pseudo-agents and agents. Pseudo-agents rank lower in sentience than humans, as is illustrated by the examples below:

(25) a. *John grudgingly blew up the barn.*
     b. *??The computer virus grudgingly disabled the firewall.*
     c. Jan   blies   tegen   zijn   zin   de
         Jan   blow up\PST.3SG   against POSS   wish DEF
         schuur op.
         barn   VPR
         'Jan blew up the barn against his will.' (Dutch)
     d. ??De AI   schakel-de   tegen   zijn   zin   de
         DEF AI   switch-PST.3SG   against POSS   wish DEF
         firewall uit.
         firewall off
         'The AI switched off the firewall against its will.'

Due to their lower sentience, the subject referents in (25b) and (25c) do not pattern with adverbs expressing emotional states too well. As animacy is inherently anthropocentric, emotional faculties are associated with higher animacy. Conversely, entities incapable of emotion (in the broadest sense of the word) will be ranked lower. Rather than treating pseudo-agents as a new effector type, they are a class of referents that can be conceptualized as either instruments or instigators. For this reason, the range of pseudo-agents has been indicated with a dashed line in figure 37. It is most interesting to find that a power differential manifests itself:

(26) a. *The computer virus destroyed the firewall by means of the algorithm.*
b. *The algorithm destroyed the firewall by means of a set of junk files.*
c. **The algorithm destroyed the firewall with the computer virus.*
d. De AI leg-de het gegevenscentrum met
DEF AI cripple-PST.3SG DEF data center with
het virus lam.
DEF virus VPR
e. Het virus leg-de het gegevenscentrum
DEF virus cripple-PST.3SG DEF data center
met een reeks junkbestand-en lam.
with INDEF series junk file-PL VPR
f. *Het virus leg-de het gegevenscentrum
DEF virus cripple-PST.3SG DEF data center
met de AI lam.
with DEF AI VPR

In the examples (26a–26c) and (26d–26f), both relevant referents (*computer virus & algorithm* and *AI & virus*, respectively) can each be conceptualized as an instigator, as the first two sentences of each set show. However, the lower-ranking referent cannot be the instigator over a higher-ranking one, as the third sentence in each set shows. An *algorithm* is less sophisticated than a *computer virus* and a *virus* is less advanced than *AI*. This would place *AI* highest on the actionality scale, *virus* second highest and *algorithm* lowest. This principle can be formalized as the *Relative Power Principle*.

(27) **Relative Power Principle (preliminary)**: The instigating referent must be ranked higher on the actionality scale than the intermediate effector referent.

In most situations, however, this is unproblematic, as there is a clear scale difference between a human wielder and, say, a hammer. It is potentially difficult in cases where both referents are similarly ranked and when both can occupy both positions in the logical structure. A word of caution is in order here. It would be erroneous to equate pseudo-agents with those instruments that can undergo ISA. *Knife*, for instance, can never occupy the instigator position, but can undergo ISA in English. It is likely that all pseudo-agents can undergo ISA, but not all instruments that can undergo ISA are pseudo-agents.

Where are pseudo-agents located in semantic space, then? I contend that a referent must rank as autonomous (proper) on the autonomy hierarchy but must not exceed level 5 (group) to be a pseudo-agent. The black arrow in figure 36 denotes the upward direction of the actionality scale.

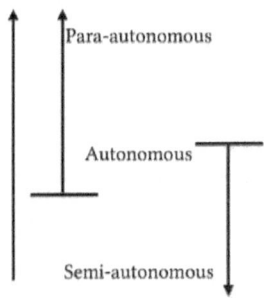

Figure 36: Semantic space of pseudo-agents.

It is now possible to indicate the portions of semantic space where forces, instruments, agents and causees are prototypically located. Pseudo-agents have simply been indicated with a dashed line and without a label, so as to make clear that I do not consider them as an effector type. As I have illustrated, there are areas where these concepts overlap (see figure 37).

4 Semantic range of instruments, agents & forces

The delineation indicated by the oval shapes is not absolute. I have stressed throughout this dissertation that animacy and related concepts are subject to gradience and fluidity. This holds for the partitioning of semantic space in figure 37 as well.

As a consequence of compounding animacy and autonomy into the actionality scale, references to 'animacy' no longer suffice to characterize the difference between forces, instruments, agent, causees and the like. Instead, their positions in semantic space would ideally be indicated by way of coordinates in a Cartesian axis system. This is obviously a very technical matter and I will go into it in section 4.3.

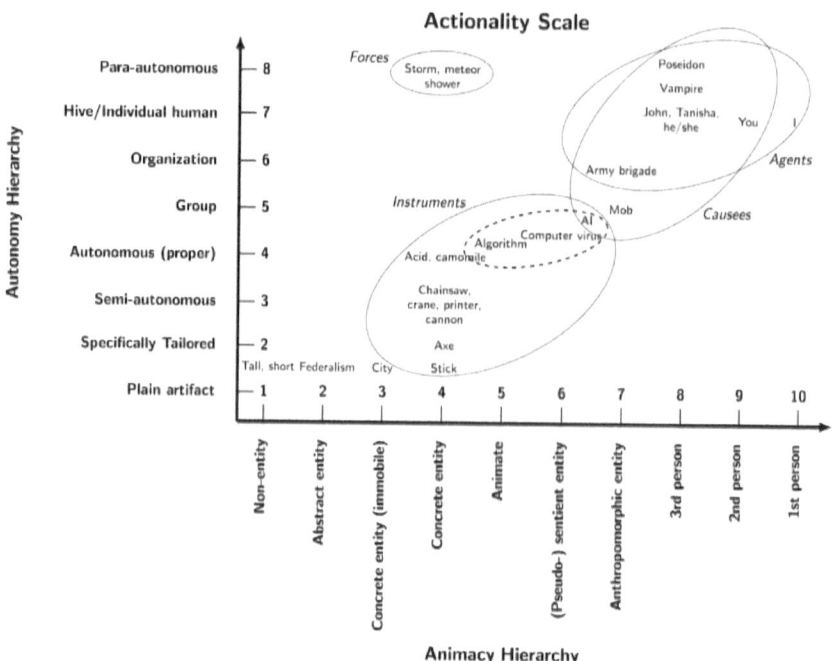

Figure 37: Range of instruments, forces, agents, pseudo-agents and causees within the actionality scale.

On a (very) minor note, one colleague pointed out that typical force arguments like *storm* can sometimes be used as instruments. For example:

(28) a. *Poseidon sank the fleet with/by means of the storm.*
b. *Poseidon used the storm to sink the fleet.*

Two remarks are in order here: 1) These are very uncommon utterances and 2) they are part of a fictitious setting in which *storm* and similar referents are commonly personified ((29a, 29b)).

(29) a. *Poseidon sent the storm to destroy the fleet and it obeyed.*
b. *Poseidon ordered the storm to destroy the fleet and it obeyed.*

Even if one were to accept the sentence in (28) as normal everyday language, then acceptability is conditioned by the status differential between instigator and instrument. Within mythology, Olympic deities are considered more powerful than natural phenomena.

4.1.5 Inherent vs. induced features

DeLancey (1984: 203ff.) and Levin & Rappaport Hovav (2005: 49), amongst others, point out that objects typically functioning as instruments can occur in subject position without actually being manipulated by an instigator. The *axe* in *the axe broke the window* (DeLancey 1984: 203) can be construed as falling due to natural circumstances, say, the referent falling off a shelf. However, such eventive construals require considerable context (Levin & Rappaport Hovav 2005: 49). This observation usually entails an inanimate object being imbued with some kind of kinetic energy (Cruse 1973: 16, 19). For instance, by adding the adjective *herunterfallend* ('falling down') to *Axt* ('axe') in German, it becomes more acceptable as a subject. Consider:

(30) a. Die   herunterfallende   Axt   zerbrach
       DEF.NOM   falling-down   axe   broke
       die   Scheibe.
       DEF.ACC   window pane
       'The falling axe broke the window pane.'
       (Alexiadou & Schäfer 2006: 44)

b. *Die Axt zerbrach die Scheibe.
   DEF.NOM axe broke DEF.ACC window pane
   'The axe broke the window.' (Alexiadou & Schäfer 2006: 44)
c. ?De steen heeft de ruit gebroken.
   DEF rock AUX DEF window break.PTCP
   'The rock broke the window.' (Alexiadou & Schäfer 2006: 44)
d. De vliegende steen heeft de ruit gebroken.
   DEF flying rock AUX DEF window break.PTCP
   'The flying rock broke the window.' (Alexiadou & Schäfer 2006: 44)
e. *The gun killed the general. (own data)
f. The bullets killed the general.

These are clear examples where the referent is imbued with kinetic energy making it eligible for a position (subject) that it is usually not eligible for. The properties in question can be considered to be induced, as falling is not an inherent property of an axe, nor is it an inherent feature of rocks to fly. In (30f) world knowledge will dictate the bullets have been fired and were in flight. The introduction of such properties has a profound influence on argument linking. In the examples in (31), the predicate requires the object to be able to move, yet the induced feature (*parked*) makes the RP incompatible with the verb's requirements:

(31) a. William drove away in the car.
     b. *William drove away in the parked car.

I believe that adnominal modification, modification by clauses and the like can be captured with the actionality scale. Rather than conceding such examples as overrides of normal examples or exceptions to the rule, I propose to directly include them in the actionality scale-approach.

I assume that referents have inherent properties. A *car*, for example, has the inherent property that it can move (see Barsalou 1992 for the conceptualization of a car in human cognition) amongst others. A *key* has the inherent ability to open a door due to the specific configuration of grooves it was designed to have (provided the target lock has the matching configuration). These properties place the referents somewhere on the actionality scale. If a feature or property is induced, the new feature matrix of the referent will assign it a new position on the scale. This in turn makes it (potentially) eligible to fill argument positions in the logical structures that it could otherwise not fill. The opposite is also possible: The introduction of a feature may move a referent to a location in the hierarchy that is outside of accessible semantic space, as the example in (31b) illustrates. If there is no information specifying otherwise, only the inherent features of a referent are relevant for linking. The examples above contained phrase-level modification. Whereas this is a very straightforward strategy to induce features, others do exist. For instance, it is possible to include modifying subordinate clauses. Consider:

(32) a. *As a result of the explosion, a stone flew across the road and broke the window.* (Cruse 1973: 20)
 b. **/?A stone flew across the road and broke the window.*

The subclause in (32a) changes the feature matrix, thereby raising the referent on the scale to a position within the accessible area of *fly*'s effector argument. Without the modifying subclause, the sentence would not be acceptable as (32b) illustrates.

This mechanism holds for all referents in relation to the argument positions of a given verb. Ergo, it is also relevant for instruments and ISA. Consider the following Dutch examples:

(33) a. *Jan dood-de de vogel met het mes.*
 Jan kill-PST.3SG DEF bird with DEF knife
 'Jan killed the bird with the knife.'
 b. **Het mes dood-de de vogel.*
 DEF knife kill-PST.3SG DEF bird
 '*The knife killed the bird.'

c. *Jan dood-de   de   vogel met het mes*
   Jan kill-PST.3SG DEF bird with DEF knife
   dat hij gooi-de.
   REL 3SG throw-PST.3SG
   'Jan killed the bird with the knife that he threw'.
d. *Het   mes   dat   Jan   gooi-de   dood-de*
   DEF knife REL Jan throw-PST.3SG kill-PST.3SG
   de   vogel.
   DEF bird
   'The knife that Jan threw killed the bird.'

Normally, the verb *kill* selects an x-argument from a portion of semantic space that *knife* is not in. However, with the induction of kinetic energy in the form of RP-level modification, the referent is 'moved' to the portion of semantic space that is accessible to *kill*'s effector argument. Sentences such as (33c–33d) are the inevitable counter-examples to any theory of instruments and ISA. My approach has the advantage that such additional information is handled with the same mechanism. It is often pointed out by my informants that typical instruments as subjects are perfectly acceptable in fairy-tale like contexts or if the instrument is personified. Consider:

(34) a. *?Nozh   razrézal   hleb.*
        knife.NOM.SG   cut.PERF.PST.3SG.M   bread.ACC.SG.M
        'The knife cut the bread.' (Russian)
     b. *?Nož   je   sekao   hleb.*
        knife.NOM AUX.3SG cut.PTCP bread.ACC
        'The knife cut the bread.' (Serbian)
     c. *?Peilis   pjov-ė   duon-ą.*
        knife.NOM cut-PST.3SG bread-ACC.SG
        'The knife cut the bread.' (Lithuanian)

The sentences in (34) are ungrammatical, except if the knife is personified. Informants report that in such cases the knife is considered a self-moving, reasoning entity. The same is true for Dutch. As Rosenbach (2008: 155) points out, animacy is not a fixed category but can be tweaked. That is to say, referents can be moved along the hierarchy to a different position. In my view, feature induction is just that: Moving the referents on the actionality scale by introducing certain features or stripping the referents of them.

In fact, personification of lower animates or inanimates is recognized in the literature (cf. Yamamoto 1999: 12–13). In my approach, personifications or anthropomorphizations can be captured with essentially the same mechanics as described above: Features are introduced into the feature matrix of the referent, giving it a different position on the scale. I propose to treat personifications as an extreme form of feature induction.

4.2 The prevalence of instruments and implements with respect to verb classes

In this section, I explore the prevalence of instruments and implements[13] with respect to the verb classes recognized by RRG. To do this, I will take canonical examples for each of these classes (adapted from Van Valin 2005: 46–47) and determine whether they allow for instruments and implements by adding these to the base structure. My prediction is that instruments can only be added to causative verb classes, as the very notion of instrument is defined over causation. However, implements are not dependent on causation and therefore they should be admissible in more cases. Implements are necessarily under the scope of a **do'**-predicate (Van Valin 2005: 55). Therefore, they should only be able to appear in LSs that have a **do'**-component.

First, let us explore states. As expected, adding a *with*-PP is inadmissible with any kind of instrumental reading. Consider examples from English, Dutch, German and French in (35).

---

[13] As implements have not yet been explored in greater detail, all implements mentioned in this section follow standard RRG-assumptions.

4 Semantic range of instruments, agents & forces

(35) a. ?*Pat is a fool with a knife.*
b. ?*Pat is   een   idioot met een   mes.*
   Pat be.PRS.3SG INDEF idiot with INDEF knife
   (Dutch)
c. ?*Pat ist   ein   Idiot mit einem Messer.*
   Pat be.PRS.3SG INDEF idiot with INDEF knife
   (German)
d. ?*Pat est   un   idiot avec un   couteau.*
   Pat be.PRS.3SG INDEF idiot with INDEF knife
   (French)

These sentences are only acceptable if the *with*-PP is interpreted as expressing an attribute of *Pat*. The attribute reading of *with*-PPs is explored further in chapter 7. Some states do not combine with a *with*-PP in any form, as (36) illustrates.

(36) a. **The cup is shattered with a rock.*
b. *???Dana saw the mountain with binoculars.*
c. *???Dana   zag   de   berg   met*
   Dana see\PST.3SG DEF mountain with
   een   verrekijker.
   INDEF Binoculars(SG) (Dutch)
d. *The cup has been shattered with a rock.*
e. *Dana looked at the mountain with binoculars.*
f. **Dana acted on the binoculars acted causing them to see the mountain.*
g. **do**´ (Dana, [**see**´ (Dana, mountain) ∧ **use**´ (Dana, binoculars)])

The sentence in (36a) is inadmissible. The variant in (36d) is not a counterexample. Rather, it is a causative achievement that has been passivized. I will go into the passivization of sentences containing an instrument in chapter 8. (36b) and (36c) are equally inadmissible. Note, however, that *look at* allows for the *with*-PP (36e) as it is an activity predicate with an implement under the scope of **do**´. It is not an instrument, because it fails the paraphrase in (36f). Therefore, (36e) corresponds to the LS in (36g).

4.2 The prevalence of instruments and implements with respect to verb classes

Activities should readily allow for implements, as they have a **do´** in their LS. The example in (3.84b) is an activity predicate with an implement. Yet, not every activity predicate allows for an implement:

(37) a. *The children cried with balloons.
 b. *De kind-eren ween-de-n met ballonn-en.
  DEF child-PL cry-PST-3PL with balloon-PL
  (Dutch)
 c. *Die Kinder wein-te-n mit Ballon-s.
  DEF child-PL cry-PST-3PL with balloon-PL
  (German)
 d. *Les enfants pleuraient avec des ballons.
  DEF child.PL cry.PST.3PL with INDEF balloon.PL
  (French)

This is due to the finer-grained semantics of *cry*. It is of such a nature that there is no tool that can possibly influence the activity. The contrast between (3.84b) and (37) shows that implements influence the activity in question in a facilitating manner: The activity is made easier for the user of the implement.

Achievements, stative semelfactives and accomplishments do not allow for implements or instruments, as their LS would predict. Consider the following examples with their Dutch equivalents.

(38) a. *The window shattered with a rock.   Achievement
 b. *De ruit verbrijzel-de met een steen.
  DEF window shatter-PST.3SG with INDEF rock
 c. ?Dana glimpsed the mountain with binoculars
  Semelfactive
 d. ?Dana ving een glimp op van
  Dana catch\PST.3SG INDEF glimpse VPR of
  de berg met de verrekijker.
  DEF mountain with INDEF binoculars(SG)
 e. *Dana acted on the binoculars, causing them to glimpse the mountain.

f. *Dana werk-te op de verrekijker in en dat
Dana act-PST.3SG on DEF binoculars VPR and CNJ
veroorzaak-te dat hij glimp een
cause-PST.3SG CNJ 3SG glimpse INDEF
van de berg opving.
of DEF mountain catch\PST.3SG

g. SEML **see'** (Lauren, mountain) ∧ **do'** (Lauren, [**use'** (Lauren, binoculars)])

h. SEML **see'** (Lauren, mountain) ∧ **do'** (Lauren, [**use'** (Lauren, verrekijker)])

Semelfactives only peripherally allow for implements ((38c–38d)), as evidenced by their marginal acceptability. The failure of the paraphrases in (38e–38f) identifies these tools as implements, corresponding with the LSs in (38g–38h).

Active accomplishments readily allow for implements, as is to be expected ((39a–39b)).

(39) a. Chris liep naar het park met
Chris run\PST.3SG to DEF park with
loopschoenen.
Running shoes-PL
'Chris ran to the park with running shoes.' (Dutch)

b. Carl ate the pizza with a fork.

c. **do'** (Chris, [**run'** (Chris) ∧ **use'** (Chris, loopschoenen)]) & INGR **be-at'** (park, Chris)

d. **do'** (Carl, [**eat'** (Carl, pizza) ∧ **use'** (Carl, fork)]) & INGR **consumed'** (pizza)

e. *Chris werk-te op de loopschoen-en in
Chris act-PST.3SG on DEF running shoe-PL VPR
en dat veroorzaak-te dat ze het park
CNJ REL cause-PST.3SG CNJ 3PL DEF park
bereik-t-en.
reach-PST-3PL

f. *Carl acted on the fork, causing it to eat the pizza.

4.2 The prevalence of instruments and implements with respect to verb classes

The tools in (39a) and (39b) are implements as they fail the causative paraphrase that identifies instruments ((39e–39f)). Now we turn to the causatives, which, according to RRG-theory, should allow for instruments. Causative states allow for instruments, as (40) illustrates. The causative paraphrase is passed, revealing the LSs in (40e) and (40f).

(40) a. *The man scared the dog with the stick.*[14]
 b. *The man acted on the stick, causing it to scare the dog.*
 c. *Der Mann verängstig-te den Hund mit*
  DEF man scare-PST.3SG DEF dog with
  einem Stock.
  INDEF stick (German)
 d. *Der Mann wirk-te auf den Stock*
  DEF man act-PST.3SG on DEF stick
  ein welcher den Hund verängstig-te.
  VPR REL DEF dog scare-PST.3SG
 e. [**do**′ (man, ∅)] CAUSE [[**do**′ (stick, ∅)] CAUSE [**feel**′ (dog, [**afraid**′])]]
 f. [**do**′ (Mann, ∅)] CAUSE [[**do**′ (Stock, ∅)] CAUSE [**feel**′ (Hund, [**afraid**′])]]

The examples in (40) can be interpreted as the man hitting the dog with the stick, causing it to be scared. However, it is also possible that there is a more indirect causal relation between the stick and the dog's being scared. For instance, the dog can be scared by the man throwing the stick in front of it or by man wildly swinging it around. Less direct forms of causation are explored in chapter 5.

Causative activities also allow for instruments:

(41) a. *Felix bounced the ball with the oar.*
 b. *Felix acted on the oar, causing it to bounce the ball.*

---

[14] The original in Van Valin (2005: 47) has a *dog* scare a *boy*. An instrument here would be somewhat less acceptable because of the dog's limited potential to wield instruments. In actionality terms, *dog* would be too low on the scale to occupy the instigator position of the expanded LS.

c. **[do′** (Felix, Ø)] CAUSE [[**do′** (oar, Ø)] CAUSE [**do′** (ball, [**bounce′** (ball)])]]
d. Felix deed de bal bots-en met
   Felix do\PST.3SG DEF bal bounce-INF with
   de roeispaan.
   DEF oar
e. Felix werk-te op de roeispaan in, wat er
   Felix act-PST.3SG on DEF oar VPR REL MSE
   toe leid-de dat de bal op en neer
   to lead-PST.3SG REL DEF ball up and down
   bots-te.[15]
   bounce-PST.3SG
f. [**do′** (Felix, Ø)] CAUSE [[**do′** (roeispaan, Ø)] CAUSE [**do′** (bal, [**bounce′** (bal)])]]

Causative accomplishments and causative achievements clearly allow instruments. In fact, due to the clarity of such examples, many examples in this dissertation are causative accomplishments or achievements. Further consider (42a) and (42d); they pass the paraphrase and so correlate with the LSs in (42c) and (42f), respectively. However, causative accomplishments can also feature implements (42g–42i).

(42) a. *Max melted the ice with the hair dryer.*
     Causative accomplishment
  b. *Max acted on the hair dryer causing it to melt the ice.*
  c. [**do′** (Max, Ø)] CAUSE [[**do′** (hair dryer, Ø)] CAUSE [BECOME **melted′** (ice)]]
  d. Max smolt het ijs met de haardroger.
     Max melt\PST.3SG DEF ice with DEF hairdryer
     (Dutch)

---

[15] The phrase *op en neer* ('up and down') was included in the Dutch paraphrase, because without the causative auxiliary *doen*, *botsen* translates as *collide*.

4.2 The prevalence of instruments and implements with respect to verb classes

e. *Max werk-te   op de   haardroger in,*
   Max act-PST.3SG on DEF Hair dryer VPR
   wat   er-toe   leid-de   dat   die   het
   REL MSE-to   lead-PST.3SG   REL DEM DEF
   ijs   smolt.
   ice   melt\PST.3SG

f. [**do**′ (Max, Ø)] CAUSE [[**do**′ (haardroger, Ø)] CAUSE [BECOME **melted**′ (ijs)]]

g. *The boy put together the bike with a manual.* (Farrell 2009: 189–190)

h. **The boy acted on the manual, causing it to put together the bike.*

i. [**do**′ (boy, Ø)] CAUSE [BECOME **together**′ (bike) ∧ **use**′ (boy, manual)] (Farrell 2009: 189–190).[16]

Causative achievements show a similar pattern:

(43) a. *Lauren popped the balloon with the pen.*
      Causative achievement

   b. *Lauren acted on the pen, causing it to pop the balloon.*

   c. [**do**′ (Lauren, Ø)] CAUSE [[**do**′ (pen, Ø)] CAUSE [INGR **popped**′ (balloon)]]

   d. *Lauren deed   de   ballon spring-en   met*
      Lauren do\PST.3SG DEF balloon burst-INF with
      een   Balpen.
      INDEF   pen (Dutch)

   e. *Lauren werk-te   op de   pen in,*
      Lauren act-PST.3SG on DEF pen VPR
      wat   er-toe   leid-de   dat   die   de   ballon
      REL MSE-to lead-PST.3SG REL DEM DEF balloon
      deed   spring-en.
      cause.AUX\PST burst-INF

---

[16] This LS is given by Farrell. While I agree that (42g) features an implement, I do not agree with the LS he proposes. I return to this issue in chapter 7.

175

4 *Semantic range of instruments, agents & forces*

    f.   [**do′** (Lauren, Ø)] CAUSE [[**do′** (balpen, Ø)] CAUSE [INGR **popped′** (ballon)]]

Likewise, causative semelfactives allow for instruments:

(44) a. *Sam flashed the light with a stick.*
          Causative semelfactive
      b. *Sam acted on the stick, causing the light to flash.*
      c. [**do′** (Sam, Ø)] CAUSE [[**do′** (stick, Ø)] CAUSE [SEML **do′** (light, [**flash′** (light)])]]
      d. *Sam deed   de   lamp flits-en   met   een*
          Sam do\PST.3SG DEF lamp flash-INF with INDEF
          stok.
          stick (Dutch)
      e. *Sam werk-te   op de   stok in,*
          Sam act-PST.3SG on DEF stick VPR
          wat er-toe leid-de   dat die de lamp
          REL MSE-to lead-PST.3SG REL DEM DEF lamp
          deed   flits-en.
          cause.AUX\PST flash-INF
      f. [**do′** (Sam, Ø)] CAUSE [[**do′** (stok, Ø)] CAUSE [SEML **do′** (lamp, [**flash′** (lamp)])]]

The only way to express (44a) in Dutch is to use a causative auxiliary *doen* ((44d)).

Causative active accomplishments that feature an instrument are a bit more complex. Consider an example with its logical structure:

(45) a. *Mary fed the pizza to the child.*
      b. [**do′** (Mary, Ø)] CAUSE [**do′** (child, [**eat′** (child, pizza)]) & INGR **consumed′** (pizza)]
      c. *Mary fed the pizza to the child with a fork.*

What LS would fit (45c)? The paraphrase in (46a) is clearly not acceptable, ruling out the LS in (46b).

4.2 The prevalence of instruments and implements with respect to verb classes

(46) a. *Mary acted on the fork, causing to it to force the child to eat.
 b. *[**do**′ (Mary, Ø)] CAUSE [[**do**′ (fork, Ø)] CAUSE [**do**′ (child, [**eat**′ (child, pizza)]) & INGR **consumed**′ (pizza)]]
 c. [**do**′ (maejto, Ø)] CAUSE [[**do**′ (usi, Ø)] CAUSE [BECOME **have**′ (yoem, mansana)]]
 d. U maejto-Ø usi-ta mansana-ta
    DET teacher-NOM child-ACC apple-ACC
    yoem-ta miik-tua-k.
    man-ACC give-CAUS-PERF (Yaqui, Uto-Aztecan)
    'The teacher made the child give the man the apple.'
    (Guerrero & Van Valin 2004: 312)

However, the Yaqui sentence in (46d) is acceptable with its corresponding LS in (46c). However, in (46d), event 1 is *the teacher* causing *the child* to give *the apple*, and event 2 is *the child* giving the man *the apple*. The sentence in (45a), however, describes an event 1 where *Mary* causes the *child* to eat and event 2 is the eating and finishing event. Adding an instrument ((45c)), modifies both events taken together, not just one of them. By contrast, *child* in (46d) does not modify the whole event. Therefore, an appropriate paraphrase of (45c) is given in (47) below.

(47) Mary caused the child to eat and finish the pizza and used a fork to accomplish this.

To capture the scope that the instrument has, I propose the LS in (48).

(48) [[**do**′ (Mary, Ø)] CAUSE [**do**′ (child, [**eat**′ (child, pizza)]) & INGR **consumed**′ (pizza)] ∧ [**do**′ (Mary, [**use**′ (Mary, fork)])]]

It is necessary to repeat the **do**′ predicate at the end to ensure the right scope relations. As the *fork* is the y-argument of a **use**′-predicate, it is an implement in this example. It cannot be an instrument, because it is not an effector-argument (x-argument of **do**′) anywhere.

Caused motion verbs do allow for instruments as (49) illustrates.

4 *Semantic range of instruments, agents & forces*

(49) a. *Sonia moved the hay bale to the hangar with a crane.*
b. *Sonia acted on the crane causing it to move the hay bale to the hangar.*
c. [**do´** (Sonia, Ø)] CAUSE [[**do´** (crane, Ø)] CAUSE [**do´** (hay bale, [**move´** (hay bale)]) & INGR **be-at´** (hangar, hay bale)]]

It seems that causative active accomplishments allow for instruments, similar to the other causative classes. However, if the tool has scope over the entire event, only an implement is possible. It is quite likely that the microsemantics of the predicate will be influential in determining whether an instrument or an implement is realized.

This section provided an overview of verb classes and their ability to occur with instruments or implements. It was shown that, confirming the prediction, implements require the presence of a **do´** in the logical structure. Instruments, on the other hand, require at least one causal operator in the LS. It was shown that causative active accomplishments were capable of having both. Causees taking instruments complicate matters considerably and this matter will be explored in chapter 7. A summary of verb classes and instruments/implements is given in table 17.

Verb class	Takes
State	None
Activity	Implement
Achievement	None
Semelfactive	Implements (peripherally)
Accomplishment	None
Active Accomplishment	Implement
Casuative state	Instrument
Causative activity	Instrument
Causative achievement	Instrument
Causative accomplishment	Instrument and implement
Causative semelfactive	Instrument
Causative Active Accomplishment	Instrument and implement

Table 17: Verb classes and the prevalence of instruments and implements.

The mechanics behind the expansion of the base logical structures with implements, instruments and the subsequent linking to syntax will be the topic of chapter 8.

4.3 Integrating the actionality scale with logical structures

Generally speaking, RRG recognizes that selectional restrictions can be placed on argument positions (Van Valin 2013: 88). RRG has adopted Pustejovsky's Qualia theory as an important mechanism to account for selectional restrictions. It allows one to annotate argument positions in terms of qualia features: Annotated positions can only be filled by referents that meet the requirements expressed by the annotation. For instance, if the referent has to be spherical in nature, there will be an annotation on the argument position with that information in the *formal role*. This constitutes a type of hard constraint. In order to make soft-constraint selectional restrictions in RRG more explicit and put them in

4 Semantic range of instruments, agents & forces

line with my approach on instruments, I propose to connect the actionality scale with the argument positions in the LS, similar to qualia-annotations.

I assume that a number of referents with similar features are acceptable to fill a given argument position. Rather than decomposing the actionality scale into several features belonging to the qualia roles and specifying ranges for each of them, I propose to directly plug in the actionality scale into the LS. Qualia and the actionality scale are complementary: Qualia annotations can provide very precise information about a referent. For instance, it can specify that a referent filling a given argument position must be able to create lines on a surface (i.e. write). By contrast, the actionality scale can provide a very general range from which referents can be drawn, without zeroing in on very precise attributes. Even though this might seem straightforward on a conceptual level, it is important to provide a technical account for it.

I have proposed the actionality scale explicitly as a Cartesian axis-system. It is therefore possible to define coordinates in the system. However, in most cases we cannot simply annotate an argument position with a simple set of coordinates because that would constitute a hard constraint. We would in effect be coercing the argument position to be filled with a very specific referent (or type of referent). This is a possibility for dealing with verbs with rather specific requirements such as those that lexicalize agency. Because most verbs are flexible with respect to their slot fillers, we have to devise something more complex. The coordinate approach provides us with a powerful system to do so, however. As I have defined the axes explicitly, it is possible to express referent requirements in a variety of ways: This approach allows us to specify whole regions of semantic space or minimum requirements on one or both axes. Consider the requirements[17] in (50) with their formulations. Recall that the x-axis is the animacy hierarchy and the y-axis is the autonomy hierarchy.

---

[17] These coordinates are randomly chosen. They are for illustration purposes only.

4.3 Integrating the actionality scale with logical structures

(50) a. (5, 2) Filler must be at these exact coordinates.
b. (5, Ø) Filler must have a value of 5 on the x-axis. Y-axis is unspecified.
c. (Ø, 5) Filler must have a value of 5 on the y-axis. X-axis is unspecified.
d. (5, 2) ↔ (5, 6) Filler must have a value between the coordinates indicated.
e. (5↑, 2↑) Filler must have an x-value of 5 or higher and a y-value of 2 or higher.
f. (5↓, 2↓) Filler must have an x-value of 5 or lower and a y-value of 2 or lower.
g. (5↓, 2↑) Filler must have an x-value of 5 or lower and a y-value of 2 or higher.
h. (Ø, Ø) Both the x- and the y-axis are unspecified.

This system allows for an immense range of possible combinations, only a subset of which is displayed here. It is very important, however, to point out that the actionality scale and its coordinate-based component are still parts of human cognition. They are modeled loosely on mathematical concepts yet do not describe a mathematical universe. Determining whether a referent has an x-value of exactly 5 or is in fact a bit higher or lower is difficult and will in all likelihood be different for different speakers. Consider then, what an annotated logical structure could look like:[18]

(51) [**do**′ (x, Ø)] CAUSE [[**do**′ (y, Ø)] CAUSE [INGR **pred**′ (z)]]
       (5↑, 2↑)   (4,1) ↔ (5,3)   (Ø, Ø)

I have opted for a second line of information instead of the usual qualia-annotation as subscripts for the simple reason of legibility.

---

[18] Here too, the numbers are intended for illustration purposes only.

4.4 The three problems revisited

Three problems with respect to ISA were introduced in chapter 3. The first problem relates to variation with respect to instruments: With the same predicate, some instruments allow for ISA whereas others do not. Consider:

(52) a. *John destroyed the sign with the bomb.*
 b. *The bomb destroyed the sign.*
 c. *John destroyed the sign with the sword.*
 d. **The sword destroyed the sign.*

The actionality scale can account for this: The acceptability of ISA depends on the position of the instrument's referent on the scale. The referents have to be high enough on the actionality scale relative to the predicate for ISA to take place. *Sword* is simply not high enough, but *bomb* is. Both referents rank as concrete entities on the animacy hierarchy, but *sword* ranks lower than *bomb* on the autonomy hierarchy: The former is *non-autonomous* whereas the latter is *semi-autonomous*. The semantics of the predicate exclude *sword* because it is not located in the correct portion of semantic space. However, it would be too quick to conclude that languages will set a general lower limit for ISA in terms of the actionality scale. The problem is that – within the same language – the same referent can undergo ISA with some predicates but not with others, even if both are causally embedded. This can be illustrated by keeping the instrument the same, but varying the predicate: For example, ISA is not possible in (53a–53b), (53e–53f) and (53k–53l) whereas it is possible in (53c–53d), (53g–53h) and (53i–53j).

(53) a. *John opened the parcel with the knife.*
 b. **The knife opened the parcel.*
 c. *Greg shattered the window with the knife.*
 d. *The knife shattered the window.*
 e. *The assassin murdered the mayor with a spear through the heart.*
 f. **The spear murdered the mayor.*

g. *The assassin killed the mayor with a spear through the heart.*
h. *The spear killed the mayor.*
i. *The cook cracked open the coconut with the hammer.*
j. *The hammer cracked open the coconut.*
k. *The cook opened the door with the hammer.*
l. **The hammer opened the door.*

The *murder* example is analyzed as the predicate lexicalizing agency (Van Valin & Wilkins 1996) which is why it is incompatible with a non-human actor. Traditionally, RRG includes a special operator ('big' DO) in the logical structure that is said to express lexicalized agency as is the case in (53e–53f). But predicates without lexicalized agency also play a role, as I have shown in (53a–53d) and (53i–53l). It would be erroneous to claim that *open* lexicalizes agency the same way that *murder* does, because *open* is compatible with non-human actors. Consider (54a–b):

(54) a. *John opened the container with a crane.*
 b. *The crane opened the container.*
 c. *John unwillingly opened the parcel with a knife.*
 d. **The assassin unwillingly murdered the mayor.*

Furthermore, *open* is compatible with agency-canceling adverbs (54c), contrary to the example in (54d). However, I believe it is possible to use the actionality scale as a single account for all these examples: Each individual predicate will impose selectional restrictions on the fillers of its argument positions. Only if the filler of the instrument slot is similar enough to the requirements for the instigator slot can it be assigned actorhood. It is not surprising then that a higher-ranking referent like *crane* is a better choice for actor than the lower-ranking knife. By contrast, the selectional requirements of shatter are less strict and do allow for lower-ranking referents as actors (such as rock, stick and the like). Ergo, the actionality scale can also provide a solution to the second problem.

The actionality scale can equally provide a solution to the third problem. By way of the very same system of selectional restrictions, language

4 Semantic range of instruments, agents & forces

differences with respect to ISA can be captured. For example, the English verb *cut* imposes looser restrictions on the argument position than any of its Dutch equivalents.[19] Afrikaans, by contrast, patterns like English:

(55) a. *Tanisha cut the bread with the knife.* (English)
      b. *The knife cut the bread.*
      c. *Tanisha sneed het brood met het mes.*
         Tanisha cut\PST.3SG DEF bread with DEF knife (Dutch)
      d. **Het mes sneed het brood.*
         DEF knife cut\PST.3SG DEF bread
      e. *Tanisha sneed het brood met het mes door.*
         Tanisha cut\PST.3SG DEF brood with DEF mes VPR
      f. *???Het mes sneed het brood door.*
         DEF knife cut\PST.3SG DEF bread VPR
      g. *Johan het die brood met 'n mes ges-ny.*
         John AUX(PST) DEF bread with INDEF knife PTCP-cut
         'John cut the bread with a knife.' (Afrikaans)
      h. *Die mes het die brood ge-sny*
         DEF knife AUX.(PST) DEF bread PTCP-cut
         'The knife cut the bread.'

Similarly, Turkish seems to be less restrictive than Bulgarian (56a–56d) and Estonian seems to be more tolerant than Russian (56e–56h):

(56) a. *John ekmeğ-i bıçak-la kes-ti.*
         John.NOM bread-ACC.SG knife-INS cut-PST.3SG
         'John cut the bread with a knife.' (Turkish)

---

[19] Whereas (55d) is completely ungrammatical, (55f) is slightly less bad.

b. ?Bıçak ekmeğ-i kes-ti.
   knife.NOM bread-ACC.SG cut-PST.3SG.
   'The knife cut the bread.'
c. Džon narjaza hljaba s nož.
   John cut.PERF.PRS.3SG bread.DEF with knife
   'John cut the bread with a knife.' (Bulgarian)
d. ???Nožŭt srjaza hljaba.
   knife.DEF cut.PERF.PRS.3SG bread.DEF
   'The knife cut the bread.'
e. John lõika-s-Ø leiba noa-ga.
   John.NOM cut-PST-3SG bread-PART knife-COM
   'John cut the bread with the knife.' (Estonian)
f. Nuga lõika-s-Ø leib-a.
   knife.NOM cut-PST-3SG bread-PART
   'The knife cut the bread.'
g. Jon otrezal hleb
   John cut.PERF.PST.3SG.M bread.ACC.SG.M
   nozhom.
   knife.INS.SG.M
   'John cut the bread with the knife.' (Russian)
h. *Nozh razrézal hleb.
   Knife.NOM.SG cut.PERF.PST.3SG.M bread.ACC.SG.M
   'The knife cut the bread.'

Even within the same language family, there can be substantial differences. The alternation between (56a) and (56b) is perfectly possible in Portuguese, somewhat strange but still grammatical in Spanish and utterly ungrammatical in Romanian (Hugo Cardoso, Thomas Brochhagen & Adina Dragomirescu, p.c.). Higher-ranking referents, such as *acid*, seem to be unproblematic in most languages:

(57) a. Jon-ek ate-a honda-tu
        John-ERG door-DET(SG.ABS) damage-PTCP
        du azido-a-rekin.
        AUX acid-DET(SG)-COM
        'John damaged the door with the acid.' (Basque)

b. Azido-a-k   ate-a   honda-tu
    acid-DET(SG)-ERG door-DET(SG.ABS) damage-PTCP
    du.
    AUX
    'The acid damaged the door.'
c. John bâ   (ân)   asid be (ân)   dar   âsib   resând.
    John with   DEM   acid to DEM   door damage   arrive
    'John damaged the door with acid.' (Persian)
d. (Ân) asid be (ân)   dar   âsib   resând.
    DEM acid to DEM   door damage arrive
    'The acid damaged the door.'
e. Ʒon-ma   da-a-zian-a   k'ar-eb-i
    John-ERG PR-NV-damage-AOR.S.3SG   door-NOM
    mžav-it.
    acid-INS
    'John damaged the door with the acid.' (Georgian)
f. Mžava-m da-a-zian-a   k'ar-eb-i.
    acid-ERG PR-NV-damage-PST.AOR.S.3SG   door-PL.NOM
    'The acid damaged the door.'
g. Jón   skemm-d-i   dyr-nar   með
    Jón.NOM.SG damage-PST-3SG   door-DEF.ACC.PL   with
    sýr-u.
    acid-DAT
    'John damaged the door with the acid.'(Icelandic)[20]
h. Sýran   kemm-d-i   dyr-nar.
    Acid-DEF.NOM.SG   damage-PST-3SG   door-DEF.ACC.PL
    'The acid damaged the door.'

Even though individual languages vary, some generalizations across languages present themselves. For instance, not a single Slavic language in the sample allowed for the example in (56b). Generally, Slavic seems to be fairly restricted with respect to ISA, whereas English and Portuguese are the most liberal languages in the sample.

---

[20] *Dyr* is plural in Icelandic (Felix Knuth, p.c.).

All three problems can be accounted for with the same approach based on the actionality scale. As I have shown, I propose to follow Grimm in assuming that argument positions are open to different sections of semantic space. In RRG-terms, this translates to argument positions in the logical structure being open to different sections of the scale. For example, the verb *kill* will have higher requirements than *cut* and *murder* will have even higher requirements than *kill*. Higher requirements translate to smaller portions of semantic space that referents can be drawn from. In other words, the three problems can be accounted for by the same system: Accessible regions of semantic space, dependent on the predicate and the language. By plugging the actionality scale into qualia theory, it can be integrated in a practical system of linking from semantics to syntax.

4.5 A different approach to the semantic range

In this chapter, I proposed an overhaul of the concept of animacy. More specifically, I proposed including a second axis, which I dubbed *autonomy*, so as to arrive at a Cartesian axis system that allows us to classify the referents of arguments more precisely. Furthermore, the use of such a system allows us to define regions of semantic space along principled lines which are directly compatible with RRG's linking system. However, in the CRC 991, Barsalou's (1992) frames are recognized as a universal format of human cognition (Löbner 2014: 23–24, 2015: 15) and are being developed to be applicable across different scientific fields (e.g. Petersen 2007/2015, Kallmeyer & Osswald 2013). As such, it is possible to provide a frame analysis of the concepts explored in this chapter. In this section, I will propose a very preliminary modeling of the actionality scale in terms of a multiple inheritance hierarchy (Osswald 2002: 12ff.). Osswald (p.c.) points out that my actionality scale-approach is useful for capturing some of the properties of referents, especially those concerning instruments, causees and the like. However, it is difficult to translate the actionality scale into the CRC's frame approach without an intermediate

4 Semantic range of instruments, agents & forces

step, as the architecture of the actionality scale does not allow for a direct translation. That is to say, it first has to be translated into another format. This section is intended to explore the intermediate step that is necessary for a translation into frames. According to Osswald (2002: 13), multiple inheritance hierarchies are an example of a multidimensional classification approach. That is, concepts inherit from *several* superordinate concepts; instead of just one as is the case with the simpler, taxonomic trees. Osswald (2002: 13) points out that with multiple inheritance hierarchies, the concepts are not to be considered subconcepts, but rather as instances of the combination of their superordinates. Such an analysis of the actionality scale is given in figure 38. I have taken concepts of the actionality scale's two axes and used them as concepts in the branches of the tree-structure. For the sake of clarity, figure 38 only shows the feature values (in terms of connecting lines) that are defining characteristics of the concept at hand. For example, human referents are defined as [+sentient] and [+animate]. Needless to say, in prototypical cases, they are also [+movable]. However, non-defining features have not been connected to the concepts to keep the general overview intact. The top section of the animacy hierarchy related to reference (1st person, 2nd person, and 3rd person) has not been included in the tree for the sake of simplicity. Example referents are given in italics.

4.5 A different approach to the semantic range

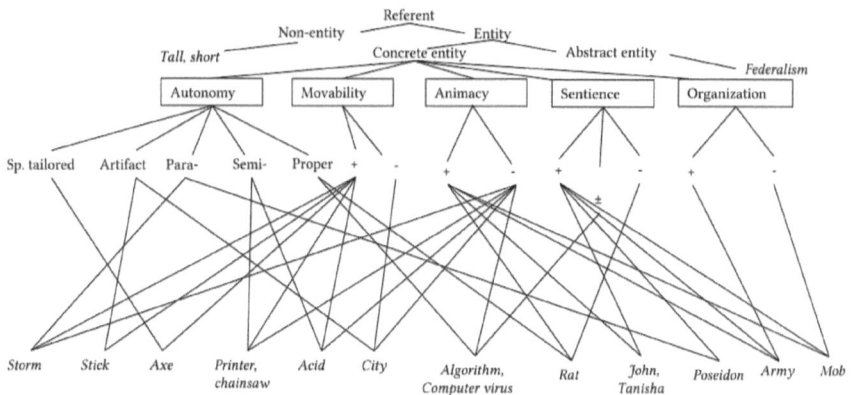

Figure 38: Preliminary Multiple Inheritance Hierarchy analysis of the actionality scale.

Figure 38 reveals that certain features might outrank others. For instance, if a referent is [+sentient], it will automatically be considered autonomous (proper). It is indeed difficult to conceptualize an entity that is [+sentient] and non-autonomous. The graph in figure 38 can be used in future work as a starting point to model the actionality scale with the CRC's frame approach. Doing so here would be beyond the scope of this dissertation.

5 Instruments and causation: A Force Dynamic view

In chapter 3, it became apparent that instruments are – in many if not most approaches – considered to be causally involved in the state of affairs described by the verb. Usually however, the causal role of the instrument is not explored systematically. At most, reference is made to a feature CAUSE that is connected to the instrument's referent or argument. In RRG, for example, instruments are causally embedded. That is to say, they are part of a subevent under the scope of a CAUSE-operator and the event itself takes scope over another CAUSE-operator. The literature on causation is vast and spans several disciplines, such as physics, linguistics, philosophy and psychology. The CAUSE operator goes back to generative semantics with which it intended capture the concept of causation. Since then, many approaches have made use of the single CAUSE-operator. Generative grammar for instance, has experimented with CAUSE as occupying a certain position in the syntactic structure (Wechsler 2006: 651). Others have used CAUSE as a purely semantic component or operator, such as RRG. This chapter is not intended to provide an overview of all of these. Rather, I will explore the Force Dynamic (Talmy 1988, 2000) view with respect to instruments. Furthermore, I will propose to integrate Force Dynamics into RRG's system of lexical decomposition thereby accounting for the notion of implement. There is an important difference between Force Dynamics' and RRG's underlying view on causation: Whereas RRG assumes causation is events acting on events (Foley & Van Valin 1984: 38), Force Dynamics assumes causation consists of participants acting on participants (Talmy

1976: 67).[1] In the sections that following, I will attempt to bridge this divide.

There are three problems with the CAUSE-operator: First, reducing the complex nature of causality to a single operator or deep verb is a gross oversimplification. The second issue is related to the first: In a system like RRG, there is a fundamental disequilibrium between aspectual operators (BECOME, INGR, SEML) and causative operators (CAUSE).[2]

Also, treating CAUSE as an 'isolated primitive' is problematic. Jackendoff (1991: 12) points out that isolated primitives can never be justified and that a primitive only makes sense in connection to other primitives. However, the use of the single causal operator as a placeholder allows linguists to make generalizations in other domains (Copley & Wolff 2014: 12). In this chapter, I propose to decompose and expand CAUSE – using force dynamic concepts – into a network of causal operators suitable for RRG's logical structures. Beyond an attempt to transcend the placeholder nature of CAUSE, the refinement I will be proposing in this chapter is necessary to provide a unified theory that can capture instruments and related concepts, such as *causees*. From the multitude of frameworks pertaining to causation, I have chosen Force Dynamics (or: *FD*) for three reasons: 1) FD is a very flexible system that allows for many different configurations and combinations of configurations, 2) there is strong experimental evidence indicating that humans conceptualize causation along force dynamic lines (Wolff 2007, 2014) and 3) FD allows for a natural extension from straightforward physical causation to less canonical cases (e.g. psychological or social causation, Wolff 2014: 100, cf. Talmy 1988).

Force Dynamics is a *production model* of causation (Copley & Wolff 2014: 25, as opposed to *dependency models*) situated in the field of cognitive linguistics. Production models characterize causation in terms of energy, force and/or their transmission. Talmy (2000: 409–410) argues

---

[1] As Croft (2012: 211) points out, Talmy's diagrams essentially depict participants acting on other participants. Talmy's examples, however, often have events acting on events.
[2] RRG (Van Valin 2005: 42) does recognize three types of causation (*coercive, non-coercive* and *permissive*) but these distinctions are seldom used.

that the dynamics of force play a fundamental role in human cognition and as such FD permeates all aspects of grammar and language. FD not only permeates language, it also manifests itself in the conceptualization of other domains such as psychology, physics, the social domain and others. FD initially developed out of the notion of causation, generalizing it to a closed-class grammatical category. That is, Talmy (2000: 411) argues that FD should be included in the set of more recognized fundamental semantic categories like number or mood. As causation is seen as the interaction of participants, FD allows for the decomposition of the usually primitive notion of causation (as far as linguistics is concerned, Copley & Wolff 2014: 11) into more granular primitives. An interesting feature of the FD-system is that configurations can be embedded into one another (see reason 1) above): Talmy (2000: 435) calls this *open-ended generativity*. This concept will play an important role in my proposed integration of RRG and FD.

Force dynamics can be provisionally characterized as the interaction of entities with respect to forces (Talmy 2000: 409). This includes the exertion of force on a participant, the reaction of the participant to that force, resistance to such a force etc. (Ibid.). In other words, the various types of causation are captured as specific configurations of participants. As different subtypes of causation are seen as combinations of several factors, FD can naturally capture less canonical causative notions such as *helping* and notions that are traditionally not seen as a type of causation at all (e.g. *prevention*). However, standard RRG (Van Valin & LaPolla 1997: 470ff.) does consider these notions as part of 'larger' causation.

5.1 Fundamentals of Force Dynamics

Talmy (2000: 413) distinguishes between two primary force entities: One that is focused on (the *agonist*) and the other, non-focused force that opposes the agonist (the *antagonist*). These entities are prototypically distinct real-world participants or individuals, but they do not need to be. It is entirely conceivable to have two opposing psychological states within one and the same individual as force entities.

5 Instruments and causation: A Force Dynamic view

The agonist (or: *Ago*) is represented by a circle and the antagonist (or: *Ant*) is represented by a concave figure. Each force entity has an intrinsic force *tendency*: either towards action (represented with >) or towards rest (represented with ●). In practice, often only the agonist's force tendency is marked, because the antagonist is assumed to have the opposite tendency by definition. One of the two force entities will be the stronger and one will be the weaker. The stronger is indicated with a + sign, the weaker (if necessary) with a – sign. The *resultant* is the outcome of the interplay between these factors (Talmy 2000: 414–415). The resultant is represented as a line beneath the agonist, with either an arrowhead or a dot to mark the outcome of the interaction between agonist and antagonist. The interaction between agonist and antagonist is termed *impingement*. Talmy (2000: 486) proposes the 'deep morpheme' ACT ON as an expression of impingement. In the previous chapters, I have employed a causative paraphrase containing an 'act on-sequence' to ascertain whether a tool is an instrument or not. This paraphrase not only aims at making the LS explicit but also intends to make the impingement between the different participants explicit. Figure 39 below is a summary of a typical FD-configuration. In all graphs, the circle always represents the agonist and the concave figure always represents the antagonist. In my graphs, these figures will always occupy the same positions (contrary to Talmy's representations) for the sake of clarity; the crucial differences between them are the respective values in the figures.[3]

---

[3] The terminology that Talmy uses (*agonist* and *antagonist*) is potentially confusing with respect to the intuitive meaning of these terms. For example, the antagonist can act on the agonist, even though a pre-theoretical interpretation would always have the agonist as the participant that acts on another. As these terms are standard in the relevant literature, I have chosen to keep them.

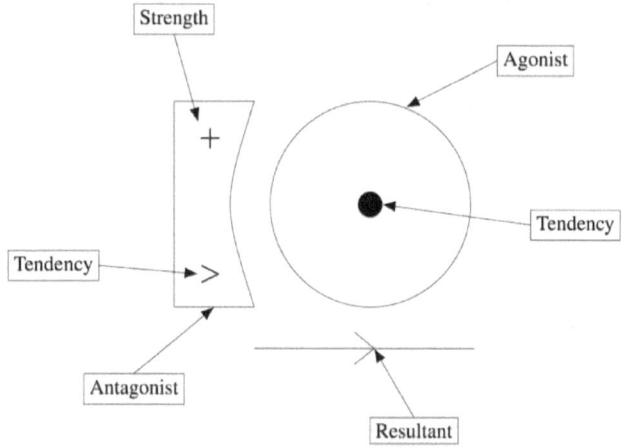

Figure 39: An overview of a force dynamic configuration.

The distinctions introduced thus far allow a formulation of four different steady-state scenarios, two of which can be classified as causative. Given an agonist with a tendency towards rest, and given a stronger antagonist, the agonist is forced or *caused* to move. The movement is caused because the antagonist's greater strength prevails over the agonist's resistance. In case the agonist is stronger, its tendency would prevail and it would remain in rest. Talmy argues that this second scenario belongs in the *despite*-category. It is also possible for the agonist to have the tendency towards action, with the antagonist being the weaker of the two entities. In this case the agonist's tendency becomes the resultant motion. This too, belongs to 'despite'. The antagonist can be considered as a *hindrance*. In other words, the agonist can manifest its tendency *despite* the antagonist's oppositions. For example, in *The knight broke through the defending lines* the referent *knight* is a stronger agonist that overcomes the weaker antagonist's opposition and thus the *knight* succeeds in his endeavor despite the opposition from the defenders. Should, however, the antagonist be stronger than the agonist, its tendency towards movement or action is blocked and the agonist is thus *caused* to rest. An example of this pattern is a sentence such as *the dam blocked the gushing*

5 Instruments and causation: A Force Dynamic view

water masses. The agonist and antagonist in *despite* and *caused* patterns are open to both values (that is, not simultaneously), as there is nothing in the theory that obliges a participant to always have the same tendency. The *despite* and *caused* patterns thus partition the four arrangements of the primary steady-state oppositions. These four possibilities are represented graphically (adapted from Talmy 2000: 415) in figure 40:

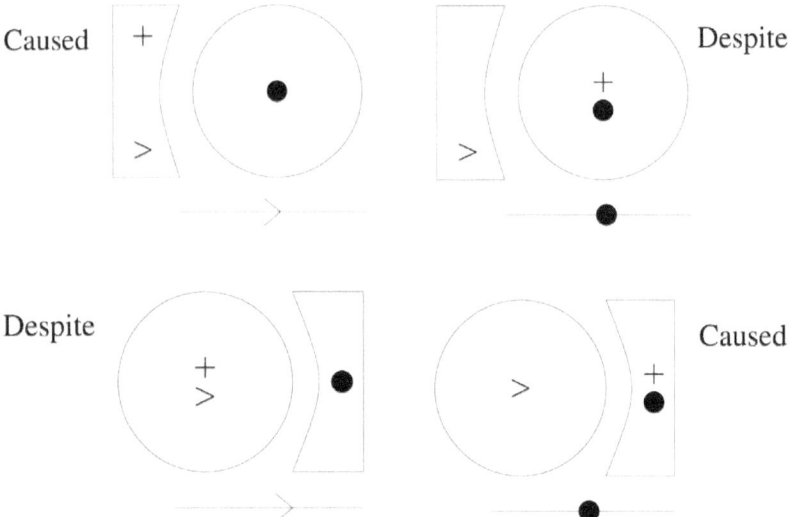

Figure 40: Primary steady-state oppositions.

According to Talmy (2000: 417), these patterns can be directly or indirectly expressed by linguistic expressions, usually by certain closed-class elements (such as conjunctions). Talmy (2000: 418) considers causation as a phenomenon whereby the resultant state of the agonist is the opposite of its intrinsic force tendency. As I pointed out before, linguistic expressions can express information or states of affairs from various domains: From purely physical events to psychological or social events. Yet, despite these widely varying contexts, the fundamental force dynamic mechanisms are the same (Talmy 2000: 412–413). Basic physical configurations can account for the complex inter- or intrasocial patterns by virtue of metaphoric extension[4] (Talmy 2000: 435 & De Mulder 2012: 4): Such extensions allow the language-user to conceptualize forces in other domains with the concepts used to capture the force dynamics of participants in the physical realm. In this regard, it is somewhat reminiscent of older scientific models and naïve physics (Talmy 2000: 455ff.).

5.1.1 Further patterns

Apart from these primary steady-state patterns,[5] force dynamic patterns can also include change over time. Adding changes over time to the steady-state patterns results in change of state patterns (Talmy 2000: 417). This is a natural consequence of the system, as it allows for the factors that have already been discussed to potentially vary: 1) The interaction between agonist and antagonist can change and 2) the strength of the participants can vary over time.

Changing impingement entails that force is not continuously exerted on the agonist. Rather, the state of exerting force is stopped or initiated at a certain point in time: The antagonist (in the most prototypical cases) leaves or enters the state of impingement. A change of impingement is indicated graphically with a dashed arrow. If desirable, the resultant can consequently be divided by a slash separating the state of the agonist before and after. An example configuration is given in figure 41.

---

[4] Metaphoric extension or metaphoric *transfer* (De Mulder 2012: 2).
[5] The patterns discussed so far are considered *steady-state* because there is no change in the participants' values, that is, their tendencies remain the same and maintain the same strength over time.

5 Instruments and causation: A Force Dynamic view

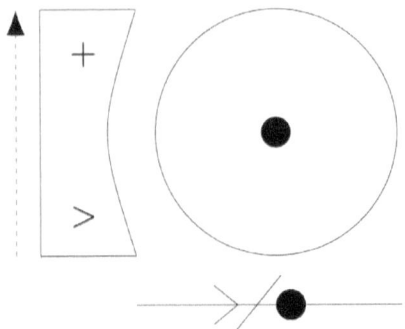

Figure 41: Example configuration with disengaging antagonist and two-state resultant.

Causation proper was defined above as a situation where the resultant is contrary to the agonist's tendency. Including change over time as a parameter allows for a distinction between *onset* and *extended causation*. *Onset causation* can be characterized as follows: At a certain point in time, the antagonist exerts a (non-continuous) force on an agonist forcing it into a state contrary to its tendency. There is, thus, onset causation of action (e.g. *throw* or German *schubsen*) or onset causation of rest (e.g. *tackle*). In cases where the antagonist exerts continuous force (as in figure 40), causation is considered to be *extended causation* (e.g. German *schieben*).

If a stronger antagonist ceases to exert force (i.e. cessation of impingement), the agonist will realize its intrinsic tendency. This is known as *onset letting*. Parallel to onset vs. extended causation, Talmy points out that there must be patterns where impingement *never* takes place. As FD is characterized by the interaction (of whatever kind) of the participants, Talmy (2000: 420–421) considers such patterns as derived from the steady-state patterns where impingement does take place. Therefore, he calls them *secondary steady-state patterns*. Any pattern where a stronger antagonist never impinges on the agonist, allowing it to realize its intrinsic force tendency, constitutes *extended letting*.

Summarizing, causation is a pattern where impingement leads to a resultant that is the opposite of the agonist's tendency. Letting is the *cessation* or *absence* of impingement, allowing the agonist to realize its intrinsic tendency.

It is important to note that FD recognizes *onset* and *extended* versions of both causation and letting. Contrary to extended letting, onset letting is a situation where the antagonist disengages thereby precipitating a *performance*. It could be argued that even with extended letting, it is the antagonist's non-impingement that is responsible for the resultant. Causation and letting can thus be considered to be part of causality in the broadest sense of the word.

With both of them, the antagonist's performance directly determines the outcome of the resultant. This *performance* can be positive (impingement with the agonist) or negative (avoiding or ceasing impingement with the agonist). In both cases, however, the antagonist *does something* (even if that is the absence of action), which is ultimately responsible for the outcome. I propose to call this *relevant performance*. With letting, the antagonist could potentially capitalize on its greater strength but does not do so. It is the *potential* power of the antagonist to affect the resultant that I consider to be central to its inclusion in broader causation. It should be noted that Talmy (2000: 421) also recognizes the importance of the potential for engagement in motivating the existence of the secondary steady-state patterns.

In the case of the *despite*-category, action is taken on the part of antagonist but it is ultimately irrelevant for the outcome as the agonist is stronger. I will refer to this *irrelevant performance*. I propose to include *causation* and *letting* in the notion of *broader causation* (cf. Van Valin & LaPolla 1997). Table 18 compares Talmy's key concepts with my proposed matrix. The shaded area indicates causation in the broader sense of the word.

5 Instruments and causation: A Force Dynamic view

Performance	Relevant	Irrelevant
Positive	Causation	Despite
Negative	Letting	While[6]

Table 18: Performance matrix.

The shaded area covers the force dynamic patterns that are relevant for my proposal: I will argue that there are four linguistically relevant types of causation, two of which correlate to the upper shaded cell and two of which correlate to the lower shaded cell. The other cells are not relevant for my approach and will not be explored any further.

5.1.2 Instruments in relation to causation

Talmy, like many other linguists, treats instruments in terms of participants in a causative situation. For Talmy, such a causative situation consists of three components: An event 1, an event 2 and a causal relation between them. Essentially, a causal relation entails that event 2 only takes place as a result of event 1 having taken place (Talmy 2000: 479). If event 1 were not to happen, event 2 would likewise not happen. Even though counterfactual theories of causation are part of the dependency models, counterfactuality can be used as a testing tool (Wolff 2007: 82).

Consider the crude characterization and an example in (1) (adapted from Talmy 2000: 482). The notation in (1d) is a more precise, Davidsonian notation of the same event.

(1)   a.   [Event 1] CAUSE [Event 2]
         b.   [The window broke]$_{E2}$ (as a result of)$_{CAUSE}$ [the ball's sailing into it]$_{E1}$.
         c.   [The ball]$_{E1}$ [broke the window]$_{E2}$
         d.   Break(e_2, window) & Sail into(e_1, ball, window) & Cause (e_1, e_2)

---

[6] Talmy does not readily provide a notion to fill this slot with. I therefore propose *while* as a description of two participants who are involved in completely unrelated actions or states. For example: *Joan read while Jack played the video game.*

Contrary to the illustration I used above, Talmy essentially rejects the 'deep verb' CAUSE as it is an oversimplification of a more diverse semantic reality. It is often the case that, in language, only a participant of event 1 is made explicit. In sentence (1c), only a participant of E1 (*ball*) is specified, but the participant is conceptually embedded within the event specified by E1. Also, the causal relation is implied in (1c) whereas it is made explicit in (1b).

To satisfy the requirements for causality, E1 and E2 must share the caused event's (E2) *figure-functioning element* (Talmy 2000: 486). This element must, at the same time, be the *ground* of E1 on which another figure impinges (see above). Figure and Ground are concepts Talmy adopted from Gestalt-psychology and reinterpreted for the domain of linguistics (Talmy 2000: 184):

(2) The Figure is a moving or conceptually movable entity whose site, path, or orientation is conceived as a variable, the particular value of which is the relevant issue.
(3) The Ground is a reference entity, one that has a stationary setting relative to a reference frame, with respect to which the Figure's site, path, or orientation is characterized.

The figure of E1 (the causing event) can be considered the instrument of the whole causative situation. In other words, instruments have a double role, which Talmy (2000: 487) calls *multirelational embedding*. A schematic summary of a causative situation with an instrument is given in figure 42.

5 Instruments and causation: A Force Dynamic view

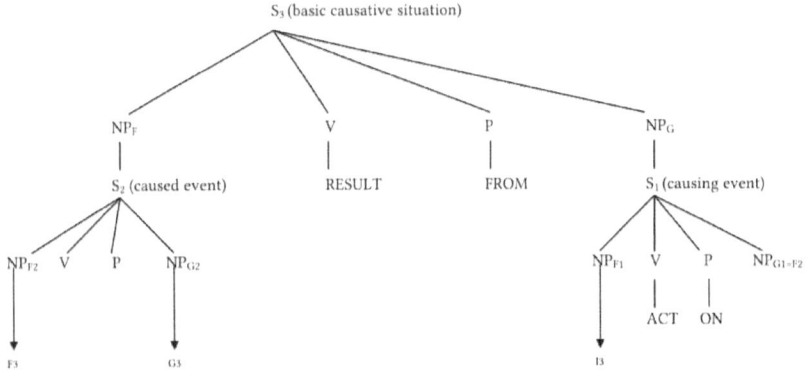

Figure 42: Structure of a basic causative event with an instrument.

F refers to *Figure*, G to *Ground* and I to *Instrument*. A number 1 refers to the causing event, number 2 refers to the caused event and 3 refers to the entire causative situation. Consider the following example:

(4) [John] cut [the bread] [with the knife]
    $G_1=F_2$ G_2 F_1
    F_3 G_3 I_3

This view diverges somewhat from RRG's conception of instruments. In Talmy's approach, the instrument is conceived of as a component of the causing event, but not explicitly of the caused event. The illustration above can be paraphrased: John acts on the knife (S_1) and John cuts the bread (S_2). Both events share John as the author, but not the knife. Talmy elevates the instrument to the level of the whole causative event. From an RRG-point of view, this is somewhat odd. In RRG's logical structures, the instrument argument is under the scope of a CAUSE operator, but simultaneously has a CAUSE-operator under its own scope. If any element should be shared between two events, it should be that which is acted on (in S_1) and which, in turn acts on another element (in S_2). Consider the complete LS for (5).

(5) [**do**′ (John, [**use**′ (John, knife)])] CAUSE [[**do**′ (knife, [**cut**′ (knife, bread)])] CAUSE [BECOME **cut**′ (bread)]]

Knife is acted upon by *John* and in turn acts on the *bread*, leading to the result of the bread being cut. I do agree with Talmy in giving the instrument a prominent place in the state of affairs, but I disagree as to the nature of this position. As it is, Talmy's instrument characterization is incompatible with RRG's logical structures. I will not be using his characterization in my effort to integrate FD with logical structures.

5.1.3 Integrating Force Dynamics with logical structures

In the following sections, I will propose an integration of force dynamic configurations with RRG's logical structures. In this section, I will integrate FD with RRG using simple, straightforward examples. That is to say, the type of causation is very direct: There is prototypical physical manipulation of one entity by another. In section 5.3, I will propose a diversification of the single causal operator itself. The FD-patterns can thus be considered as a decomposition of the notion of CAUSE (here, in its most prototypical sense). Consider the following examples featuring an instrument:

(6) a. *The terrorists destroyed the car with a bomb.*
 b. [**do**′ (terrorists, Ø)] CAUSE [[**do**′ (bomb, Ø)] CAUSE [INGR **destroyed**′ (car)]]
 c. *Mary cut the cake with a knife.*
 d. [**do**′ (Mary, Ø)] CAUSE [[**do**′ (knife, Ø)] CAUSE [BECOME **cut**′ (cake)]]

In these examples, an agent impinges upon an instrument, which in turn causes the coming about of an event. The instrument impinges upon the patient in much the same way. In (6c), this is very clear: The knife makes contact with the cake, splicing it into pieces as a result. In (6a), the impingement is essentially the same, even though there is some conceptual difference. It is the bomb's behavior (exploding) that impinges on the car, rather than the object itself. In both examples, there are three subevents, linked together in a causal chain. To make the nature of CAUSE

5 Instruments and causation: A Force Dynamic view

more explicit, I propose to use FD-configurations as a model. As both CAUSE-operators in each of the examples express a 'classical' causative situation, they can be described with the same, basic FD-configuration: In the first section of the chain, a stronger antagonist with a tendency towards action (*terrorists* and *Mary*) impinges on an agonist with a tendency towards rest (*bomb* and *knife*). Both instruments have a tendency towards rest, as bombs and knives are designed to be handled by someone. If they are not manipulated, they do not 'act'. The resultant of the first sequence is the antagonist of the second sequence. In this sequence, the antagonist is again stronger than the agonist, leading to an action-resultant. To indicate that the resultant of the first sequence is an agonist that has been caused to move and that this determines the antagonist's force tendency in the second sequence, I have added an arrow from the first resultant intersecting with the second arrow from *bomb*. The configuration for (6c–6d) is similar. It is given in figure 44.

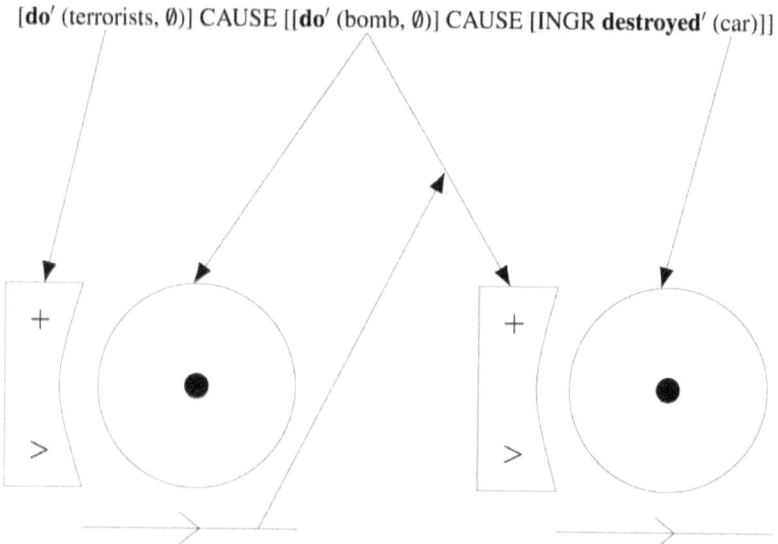

Figure 43: Force dynamic configurations in a standard instrument construction.

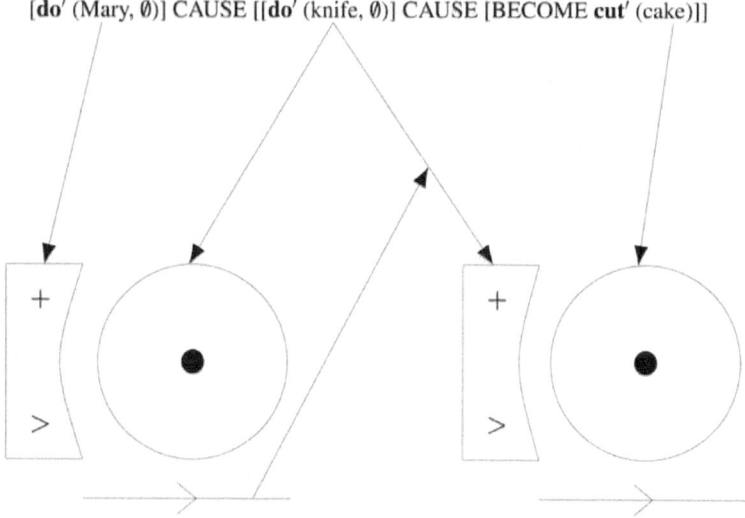

Figure 44: Force dynamic configurations in a standard instrument construction (II).

5.1.4 Force Dynamics: More than causation

Talmy points out that Force Dynamics is a category that permeates the whole of grammar. For instance, it can manifest itself in conjunctions (e.g. *despite*). Even though Force Dynamics was developed to capture causation and related concepts, I believe it is crucial to expand FD's role as a category in grammar even further. I propose to treat FD as a category that permeates language on several levels and as such, it will be active ubiquitously. Consider the examples in (7):

(7) a. *Sarah carried the box.*
    b. *John touched the wall.*

Carry and *touch* are definitely not causative predicates, yet the force dynamic configuration is clear. One participant (*Sarah* or *John*) impinges on another (*box* or *wall*), even though the resultant is not made clear linguistically. As FD patterns play a basic conceptual structuring role (Talmy 2000: 411), I assume they are also active on the micro-level. This

5 Instruments and causation: A Force Dynamic view

micro-level is to be understood as an FD-configuration of participants *within* the same (sub)event.

This distinction raises an important matter though: If we assume that force dynamic configurations operate everywhere (including on the micro-level), what distinguishes a (linguistically) non-causative configuration from a causative one? I propose to treat force dynamic configurations as linguistically causative, iff the agonist and the antagonist are members of separate sub-events. This fits RRG's logical structures naturally, as was shown in section 5.1.3. Consider the example in (6a). Its LS has three subevents: The activity on the part of terrorists, the bomb performing an activity and the ingressive event of the car transitioning from an intact to a destroyed state. In my proposal, force dynamic configurations are at play within each of the subevents (i.e. the micro-level). These have now been added to the LS. Each of the three subevents taken in itself is non-causative. However, on the macro-level, the *terrorists* impinge on the *bomb* and the *bomb* impinges on the car. These two impingements occur *across* the individual subevents: The causal operator is a specification of the precise type of impingement between the two participants in question. I have repeated the (complete) LS from (6a), but with the micro-level added. Contrary to *terrorists, bomb* does not have a micro-configuration, as there is no interaction between two participants within the subevent. This is illustrated in figure 45.

In short, under my combined use of FD and RRG, linguistic causation is only present if there is impingement on the macro-level, i.e. *across* subevents. Impingement *within* subevents (i.e. the micro-level) does not manifest itself as linguistic causation.

5.1 Fundamentals of Force Dynamics

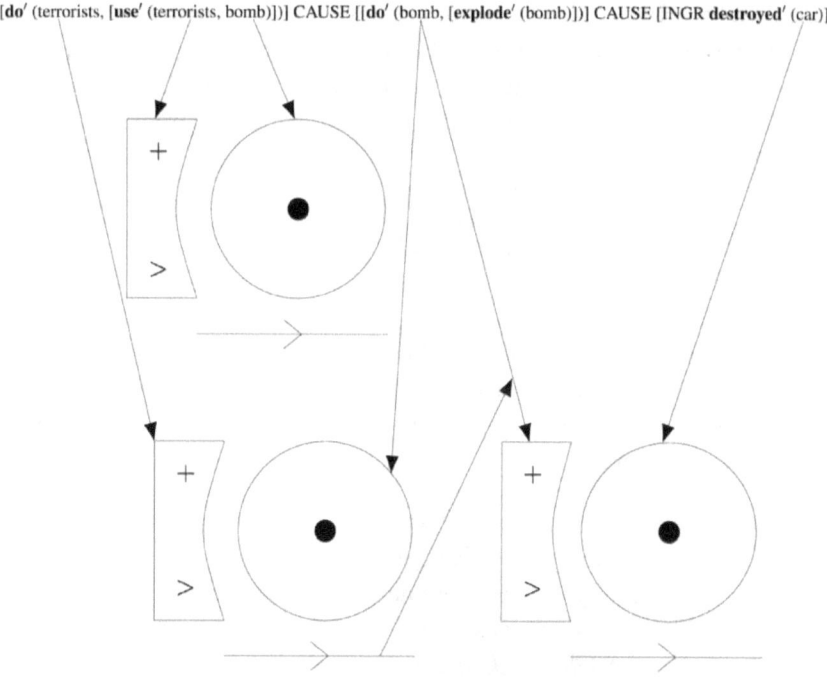

Figure 45: Standard instrument construction with micro- and macro-configurations.

5.1.5 Configurations of volition and Holisky's principle

Volition and/or intention plays an important role in many descriptions of language and in many frameworks. For instance, RRG ties in intention with agency. Agency is thus considered as a property that an effector has when it is intentionally performing the action identified by the verb. Consider:

(8) a. *John killed the deer.*
    b. *John accidentally killed the deer.*
    c. *John intentionally killed the deer.*

207

5 Instruments and causation: A Force Dynamic view

In standard RRG-terms, *John* in (8a) is an agent by virtue of being a human effector. Human effectors are read, by Holisky's principle, as agents unless there is evidence to the contrary as is the case in (8b). In (8c), *John* is an agent and this is confirmed by *intentionally*. This is not only relevant for instigators, such as in (8), but also for other human referents. Consider the causees below:

(9) a. *Elise made John walk.*
 b. *Elise had John walk.*
 c. *Elise let John walk.*

In (9a), *John* is not acting willingly, contrary to (9c), where a non-volitional reading of the causee is impossible. In (9b), both a volitional and a non-volitional reading are possible. This can be tested by adding additional information:

(10) a. **Elise made John walk and he willingly did it.*
 b. *Elise made John walk against his will.*
 c. *Elise had John walk and he willingly did it.*
 d. *Elise had John walk and he did it against his will.*
 e. *Elise let John walk and he willingly did it.*
 f. **Elise let John walk against his will.*

Examples (10a) and (10f) yield contradictions, whereas (10b) and (10e) confirm the default reading. Both pieces of information are compatible with (10c) and (10d), however, signaling that the English causative auxiliary *have* is compatible with both readings. This is connected to the strength of causation, which I will discuss in section 5.3. As far as volition and intention are concerned, I assume that FD can provide a principled account. In short, I will argue to treat volition and intention as properties of the referents that can come about by context, constructions, pragmatics, adverbs, subclauses and the like. Practically speaking, I propose to subject these concepts to an FD-analysis.

Force Dynamics assumes that FD-configurations do not only hold between singular individuals but can also apply within the individual self. Talmy (2000: 431) calls this concept the *divided self*. The force dynamic participants within the self are elements of the psyche, such as base

5.1 Fundamentals of Force Dynamics

desires, urges, reservations about a certain topic, self-restraint etc. Talmy (2000: 431) points out that the divided self is often made explicit in language. Consider:

(11) a. *I held myself back from responding.*
b. *I refrained from responding.*

In the previous section, I proposed to differentiate between two levels of FD-configurations: *Macro*-level configurations and *micro*-level configurations. In addition to these, I propose to include a third level: *Nano*-level configurations. Nano-level force dynamic configurations are FD-patterns within a single participant. Or, put in RRG-terms, within the filler of an argument position of the LS. These three levels are related to each other via the concept of *open-ended generativity*. The resultant of a lower-level configuration is the agonist (or antagonist) of the higher level. I will illustrate this system by means of two examples. The first example contains a base example sentence, whereas the second is characterized by an expanded version of the first example. The matching graphs illustrate the underlying force dynamic configurations.

(12) *John broke the window.*[7]

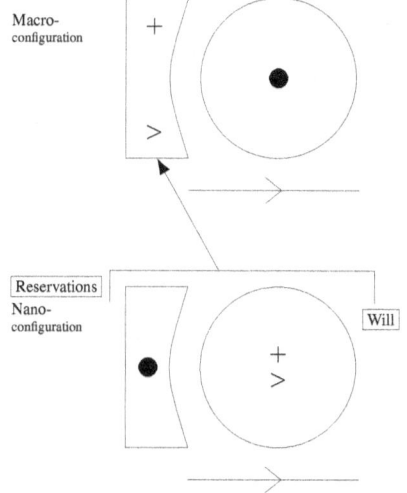

---

[7] *John* is to be identified with the antagonist and *window* is to be equated with the agonist.

5 Instruments and causation: A Force Dynamic view

Following Holisky's Principle, *John* is read as an agent. On the macro-level, *John* is the antagonist impinging on an agonist (*window*). The antagonist has a tendency towards action, whereas the agonist has a tendency towards inaction. The antagonist is stronger, resulting in an action resultant, which is, in this case, a breaking of the window. As agonist and antagonist belong to two different subevents in the logical structures, this configuration will manifest as linguistically causative. On the nano-level, John's *will* is the agonist (towards action) and his reservations about the breaking event function as the antagonist (tendency towards rest). The agonist is stronger and manifests its force tendency in the nano-resultant (towards action). The nano-resultant in turn acts as the antagonist on the macro-level (i.e. the macro-resultant). In the sentence in (13), the macro-configuration is the same as in (12), evidenced by the fact that the event took place very much the same way. The main difference is that *John* performed the action but this was not concordant with his will. This can be captured by assuming a different nano-configuration: John's will is again the agonist, but has a tendency towards rest. The antagonist is some pressure on *John* to break the *window*. This 'pressure' can be a contextually relevant individual ordering John to perform the action, but it could also be John's clumsiness that overrides his will. The nano-resultant is the same as in (12), manifesting itself in the very same way in the macro-configuration. Despite a different nano-configuration, the same macro-configuration comes about. Holisky' principle will set the nano-configuration to the one in (12) by default. By adding extra information, it can be altered.

(13) John broke the window, but he didn't really want to.

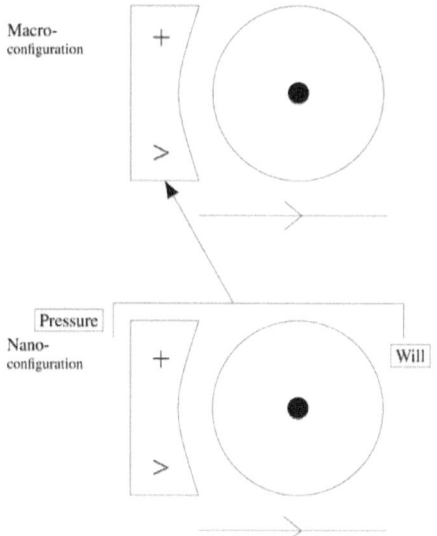

The behavior of causees can be captured in much the same way. I will illustrate this with English causative auxiliaries. These are given in (14) through (16). In the b- and c-versions, I have added elements aimed at fleshing out their causees' volition. The d-versions contain a subclause to illustrate that there is no counterfactuality: The event described actually took place. In English, *make* and *have* are implicatively causal, meaning that the event necessarily took place (Van Valin 2005: 42). *Let*, on the other hand, is not implicative. That is to say, the result could have taken place, but this is not necessary. This is shown in (15d–15e). To avoid unnecessary complication, I will use the implicative reading of *let* for the present discussion.

(14) a. *John made Bill run.*
      b. *John made Bill run against his will.*
      c. **John made Bill run and he willingly did.*
      d. **John made Bill run, but Bill didn't run.*

5 Instruments and causation: A Force Dynamic view

(15) a. John let Bill run.
      b. *John let Bill run against his [Bill's] will.
      c. John let Bill run and he willingly did.
      d. John let Bill run, but Bill didn't run.
      e. John let Bill run and he ran.

(16) a. John had Bill run.
      b. John had Bill run against his will.
      c. John had Bill run and he willingly did.
      d. *John had Bill run, but Bill didn't run.

(17) John made Bill run.

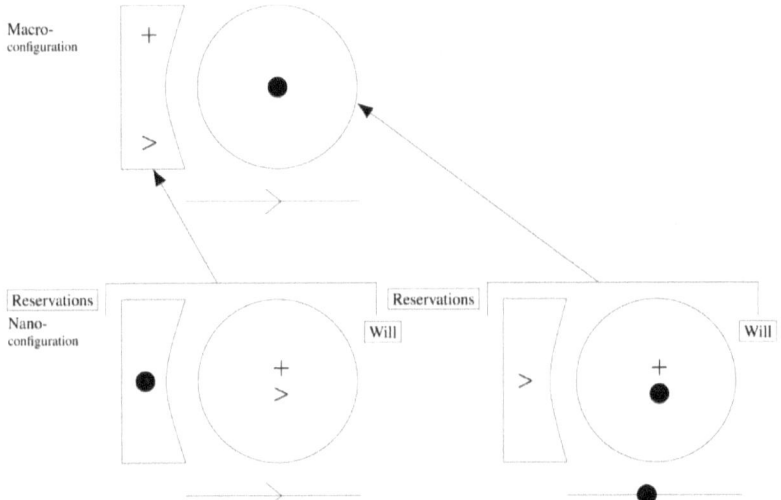

In (17), similar mechanics are at work as with the example in (12): On the macro-level, *John* is the antagonist (with a tendency towards action) and *Bill* is the agonist (with a tendency towards rest). As the antagonist is stronger, its tendency prevails and the result is action, in this case a running event. On the nano-level, there is a configuration for each of the participants as both are human. *John*'s configuration is the same as in (12). Bill's configuration, on the other hand, looks somewhat different: Bill's will is the agonist with a tendency towards rest. The antagonist can be his reservations concerning his own inaction, for example. As the agonist is stronger, the result is rest, which translates to an agonist with a tendency towards rest on the macro-level. In the end, this tendency is overcome by a stronger macro-antagonist.

(18) John let Bill run.

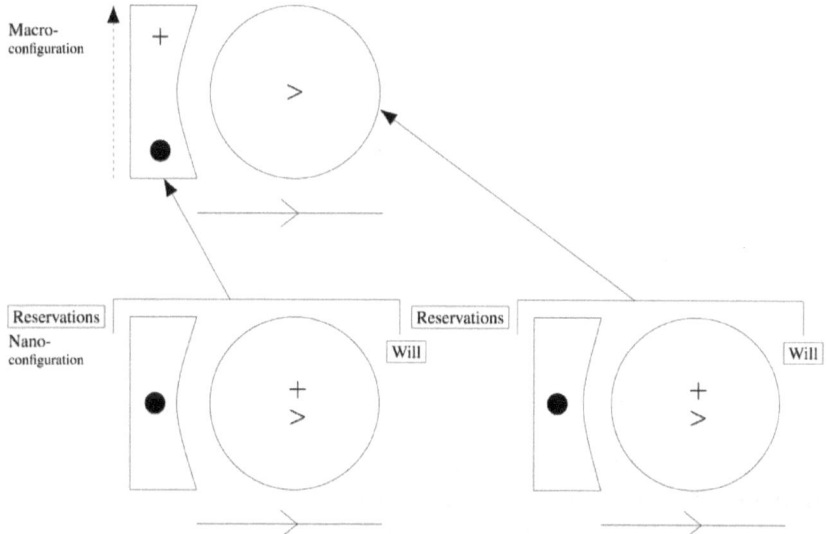

In (18) the situation is the reverse: *Bill*'s nano-configuration is one where his will (the nano-agonist with a tendency towards action) overcomes a weaker nano-antagonist (again, the referent's reservations or psychological pressure), leading to a resultant in action. The nano-resultant translates to a macro-agonist with a tendency towards action. *John*'s nano-configuration equally has an action-resultant: *John*'s will is an agonist towards motion and the antagonist *is John*'s reservations. As the agonist is stronger, the resultant is towards action which translates to a macro-antagonist. Here, however, we find a different macro-pattern: *let* expresses the cessation of impingement. The antagonist originally had a tendency towards inaction, blocking the realization of *Bill*'s macro-force tendency. *John*'s nano-resultant (action) thus translates to the removal of a blockage (i.e. the cessation of impingement). This is represented with a dashed, upward arrow (to the left of the macro-antagonist in (18)).

5 Instruments and causation: A Force Dynamic view

(19) John had Bill run.

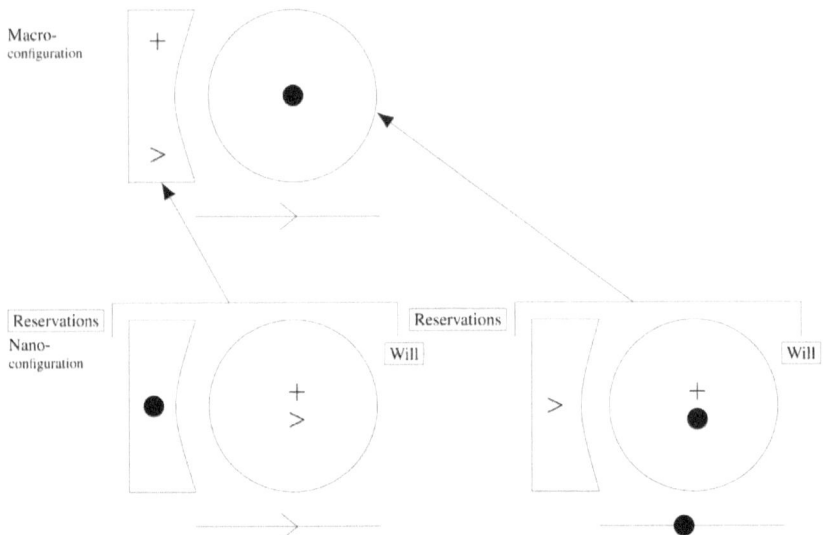

The pattern in (19) allows for a complex configuration, or rather, a set of configurations. On the macro-level, the same basic causative pattern occurs: Bill is an agonist in rest, and the stronger macro-antagonist (*John*) impinges on Bill, leading to a resultant in action. If *Bill* is acting non-volitionally in (19) – as in the *make*-construction – the matching nano-pattern is the same. However, if the causee is acting volitionally, a different nano-pattern exists. It cannot be the same nano-pattern as in the *let*-construction, because the force dynamic configuration is fundamentally different: In the *let*-construction, a blockage is removed allowing the agonist to realize its force tendency. From a conceptual point of view, the nature of volition is also different with *let* and *had*: *had* expresses an agonist that is acting counter its tendency. If the agonist were realizing its force tendency toward action, then there would be no need for coercion on the part of the antagonist. In other words, if *Bill* were genuinely acting volitionally, there would be no need for John to urge him into doing so. This is fundamentally different from *let* where a removal of pressure enables *Bill* to pursue what he really wants to do. *Bill*'s 'volition' in *had* could better be characterized as the absence of

5.1 Fundamentals of Force Dynamics

unwillingness: *Bill* is not against the action described by the verb, but without intervention by *John*, he would not perform the action. By way of illustration, imagine the following scenario: *Bill* would like to go for a run, but cannot bring himself to doing that, because of job-related pressure (e.g. grading exams). *John* (Bill's boss) urges *Bill* to go for a run. In other words, *John* overrides *Bill*'s nano-antagonist, allowing *Bill*'s nano-agonist to realize its tendency. The difference with true volition is that in a case of true volition, the participant's nano-agonist is strong enough to manifest itself directly. In the case of *pseudo-volition*, the causee's will can only manifest itself through the agent's intervention. Therefore, as far as the second FD-configuration is concerned, the nano-agonist has a tendency towards action, but the nano-antagonist is stronger and thus the resultant is towards rest. The nano-resultant has the same value as in the non-volitional reading. The volitional nano-configuration for the causee is given in (20).

(20)

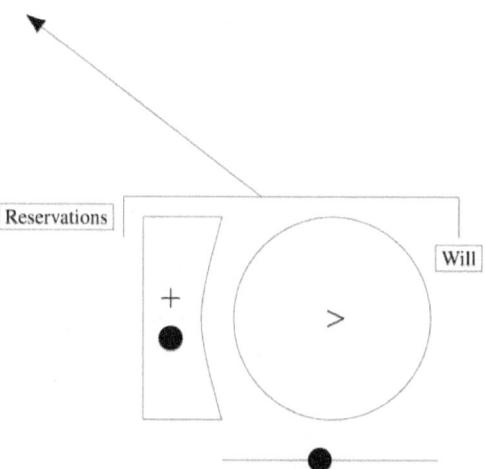

The precise nano-configuration and, thus, the precise reading are determined by Holisky's principle: In absence of information to the contrary, the pseudo-volitional reading is selected. Languages have multiple

215

marking possibilities to mark causees differentially, thereby conditioning pragmatic and semantic differences. This will be explored further in chapter 8. Certain languages have marking on the causee to disambiguate the type of causation or supply information regarding the causee's volition (see section 5.3.2).

Summarizing, the same macro-pattern is shared by all three causative auxiliary constructions: An entity in rest is impinged upon, leading to an action macro-resultant. The *had*-construction is special in that it allows for two readings of the causee: It may be volitionally acting or non-volitionally acting. The *make*-construction only allows for one nano-configuration (non-volitional) whereas the *let*-construction only allows for the other (volition). The main difference between the *make*- and *have*-constructions is the strength of causation. This is an element that is not given a lot of prominence in Talmy's account. There is no means to indicate degrees of 'stronger antagonist'. In section 5.3, I will propose to enrich causation in the logical structures by introducing the concept of strength of causation.

In the previous sections, I have shown that Force Dynamics is a powerful explanatory tool. I have proposed a distinction between three levels of configurations: 1) The nano-level, 2) the micro-level and 3) the macro-level. The first two levels do not contribute to linguistic causation, but are levels of representation that can be relevant for notions like volition, intention and fine-grained semantic or pragmatic interpretation. The macro-level is a level that is primarily relevant to account for the causal relations that affect instrument and causees. These three levels are defined over levels in the logical structure: The macro-level concerns configurations *across* subevents, the micro-level concerns configurations *within* subevents, and the nano-level concerns configurations within the *fillers* of argument-positions. I have also shown that through force dynamic configurations, a principled difference between volition and pseudo-volition arises.

5.2 Implements as facilitating instruments

In this chapter, I have presented an analysis of causality with respect to instruments by integrating FD with RRG's logical structures. However, implements are not causally embedded. Nevertheless, I argue in favor of analyzing implements with FD as well. At present, implements are characterized by the **use'** (x, y) predicate preceded by a connective (∧). I believe RRG's conception of implements could stand to gain a lot by making the nature of this connective more explicit. In RRG's current conception, the connective simply means *and simultaneously*. There is no compelling reason why the use-predicate should be in any way conceptually linked with the first subevent. It could in effect be describing completely unrelated actions (Sebastian Löbner, p.c.): There is no clear reason why (21a) could not link back to (21b).

(21) a. *Abdul ate cereal and he used a pencil.*
   b. **do'** (Abdul, [**eat'** (Abdul, cereal) ∧ **use'** (Abdul, pencil)])

I believe it is therefore crucial to explore the nature of the relation that implements bear to the rest of the event. To do this, I will use my modified FD-proposal including micro- and macro-configurations. Assigning a specific FD-configuration to implements provides a strong cognitive basis for treating them as fundamentally distinct from the causally embedded instrument relation.

5.2.1 *Helping* as weaker causality

In a large-scale study on the micro-semantics of English verb classes, Koenig et al. (2008) argue in favor of a weaker causal relation called *helping* between certain participants in the sentence.

From a force dynamic perspective, *helping* (Wolff 2014: 108) is a very specific force configuration where one participant has a tendency towards the end-state and the other participant has the same tendency. This essentially means that a given event is made easier or *facilitated* by the occurrence of another: Due to the presence of the second event, the first event is made easier to perform on the part of the author of the

5 Instruments and causation: A Force Dynamic view

event. As I have illustrated in previous sections, Force Dynamics allows for the composing of the resultants of configurations into larger configurations. That is to say, a resultant of configuration 1 can be the agonist (or antagonist) of configuration 2. How does this relate to RRG-style implements and the **use′** predicate? Consider a prototypical instance of a sentence with an implement:

(22) *John ate soup with a spoon.*

Rather than assuming that there is a causal chain, there is a very specific FD-configuration: *helping*. With my distinction between levels of FD-configurations, it is possible analyze the two subevents separately on the micro-level.

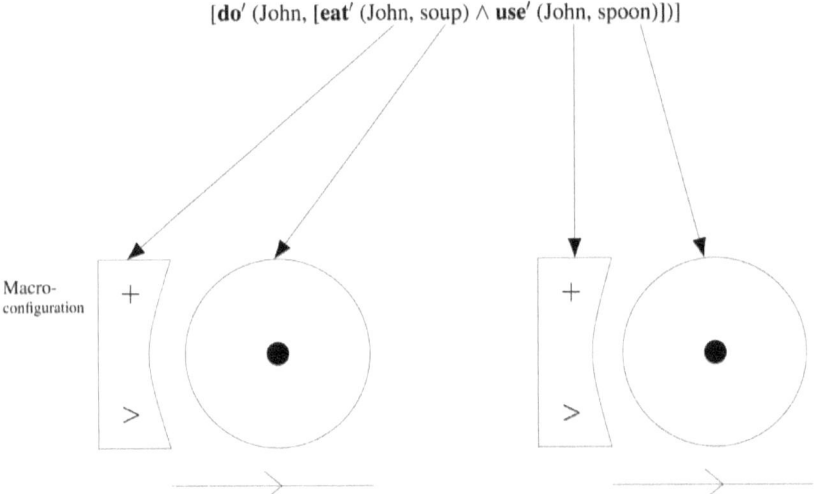

Figure 46: Micro-FD configurations for an implement construction.

The two force dynamic configurations above are, by themselves not the helping configuration. They both describe similar events: An antagonist (*John* in both) impinges on a weaker agonist with a tendency towards rest (*soup* and *spoon*, respectively). The result is an agonist in action. Recall that this does not constitute causation in a linguistic sense. A *helping* relation is essentially a configuration where the agonist has a tendency and the antagonist has the same tendency (Wolff 2014: 108). Following Koenig, helping is essentially making a certain effect or event easier, not causing it. In terms of logical structures, the subevent that the use-predicate describes makes the other subevent easier. This stands to reason conceptually: Eating soup is easier with a spoon than without one. This can be captured naturally with FD-configurations. The whole first micro-configuration functions as a stronger agonist with a tendency towards action on the macro-level. The whole second micro-configuration functions as the macro-antagonist that equally has a tendency towards action. The tendencies of the two macro-participants do not oppose each other, rather they compound each other, making the resultant tendency stronger.[8] This configuration constitutes a typical helping relation inforce dynamic terms. The entire configuration for (22) is given in figure 47. This FD-configuration shows the interaction between the two subevents in a principled way. The occurrence of the connective does not mean that there is no interaction between the two subevents. Rather, the simultaneous occurrence of the second subevent with the first facilitates the occurrence of the first subevent. The connective may not show this, but the FD-based decomposition of the sequence ∧ **use**´ does.

---

[8] The increased tendency in the macro-resultant is not indicated graphically as it is implied by the rest of the macro-configuration.

5 Instruments and causation: A Force Dynamic view

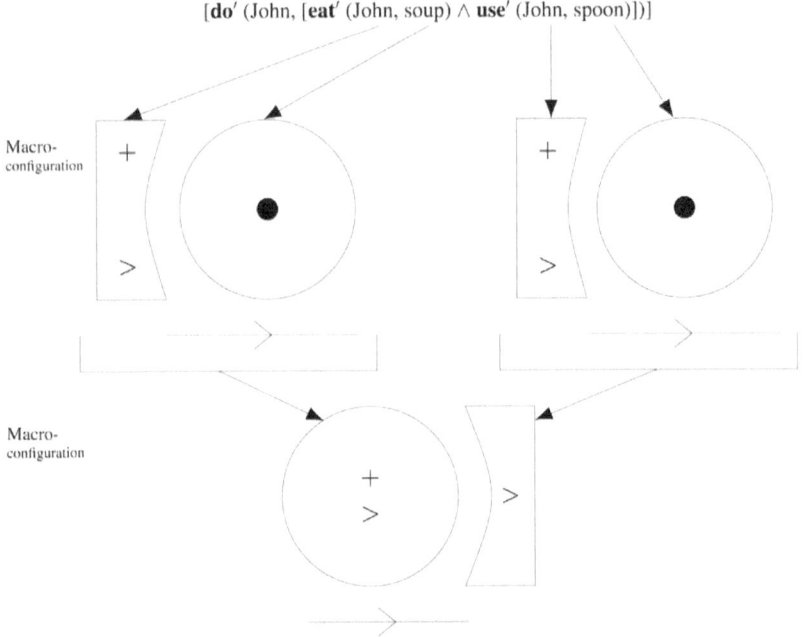

Figure 47: Micro- and macro-configurations
for an implement construction.

5.2.2 Identifying implements and instruments: a new diagnostic

In chapter 3, I argued against ISA as the motivation for the instrument-implement distinction. If ISA is no longer an adequate tool to distinguish implements from instruments, then a new way of detecting them is required.

In previous chapters, I have tacitly been using a paraphrase to identify instruments. As instruments are defined over causal embedding, any paraphrase should 1) make the logical structure explicit and 2) should also correctly identify instruments that would be ranked as implements when ISA is used as a diagnostic. I propose the diagnostic in (23).

(23) X acted on Y, causing it to V.

5.2 Implements as facilitating instruments

This diagnostic is aimed at making the logical structure as explicit as possible. If the test fails, then the tool is an implement and not an instrument. This is illustrated by the examples below:

(24) a. *Mary cut the cake with the knife.*
      b. *Mary acted on the knife, causing it to cut the cake.*
      c. *The knife acted on the cake, causing it to become cut.*
      d. [**do´** (Mary, Ø)] CAUSE [[**do´** (knife, Ø)] CAUSE [BECOME **cut´** (cake)]]

It is important to provide validation for each causal operator in the chain. The test in (24b) validates the first operator in (24d) and the test in (24c) validates the second causal operator. The paraphrase test fails in (25b), showing that there cannot be a causal operator. The failure of (25b) and (25c) means that (25d) is incorrect as the LS of (25a). The correct LS is given in (25e).

(25) a. *Mary ate soup with a spoon.*
      b. **Mary acted on the spoon, causing it to eat soup.*
      c. **The spoon acted on soup, causing it to become consumed.*
      d. *[**do´** (Mary, Ø)] CAUSE [[**do´** (spoon, Ø)] CAUSE [BECOME **consumed´** (soup)]]
      e. **do´** (Mary, [**eat´** (Mary, soup) ∧ **use´** (Mary, spoon)])

The paraphrase in (23) can identify instrument positively and implements negatively. Is there a test that identifies implements positively and instruments negatively? In sentences containing causation, there is a relation between – at least – two entities (or events) or between an entity and an event (Talmy 2000: 476–477). This relation must, at the very least, be one of entity A affecting entity (or event) B. If A and B are unrelated, then there is no causation. Consider (adapted from Talmy 2000: 476–477):

(26) a. *Joan emptied the tank.*
      b. *Joan read a book and the tank emptied.*
      c. *Joan pulled the plug and the tank emptied.*
      d. *Joan emptied the tank by pulling the plug.*

5 *Instruments and causation: A Force Dynamic view*

In (26c), entity A (Joan) performs an action which is directly related to the event where the tank (entity B) loses its contents. Therefore, it is truth-conditionally equivalent to (26a) and (26d) but not to (26b).

Talmy points out that an alteration of B's characteristics constitutes a facilitating relation. This relation cannot be paraphrased with usual causative forms, but rather with verbs like *help*. As I explained in the previous section, the macro-agonist's tendency (figure 47) is compounded and reinforced. With such reinforcement, the agonist's identity is not altered but its characteristics are: The eating event takes place as it would without the 'helper', but its characteristics are altered in that the mode of eating is changed (and more efficient). Consider the following supposed paraphrases of (26a) that Talmy (2000: 477) proposes, in a slightly adapted form:

(27) a. **Joan emptied the tank by enlarging the hole.*
b. *Joan helped the tank empty by enlarging the hole.*
c. **Joan caused the tank to empty by enlarging the hole.*
d. *?Joan made the tank become empty by enlarging the hole.*

In (27b), Talmy argues that the characteristics of B are changed, but not the identity. The formulations in the other sentences are expressions of causation, i.e. they change the identity of B. The activity of enlarging an already existing hole only changes characteristics (i.e. size) but not the identity (i.e. the hole already exists). Therefore, the expressions of a characteristics' change in (27a), (27c) and (27d) are incompatible with (26a) as it expresses an identity change. Notice that the examples become acceptable when they are paired with an expression of change in identity rather than with the expression of a change in characteristics:

(28) a. *Joan emptied the tank by pulling the plug.*
b. *Joan caused the tank to empty by pulling the plug.*
c. *Joan made the tank become empty by pulling the plug.*

In (29), two different potential test-formats using *help* are given.

(29) a. *Using a knife helped Mary to cut a cake.*   Instrument
b. *Using a spoon helped Abdul eat the soup.*   Implement

5.2 Implements as facilitating instruments

c. The knife helped Mary to cut the cake.   Instrument
d. The spoon helped Abdul eat the soup.   Implement

These formats are problematic, however, as both instruments and implements would pass. A test aimed at positively identifying implements must target the change in characteristics rather than using the verb *help*. Recall that my treatment of implements assumes that the other subevent is made *easier* and that this constitutes a change in characteristics. The causal paraphrase tests for a specific relation that is decomposed in terms of an FD-configuration. By way of parallel, an implement-test should test for the most salient feature of the *helping*-configuration. However, adding the sequence *made easier by using* does not produce any significant results because, again, both instruments and implements pass. Consider:

(30)   a.   Mary cut the cake with the knife.   Instrument
       b.   Mary's activity of cutting the cake was made easier by using the knife.
       c.   Abdul ate soup with a spoon.   Implement
       d.   Abdul's activity of eating the soup was made easier by using a spoon.
       e.   Joan watched the birds with binoculars.   Implement
       f.   Joan's activity of watching birds was made easier by using the binoculars.
       g.   Ragnar broke the window with a rock.   Instrument
       h.   Ragnar's activity of breaking the window was made easier by using the rock.

I assume that the examples in (30) are not useable for a similar reason that the *help*-test does not work: The micro-semantics of the verb or construction used in the test are wider than the semantics one wishes to aim for, which means that instruments and implements cannot be distinguished. I propose two formats for positively identifying implements. One follows the same logic of making the LS explicit. In this case, the nature of the connective is made explicit by adding α *[and simultaneously]* β. The second test is the use of the verb *facilitate*. Contrary to the verb *help* or the sequence *made easier by*, the results are acceptable when applied to a sentence containing an implement but are very odd when applied to sentences containing an instrument. These are given in (31).

(31) a. *Mary cut the cake with the knife.* Instrument
 b. *??Mary cut the cake and simultaneously used the knife.*
 c. *??The knife facilitated the cutting of the cake.*
 d. *Abdul ate soup with a spoon.* Implement
 e. *Abdul ate the soup and simultaneously used the spoon.*
 f. *The spoon facilitated the eating of the soup.*
 g. *Joan watched the birds with binoculars.* Implement
 h. *Joan watched the birds and simultaneously used the binoculars.*
 i. *The binoculars facilitated the bird watching.*
 j. *Ragnar broke the window with a rock.* Instrument
 k. *??Ragnar broke the window and simultaneously used the rock.*
 i. *??The rock facilitated the breaking of the window.*

The tests produce very strange results for the examples containing instruments for two reasons: The first test separates the use of the instrument from the main subevent. As the use of the instrument is a precondition for the result state to come about (expressed by the embedding in a causal chain), separating the instrument subevent from the other(s) yields very strange results. Sentences containing implements are perfectly acceptable because the second subevent is not a precondition for the main subevent to occur. The second test uses a very specific verb whose semantics are much closer to the semantics of the helping-relation than those of the verb *help*. In other words, both tests make the force dynamic logic behind the $\alpha \wedge$ **use'** relation explicit. The schematic format for the first test is given in (32a) and that of the second is given in (32b). Depending on the language, the format of these tests might have to be adapted somewhat. For instance, the verb *facilitate* might not have a direct equivalent in every language.

(32) a. X V-ed and simultaneously used Y.
 b. Y facilitated the V-ing.

If a tool passes the causal paraphrase but not the two implement tests, then it is an instrument. If it passes the two implement tests but not the causal paraphrase, it is an implement. A summary of these tests is given in table 19.

	Instrument (CAUSE **do´** (x, Ø))	Implement (∧ **use´** (x, y))
Causal paraphrase	Yes	No
and simultaneous-ly-test	No	Yes
Facilitate-test	No	Yes

Table 19: Summary of diagnostics for instruments and implements.

5.3 A proposal for enriched causation

In the previous sections of this chapter, I have argued for the direct relevance of different configurations with respect to instruments, implements, causees and the like.

In standard RRG, causation is represented with the single causal operator CAUSE. However, the causal component in the logical structures is still very much an oversimplification, as Van Valin (2005: 42) points out himself. Drawing on insights from the study of instruments and intermediate effectors, this section is intended as a first proposal for expanding the notion of causation in the logical structures.

Van Valin (2005: 42) recognizes three types of causation: *direct* (or coercive), *indirect* (or non-coercive) and *permissive* causation. Despite this, RRG largely only uses a single causal operator in the logical structures.[9] Consider the examples in (33).

---

[9] The three subtypes are not used productively in the RRG-literature.

(33) a. *Eric made Bill call a taxi.* (Direct causation)
     b. *Eric had Bill call a taxi.* (Indirect causation)
     c. *Eric let Bill call a taxi.* (Permissive causation)

The first two types are amalgamated into CAUSE and the letter is to be represented by LET. However, in practice, all three are reduced to the single CAUSE-operator. Up to now, it was tacitly assumed that the different types of causation bore little relevance to the linking of semantics to syntax. In the following section, I will explore my conception of direct and indirect causation, as they are different from standard RRG.[10] This proposal entails neutralizing causative relations to arrive at four generalized causative relations (or GCRs). I argue that Talmy's notion of impingement is central to causation and to the approach I am proposing here.

5.3.1 Relevant dimensions for neutralization

I propose a model for GCRs based on the nature of the *interaction* between the agonist and antagonist. I contend that the interaction of the antagonist and the agonist can be defined in terms of two features: [±impingement] and [±direct]. [±direct] refers to the type of interaction: [+direct] is any type of physical interaction between agonist and antagonist, whereas [-direct] is any other type. These two features yield a matrix with four cells, each one corresponding to one of the GCRs. Note that I define [±direct] different from similar concepts in other approaches. Kemmer and Verhagen (1994: 121–122), for instance, define indirect causation as causation where an 'intermediary transmitter' is present. Direct causation, by contrast, is defined as causation that holds between two participants directly. Van Valin (2005: 42) roughly equates direct causation with a coercive form of causation. In my proposal [±direct] refers to the strength of the interaction. I treat prototypical direct causation as a case where direct physical manipulation (*full-contact impingement*) is present between the agonist and the antagonist. Typical instances of full-contact impingement are instrument constructions: An

---

[10] In the relevant literature, there is an abundance of differing definitions of *direct* and *indirect* causation (see Martin & Schäfer 2014: 241ff.).

instigator directly physically handles the instrument to arrive at a certain result. Most causees, on the other hand, will only be 'handled' non-physically. In a sentence like *John had Mary cut the cake*, the default reading will be one where Mary acts volitionally (see section 5.1.5). The most likely interpretation of this sentence is one where John asked Mary to perform the action. This is similar to Van Valin's conception of non-coercive causation. However, direct causation in my proposal is primarily connected to instruments. This does not mean that I treat examples like *John made Mary cut the cake* as indirect. In this case, it is not a request but a command or some form of coercion. There is no direct physical manipulation in this case, yet the type of causation is also direct. I propose to treat such cases as *semi-contact impingement*. I assume that the full-contact type of impingement is cognitively the more basic of the two. Semi-contact impingement is conceptually derived from the former through the process of metaphoric extension, the same process that allows for the inclusion of non-physical agonists and antagonists in FD-configurations. Consider the example in (34).

(34) a. *The soldier made John enter his password at gunpoint.*
b. *John broke the window by pushing Todd into it.*

In (34b), an animate is directly physically manipulated: *John* pushes *Todd* into the window, thereby breaking it. In (34a), the *soldier* does not use *John* as a tool to type in a password. Rather, there is a very high degree of coercion (expressed by *at gunpoint*) that conceptually lowers the causee's autonomy to that of *Todd* in (34b) or to that of a typical instrument. This process is part of the metaphorical extension from full-contact impingement to semi-contact impingement. Therefore, both sentences in (34) contain [+direct] impingement and are cases of direct causation.

The feature [±impingement] is fairly straightforward. [±impingement] refers to the standard concept of impingement in Force Dynamics as it was presented in the previous sections: Impingement is the coming in contact of an antagonist with an agonist. This feature is a neutralization as well: [+impingement] thus refers to any situation where an antagonist and an agonist are in a state of impingement, be it of the onset-type or the extended type. Consider (35).

5 Instruments and causation: A Force Dynamic view

(35) a. *The doctor cured the patient with the drug.*
b. *The lumberjack cut down the tree with a chainsaw.*

In (35a), the *doctor* cures the *patient* by administering a *drug*. As the doctor only physically manipulates the *drug* in the beginning phase of the event, this sentence illustrates the onset-type. By contrast, in (35b), the *lumberjack* physically handles the *chainsaw* throughout the event. (35b) is an example of the extended impingement type. In chapter 3, I argued against Kamp & Rossdeutscher's (1994) and Alexiadou & Schäfer's (2006) idea that the distinction between onset causation and continuous causation is relevant for the discussion of instruments. I have therefore lumped these two concepts together under [+impingement]. The value [-impingement] is slightly different. [-impingement] is primarily defined by the cessation of impingement. Consider:

(36) a. *John let the pen fall.*
b. *Sarah allowed her daughter to go to the movies.*

In (36), stronger antagonists (*John* and *Sarah*) cease impinging on the agonist (*pen* and *her daughter*), allowing the latter to realize their force tendencies. The main difference between (36a) and (36b) is the directness of impingement: (36a) is an expression of [+direct] and (36b) expresses [-direct]. The *pen* has the innate tendency to fall as it is pulled on by gravity[11] John holds the pen, thereby physically manipulating it. The impingement ceases and the pen is allowed to manifest its force tendency. In (36b), there is psycho-mental impingement between Sarah and her daughter. This impingement also ceases, allowing her daughter to realize her tendency.

With respect to [-impingement], there is an added difficulty. The extended form of [-impingement] is that which Talmy calls 'extended letting': The antagonist could impinge, but does not do so at any point. This raises the question of whether extended [-impingement] can really

---

[11] Copley & Harley (2014: 132) call the collection of all innate tendencies of all objects and entities the *normal field*. The pen's tendency to fall due to gravity is an example of a force tendency belonging to the normal field.

5.3 A proposal for enriched causation

be considered a type of causation. It is possible to interpret (37a) and (37b) as cases of extended letting. Consider:

(37) a. *John saw the pen roll towards the edge of the table but he just let it fall.*
 b. *Even though Sarah had her reservations about it, she didn't say a word and let her daughter go to the movies.*

In both examples in (37), the antagonist stays away during the entire event, despite their potential for successful impingement. Answering this question, however, is beyond the scope of this dissertation as I am primarily concerned with direct and indirect causation. I have summarized the features and their underlying neutralizations in figure 48.[12]

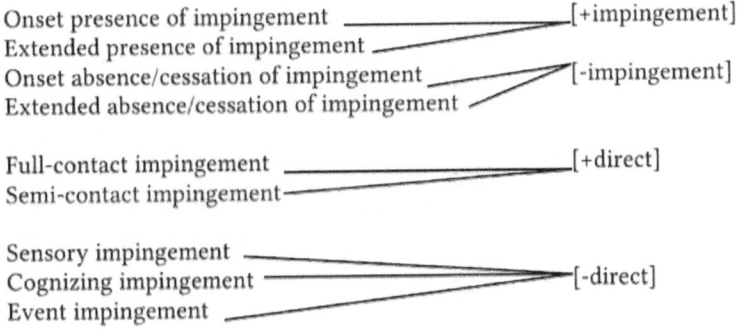

Figure 48: Feature neutralizations.

For clarification purposes, I will briefly elaborate on the other features in the figure. *Sensory impingement* refers to the antagonist being sensory input. For example: If a driver sees a car accident which prompts them to stop and help, then the impingement is of a sensory nature, rather than a direct physical one. The same applies to *cognizing impingement* where it is reasoning or communication that causes a participant to act. Examples include someone being talked into doing something. *Event impingement*

---

[12] I do not claim to present an exhaustive list of the base relations.

5 Instruments and causation: A Force Dynamic view

refers to a whole event as antagonist. For example, *the military assault* in *the military assault made him take a different road.*

The matrix below summarizes the four proposed types of causation that are relevant for linking (proposed LS-operators for each respective type are given between brackets):

	[+direct]	[-direct]
[+impingement]	Direct (CAUSE)	Indirect (IND)
[-impingement]	Enabling (LET)	Permissive (ALLOW)

Table 20: Matrix of proposed types of causation and their operators.

Direct and indirect causation have the same FD-patterns, the main difference being strength. The same is true for enabling and permissive causation. I propose to add an exclamation mark to mark strength/directness.[13] Direct and enabling causation are set apart from indirect and permissive causation, respectively, by the use of the exclamation mark. The difference in directness is also a difference in strength.

The patterns with direct interaction will be indicated by an exclamation mark marking the antagonist. The FD-configurations for the four causal relations are given in figure 49 below.

---

[13] As strength is the scalar dimension underlying all four relations, [±direct] can also be considered as differences in strength (see figure 51 below).

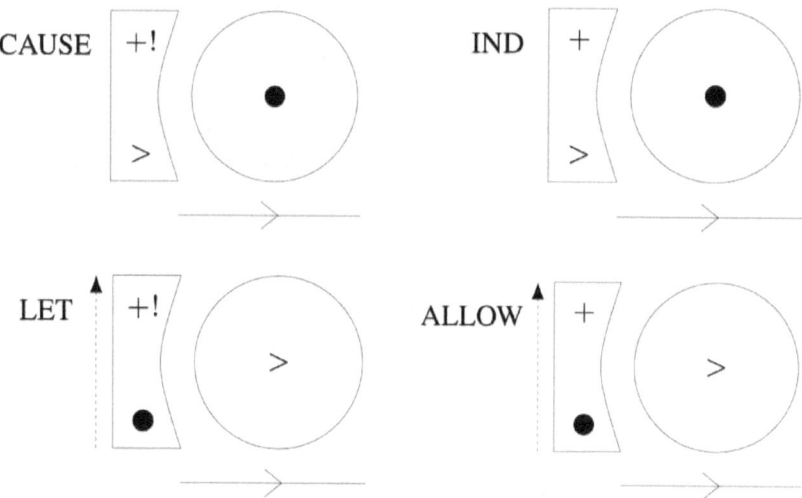

Figure 49: Force dynamic configurations underlying the four principle causal operators.

5.3.2 Neutralization of causation

As I showed in chapter 3, RRG treats thematic relations as neutralizations of lower-level verb-specific relations. In turn, thematic relations are neutralized into generalized semantic roles (GSRs) called macroroles. It is this level that is relevant for linking purposes. I propose to treat causation in very much the same way. Talmy (2000: 472–475) presents a list with about a dozen different causative relations, each with a separate deep verb. Internal ordering is motivated by differences is foregrounding,
continuity and the like. Although Talmy provides a principled account of derivations from the deep structure to a surface structure, I do not follow his approach for two reasons: 1) A derivational account is fundamentally incompatible with the framework used in this dissertation and 2) I do not consider such an overly differentiated view of causation to be a plausible basis for linking to morphosyntax. However, I do agree with Talmy that each of the causative relations in the list is important for interpretative purposes in the same way that thematic relations are also interpretationally important. For example, the distinction between plain human

5 Instruments and causation: A Force Dynamic view

effector and agent is relevant for the interpretation of the sentence uttered. I argue that this is also true for causation: The neutralized level of causation, akin to the macrorole level, is important for linking, whereas lower-level causative distinctions can be relevant for the precise interpretation of the content.

What Talmy labels *autonomous event* is not recognized here as causation. In the sense of phyiscs, there very well might be causation at play, but this is not linguistically relevant. Even though Talmy stresses the distinction between the physical conception of the world and the human-mental conception of the world several times, he (2000: 472) remarkably enough recognizes autonomous events as a subtype of causation. Including autonomous events as causative opens up the door for'implicit causation' or similar concepts under which almost everything could be accounted for as causative (to some extent). I do not recognize autonomous events as causative as far as language is concerned, because they fail standard causative tests:

(38)   a.   *The ice melted.*
        b.   **Ø caused the ice to melt.*
        c.   **Ø is the cause of the ice's melting.*
        d.   **The ice melted because of Ø.*

The lack of a second argument blocks any possibility of semantic causation. The necessity for a second argument was also pointed out in chapter 2. All subtypes of causation that do not pass these tests have been omitted. I have also left out the causative types motivated by a differing number of elements in the causal chain. In RRG, a causal chain is simply a series of causative operators, whatever their nature. In this view, the interpretation of the number of elements in a causal chain is a property of the whole chain, not just of a single operator.

The figure below is a proposal for *causative neutralization* based on Talmy's (2000: 472–475) subtypes of causation. The subtypes proposed by Talmy can be neutralized to one of the four causative relations I proposed in the previous section. The proposal is by no means exhaustive and is to be seen as a starting point for the concept of *general causative relations*. The base and intermediate causative relations could and should

5.3 A proposal for enriched causation

be investigated further and expanded considerably. This is a topic for future research in its own right. As the lowest-level causal relations are conceptual in nature, this list could grow quite substantially.

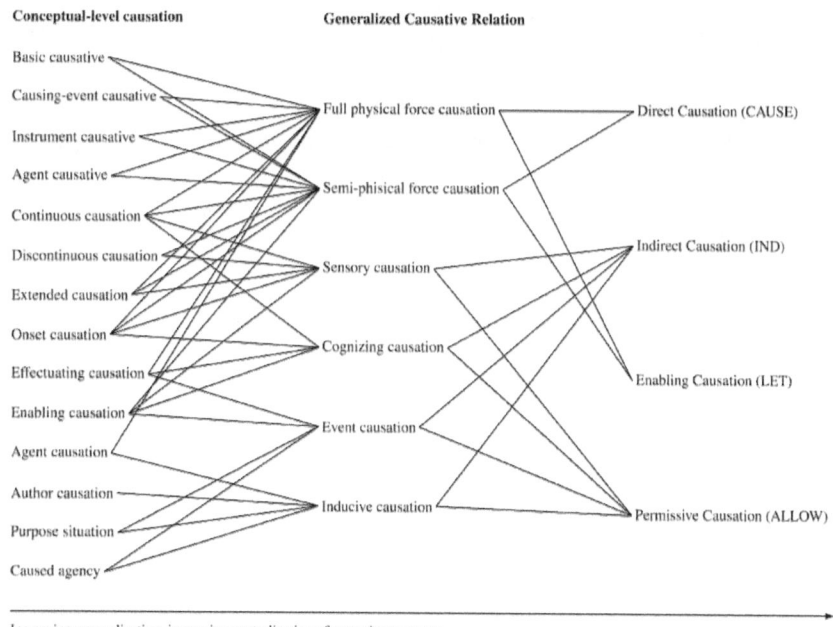

Figure 50: Neutralization of conceptual causation to generalized causative relations.

I also propose to rank the four causal operators on a scale according to strength: The strength of interaction cross-cuts the dimensions of [±impingement] and [±direct]. I assume that [±impingement] is the more important feature and I rank it higher than [±direct]. Direct manipulation is more coercive than indirect. *Ordering* someone to perform an activity is more direct than *asking* someone to do something. It will also require greater strength (either literally or metaphorically): One can only order someone if there is a solidified power differential. That is, the antagonist has to be inherently more powerful than the agonist. Enabling and permissive causation are judged to be weaker than direct and indirect causation, because in these two types impingement ceases.

5 Instruments and causation: A Force Dynamic view

Internally, the former two types are distinguished from each other over the same logic of strength. Enabling causation involves direct interaction, whereas permissive causation involves indirect interaction. The first value for each operator is impingement, the second is directness. I have summarized the four generalized causative relations in figure 51. It also includes *helping*-causation as it was introduced in section 5.2. I treat *helping*-causation as a weak form of causation (cf. Koenig et al. 2008) and distinguish it from *strong* forms of causation (the four GCR types explored in this chapter).

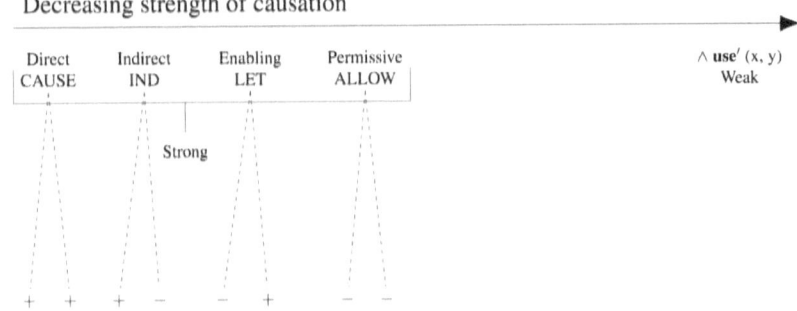

Figure 51: Causal operators ordered according to strength of causation.

On a final note, languages do not always unambiguously mark the type of causation in a given context (also see chapter 7).[14] In fact, there can be a high degree of uncertainty, which mainly concerns the strength-principle (even on a micro-level). Consider:

(39) a. *Bill had Eric make him some coffee.*
      b. *The supervisor had his employee make him some coffee.*
      c. *The general had the sergeant clean the toilet.*

In (39b), the semantic content of the agonist and the antagonist makes clear that this is rather a type of weak order (as opposed to *made* which

---

[14] According to Wolff (2014: 107), people are often uncertain about the magnitude of forces (in my approach: strength of causation), which has consequences for how causality is described and represented.

expresses direct coercion). (39a), by contrast, is quite unclear. It has two obvious but different interpretations: 1) the same as in (39b) or 2) a request between equals (e.g. friends).

English has three causative auxiliaries: *make, have* and *let*. The first expresses direct causation, the second expresses indirect causation and the third expresses both enabling and permissive causation. Dutch, by contrast, has only two auxiliaries: *doen* expresses direct causation and *laten* expresses everything else. German has an even more restricted set; it only has *lassen*. Despite the fact that the English auxiliaries typically express a type of causation, there can be some overlap or unclarity owing to context. For example, in (39c), the semantic content of the referents would suggest a direct order on the part of the antagonist, making this direct causation. Yet, the indirect auxiliary is chosen. If the antagonist is inherently more powerful or more authoritative than the agonist, the precise nature of the causation (*direct* vs. *indirect*) is often a grey area. Some languages (but not English) use differential causee-marking, for various purposes. One such purpose is to disambiguate that which I have called the strength of causation. Consider Dutch, for example.

(40) a. *Thomas liet   Charlotte de   brief lezen.*
Thomas let\PST.3SG Charlotte DEF letter read.INF
'Thomas let Charlotte read the letter.'
b. *Thomas liet   de   brief door Charlotte lezen.*
Thomas let\PST.3SG DEF letter PREP Charlotte read.INF
'Thomas let read the letter by Charlotte.'
c. *Thomas liet   de   brief aan Charlotte lezen.*
Thomas let\PST.3SG DEF letter PREP Charlotte read.INF
'Thomas let read the letter to Charlotte.'
d. *Thomas deed   Charlotte de   brief lezen.*
Thomas do\PST.3SG Charlotte DEF letter read.INF
'Thomas made Charlotte read the letter.'

5 Instruments and causation: A Force Dynamic view

e. *Thomas deed   Charlotte de   brief lezen
Thomas do\PST.3SG Charlotte DEF letter read.INF
en ze deed   dat met plezier.
and she do\PST.3SG that with pleasure
'Thomas made Charlotte read the letter and she did so willingly.'

f. ?Thomas liet   de   brief door Charlotte lezen
Thomas let\PST.3SG DEF letter by   Charlotte read.INF
en ze deed   dat met plezier.
and she do\PST.3SG that with pleasure
'Thomas had Charlotte read the letter and she did so willingly.'

The auxiliary in (40a) expresses indirect and permissive/enabling causation.[15] As was the case in the FD-analysis containing a causee that can be read as volitional and non-volitional, (40a)'s causee is ambiguous with respect to Charlotte's volition. Adding the preposition *aan* in (40c) triggers a strongly volitional reading, making the type of causation permissive/enabling. By adding door in (40b), the volitional reading of Charlotte is made less strong (but not canceled), setting the reading to that of indirect causation. Even though it is a stronger form of causation than without the marking, it is still weaker than if doen is used (40d–40f).[16]

These examples illustrate that volition correlates with the strength of causation: Direct causation is incompatible with a volitional causee. Therefore, more inanimates will be found under the scope of direct causation than animates. The weaker the causation is, the more acceptable a volitional causee becomes and vice versa. For example, Verhagen & Kemmer (1997: 65, 71) show that, in case of an animate causer, 79% of causees under the scope of *doen* are inanimate (where volition is hardly relevant) and 21% are animate. With *laten*, there is a higher degree of animate causees (49%) than with *doen*. I will explore causee-marking further in chapter 8. Kemmer & Verhagen (1994: 122) furthermore report

---

[15] In Dutch, just like in English, no morphological distinction is made between permissive and enabling causation.
[16] This disambiguation strategy is only open to a subset of Dutch verbs (Verhagen & Kemmer 1997: 77).

that (in English) a decrease in the causee's autonomy correlates with more direct forms of causation (i.e. *make*-construction). This ties in with my actionality scale-approach proposed in chapter 4: The higher a referent is located on the actionality scale, the more likely it will be under the scope of non-direct forms of causation (IND, LET, ALLOW) and vice versa.

5.3.3 Enriched causation in the logical structures

I recognize the fact that the placeholder nature of CAUSE can have advantages in the scientific study of language. Nonetheless, I propose to include the four causal operators in RRG's inventory. By way of illustration, some examples are given in (41). The examples in (41g–41h) and (41i–41j) are a case of enabling and permissive causation, as made clear by the information given in the brackets. Bear in mind that languages usually do not directly distinguish between enabling and permissive causation, even though a cognitive difference exists.

(41) a. *Todd broke the console with a rock.*
 b. **[do′** (Todd, Ø)] CAUSE [[**do′** (rock, Ø)] CAUSE [BECOME **broken′** (console)]]
 c. *Jean a fait couper le pain à Marie.*
 Jean AUX.3SG make.PTCP cut DEF bread to Marie
 'Jean made Marie cut the bread.'
 d. **[do′** (Jean, Ø)] CAUSE [[**do′** (Marie, Ø)] CAUSE [BECOME **cut′** (bread)]]
 e. *Jean a fait couper le pain par Marie.*
 Jean AUX.3SG make.PTCP cut DEF bread by Marie
 'Jean had Marie cut the bread.'
 f. **[do′** (Jean, Ø)] IND [[**do′** (Marie, Ø)] CAUSE [BECOME **cut′** (pain)]]
 g. *Todd heef-t John lat-en lop-en.*
 Todd AUX-3SG John let-INF run-INF
 'Todd let John run.' (by releasing him from his grip)
 h. **[do′** (Todd, Ø)] LET [**do′** (John, [**run′** (John)])]

i. *Todd heef-t   John lat-en   lop-en.*
   Todd AUX-3SG John let-INF run-INF
   'Todd let John run.' (by giving him permission to do so)
j. [**do´** (Todd, Ø)] ALLOW [**do´** (John, [**run´** (John)])]

In many cases, the precise nature of causation will be underspecified. For instance, the French nuclear *faire*-construction can express both direct and indirect causation. The difference is signaled by the marking of the causee (*à* for direct, *par* for indirect causation). Rather than assuming there are two *faires* in the lexicon with a different LS, it is preferable to assume an underspecified causal operator. To represent this underspecification in the LS, I propose to use italicized *CAUSE*. In Van Valin & LaPolla (1997: 121), italicized *CAUSE* represents the main cause in a causal chain. However, this practice was discontinued in subsequent work. I therefore propose to reintroduce it, albeit with a different meaning. In the examples above in (41), the causal operators were not kept underspecified, which they, strictly speaking, should be. In (41), I used the very specific operators for illustration purposes only.

5.4 Conclusion

In this chapter, I have explored the causative semantics of instruments and implements. Furthermore, I have proposed a merger of FD with RRG's logical structures. In the introduction, a philosophical distinction between the two frameworks was mentioned: RRG treats causation as events acting on events, whereas FD assumes participants act on participants. Even though this constitutes a deeper philosophical issue that surpasses the goals of this dissertation, my approach attempts to bridge the gap between these points of view: On the micro-level, participants act on participants (within one subevent). As such, it does not constitute linguistic causation. On the macro-level, participants act on participants *across* subevents. In other words, a participant acts on another participant, but it is embedded in a proper subevent rather than being a participant in isolation (as is the case on the micro-level). My approach does not exclude events acting on events in their entirety.

6 The Instrument-Subject Alternation and subtypes of instruments

In this chapter, I explore ISA in more detail. In particular, I argue that ISA and several similar phenomena are best treated as constructions. Goldberg (2003: 222) points out that a wide array of semi-idiomatic expressions exists in every language and that they can be accounted for in terms of constructions, that is, as schematized form-meaning pairings (cf. Goldberg 2003: 219). Constructions are also recognized by RRG as a means to capture the language-specific properties of languages while still referring to general principles (Van Valin 2005: 132). One reason to capture ISA in terms of constructions is that there is a great deal of cross-linguistic variation with respect to ISA. For instance, English and Portuguese seem to be very productive, whereas Dutch is very restrictive. German, on the other hand, primarily allows for it with a very specific reading. I will also make a claim in favor of a new naturalness condition as a means to govern contextual factors. Furthermore, there are a number of expressions that superficially resemble ISA, yet show various morphosyntactic differences. I agree with Goldberg (1995: 8) that different constructions are associated with (slight) differences in meaning.

6.1 Delineating instruments in subject position from other inanimates in subject position

I claim that there is a fundamental distinction between cases of ISA and cases where other inanimates occupy the subject position. In the latter

6 The Instrument-Subject Alternation and subtypes of instruments

case, inanimates such as forces occupy the highest argument position in the LS. By the very nature of instrument constructions (i.e. causal embedding), intransitive predicates can never feature an instrument as their only argument. Inanimates as the only argument of an intransitive predication (e.g. *Snow* in *The snow melted*) are of no concern to the current study. In other words, only transitive predications with an inanimate subject are relevant and many of those are force-effectors. In chapter 4 (table 16), several tests were proposed to distinguish these from instruments in subject position. Only those transitive predictions where the inanimate cannot conceivably be a force are relevant. Consider:

(1)   a.   *The bomb destroyed the car.*
       b.   *The grenade killed the civilian.*
       c.   *The terrorists destroyed the car with the bomb.*
       d.   *The soldier killed the civilian with the grenade.*

In (1a–1b), *bomb* and *grenade* can be considered instruments undergoing ISA, as the corresponding sentences in (1c–1d) are plausible correlates. If a plausible instigator is not readily available, it can become difficult to distinguish (2a) from (2b):

(2)   a.   [**do´** (terrorists, Ø)] CAUSE [[**do´** (bomb, Ø)] CAUSE [BECOME **destroyed´** (car)]]
      b.   [**do´** (bomb, Ø)] CAUSE [BECOME **destroyed´** (car)]
      c.   *The bomb went off by itself and destroyed the car.*
      d.   **The bomb destroyed the car with its shrapnel.*

In (2b), the *bomb* is interpreted as having gone off by itself as is illustrated by the acceptability of (2c). The example in (2c) shows that *bomb* can be the highest-ranking x-argument. However, it cannot be a force or a pseudo-agent because it cannot take an instrument itself ((2d)). The question is then, whether there is a plausible instigator or not. If not, then LSs like the one in (2b) have to be assumed. If yes, then typical ISA-LSs have to be assumed (see section 6.2). The plausibility of the instigator will be explored further in section 6.3.

6.2 Mechanics & purpose

ISA involves a process (*metonymic clipping*, Van Valin & Wilkins 1996: 301) whereby the initial effector is left unspecified. As a consequence of leaving the instigator unspecified, it can no longer receive the actor macrorole. Instead, it is assigned to the highest available effector, the instrument. This is illustrated in (3b) and (3c).

(3) a. *Jack cut the bread with a knife.*
 b. [**do´** (Jack, Ø)] CAUSE [[**do´** (knife, Ø)] CAUSE [BECOME
      A   NMR
   cut´ (bread)]]
      U
 c. [**do´** (Ø, Ø)] CAUSE [[**do´** (knife, Ø)] CAUSE [BECOME **cut´**
   (bread)]]   A
      U

Provided ISA is possible in the language under investigation, why do languages use this construction? In this matter, I believe Schlesinger's (1989: 191) naturalness condition 2 should be reanalyzed as the *driver* of the construction called ISA. The condition is repeated in (4).

(4) **Naturalness Condition 2**: To the extent that attention is drawn to the instrument by means of which an action is performed and away from the instigator of the action, the former will be naturally expressed as the sentence subject.

Naturalness condition 2 does not capture *when* ISA is natural but rather *why* speakers would choose to express an instrument as a subject. In the examples in (1a–1b) focus is put on the instrument by leaving out the instigator. This is quite similar to the motivation behind the passive: By assigning PSA-hood to the undergoer-argument, it becomes more topical as PSAs are the topic by default. Contrary to actor selection, undergoer selection can be variable and this is RRG's strategy to capture phenomena like dative shift. In a sentence like *Pat gave Chris the gift* the undergoer is assigned to the argument that is neither highest nor lowest on the AUH. In other words, variable undergoer selection allows for the modulation of topicality. There is evidence in favor of the more topical of two potential undergoers being chosen as undergoer in case of variable undergoer selection (Van Valin & LaPolla 1997: 423). As actor selection is not variable, it cannot be modulated for pragmatic effect. Phenomena like ISA are therefore not unexpected: By leaving the highest-ranking argument unspecified, the actor role is assigned by default to the highest specified argument. In turn, this argument is selected as the PSA (in an active sentence), making the instrument the topic. Rather than treating (4) as a condition for ISA to take place, I treat it as a reason for ISA to take place. I propose to label it as the 'Instrument-effector as Actor-construction' as the notion of subject is not directly relevant in RRG (see chapter 2). A preliminary constructional schema for ISA is given in table 21.

Construction: English Instrument as Actor-construction	
Syntax:	template: default (see principle in (2.13))
	PSA: Standard rules for accusative systems
Morphology:	PSA: no explicit morphology
	Verb agreement: Default
Semantics:	(1) x-argument of initial **do'** is unspecified
	(2) Actor-macrorole is assigned to highest specified x-argument of **do'**
	(3) highest specified x-argument of **do'** must have minimum actional status as defined by argument position
Pragmatics:	Instrument-effector is default topic

Table 21: Constructional schema for the *instrument-subject alternation* (preliminary).[1]

In chapter 4, it was also established that the acceptability of an instrument-effector bearing the actor macrorole is dependent on its referent's position on the actionality scale: The referent must rank above a certain

---

[1] *Standard rules for accusative systems* in the schema is a reference to the principles governing PSA-assignment in accusative constructions (Van Valin 2005: 100): The highest ranking direct core argument in terms of the PSA-selection hierarchy becomes the PSA. I have adopted this notation here for the sake of simplicity.

cut-off point relative to the predicate's requirements before ISA is possible. This is represented in the section *semantics* as point (3). I will revisit this in section 6.4.

6.3 A new *naturalness condition* as a prerequisite for ISA

In chapter 3, I pointed out that ISA is a construction that seems to be constrained by the requirement of an event link. All subevents described by the sentence have to be in a meaningful relation to each other. That is to say, before ISA can be applied, all components of the event represented in the 'unshifted' sentence must be immediately causally linked. I propose to capture this with a condition relating to the subevents in the logical structure:

(5) **Natural Event Condition**: A complex event E is a natural event iff subevent E_1 immediately causes (or can immediately cause) subevent E_3 if subevent E_2 were removed from the structure of the matrix event E.

Why is such a condition needed? As the instigator position in an ISA-construction is not lexically filled but contextually supplied, it becomes necessary to decide what can and what cannot be a realistic instigator. If there is no realistic instigator (from a linguistic point of view), then there is no ISA. Rather, the participant under investigation actually occupies the initial position in an LS, whatever its nature might be.[2] Without any principled limits on what can count as an instigator, it is possible to argue for increasingly outlandish candidates for instigatorhood. For example, it has been claimed that *grenade* is an instrument manipulated by the implicit instigator *gravity* in (6a). The intended situation is one where due to gravity's effects, a grenade rolls off of a shelf and explodes. Intuitively, gravity cannot be held responsible for the destruction of the shed here. Without

---

[2] That is to say, that LS can be very different from any assumed instrument-LS.

6   *The Instrument-Subject Alternation and subtypes of instruments*

the natural event condition, there is no way to rule out such a claim, however. I propose the natural event condition to fulfill precisely this role: It rules out *gravity* as the instigator. Even though the supposed underlying logical structure seems admissible ((6b)), it does not hold up to scrutiny. Linking the LS to syntax, as in (6c), results in a very peculiar sentence. The reason for this is given in (6d). Here, E_2 is removed from the LS and the resulting structure is linked to syntax ((6e)) with a non-sensical result. By contrast, positing *terrorists* as an instigator is acceptable ((6f–6i)).

(6)   a.   *The grenade destroyed the shed.*
       b.   [**do´** (gravity, Ø)] CAUSE [[**do´** (grenade, Ø)] CAUSE
             E_1 E_2
           [INGR **destroyed´**(shed)]]
           E_3
       c.   **Gravity destroyed the shed with the grenade.*
       d.   [**do´** (gravity, Ø)] CAUSE [INGR **destroyed´** (shed)]
            E_1 E_3
       e.   **Gravity destroyed the shed.*
       f.   [**do´** (terrorists, Ø)] CAUSE [[**do´** (grenade, Ø)] CAUSE
            E_1 E_2
           [INGR **destroyed´** (shed)]]
           E_3
       g.   *The terrorists destroyed the shed with the grenade.*
       h.   [**do´** (terrorists, Ø)] CAUSE [INGR **destroyed´** (shed)]
            E_1 E_3
       i.   *The terrorists destroyed the shed.*

These examples show that the natural event condition can distinguish an acceptable instigator from a non-acceptable one. This seems straightforward, but it can also account for less clear examples where there is no (linguistically) plausible instigator at all. Consider the example in (7). Despite the oddity of the sentence in (7a), its corresponding structure in (7b) seems well-formed. Removing E₂ reveals that is not acceptable. The structure in (7c) would inevitably link into the somewhat strange sentence[3] in (7d).

(7) a. *The WW II-soldier killed the modern-day civilian with the landmine.
  b. [**do'** (WW II-soldier, Ø)] CAUSE [[**do'** (landmine, Ø)] CAUSE [BECOME **dead'** (modern-day civilian)]]
  c. [**do'** (WW II-soldier, Ø)] CAUSE [BECOME **dead'** (modern-day civilian)]
  d. *The WW II-soldier killed the modern-day civilian.
  e. *The WW II-soldier killed the civilian in 2015.

It would be possible to claim that a WW II-soldier who is still alive today can provide an adequate, though unlikely, context for the sentences in (7d) and (7e). The qualification *WW II-soldier* to denote the former soldier in this unlikely scenario is strange as it is hardly relevant for the description of the killing event. In this respect, replacing *WW II-soldier* with *WW II-landmine* does yield an acceptable sentence as the landmine does not cease to be one over time (and its origins are irrevocably WW II), whereas the soldier did cease to be a WW II-soldier by the time WW II ended. This is especially important linguistically, as sentences where an immediate event-link is absent are highly marked. One cannot simply apply transitive reasoning: The WWII-soldier planted the landmine and the landmine killed the civilian in 2015. According to typical transitive reasoning, the WW II-soldier caused the civilian's death. Yet, despite the straightforwardness of transitive logic, sentences like the one in (7e) are still marked or even ungrammatical. Language seems to require the existence of a

---

[3] Representing information like *modern-day* as adverbial information of the type *in 2015* would place it in the logical structures as well. Adverbial information is usually not represented in the LS for reasons of economy and clarity. The consequences of removing E₂ would have the same effect though: The result would be a very similar, odd sentence ((7e)). Therefore, I will keep the compounds in (7) to make this point clear.

plausible, immediate link between all subevents for the sentence to be acceptable. This point can be made clearer by pulling the subevents even further apart temporally.

(8) a. *The bomb destroyed the house in 2015.*
     b. *John destroyed the house in 2015 with a bomb.*
     c. **The Austro-Hungarian general destroyed the house in 2015 with the bomb.*
     d. **The Austro-Hungarian general destroyed the house in 2015.*
     e. *The bomb went off and destroyed the house because it had degraded too much.*
     f. **The degradation process destroyed the house with the bomb.*

The examples in (8c–8d) illustrate that it is not plausible to posit a general of state that ceased to exist almost a century ago as the instigator of the destruction event in 2015, even though this person would be the instigator under transitive reasoning. A contemporary individual (*John*) is admissible, as is no instigator at all ((8e)). Positing the degradation process as instigator is not possible linguistically speaking ((8f)). If there is no realistic instigator, there cannot be a corresponding unfilled slot in the LS.

To refute ever more outrageous and potentially infinitely regressing claims regarding an 'implicit' effector, it is crucial to put a limit on context. The natural event condition provides a principled way to do this: Remove E_2 from the proposed sentence's LS and apply the linking algorithm. RRG (Van Valin 2005: 59) considers the section of logical structure that is associated with the instrument position as an expansion of a more basic LS. If a sentence with an instrument is posited, then it stands to reason that removing the instrument section (i.e. E_2) must result in a base LS that links into an acceptable sentence. It is now possible to draw up a complete constructional schema for ISA. It is given in table 22.

Construction: English Instrument as Actor-construction	
Syntax:	Template: default
	PSA: Standard rules for accusative systems
Morphology:	PSA: no explicit morphology
	Verb agreement: Default
Semantics:	(1) x-argument of initial **do´** is unspecified
	(2) Actor-macrorole is assigned to highest specified x-argument of **do´**
	(3) highest specified x-argument of **do´** must have minimum actional status as defined by the argument position
Pragmatics:	(1) Instrument-effector is default topic
	(2) Natural Event Condition must be met

Table 22: Constructional schema for the *instrument-subject alternation* (complete).

6.4 Actionality constraint

In chapter 4 I proposed that ISA is only possible if the position of the instrument on the actionality scale is high enough relative to the predicate's requirements. More specifically, I have claimed that the instrument-referent has to occupy a position that is within the instigator's accessible semantic space. The crucial axis here is autonomy: The instrument's autonomy value must crucially be within the range specified for the instigator. This can be handled in structural terms: In chapter 4 I introduced a system for translating the actionality scale into a type of annotation. I propose to formalize my 'positional' claim in terms of the actionality constraint (AC) which constrains the occurrences of ISA. Without such a constraint, every instrument would be able to undergo ISA due to its causally embedded nature.

6 The Instrument-Subject Alternation and subtypes of instruments

(9) **Actionality Constraint**: Save for other restrictions, an instrument effector can undergo the Instrument-Subject Alternation iff its y-value on the actionality scale falls within the instigator's y-value range as determined by the predicate.

I will illustrate this constraint with the simple examples in (10). Consider:

(10) a. *Jack cut down the tree with the axe.*
b. [**do´** (Jack, Ø)] CAUSE [[**do´** (axe, Ø)] CAUSE [BECOME **cut down´** (tree)]]   Jack: (8, 7) axe: (4, 2) tree: (3, 1)
c. [**do´** (x, Ø)] CAUSE [[**do´** (y, Ø)] CAUSE [BECOME **cut down´**(z)]] x-position: (7↑, 3↑) y-position: (4, 2) ↔ (4↑, 7) z-position: (Ø, Ø)
→ Y-value of instrument-effector is not within instigator's potential range: AC not satisfied, ISA not possible.
d. **The axe cut down the tree.*
e. *Jack cut down the tree with the chainsaw.*
f. [**do´** (Jack, Ø)] CAUSE [[**do´** (chainsaw, Ø)] CAUSE [BECOME **cut down´** (tree)]] Jack: (8, 7) chainsaw: (4, 3) tree: (3, 1)
g. [**do´** (x, Ø)] CAUSE [[**do´** (y, Ø)] CAUSE [BECOME **cut down´** (z)]] x-position: (7↑, 3↑) y-position (4, 2) ↔ (4↑, 7) z-position: (Ø, Ø)
→ Y-value of instrument-effector is within instigator's potential range: AC satisfied, ISA possible.
h. *The chainsaw cut down the tree.*

The numbers in the examples in (10) may not intuitively convey the actionality differences. Bear in mind, however, that the difference between autonomy level 2 and level 3 marks the difference between non-autonomous entities (e.g. *axe*) and semi-autonomous entities (e.g. *chainsaw*). Despite the fact that the numbers might suggest otherwise, the conceptual difference is quite profound.

I roughly determined the minimum/maximum values for each position by testing: I filled the argument positions with referents from all ranges of the actionality scale. The results are given in the bare LSs in (10c) and (10g). Should further selectional restrictions be imposed by the language (e.g. shape of a referent), then these are captured with qualia annotations rather than with actionality values. The AC is intended to be universal, but it follows language-specific preferences. For instance, in Icelandic and Lithuanian, *chainsaw* is not high enough on the autonomy scale. In other words, the minimum requirements the Icelandic predicate imposes on its instigator position are higher. Consider:

(11) a. *Keðjusög-in   fell-d-i   tré-ð.
        chainsaw-DEF.NOM.SG fell-PST-3SG tree-DEF.ACC.SG
        'The chainsaw cut down the tree.' (Icelandic)
    b. *Pjūklas nupjov-ė   medį.
        chainsaw cut-PST.3SG tree.ACC.SG
        'The chainsaw cut down the tree.' (Lithuanian)

6.5 Ability readings vs. ISA

In chapter 3, it was briefly pointed out that some apparent instances of ISA are actually primarily interpreted as utterances conveying a meaning of the tool possessing a certain ability. Informants of some languages confirm that there is a strong preference for this kind of interpretation over an ISA-interpretation. Consider the German examples in (12):

(12) a. *Das Messer schneid-et   (das) Brot.*
        DEF knife   cut-PRS.3SG (DEF) bread
        'The knife cuts the bread.'
    b. *Der Schlüssel öffn-et   die Tür.*
        DEF key   open-PRS.3SG DEF door
        'The key opens the door.'
    c. *Das Tuch mach-t   den Tisch sauber.*
        DEF rag make-PRS.3SG DEF table clean
        'The rag cleans the table.'

The sentences in (12a–12c) are preferentially interpreted as their tools having the ability to cut something, to open something and to clean something. Typical ISA-readings are dispreferred, although this is also a matter of gradation: (12a) and (12b) are more acceptable with an ISA-reading than

(12c), whose ISA-reading was unanimously rejected by informants. Whereas German generally prefers ability-readings to ISA-readings, in some languages it depends on the kind of referent. Consider the examples from Serbian in (13).

(13) a. *Nož je sekao hleb.
  knife AUX.3SG cut.PTCP bread.ACC
  'The knife cut the bread.'
 b. Deterdžent je uklonio masne fleke
  detergent AUX.3SG remove.PTCP.M fat.ACC stain.ACC
  u rerni.
  in oven.LOC
  'The detergent removed the fat stain from the oven.'

The example in (13a) is not grammatical, save for personifications (see section 4.1.5). The example in (13b) is ungrammatical with an ISA-interpretation, but is acceptable with an ablity-reading (in the present tense). It seems that Serbian puts limitations on the ability-reading: *Detergent* ranks higher than *knife* on the autonomy hierarchy. Serbian thus seems to allow ability-readings only if the referent is considered to be acting autonomously.

Even though ISA and ability-readings are superficially difficult to distinguish, the latter are subject to certain restrictions. These utterances convey very general information about a very specific referent: They express that a specific referent can do something specific. It is therefore more natural for them to appear in the present tense, similar to other, general statements. In (14), the statements are odd because they contradict the supposed general nature of the referent. The more information is added that distorts the general nature of the referent, the less acceptable the statement becomes.

(14) a. *Das Messer schneid-et das Brot.*
  DEF knife cut-PRS.3SG DEF bread (Present)
  'The knife cuts/can cut the bread.'
 b. ?*Das Messer schnitt das Brot.*
  DEF knife cut\PST.3SG DEF bread (Past)

c. ??*Das Messer schnitt das Brot gestern.*
   DEF knife cut\PST.3SG DEF bread yesterday
   (Past+*yesterday*)
d. ???*Das Messer hat das*
   DEF knife AUX.3SG DEF
   Brot gestern ge-schnitt\-en.
   bread yesterday PTCP-cut\-PTCP
   (Perfect+*yesterday*)
e. *Der Schlüssel öffn-et die Tür.*
   DEF key open-PRS.3SG DEF door (Present)
   'The key opens/can open the door.'
f. ?*Der Schlüssel öffne-te die Tür.*
   DEF key open-PST.3SG DEF door (Past)
   'The key opened/could open the door.'
g. ??*Der Schlüssel öffne-te die Tür gestern.*
   DEF key open-PST.3SG DEF door yesterday
   'The key opened the door yesterday.' (Past+*yesterday*)
h. ???*Der Schlüssel hat gestern die Tür*
   DEF key AUX.3SG yesterday DEF door
   ge-öffn-et.
   PTCP-open-PTCP (Perfect+*yesterday*)
i. ?*Der Schlüssel öffn-et für gewöhnlich*
   DEF key open-PRS.3SG usually
   die Tür, heute aber nicht.
   DEF door, today but not
   'The key usually opens the door, but not today.'
j. The key opened the door today, but failed to do so yesterday.

The example in (14i) is contradictory: It implies that the key usually has the ability to unlock the door, but does not possess this ability today. The English equivalent in (14j) is perfectly acceptable with an ISA-reading. The key opened the door, but could not do so yesterday (because, for instance, the lock was blocked by another object).

An ability reading can be isolated by supplying extra information: The utterances become more acceptable if 1) demonstratives singling out a

6 The Instrument-Subject Alternation and subtypes of instruments

specific referent are used, 2) if they are compared to another referent ((15b)) in terms of ability to do something and 3) when certain ability adverbs are used ((15i)). Applying contrastive stress to the demonstrative makes the examples even more acceptable (15c–15d). Furthermore, (15a-15b) can be paraphrased as (15e–15f) or (15g–15h), which uncontroversially express ability.

(15) a. *Dieses   Messer schneid-et   das Brot.*
           DEM.PROX knife cut-PRS.3SG DEF bread
           'This knife cuts the bread.'
    b. *Dieses   Messer schneid-et   das Brot,*
           DEM.PROX knife cut-PRS.3SG DEF bread
           das andere jedoch   nicht.
           DEF other   on the other hand not
           'This knife cuts the bread, the other one does not.'
    c. *DIESES   Messer schneid-et   das Brot.*
           DEM.PROX knife cut-PRS.3SG DEF bread
           'THIS knife cuts the bread.'
    d. *DIESES   Messer schneid-et   das Brot,*
           DEM.PROX knife cut-PRS.3SG DEF bread
           das andere jedoch   nicht.
           DEF other   on the other hand not
           'THIS knife cuts the bread, the other one does not.'
    e. *Dieses   Messer hat   die Fähigkeit*
           DEM.PROX knife   AUX.3SG DEF ability
           das Brot zu schneid-en.
           DEF bread to cut-INF
           'This knife has the ability to cut the bread.'
    f. *Dieses   Messer hat   die Fähigkeit das Brot*
           DEM.PROX knife   AUX.3SG DEF ability   DEF bread
           zu schneid-en, das andere jedoch   nicht.
           to cut-INF   DEF other   on the other hand not
           'This knife has the ability to cut the bread, but the other one does not.'

g. *Dieses   Messer kann   das Brot schneid-en.*
    DEM.PROX knife   can.PRS.3SG DEF bread cut-INF
    'This knife can cut the bread.'
h. *Dieses   Messer kann   das Brot schneid-en,*
    DEM.PROX knife   can.PRS.3SG DEF bread cut-INF
    das andere jedoch   nicht.
    DEF other   on the other hand not
    'This knife can cut the bread, but the other one cannot.'
i. *Das Messer schneid-et   das Brot leicht.*[4]
    DEF knife   cut-PRS.3SG DEF bread easily
    'This knife cuts the bread easily.'

If a demonstrative is added to the undergoer argument, the sentence becomes even more natural, which is also true for the English equivalent in (16b).

(16) a. *Dieser   Schlüssel öffn-et   jene   Tür.*
         DEM.PROX key   open-PRS.3SG DEM.DIST door
     b. *This key opens that door.* (Alexiadou & Schäfer 2006: 44)

This extra information cannot readily be added to ISA-readings. Consider the following examples from English, with the basic sentence in (17a) and the basic ability-reading in (17d). (17b) is an ISA version of (17a) and (17e–17f) are paraphrases of the ability-reading. Adding demonstratives to ISA-sentences is less acceptable as (17c) shows. By contrast, using demonstratives is preferred with ability-readings in English.

(17) a. *John cut the bread with the knife.*
     b. *The knife cut the bread.*
     c. *?This knife cut the bread.*
     d. *This knife cuts the bread.*
     e. *This knife has the ability to cut the bread.*
     f. *This knife can cut the bread.*

---

[4] Interestingly, informants rejected the use of *einfach*, even though it has the same meaning as *leicht*.

6 *The Instrument-Subject Alternation and subtypes of instruments*

If demonstratives are not used, it is not always straightforward to distinguish between an ability reading and ISA. In (18), the sentence can be interpreted as ISA (say, when the situation is being described as it unfolds) or as an ability. A certain degree of ambiguity has to be taken into account.

(18) *The knife cuts the bread.*

As the ability and the ISA reading are fundamentally distinct, I propose two different logical structures for them. The ISA-logical structures were given in section 6.2.

There is some similarity between these ability readings and so-called *middle constructions*, such as the Croatian example in (19). Both ability-readings and middle constructions prefer the present tense (in English and Dutch at least), for example.

(19) *Knjig-a   se   dobro čita-Ø*
      book-F.SG.NOM REFL good read-3SG.PRS
      'The book reads well.' (Van Valin & LaPolla 1997: 416)

Van Valin & LaPolla analyze middle constructions as attributive constructions where the adverb is an obligatory part of the LS. The LS for (19) is given in (20) (after Van Valin & LaPolla 1997: 417).

(20) **be′** ([**do′** (Ø, [**read′** (Ø, knjig-)])], [**good′**])

There are also important differences: Stalmaszczyk (1993: 135) points out that middle constructions require the presence of a modifier such as an adverbial. Such modifiers are absent from ability constructions. Furthermore, middle constructions attribute a property to the logical object of the verb (Stalmaszczyk 1993: 134), as is also apparent from the LS in (20). By contrast, ability readings attribute a property to the instrument rather than to the lowest-ranking argument. From an RRG point of view, positing a manner adverb in the LS for the ability construction would not be admissible, because everything that is specified in the LS must be present in the syntax and vice versa (cf. the Completeness Constraint). As the ability-readings do not have an overt adverb, it is impossible to posit one in the LS. Rather, I propose to capture such constructions with RRG's modal operator *ability*. I therefore propose the LS in (21). Essentially, it is a basic decomposition for *cut*, but with a modal operator added. The more general LS-template is given in (21b).

(21) a. [**do**′ (∅, ∅)] CAUSE <$_{MOD}$*ABIL*<[[**do**′ (knife, ∅)] CAUSE [BECOME **cut**′ (bread)]]>>
 b. [**do**′ (∅, ∅)] CAUSE <$_{MOD}$*ABIL*<[[**do**′ (x, ∅)] CAUSE [BECOME/INGR **pred**′ (y)]]>>

The presence of this modal operator is obligatory and can have an influence on the occurrence of other operators. For instance, event quantification is incompatible with this structure, as (22) illustrates.

(22) **Dieses Messer schneidet das Brot 4 Mal.*
 DEM knife cut.PRS.3SG DEF bread 4 times
 'This knife cuts the bread 4 times.'

It is possible to treat the ability reading as a construction, captured in a constructional schema, specifying the tense the utterance must be in: The facts that demonstratives, present tense and comparisons make these utterances more natural are fairly ad hoc and possibly language-specific facts. RRG's constructional schemas provide an ideal format to represent this. The core component of the semantic side of the schema will be the LS in (21b).

What about language variation with respect to this construction? In Dutch, for example, the German ability constructions in (14a–14h) are ungrammatical ((23a–23b)). To express the same content, a modal auxiliary (*kan*) must be used ((23c–23d)).

(23) a. **Dit mes snijd-t het brood.*
 DEM.PROX knife cut-PRS.3SG DEF bread.
 'This knife cuts the bread.'
 b. **Dit mes snijd-t het brood, maar het*
 DEM.PROX knife cut-PRS.3SG DEF bread but DEF
 andere mes niet.
 other knife not
 'This knife cuts the bread, but other knife does not.'

c. *Dit   mes   kan   het brood snijd-en.*
   DEM.PROX knife can.PRS.3SG DEF bread cut-INF
   'This knife can cut the bread.'
d. *Dit   mes   kan   het brood snijd-en,*
   DEM.PROX knife can.PRS.3SG DEF bread cut-INF
   maar het   andere mes   kan   dat niet.
   but DEF other knife can.PRS.3SG DEM not
   'This knife can cut the bread but the other one cannot.'

In Greek, a demonstrative *must* be used with the instrument to arrive at an ability reading, contrary to German where the use of demonstratives only makes the utterance more acceptable. In Greek, (24b) is strange because it neither conveys the ability reading of (24a), nor is there a real generic reading as the plural would be required (24c).

(24) a. *Afto to macheri kovi   psomi.*
        DEM DET knife   cut.PRS.3SG bread.ACC.
        'This knife cuts bread.'
     b. *?To macheri kovi   psomi.*
        DET knife   cut.PRS.3SG bread.ACC
        'The knife cuts bread.'
     c. *Ta   macheria kovun psomi.*
        DET.PL knife.PL cut.3PL bread.ACC
        'Knives cut bread.'

A reason for languages like German to restrict tools in subject position to an ability reading can be explained with Fauconnier's notion of unexpectedness (2011: 541): As inanimates like *knife* are poor 'agents', their occurrence as subject is unexpected. 'Unexpected subjects' are cross-linguistically restricted. The German-specific restriction seems to be that any such sentence must be interpreted as an ability-reading. The constructional schema for the German ability construction is given in table 23.

Construction: German Ability-construction	
Syntax:	Template: default
	PSA: Standard rules for accusative systems
Morphology:	PSA: NOM
	Verb agreement: Default
	Verb tense: Present
	PSA-Determiner: Demonstrative
Semantics:	(1) *Comment* expresses ability of referent realized as *Topic*.
	(2) Normal actionality requirements for x-initial argument in LS may be overridden.
	(3) *ABIL*-operator obligatory in LS
Pragmatics:	Predicate focus

Table 23: The German ability construction.

6.6 General statements vs. ISA

Somewhat related to the ability reading are generic statements with tools or other inanimates in subject position. Consider:

(25) a. *Guns kill people.*
b. *Capitalism exploits the working class.*
c. *Poverty disrupts society.*
d. *Knives kill people.*
e. *Trucks clog the roads.*

General statements like these express a behavioral property of the x-argument. Following Geurts (1985: 251), I assume that generic statements essentially convey *stereotypes* about the referent in question. *Knives*, for example, cannot only be used to kill but also to cut up food or to craft tools. Similary, *trucks* often cause traffic congestion on highways, but not every occurrence of a truck leads to clogging of the road it is on. Like ISA, such statements are subject to several constraints. For example, they become less acceptable in the past tense.

6 The Instrument-Subject Alternation and subtypes of instruments

(26) a. ?*Guns killed people.*
    b. ?*Capitalism exploited the working class.*
    c. ?*Poverty disrupted society.*
    d. ?*Knives killed people.*
    e. ?*Trucks clogged the roads.*

All of the versions in (26) would only be valid if the referent no longer existed. For instance, (26b) would be perfectly acceptable if capitalism did not exist anymore, as evidenced by (27a). Similarly, (26e) is only acceptable if trucks were a vehicle of the past, as evidenced in (27b).

(27) a. *Feudalism exploited the farming class.*
    b. *Wheelbarrows clogged the roads.*

Krifka (1995: 255) argues in favor of a generic operator *GEN* that is dependent on a modal background to account for generic statements. Genericity and its semantics are highly complex topics and are beyond the scope of this dissertation. Nonetheless, I propose to roughly follow Krifka and introduce *GEN* as an operator in the LS. GEN in my proposal can be characterized as a status operator modifying an LS in the sense that the LS is usually valid for the state of affairs described by that LS. A provisional characterization of GEN, loosely modeled after Krifka's (1995: 255) proposal and the LS of (25b) are given in (28a) and (28b), respectively. ISA is not necessarily incompatible with the GEN-operator, as the example in (28c–28d) illustrates.

(28) a. **GEN**: An LS α, describing a matrix state of affairs β, is considered generic iff $\exists(\beta)$ which consists of states of affairs Xa through Xn and iff more states of affairs of matrix (β) are true than false.
    b. <$_{STA}$*GEN*<[**do**´ (capitalism, [**exploit**´ (capitalism, working class)])]>>
    c. *Keys open doors.*
    d. <$_{STA}$*GEN*<[**do**´ (Ø, Ø)] CAUSE [[**do**´ (keys, Ø)] CAUSE [BECOME **open**´ (doors)]]>>

A very basic constructional schema is given in table 24.

Construction: English General Property construction	
Syntax:	Template: default
	PSA: standard rules for accusative systems
Morphology:	PSA: no explicit morphology
	Verb agreement: default
	Verb tense: present
Semantics:	(1) *Comment* expresses a stereotypical property or feature of referent realized as *Topic*.
	(2) Normal actionality requirements for x-initial argument in LS overridden.
	(3) *GEN*-operator obligatory in LS
Pragmatics:	Predicate focus

Table 24: Constructional schema for English General Property construction.

6.7 Subtypes of instruments

Conceptually, both implements and instruments are used by a wielder to perform an action, as evidenced by the **use'**-predicate that both share in their LS.[5] The instrument-implement distinction constitutes a first split in the class of 'tools'. With the analysis of ISA, it is now possible to distinguish two subtypes of instruments: *free* and *blocked* instruments. This is given in figure 52.

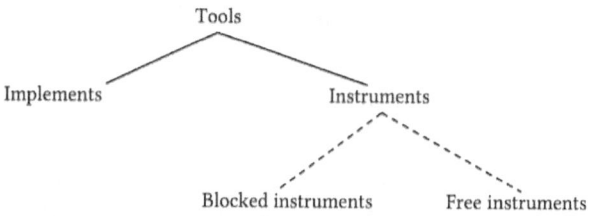

Figure 52: Split between free & blocked instruments and implements.

---

[5] In case of instruments, the predicate is present in the 'full' LS.

6.7.1 Free instruments & blocked instruments

Both free and blocked instruments are instruments: They both occupy the same LS-position. The main difference is that the former can undergo ISA whereas the latter cannot. This distinction is thus clearly of a different magnitude than the one between instruments and implements. The most crucial property of this distinction is that it is relative: What is a free or a blocked instrument depends on 1) the requirements imposed by the predicate on the argument slot fillers and 2) the individual language. Therefore, free and blocked instruments are not considered subtypes of effector. Rather, the distinction is a purely terminological one, which is reflected in the dashed lines in figure 52.

6.7.2 Conjoined instruments & conjoined implements

So far, the examples in this thesis only feature one referent per instrumental phrase. Few in the relevant literature explicitly deal with multiple instruments per phrase. I propose to term instrument RPs that contain multiple referents *conjoined instruments*. This is illustrated in the examples below:

(29) a. *Jack opened the door with the key and the swipe card.*
(adapted from Webb 2008: 19)
b. *John cut the bread with the knife and the box cutter.*
c. *Seymour sliced the salami with a knife and a scalpel.*
(Lakoff 1968: 8)

These instruments seem fairly straightforward. They pass the causal paraphrase both in their conjoined form and when taken individually:

(30) a. *John acted on the knife and the box cutter causing them to cut the bread.*
b. *John acted on the knife causing it to cut the bread.*
c. *John acted on the box cutter causing it to cut the bread.*
d. *John cut the bread with the box cutter and the knife.*

6.7 Subtypes of instruments

Furthermore, the phrase-internal order of the referents can be switched without a change in meaning ((30d)). Conceptually, the referents are performing the causing action independently from each other. The *knife* and the *box cutter* essentially perform the same activity but are not dependent on each other. One can imagine *John* holding the knife in his left hand and the box cutter in his right hand. For these reasons, I consider them to *symmetrically conjoined instruments*. The entry in the logical structure is similar to that of comitatives. The connective symbol expresses that the order of the two referents is essentially irrelevant. The logical structures of (31a) and (31b) are given in (31d) and (31e), respectively.

(31) a. *John cut the bread with the box cutter and the knife.*
 b. *John destroyed the sign with the chainsaw and the machine gun.*
 c. *John destroyed the sign with the machine gun and the chainsaw.*
 d. [**do′** (John, Ø)] CAUSE [[**do′** (box cutter ∧ knife, Ø)] CAUSE [BECOME **cut′** (bread)]]
 e. [**do′** (John, Ø)] CAUSE [[**do′** (chainsaw ∧ machine gun, Ø)] CAUSE [BECOME **destroyed′** (sign)]]

What are the implications for ISA, then? As I have shown, there are referents that are clearly causally embedded (i.e. they pass the causal paraphrase) but still cannot undergo ISA. It was argued that this is due to a language-specific constraint related to the actionality scale. With respect to symmetrically conjoined instruments, ISA with the conjoined phrase is only possible if each referent individually can undergo ISA. Consider, for example, example (32b) with *sword* instead of *machine gun*. The referent *sword* is causally embedded, yet cannot undergo ISA because it is too low on the actionality scale:

(32) a. *John destroyed the sign with the sword.*
 b. *John acted on the sword causing it to destroy the sign.*
 c. **The sword destroyed the sign.*
 d. **The sword and the machine gun destroyed the sign.*

6 The Instrument-Subject Alternation and subtypes of instruments

The ISA-acceptability of conjoined instruments thus depends on the ISA-acceptability of its 'weakest' component.

Instruments can also be conjoined *asymmetrically*. Consider, for instance, the examples (after Schlesinger 1989: 199) in (33).

(33) a. *Jennifer made a hole in the wall with a hammer and a chisel.*
b. *Jeffrey wounded the president with a rifle and two bullets.*
c. **A hammer made a hole in the wall.*
d. *A chisel made a hole in the wall.*
e. *Two bullets wounded the president.*
f. **A rifle wounded the president.*

Similarly to the symmetrically conjoined instruments, there are two instrument-referents in one *with*-PP. Schlesinger argues that ISA can only take place with the latter of the two referents, as (33c–33d) and (33e–33f) illustrate, at least when referring to the situation in the unshifted sentences. Note that if the instrumental phrases only contain the first referent ((34a)), ISA becomes possible (34b)):

(34) a. *Jennifer made a hole in the wall with the hammer.*
b. *The hammer made a hole in the wall.*

There is a straightforward reason why the sentences in (33c) and (33f) are not grammatical. There is a sequential order between the two referents in (33a) and (33b). In the scenario described in (33a), the hammer acts on the chisel which in turn acts on the wall, causing it to be breached. The hammer thus does not directly act on the wall. This is similar in (33b), where the rifle (more accurately, its internal mechanics) acts upon the bullets in the chamber, which in turn act on the referent *president*, causing him to be wounded. This can be captured quite naturally with Croft's causal chains. Consider the partial causal chain for the hammer and chisel example.

6.7 Subtypes of instruments

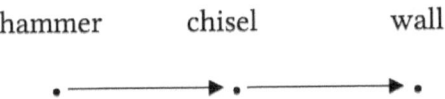

Figure 53: Partial causal chain.

The hammer transfers 'force' to the chisel, which brings about the result state. This ordering is conceptually determined, as world knowledge dictates that a hammer acts on a chisel to breach something, not vice versa. That this ordering is linguistically relevant is also illustrated by the reduced acceptability of the sentence when switching the referents.

(35) a. ?*Jennifer made a hole in the wall with a chisel and a hammer.*
 b. ??*Jennifer made a hole in the wall with chisel and hammer.*

I contend that the information regarding the conceptual interaction between hammer and chisel is reflected in the semantics. In English, this manifests itself in a preferred order of referents. The question remains how to represent this information in RRG. Introducing an extra CAUSE-operator in the logical structure does not adequately capture the nature of conjoined instruments. Consider:

(36) a. *Jennifer acted on the chisel, causing it to make a hole in the wall.*
 b. *Jennifer acted on the hammer, causing it to act on the chisel, causing it to make a hole in the wall.*
 c. *Jennifer made Bill destroy the barn with a cannon.*
 d. *Jennifer acted on Bill, causing him to destroy the barn.*
 e. **Jennifer acted on the cannon, causing it to destroy the barn.*

The example in (36e) is not acceptable because *Jennifer* does not directly act on the *cannon*. Rather, she acts on *Bill* who in turn acts on the *cannon*. In cases such as these, it is felicitous to assume that there is an extra causal sequence (also see chapter 7). This is different for (33a): *Jennifer* acts on both instruments simultaneously and one of the instruments acts on the other. Because *Jennifer* directly manipulates both instruments, including an additional CAUSE-operator is not an option. This is illustrated by the acceptability of (36a–36b). Conjoined instruments also usually occur as one argument, as evidenced by the single occurrence of *with*. Qualia theory is able to capture this information. The formal quale contains information that distinguishes the object in a larger domain. In this case, the typical position as anterior to and used in conjunction with a chisel can be captured. The telic quale stores information pertaining to the function of the object, in this case, the transmission of force from one to the other. An example of such a qualia-based notation for *hammer* and *chisel* is given in (37). Consider (37).

(37) **hammer** (x)
    a. Const: **impact tool′** (x)
    b. Form: **tool′** (x) ∧ **tool′** (y)
    c. Telic: **do′** (x, [**hit′** (x, y)])
    d. Agentive: **artifact′** (x), [**do′** (a, ∅)] CAUSE [[**do′** (x ∧ y)] CAUSE [...]]

chisel (y)
    a. Const: **tool′** (y)
    b. Form: **tool′** (x) ∧ **tool′** (y)
    c. Telic: **do′** (x, [**hit′** (x, y)])
    d. Agentive: **artifact′** (y), [**do′** (a, ∅)] CAUSE [[**do′** (x ∧ y)] CAUSE [...]]

A further argument in favor of such a notation and against introducing an extra causal operator is that ISA is possible with the conjoined instrument in its entirety:

(38)   *The hammer and chisel made a hole in the wall.*

Such an alternation is hard to account for if there were an extra CAUSE-operator in the logical structure. Consider:

(39)   a. *Bill made John cut down the tree with a chainsaw.*
           b. **John and the chainsaw cut down the tree.*

6.7 Subtypes of instruments

Instead, using asymmetric conjunction allows for linking in ISA in a natural way. The actor macrorole is assigned to the instrument argument, irrespective of whether it is conjoined or simple.[6]

Schlesinger pointed out that only the second referent of a conjoined instrument (my wording) can undergo ISA. This can now be explained: Due to the asymmetric nature of the conjoined instrument, only the referent that directly causes the change of state in the affected participant can undergo ISA. The qualia-based notation captures this. The consequences are that 1) either the whole phrase undergoes ISA with the fixed ordering as imposed by the qualia notation or 2) the referent that directly causes a change of state undergoes ISA. The first referent cannot be selected to undergo ISA.

So far, I have discussed conjoined *instruments*. However, it is also possible to conjoin implements. Consider:

(40) a. *Mary ate the soup with the spoon and the cup.*
     b. *Pat looked at the birds with the binoculars and the telescope.*

The referents in these examples fail the causal paraphrase, both when conjoined and individually:

(41) a. **Mary acted on the spoon and the cup causing them to eat the soup.*
     b. **Mary acted on the spoon causing it to eat the soup.*
     c. **Mary acted on the cup causing it to eat the soup.*
     d. **Pat acted on the binoculars and the telescope causing them to see the birds.*
     e. **Pat acted on the binoculars causing it to see the birds.*
     f. **Pat acted on the telescope causing it to see the birds.*

---

[6] It is possible to read *hammer and chisel* as a symmetrically conjoined instrument. For instance; Jennifer makes a hole in the wall, holding the hammer in her left hand and the chisel in her right hand. Even though this is possible, it is an unlikely reading. World knowledge dictates that both tools are used sequentially and not parallel to each other.

6 The Instrument-Subject Alternation and subtypes of instruments

The causal paraphrase shows that these referents are not causally embedded and are thus implements. These referents are symmetrically conjoined, as one can switch them around without any semantic difference:

(42) a. *Mary ate the soup with the cup and the spoon.*
b. *Pat looked at the birds with the telescope and the binoculars.*

I propose to represent conjoined implements in the logical structure the same way I represent symmetrically conjoined instruments:

(43) a. ... ∧ **use′** (Mary, spoon ∧ cup)
b. ... ∧ **use′** (Pat, binoculars ∧ telescope)

Contrary to instruments, however, implements can only be conjoined symmetrically. The fixed ordering of asymmetrically conjoined instruments encodes a form of 'internal causation'. This is incompatible with the lack of causal embedding that is inherent to implements.

One word of caution is warranted here though. It is possible to posit counterexamples that feature referents that typically occur as instruments (e.g. *knife*). Consider:

(44) a. *Mary ate the food with the knife and the spoon.*
b. **Mary acted on the knife and the spoon causing them to eat the food.*
c. **Mary acted on the spoon causing it to eat the food.*
d. **Mary acted on the knife causing it to eat the food.*
e. *Mary ate the food with the knife.*

However, as the paraphrases show, *knife* is not causally embedded. It is perfectly possible to eat food with a knife ((44e)), despite it being a rather inefficient method to do so. Just because the referent *knife* usually occurs as an instrument, it does not entail that it can never occur as an implement.

I have illustrated that it is possible to conjoin instruments with instruments and implements with implements. For implements, it is only possible to conjoin symmetrically, as asymmetric conjoining is incompatible in absence of a causal chain. Instruments can be conjoined symmetrically and asymmetrically. In the latter case, conceptual information is linguistically relevant and represented in the logical structure. ISA is (obviously) only possible with conjoined instruments, as only these pass the causal paraphrase. There are several restrictions with respect to ISA: 1) Both instruments must be able to undergo ISA individually and 2) (in case of asymmetric conjoining) only the referent directly causing the change of state can undergo ISA or the conjoined phrase as a whole.

6.8 Conclusion

In this chapter, I illustrated that ISA is a construction that can be used to obscure the instigator of a causal chain by leaving the corresponding argument slot unspecified. This assigns the actor macrorole to the instrument-effector, as actorhood has to be assigned to the highest overt argument in the LS. I also explored the restrictions that accompany ISA. ISA can only take place if 1) there is a causal chain, 2) the instrument's referent is high enough on the actionality scale relative to the predicate's requirements and 3) if there is a plausible instigator recoverable from context. To capture 3) I proposed the Natural Event Condition. By positing a certain referent as instigator and removing the subevent containing the instrument, the naturalness of a causal chain is tested for. If the remaining causal chain is inadmissible, there is no natural event and if this is the case, the inanimate referent is not an instrument undergoing ISA but it rather occupies the highest argument position in the LS in its own right. The mechanics and all of the restrictions concerning ISA are captured in a constructional schema (table 22).

Furthermore, I explored two phenomena superficially similar to ISA: The ability-reading and the generic reading. Rather than describing a state of affairs as it unfolds as is the case with ISA, the ability-reading attributes a certain ability to perform an action to a referent, which is, in this case, an inanimate usually encountered as an instrument-effector. The generic reading attributes a certain fact or state of affairs to an inanimate usually used as an instrument. Both the generic reading and the ability reading are captured by positing an operator in the LS: *GEN* and *ABIL*, respectively.

7 Delimiting instruments from instrument-like participants

In the introduction, it was explained that in many languages the marking typically employed for instruments has a wide range of other functions. Some of these functions are clearly adverbial in nature and are not an object of the present study. So far, I have explored the prototypical cases of instruments and the related concept of implements. However, there are several cases where a certain constituent superficially resembles an instrument, such as in (1).

(1) a. *John ran to the store with the hammer.*
    b. *The woman with the book left the room.*
    c. *Jan ren-de naar de winkel met de hamer.*
       Jan run-PST.3SG to DEF store with DEF hammer (Dutch)
    d. *De vrouw met het boek verliet de kamer.*
       DEF woman with DEF book leave\PST.3SG DEF room

The status of such constituents is far from clear. This chapter is intended to explore their properties and how they can be captured in RRG. Reference is also sometimes made to human instruments. I treat these as causees and I will explore their status in relation to instruments. By delineating such concepts from instruments and implements, I aim at providing a sharper definition of the instrument notion.

7.1 Causees

The intermediate effector position is not restricted to inanimates (or lesser animates) only. In fact, causees can be considered as a kind of human instrument and there appear to be great parallels between them: The causee is acted upon to perform an activity similar to an instrument. Neither causees nor instruments are 'primary causers', to use Schlesinger's (1989: 194) terms, but entities *caused to do* something. It then stands to reason that examples with causees and instruments should pass the same causal paraphrase testing that I have been applying thus far. Consider (3a–3c) compared to (3d–3f):

(3) a. *Jean   a   fait   couper le   pain à   Marie.*
       Jean AUX.3SG make.PTCP   cut   DEF bread to Marie
       'Jean made Marie cut the bread.' (French)
    b. *Jean   a   agit   sur Marie, ce qui a*
       Jean AUX.3SG act.PTCP on Marie REL AUX.3SG
       causé   qu'elle   coupe   le   pain.
       cause.PTCP that=3SG.F cut.3SG DEF bread
       'Jean acted on Mary, causing her to cut the bread.'
    c. *Marie   a   agit   sur   le   pain, ce qui*
       Marie AUX.3SG act.PTCP on DEF bread   REL
       a   causé   qu'il   est   coupé.
       AUX.3SG cause.PTCP that=3SG.M AUX.3SG cut.PTCP
       'Mary acted on the bread, causing it to be cut.'
    d. *Jean   a   coupé   le   pain avec un   couteau.*
       Jean AUX.3SG cut.PTCP DEF bread with INDEF knife.
       'Jean cut the bread with a knife.'
    e. *Jean   a   agit   sur   le   couteau, ce qui*
       Jean AUX.3SG act.PTCP on DEF knife   REL
       a   causé   qu'il   coupe   le   pain.
       AUX.3SG cause.PTCP that=3SG.M cut.3SG DEF bread.
       'Jean acted on the knife, causing it to cut the bread.'

f. Le couteau a agit sur le pain, ce qui
DEF knife AUX.3SG act.PTCP on DEF bread REL
a causé qu'il est coupé.
AUX.3SG cause.PTCP that=3SG.M AUX.3SG cut.PTCP
'The knife acted on the bread, causing it to be cut.'

The logical structures for (3a) and (3d) will look very similar. They are given in (4).

(4) a. [**do′** (Jean, Ø)] CAUSE [[**do′** (Marie, Ø)] CAUSE [BECOME **cut′** (pain)]]
 b. [**do′** (Jean, Ø)] CAUSE [[**do′** (couteau, Ø)] CAUSE [BECOME **cut′** (pain)]]

If causees and instruments arguably occupy the same position in the logical structure, why and how do we distinguish between them? If they occupy the same position and pass the same tests, then would it not be simpler to treat them as the same category? One argument in favor of keeping these notions separate is that languages usually have different preferred linking strategies for them. In French, causees (under the scope of direct causation) prefer the dative marker *à* combined with a nuclear juncture, whereas instruments prefer the preposition *avec*. In English, instruments prefer the linking strategy with a *with*-PP, whereas causees prefer a (complex) construction with a causative verb. The example in (5d) is inadmissible because *rock* is too low on the actionality scale to be a realistic causee. As an instrument, it is incompatible with a typical expression of causees (*make*-construction). Consider English, German ((5e–5h)) and Dutch ((5i–5l)):

(5) a. *I had Bill break the window.*
 b. *?I broke the window with Bill.*[1]
 c. *I broke the window with the rock.*

---

[1] This sentence is perfectly acceptable if it is interpreted as a comitative construction. As a causee construction, however, it is of questionable acceptability. The same holds for the German and Dutch equivalents in (5).

d. *I made the rock break the window.
e. Ich   ließ   Erich   das   Fenster   einschlag-en.
   1SG   let\PST.1SG   Erich   DEF   window   bash in-INF
f. ?Ich   schlug   das   Fenster   mit   Erich   ein.
   1SG   bash in\PST.1SG DEF   window   with   Erich   VPR
g. Ich   schlug   das   Fenster   mit   einem
   1SG   bash in\PST.1SG DEF   window   with   INDEF
   Stein ein.
   rock   VPR
h. *Ich   ließ   einen   Stein   das   Fenster
   1SG   let\PST.1SG   INDEF   rock   DEF   window
   einschlag-en.
   bash in-INF
i. Ik   deed   Erik   het   raam
   1SG   make\PST.1SG   Erik   DEF   window
   ingooi-en.
   throw in-INF
j. ?Ik   gooi-de   het   raam   in   met   Erik.[2]
   1SG   throw-PST.1SG   DEF   window VPR   with Erik
k. Ik   gooi-de   het   raam   in   met   een
   1SG   throw-PST.1SG   DEF   window VPR   with INDEF
   steen.
   rock
l. *Ik   deed   de   steen   het   raam
   1SG   make\PST.1SG   DEF   rock   DEF   window
   ingooi-en.
   throw in-INF

There are some arguments that can be realized with typical instrument-marking, despite being a causee. Consider the following examples: (6c) is an LS corresponding to (6a). A paraphrase of (6a) is given in (6b).

---

[2] The Dutch verb *ingooien* (literally: *throw in*) is the most direct equivalent of English *break* in this context.

(6) a. *The general captured the city with only a handful of soldiers.*[3]
 b. *The general made the soldiers capture the city.*
 c. [**do**′ (general, Ø)] CAUSE [[**do**′ (soldiers, Ø)] CAUSE [BECOME **captured**′ (city)]]
 d. *The soldiers captured the city.*

In (6a) typical instrumental marking is employed for the causee. There is a good reason not to treat *soldiers* as an instrument, but as a real causee: If ISA were applied as in (6d), Holisky's principle would link it back to an LS with the argument as an agentive instigator. It is given in (7a). Further compare (7a) to (7b–7c).

(7) a. [**do**′ (soldiers, Ø)] CAUSE [[**do**′ (Ø, Ø)] CAUSE [BECOME **destroyed**′ (city)]]
 b. *The soldiers destroyed the city with a catapult.*
 c. [**do**′ (soldiers, Ø)] CAUSE [[**do**′ (catapult, Ø)] CAUSE [BECOME **destroyed**′ (city)]]

The default interpretation of (6d) is one where the soldiers themselves act as the instigator. The same applies to (5a) if one were to attempt ISA:

(8) a. *Bill broke the window.*
 b. [**do**′ (Bill, Ø)] CAUSE [BECOME **broken**′ (window)]

It was illustrated by the examples in (5) that human referents are not compatible with instrument-marking (in this function, see footnote 80) and inanimates are not compatible with causee-marking. However, the referent of *soldiers* is a group of humans. Groups and organizations are usually considered less animate than individual humans in most approaches to animacy. In my actionality scale, they rank as anthropomorphic entities on the animacy hierarchy (just like *Bill*, for instance), but they are lower in autonomy than individuals. In short, their position on the actionality scale is lower than that of *Bill*. This has a reflex in linking preferences in English. *Soldiers* allows for both the *made*-strategy and the *with*-strategy.

---

[3] This sentence can also have a comitative reading. However, world knowledge of how military organizations operate makes this reading somewhat unlikely.

7 Delimiting instruments from instrument-like participants

Most referents are only compatible with one strategy but lower-ranking causees will typically allow for both. This is equally true for Dutch and German:

(9) a. De generaal vernietig-de de stad **met**
DEF general destroy-PST.3SG DEF city with
de soldaten.
DEF soldiers (Dutch)
b. De generaal **deed** de soldaten de stad
DEF general make\PST.3SG DEF soldaten DEF city
vernietig-en.
destroy-INF
c. Der General zerstör-te die Stadt **mit**
DEF general destroy-PST.3SG DEF city with
den Soldaten.
DEF Soldiers (German)
d. Der General **ließ** die Soldaten die
DEF general let\PST.3SG DEF soldiers DEF
Stadt zerstör-en.
city destroy-INF

It is clear from the examples discussed thus far that a typical causee occupies a higher position on the actionality scale than a typical instrument. However, it would be too simple to assume that the differences in actionality can provide a complete answer. There are cases where referents can be either an instrument or a causee (or be ambiguous).

(10) a. *John broke the window with the dog. (by throwing the dog)*
b. *John had the dog break the window. (by ordering the dog)*
c. *The dog broke the window with a stick.*

Again, *dog* can be a real causee, as applying ISA to (10b) would rather link back to an LS with *dog* as instigator as evidenced by its instrument-taking potential ((10c)). The referent *dog* changes actionality status between (10a) and (10b). In (10a), *dog* refers to the dog's body as a physical object, rather

274

than to the dog as a whole. In terms of actionality status, *dog* in (10a) is much lower on the scale than it is in (10b). Therefore, in (10a), it is an instrument as it is too low to be a realistic candidate for causeehood. This is parallel to more commonplace instruments and causees: Instruments like *rock* have to be manipulated more directly than referents like *soldiers* or *Bill*. The former requires physical handling on the part of the manipulator, whereas the latter do not due to their position on the actionality scale. Typical causees are much higher on the scale than typical instruments with only very few referents that can be conceptualized as both. This difference in actionality has repercussions for the type of causation that each is under the scope of (or can be). In chapter 5, I explored an expanded system of causal operators in RRG's logical structures and I suggested representing indirect causation with a different causal operator. Causees can be under the scope of direct or indirect causation, whereas instruments can only be under the scope of direct causation. To illustrate this difference, consider the French examples in (11). The LS in (11e) underlies both (11a) and (11c) and has the underspecified causal operator as introduced in chapter 5.

(11) a. *Jean   a   fait   couper le   pain   à Marie.*
        Jean   AUX.3SG make.PTCP cut   DEF bread to Marie
        'Jean made Marie cut the bread.'
   b. [**do'** (Jean, Ø)] CAUSE [[**do'** (Marie, Ø)] CAUSE [BECOME **cut'** (pain)]]
   c. *Jean   a   fait   couper le   pain   par Marie.*
        Jean   AUX.3SG make.PTCP cut   DEF bread by Marie
        'Jean had Marie cut the bread.'
   d. [**do'** (Jean, Ø)] IND [[**do'** (Marie, Ø)] CAUSE [BECOME **cut'** (pain)]]
   e. [**do'** (Jean, Ø)] *CAUSE* [[**do'** (Marie, Ø)] CAUSE [BECOME **cut'** (pain)]]
   f. *Jean   a   coupé   le   pain   avec un couteau.*
        Jean   AUX.3SG cut.PTCP   DEF bread with INDEF knife
        'Jean cut the bread with a knife.'

7 Delimiting instruments from instrument-like participants

g. [**do′** (Jean, Ø)] CAUSE [[**do′** (couteau, Ø)] CAUSE [BECOME **cut′** (pain)]]
h. *Jean a fait couper le pain à
    Jean AUX.3SG make.PTCP cut DEF bread to
    le couteau.
    DEF knife
    '*Jean made the knife cut the bread.'
i. *[**do′** (Jean, Ø)] IND [[**do′** (couteau, Ø)] CAUSE [BECOME **cut′** (pain)]]

The examples in (11f–11i) illustrate that the instrument can only be under the scope of direct causation. Using the causee construction is not admissible and thus the type of causation cannot be indirect, as illustrated in (11i). Even though there is a tendency for causees to be under the scope of indirect causation, they can also be under the scope of direct causation. This is illustrated by the examples in (11a–11e). Even though there is no physical manipulation in (11a) as with instruments, I assume that the directness of impingement in that example is the product of metaphoric extension of prototypical physical manipulation to socio-psychological pressure (cf. Talmy 2000: 409). In terms of the system I proposed in chapter 5, this kind of causation would count as *semi-physical*.[4] That does not mean, however, that the precise type of causation with causees is always clear. Consider for example the conversation in (12), where the second speaker asks for clarification by stressing the assumed direct nature of causation.

(12) Speaker 1: *My boss made me tidy up my office.*
    Speaker 2: *He MADE you?*
    Speaker 1: *Well, he asked me to.*

Contrary to causees, typical instruments can never be under the scope of indirect causation or any kind of causation weaker than that as evidenced by the English examples in (13).

---

4   Causees can also be under permissive and enabling causation, as was shown in chapter 5. This is irrelevant for the present discussion, however. The LSs in (11d) and (11i) have IND for illustration purposes only. I assume the underspecified *CAUSE*, however.

(13) a. *John had the sword destroy the sign.
      b. *John let the sword destroy the sign.
      c. *Abdul had the knife cut the cake.
      d. *Abdul let the knife cut the cake.

In chapter 4, it was established that pseudo-agents have special properties: They can be conceptualized as instruments or as instigators. Similar to causees operating under *direct* causation, some pseudo-agents can also operate under *indirect* causation ((14)).

(14) Evie **liet**   de   AI Michael-s   computer
      Evie let\PST.3SG DEF AI Michael-POSS computer
      lamlegg-en.
      cripple-INF (Dutch)
      'Evie had the AI-unit cripple Michael's computer.'

As pseudo-agents can be instigators in their own right, I propose to treat *AI* in the Dutch example above as a causee and not as an instrument. The potential for causeehood on the part of pseudo-agents is also indicated in the graph in figure 37 by means of the overlapping areas. In other words, pseudo-agents can be conceptualized as instigators, instruments *and* causees.

In chapter 5, it was argued that causees can act either volitionally or non-volitionally and these concepts were decomposed using FD. If the auxiliary or other causal morphology does not entail any information regarding intention, Holisky's principle applies. For example, in Quechua (15), causees can be marked with accusative, in which case they are read as acting non-volitionally (Van Valin & LaPolla 1997: 588, Van Valin & Wilkins 1996: 311–312, examples from Bills et al. 1969). If the causee is marked with the instrumental, it can be interpreted as either volitionally or non-volitionally acting, whereas accusative marking only allows for the non-volitional reading. In the former case, Holisky's principle applies.

(15) a. *Nuqa Fan-ta   rumi-ta   apa-ci-ni.*
          1SG Juan-ACC rock-ACC carry-CAUSE-1SG
          'I made Juan carry the rock.'

b. *Nuqa Fan-wan rumi-ta apa-ci-ni.*
   1SG Juan-INS rock-ACC carry-CAUSE-1SG
   'I had Juan carry the rock.'

A similar situation exists in French (Van Valin & Wilkins 1996: 311–312, examples from Hyman and Zimmer 1976). In (16a), any volitional reading on the part of the causee is blocked by the use of *à*. The use of *par* allows for both a volitional and a non-volitional reading. I will return to this issue in chapter 8.

(16) a. *J'ai   fait   nettoyer   les   toilettes   au*
        1SG=AUX do.PTCP clean.INF DEF toilets   to.DEF
        général.
        general
        'I made the general clean the toilets.'
     b. *J'ai   fait   nettoyer   les   toilettes   par*
        1SG=AUX do.PTCP clean.INF DEF toilets   by
        le   général.
        DEF   general
        'I had the general clean the toilets.'

Dutch has an auxiliary that precludes any voluntary reading of the causee (*doen*) and it has a second auxiliary (*laten*) that does not entail any information concerning volition on the part of the causee. Consider (17):

(17) a. *Lara liet   Tim het afval buiten zett-en,*
        Lara let\PST Tim DEF trash outside put-INF
        maar deed   dat tegen zijn zin.
        but do\PST.3SG DEM against POSS preference
        'Lara made Tim take out the trash, but he only did so against his will.'
     b. *Lara liet   Tim het afval buiten zett-en*
        Lara let\PST.3SG Tim DEF trash outside put-INF
        en hij deed   dat met plezier.
        and 3SG do\PST.3SG DEM with pleasure
        'Lara had/let Tim take out the trash and he did so willingly.'

c. *Lara deed   Tim het afval buiten zett-en
    Lara do\PST.3SG Tim DEF trash outside put-INF
    en hij deed   dat met plezier.
    and 3SG do\PST.3SG DEM with pleasure
    '*Lara made Tim take out the trash and he did so willingly.'

If one were to use *laten* without any further information, the causee would be interpreted as acting intentionally. By contrast, the causee in (17c) is always interpreted as acting non-intentionally. In the Dutch examples in (5.40), use of *door* fixes the reading of causation to IND[5], whereas the use of *aan* sets it to permissive/enabling. If no preposition is used, the type of causation is underspecified and the reading of the causee is determined by Holisky's principle.[6] In French too, the use of a certain preposition is indicative of the type of causation: *à* fixes the type of causation to direct causation, leaving no room for interpretation. The use of *à* constitutes 'information to the contrary' in terms of Holisky's principle. If *par* is used, causation is set to indirect and Holisky's principle determines the precise reading of causee: Adding information signaling willingness, yields a contradiction for (18a) but not for (18b).

(18) a. *J'ai   fait   nettoyer   les toilettes
         1SG=AUX   make.PTCP   clean.INF DEF toilet.PL
         au   général et   il   l'a   voulu.
         to.DEF   general and 3SG OBJ=AUX.3SG   want.PTCP
         'I made the general clean the toilets and he wanted to.'

---

[5] Recall that the use of *door* makes the volitional reading less likely but does not rule it out (see chapter 5).
[6] Verhagen and Kemmer (1997: 79) argue that if no preposition is used, the default reading is that of a non-volitional causee. My own native speaker intuitions are at odds with this and they confirm Holisky's principle. Verhagen and Kemmer argue that including *and she did a fine job* in sentences with *laten* (without a preposition) is not appropriate. There are two problems with this: 1) Such an addition is no real test for volition and 2) in my variety of Dutch it *would* be appropriate to add the sequence.

b. *J'ai   fait   nettoyer les   toilettes par*
   1SG=AUX make.PTCP clean.INF DEF toilet.PL by
   le général et il   l'a   voulu.
   DEF general and 3SG OBJ=AUX.3SG want.PTCP
   'I had the general clean the toilets and he wanted to.'

In German, there is only one causative auxiliary, *lassen* ((19)). Here, too, Holisky's principle determines whether the causee is understood as intentional or non-intentional. Contrary to French and Quechua, there is no morphological means to explicitly express a non-volitional reading. The preposition *von* is used for the purposes of disambiguation with animates, but has no further implication for the volitionality of the causee. In (19d), the argument marked by *von* indicates that *it* is the causee and not the person kissed. Without *von*, the sentence is ambiguous with respect to who is kissed.

(19) a. *Lara ließ   Tim den Müll wegbring-en.*
         Lara let\PST.3SG Tim DEF trash take away-INF
         'Lara had/made/let Tim take out the trash.'
     b. *Lara ließ   Tim den Müll wegbring-en*
         Lara let\PST.3SG Tim DEF trash take away-INF
         und er   tat   es   sogar freiwillig.
         and 3SG do\PST.3SG 3SG.O even voluntarily
         'Lara had Tim take out the trash and he even did so voluntarily.'
     c. *Lara ließ   Tim den Müll wegbring-en,*
         Lara let\PST.3SG Tim DEF trash take away-INF
         aber er tat   es   nur unfreiwillig.
         but 3SG do\PST.3SG 3SG.O only involuntarily
         'Lara had Tim take out the trash, but he only did so involuntarily.'
     d. *Lara ließ   Tim von Maria küss-en.*
         Lara let\PST.3SG Tim by Maria kiss-INF.
         'Lara had Maria kiss Tim.'

I will return to causee-marking in chapter 8. To summarize the properties of all classes of referents that can be intermediate effectors, I have provided table 25. The values in the table are valid for prototypical instruments and causees. For the sake of clarity, I have also included pseudo-agents. Bear in mind, however, that these are referents that can be conceptualized as either instruments *or* causees. *Type of causation* refers to the type they are typically found under the scope of. *Actionality* refers to the position on the actionality scale. If more than one type of causation is listed, the first one mentioned is the most usual one.

	Type of causation	Actionality
Instrument	Direct	Mid-range
Causee	Indirect/Direct	Very high
Pseudo-agent	Direct/Indirect	High

Table 25: Summary of intermediate effector classes.

7.1.1 Causees taking instruments

Since I posit that causees and instruments typically occupy the same position in the LS (at least in French), some sentences with both could potentially pose a problem. Consider:

(20) Jean a fait couper le pain
 Jean AUX.3SG make.PTCP cut.INF DEF bread
 à Marie avec un couteau.
 to Marie with INDEF knife
 'Jean made Mary cut the bread with a knife.'

Assuming that the instrument and the causee occupy the same argument position in the LS, how do we account for examples like (20)? The most natural reading of (20) is that *Jean* had *Marie* cut the bread and *Marie* used a knife to arrive at this result. Before any LS can be proposed, it has to be ascertained whether both *Marie* and *couteau* are causally embedded. This can be done by testing every individual segment of the causal chain with the causal paraphrase. Applying the test reveals that the two arguments are, in fact, causally embedded ((21a–21b)) and that *couteau* is not under the direct scope of *Jean* ((21c)).

(21)   a.   *Jean a   agit   sur Marie,   ce qui*
             Jean AUX.3SG act.PTCP on Marie   REL
             a   causé   qu'elle   coupe   le   pain
             AUX.3SG cause.PTCP that=3SG.F cut.3SG DEF bread
             avec un   couteau.
             with INDEF   knife
             'Jean acted on Mary, causing her to cut the bread with a knife.'

        b.   *Marie a   agit   sur   le   couteau,   ce qui*
             Marie AUX.3SG act.PTCP on   DEF knife   REL
             a   causé   qu'il   coupe   le
             AUX.3SG cause.PTCP that=3SG.M cut.3SG DEF
             pain.
             bread
             'Mary acted on the knife, causing it to cut the bread.'

        c.   **Jean a   agit   sur le   couteau,   ce qui*
             Jean AUX.3SG act.PTCP on   DEF knife   REL
             a   causé   qu'il   coupe   le   pain.
             AUX.3SG cause.PTCP that=3SG.M cut.3SG DEF bread
             '*Jean acted on the knife, causing it to cut the bread.'

To adequately capture what the paraphrases in (21) revealed, adding another causal sequence to the LS is the most straightforward solution. The LS of (21a) is given in (22).

(22)   [**do**´ (Jean, Ø)] CAUSE [[**do**´ (Marie, Ø)] CAUSE [[**do**´ (couteau, Ø)] CAUSE [BECOME **cut**´ (pain)]]]

There is a marginal reading of (20), where *Jean* uses the *knife* to make *Marie* do something and that something is to cut the bread. This reading of (21a) also passes the causal paraphrase. *Jean* acts on the knife, which in turn acts on *Marie* which causes her perform an activity. Bear in mind that such an interpretation is very marked and not a single informant indicated it as the default interpretation.

7.1 Causees

So far, causees so far have been intermediate effectors, i.e. as effectors followed by at least one causal operator. However, contrary to instruments, causees do not have to be intermediate. It is more apt to define them as non-initial effectors. Consider the following examples from French and Dutch:

(23) a. *Jean   a   fait   manger   Marie   avec*
      Jean   AUX.3SG   make.PTCP   eat.INF   Marie   with
      une   fourchette.
      INDEF   fork
      'Jean made Marie eat with a fork.' (French)
   b. *Jean   heef-t   Marie   met   een   vork   doe-n*
      Jean   AUX-3SG   Marie   with   INDEF   fork   do-INF
      et-en.
      eat-INF
      'Jean made Marie eat with a fork.' (Dutch)
   c. *Marie   a   mangé   avec une   fourchette.*
      Marie AUX.3SG   eat.PTCP   with INDEF fork
      'Marie ate with a fork.' (French)
   d. *Marie   at   met   een   vork.*
      Marie   eat\PST.3SG   with   INDEF   fork
      'Marie ate with a fork.' (Dutch)

The sentence in (23a) has two relevant interpretations: 1) *Jean* makes *Marie* do something, and that something is eating with a fork and 2) *Jean* makes *Marie* eat, poking her with a fork to achieve this. The LS of the first interpretation is given in (24a) and the LS of the second one is given in (24b).

(24) a. [**do**′ (Jean, Ø)] *CAUSE* [**do**′ (Marie, [**eat**′ (Marie, Ø) ∧ **use**′ (Marie, fourchette)])]
   b. [**do**′ (Jean, Ø)] *CAUSE* [[**do**′ (fourchette, Ø)] *CAUSE* [**do**′ (Marie, [**eat**′ (Marie, Ø)])]]
   c. **do**′ (Marie, [**eat**′ (Marie, Ø) ∧ **use**′ (Marie, fourchette)])

Fork in (23a) under interpretation 1) is an implement as it would fail the causative paraphrase. Furthermore, it would unambiguously be an implement in the more basic example in (23c). Its LS is given in (24c).

There is an important principle behind the phenomenon where causees take instruments: The instrument has to be lower in the LS (i.e. more to the right) than the causee governing it. In other words, there is a relative ordering: Causees normally precede instruments. Consider the examples in (25) where this principle is violated.

(25) a. *John made the cannon make Bill destroy the barn.
 b. *John made/had/let the cannon make Bill destroy the barn.
 c. *John deed   het kanon   Bill de   schuur
    John do\PST.3SG DEF cannon Bill DEF barn
    vernietig-en.
    destroy-INF
    '*John made the cannon make Bill destroy the barn.' (Dutch)
 d. *John deed   het kanon   de   schuur met Bill
    John do\PST.3SG DEF cannon DEF barn   with Bill
    vernietig-en.
    destroy-INF
    '*John made the cannon destroy the barn with Bill.'

In chapter 4, the Relative Power Principle was introduced to govern the relative ordering of pseudo-agents and instruments. The examples in (25) illustrate that this principle, or rather an extension thereof, also governs the occurrence of instruments and causees in the same sentence. An updated version of the principle is given in (26).

(26) **Relative Power Principle (final):** Save for other considerations, the referent filling an effector slot (α) in the logical structure must be ranked higher on the actionality scale than the referents of effector arguments that are embedded deeper in the logical structure than α.

This new formulation of the principle covers all cases that were covered by the provisional principle in chapter 4. In addition, it covers the distribution of causees, instruments and agents. Typical causees are just as human as typical agents, yet are tacitly assumed to be less powerful. In causee constructions the instigator is considered to be in a position of (more) power:

(27) a. *John made Bill cut down the tree.*
b. *The general had the sergeant make the call.*
c. *?The sergeant had the general make the call.*

In (27a), *John* is interpreted as having some power over Bill. If both were reversed, *Bill* would be considered as having power over *John*. This variable actionality is of the *induced* kind and depends (in this case) on contextual knowledge. I therefore regard human causees as slightly less actional than human agents. In (27b) on the other hand, this power differential is lexicalized. Switching both arguments yields a less acceptable sentence (27c).

The revised principle in (26) contains the wording *save for other considerations*. This refers to examples such as (23a) under the second interpretation. Here, the instrument ranks higher than the causee in the LS. However, as I pointed out before, such interpretations are very marked and never constitute the default interpretation. It seems that the principle in (26) is not absolute in the sense that a violation results in ungrammaticality. Deviating from (26) does, however, result in a very marked structure.

7.1.2 Expanding the effector role

In Van Valin & Wilkins (1996), the anatomy of the effector role was investigated. Three main readings of effector were distinguished: 1) agent, 2) instrument and 3) force. The authors defined the readings of the effector role according to mainly two properties, namely the position of the effector (intermediate vs. instigating) and the nature of the referent (human vs. inanimate). In the previous chapters, I have investigated forces, instruments and causees. For example, it was established that forces typically occupy a very specific section of semantic space, centered around the concept of *para-autonomous*. I believe it would be advantageous to refine the existing 1996 classification and to include two new subtypes: the *causee* and the *executor*. The executor is simply a label for non-agentive human instigators, i.e., human instigators whose default agency is canceled. Van

7 Delimiting instruments from instrument-like participants

Valin and Wilkins (1996) do recognize non-agentive human effectors, but they do not include them in the list of effector subtypes. If a subclassification of effector is not useful, it suffices to use the term *effector* or *plain effector*. For instance, if there is only single argument, such as with intransitives (e.g. *The ball is rolling*), it does not seem necessary to provide a classification beyond *plain effector*. I have not included free and blocked instruments or pseudo-agents. Pseudo-agents are not so much an effector subtype rather than a specific class of referents that can be conceptualized as both instruments and instigators. Free and blocked instruments do not constitute a subtype either, as they are both simply instruments. Recall that this distinction is purely terminological in nature: A free instrument is an instrument that can undergo ISA with a given predicate and in a certain language. *Mes* in examples (3.50e–3.50f) is a blocked instrument in Dutch but would be a free instrument in the English equivalent. Free and blocked are nothing more than labels to describe the behavior of referents; they do not imply any deeper theoretical distinction.

Feature	Effector subtypes				
	Agent	Executor	Force	Causee	Instrument
Instigator	Yes	Yes	Yes	No	No
Causation type	N/A	N/A	N/A	(In)direct	Direct
Metonymic clipping	N/A	N/A	N/A	No	Yes/No
Actionality	High	High	Para-autonomous	High	Mid
HP relevant	Yes	Yes	No	Yes	No
Volitional	Yes	No	N/A	Yes/No	N/A

Table 26: Summary of proposed effector subtypes.

Causees are listed as being under *(in)direct* causation: They can be under the scope of indirect causation, but can also be licensed under direct causation. Instruments are given the value *Yes/No* with respect to metonymic clipping. This refers to the fact that some instruments allow for ISA but others do not. The actionality row refers to the portion of semantic space that the subtype's referents are typically located in. *HP relevant* refers to whether Holisky's principle is relevant. It is only relevant for agents, executors and causees because the principle primarily affects human referents. Lexical agents or agenthood imposed by a construction are not covered. This field only concerns HP-derived agents. *Volitional* refers to whether the referent is inherently acting *volitionally* or not.

7.2 Comitatives

In RRG, comitatives are essentially conjoined arguments where one is coded with a *with*-PP (but need not be). As I pointed out in the introduction of this chapter, there is a superficial similarity in many languages between comitatives and instruments. Even though more languages make a morphosyntactic distinction between the two, most languages spoken natively in Europe do not make such a distinction (Stolz et al. 2013: WALS entry), Finnish being a notable exception. Comitatives are said to express the notion of accompaniment of two entities (Ibid.). Yet, there also appears to be a criterion of co-authorhood for the most prototypical comitatives, as shown in (28a).

(28) a. *John ran to the store with Mary.*
 b. *John ran to the store with his goldfish.*
 c. *John ran to the store with his hammer.*

In (28b), *goldfish* is not a co-author, as the animal is confined to water and cannot run parallel to *John*. Similarly, in (28c), *hammer,* being quite low on the actionality scale, cannot be co-autor of the action described by the predicate. In this section, I will explore the RRG-approach to comitatives and attempt to provide an account of examples such as (28b) and (28c).

7.2.1 True comitatives

Normal (or 'true') comitatives are treated as a linking option in RRG (Van Valin & LaPolla 1997: 379, Van Valin 2013: 73ff., cf. Jolly 1993). Essentially, these prototypical comitatives are tied in to the actor macrorole: One of the arguments will function as the actor. As far as logical structures are concerned, comitatives are treated as conjoined arguments of the form (X ∧ Y) where one of the arguments is alternatively coded in a *with*-PP. The necessary characteristic for comitatives is so-called co-authorhood. Co-authorhood is a preliminary term to denote that both arguments in question are considered to be *authors* of the state or activity. This is evidenced by two alternations that can be used as tests: 1) The ability to occur without PP-coding and 2) the interchangeability of the arguments. Regarding 1), Koenig et al. (2008: 181) suggest paraphrasing the sentence under investigation as *X and Y V-ed*. This is illustrated in (29b) and (29d), and alternation 2) is illustrated in (29b–29d). I propose to treat arguments that pass both tests as co-authors. Instruments, contrary to comitatives, does not pass Koenig's proposed paraphrase ((29f–29i)). The logical structure underlying (29a–29d) is given in (29e). I choose to use *co-authorhood* while rejecting the notion of co-agency because comitatives can be non-agentive, as shown by the acceptability of (29j–29k).

(29) a. *John walked with Sonia.*
 b. *John and Sonia walked.*
 c. *Sonia walked with John.*
 d. *Sonia and John walked.*
 e. **do´** (John ∧ Sonia, [**walk´** (John ∧ Sonia)])
 f. *John broke the cup with the hammer.*
 g. **John and the hammer broke the cup.*
 h. *Sonia cut off the leaf with a knife.*
 i. **Sonia and the knife cut off the leaf.*
 j. *Sonia and John drank all the wine together, but they did not intend to.*
 k. *Sonia drank the wine with John, but they did not intend to.*

Comitatives are primarily a morphosyntactic phenomenon, where alternative coding is used for pragmatic purposes. Both arguments can be selected as actor, or one argument can receive *with*-coding. In case of the latter, the alternatively coded argument is not selected as actor but becomes an oblique core argument and is marked by *with* following the standard linking rules for non-macrorole arguments. It is for this reason that I equally reject the alternative terminology of *co-actorhood* (instead of co-authorhood), because this would be confusing from a linking perspective. In the examples below (adapted from Van Valin 2013: 91), all three realizations again have the same underlying LS (given in (30d)), irrespective of voice-oppositions.

(30) a. *The gangster robbed the bank (together) with the corrupt policeman.*
 b. *The bank was robbed by the gangster (together) with the corrupt policeman.*
 c. *The bank was robbed by the corrupt policeman (together) with the gangster.*
 d. [**do´** (gangster ∧ corrupt policeman)] CAUSE [BECOME NOT **have´** (bank, Ø)]

Van Valin (2013: 103) points out that the qualia-properties of the referents are crucial for the comitative interpretation of *with*. In other words, the object of *with* in (30a–30b) is interpreted as being in a comitative relationship with *gangster* because its qualia-properties describe it as a human, capable of doing a certain activity. These properties are stored on the telic qualia layer (or: quale). Van Valin (2013: 100) represents these properties for a referent such as *Kim* as in (31).

(31) a. **Kim** (a)
 b. Telic: **do´** (a, [...])

This information is the reason why the sentence in (30a–30b) is interpreted as comitative rather than, say, instrumental. The arguments pass both tests for co-authorhood ((32)), because the qualia-properties of *gangster* and *corrupt policeman* are essentially the same (i.e. human, capable of performing certain activities).

(32) a. *The gangster and the corrupt policeman robbed the bank.*
      b. *The corrupt policeman and the gangster robbed the bank.*
      c. *The corrupt policeman robbed the bank with the gangster.*

7.2.2 Undergoer & NMR comitatives

Jolly (1993: 300–301) explores a phenomenon that is said to use the same mechanics as the true comitatives and can be considered the *undergoer*-version of the comitative. Consider the example in (33a) and the LS Jolly proposes for it in (33b).

(33) a. *John served the entree with the soup to his guests.*
          (adapted from Jolly 1993: 300)
      b. [**do**´ (John, Ø)] CAUSE [BECOME **have**´ (guests, entree ∧ soup)]

Jolly assumes that the RP *entree* ∧ *soup* functions along the same lines as far as argument marking is concerned: *Entree* is selected as undergoer, leaving *soup* as an NMR marked by *with*. As is the case with the more typical comitatives, the order of the nouns can be switched and the *with*-coding is not obligatory but optional:

(34) a. *John served the entree with the soup to his guests.*
      b. *John served the soup with the entree to his guests.*
      c. *John served his guests the entree and the soup.*
      d. *John served his guests the soup and the entree.*

As *serve* behaves like a dative shift verb, it is possible to assign the undergoer macrorole to *guests*, leaving *entree* ∧ *soup* as the NMR. This is given in (34c–34d). Yet, even with this alternative undergoer assignment pattern, it is possible to mark one of the arguments by *with* (35a). Here, too, the order can be switched ((35c)). The LS for (35a) is given in (35b).

(35) a. *John served his guests the entree with the soup.*
      b. [**do**´ (John, Ø)] CAUSE [BECOME **have**´ (guests, entree ∧ soup)] A $\quad$ U $\quad$ NMR$_1$
          NMR$_2$
      c. *John served his guests the soup with the entree.*

In case of two NMRs, it appears that the one that is least pragmatically salient is marked by *with*, paralleling the pragmatic assumptions surrounding variable undergoer selection. In case of variable undergoer selection, the lowest-ranking argument is selected as NMR and is marked by *with*. Compare: *John presented the pad to Eliza* vs. *John presented Eliza with the pad*. The example given in section 6.2 is one of dative shift. Dative shift verbs, contrary to transfer verbs, are exempt from marking the non-default NMR by *with* (Van Valin 2005: 114). However, the logic of pragmatic modulation in both these types of variable undergoer selection is the same. I assume that the reason for alternatively coding one of the two argument in (33a) and (35b) is driven by the same motivation: The most topical of the two arguments is left unmarked. The least topical one is marked by *with*. In the case of (33a), one is selected as undergoer and the other becomes an NMR. In (35b), one NMR is split into two. *NMR-splitting* seems to follow the same logic of pragmatic modulation by extension. It appears that the term comitative is much broader than co-authorhood and also includes (at least) a form of co-undergoerhood. As comitatives are essentially a linking-option, I will return to them in chapter 8.

7.2.3 Comitatives with inanimate components

Most comitative examples contain human referents and co-authorhood is a useful criterion. As pointed out by Schlesinger (1989: 201), sentences like *John and the key opened the door* are ungrammatical. In terms of the approach in the previous sections, the two arguments cannot be conjoined because their referents' qualia-properties do not match. Using the two paraphrases proposed above, the more basic example in (36a) is identified as an instrument construction and not as a comitative.

(36)   a.   *John opened the door with the key.*
        b.   **John and the key opened the door.*
        c.   **The key and John opened the door.*
        d.   **The key opened the door with John.*

However, it would be dubious to explain the acceptability of the sentences in (37) (adapted from Schlesinger 1989: 201f.) with matching qualia-structures.

7 *Delimiting instruments from instrument-like participants*

(37) a. *Floods and guerilla forces ravaged the area.*
b. *The battleship and the Admiral bombarded the coast.*

It is clear that the referents in these sentences are not directly similar in nature. A *battleship* is an inanimate that does not have a will of its own and is in all likelihood commanded by the other referent, *Admiral.* Yet, despite this difference, such sentences are still grammatical, contrary to the ones in (38).

(38) a. **The general and the sword cut open the suit of armor.*
b. **The farmer and the plow plowed the field.*

I propose that the conjunction of arguments is constrained by the position of their referents on the actionality scale: Only if each of the referents could function as the sole x-argument of the relevant LS can such conjunction successfully occur. The sentence **John and the key opened the door* is not admissible because it fails this requirement: *John* and *key* cannot occupy the same position (or a similar one) in the logical structure. The ability to function in the same slot depends on the referents being (rather) close in terms of the actionality scale. Consider:

(39) a. *John opened the door.*
b. [**do´** (John, Ø)] CAUSE [BECOME **open´** (door)]
c. *John opened the door with a key.*
d. [**do´** (John, Ø)] CAUSE [[**do´** (key, Ø)] CAUSE [BECOME **open´** (door)]]
e. *The key opened the door.*
f. [**do´** (Ø, Ø)] CAUSE [[**do´** (key, Ø)] CAUSE [BECOME **open´** (door)]]
g. *[**do´** (key, Ø)] CAUSE [[**do´** (levers, Ø)] CAUSE [BECOME **open´** (door)]]
h. **The key opened the door with the levers.*

In (39a–39d), *John* and *key* respectively occupy the instigator and instrument position in the logical structures. As I have shown, an instrument undergoing ISA is still in its intermediary position. It cannot be an instigator, as evidenced by (39e–39h), where an attempt to move *key* to instigator position with an additional instrument results in ungrammaticality. In (40) below, the LS is the same, because both referents could be instigators in their own right. The LS for (40a) is given in (40g).

(40)   a.   *John and the computer virus disabled Mary's computer.*
      b.   *John disabled Mary's computer.*
      c.   [**do´** (John, Ø)] CAUSE [BECOME **disabled´** (Mary's computer)]
      d.   *The computer virus disabled Mary's computer.*
      e.   [**do´** (computer virus, Ø)] CAUSE [BECOME **disabled´** (Mary's computer)]
      f.   *The computer virus disabled Mary's computer with spam.*
      g.   [**do´** (John ∧ computer virus, Ø)] CAUSE [BECOME **disabled´** (Mary's computer)]

One could argue that co-authorhood should be 'broadened' to include inanimates that are high enough on the actionality scale and that comitatives with inanimate components should be considered as ordinary, typical comitatives. As soon as there is co-authorhood, alternative coding is possible. This would be false, as the sentences in (40) do not allow for alternative coding like normal comitatives, despite being conjoined. *John* and *computer virus* are both co-authors, as evidenced by (40), yet alternative coding is not possible:

(41)   **John disabled Mary's computer with the computer virus.*

The sentence in (41) is not an admissible alternatively coded version of the one in (40a). It can only have the classic instrument reading and would always link back to the logical structure in (42).

(42)   [**do´** (John, Ø)] CAUSE [[**do´** (computer virus, Ø)] CAUSE [BECOME **disabled´** (Mary's computer)]]

It thus seems that co-authorhood is not a sufficient criterion. Even if co-authorhood is present, alternative coding is only allowed if the actionality level of the conjoined arguments is as good as identical. Prototypically, this involves two instances of the same species, class or type. The second

7 Delimiting instruments from instrument-like participants

sentence in each of the pairs below receives the standard comitative interpretation, even if the referents are inanimates.

(43) a. *The tornado and the hurricane destroyed the barn.*
b. *The tornado destroyed the barn (together) with the hurricane.*
c. *The first and the second assembly robot assembled the car.*
d. *The first assembly robot assembled the car (together) with the second assembly robot.*

There are of course instances where the structural criterion I proposed earlier is seemingly met, yet the sentence is still not admissible ((44a)). The logical structure of (44b) is given in (44c). Schlesinger believes that (44b) and (44d) describe the same state of affairs. He therefore believes that the difference in membership is what makes (44a) inadmissible. Even though I attribute some explanatory power to degrees of membership (in my proper terminology *actionality status*), I believe there is a structural explanation here. It seems strange to posit stick as an effector and, furthermore, it cannot take an instrument itself. Therefore, it cannot be an initial effector. Apart from a potential ISA-reading, contexts can be conjured up to account for (44d) where there is no instigator and the stick falls because of natural causes. Even though gravity (or other natural causes) might be an instigator in the purely physical realm, it is hardly ever constructed as an instigator linguistically. Yet, a non-ISA interpretation is quite plausible from a language user's point of view. A non-ISA interpretation would mean that the *stick* is a force, which it cannot be according to the actionality scale. Rather than assuming an exception captured by a construction or making an exception to the actionality scale, there is a much simpler solution. I propose to treat *Carol* in (44b) as a normal effector, subject to the actionality hierarchy. Example (44d), however, is to be analyzed as a predicate of location, making *stick* a mover. The requirement for predicates of motion are generally lower and the referent *stick* – by virtue of being mobile – meets the requirements for that LS's x-argument. This might seem ad hoc, but the meanings of (44b) and (44d) are actually quite distinct. The former captures a state of affairs where an individual inflicts pain on another entity. The latter denotes an object impacting another. Aktionsart-testing is difficult as *hit* is very polysemous. The Dutch and German equivalents are clearer because they use different verbs. Both *raken* and *treffen* test as achievements. Evidence for the analysis of (44d) as a motion predicate comes from Dutch and German (for example), where two different verbs are employed ((44f–44k)).

(44) a. *Carol and the stick hit the horse.* (adapted from Schlesinger 1989: 201)
 b. *Carol hit the horse.*
 c. **do**′ (Carol, [**hit**′ (Carol, horse)])
 d. *The stick hit the horse.*
 e. INGR **be-at**′ (stick, horse)
 f. Carol sloeg het paard.
  Carol hit\PST.3SG DEF horse (Dutch)
 g. De stok raak-te het paard.
  DEF stick hit-PST.3SG DEF horse
 h. *De stok sloeg het paard.
  DEF stick hit\PST.3SG DEF horse
 i. Carol schlug das Pferd.
  Carol hit\PST.3SG DEF horse (German)
 j. Der Stock traf das Pferd.
  DEF stick hit\PST.3SG DEF horse
 k. *Der Stock schlug das Pferd.
  DEF stick hit\PST.3SG DEF horse

Thus, despite the fact that both states of affairs are coded with the same verb, they relate to different logical structures, which are expressed by different verbs in Dutch and German. *Stick* cannot occupy the position that *Carol* occupies in (44c) and therefore conjunction is impossible. Therefore, the structural criterion I proposed holds: Only one can fill the argument position in the LS but the other cannot.

In this section I illustrated that inanimates can be conjoined with animates. Essentially, such cases can be treated like normal comitatives, i.e. conjoined arguments. There is a crucial condition for this to be possible: Each of the conjoinees must be able to independently function in the same position in the same logical structure.[7] I propose to use this criterion as a refinement of *co-authorhood* as the prerequisite for conjoined arguments for a given argument position. A referent's ability to function as such depends on its position on the actionality scale to a large degree (i.e. it must be in the correct portion of semantic space).

Alternative coding, however, is an option that is reserved to two co-authors that have the same actional status. Schlesinger (1989: 202) refers to this as the necessity for the degree of membership to be similar. Normal comitatives feature human referents which occupy the same position on the actionality scale. Because of this, they are not only co-authors, but the similarity in actionality also allows for the alternative linking with a *with*-PP. As soon as one of the referents is significantly lower than the other, the alternative linking option disappears because of preferred linking back to an instrument-LS. If there is no co-authorhood, the conjunction of arguments becomes impossible. As has become clear in this section and the previous one, comitatives are a much wider phenomenon than human co-authors, even though the latter constitute the prototypical instance of the class.

It is easier to generalize with my proposal than it is to generalize with statements of the type "only forces and forces or forces and agents may be conjoined". Given the fact that there is a class of referents that can be both instruments and instigators (*pseudo-agents*, see chapter 4), the discrete nature of such statements would pose challenges.

The three types of comitatives explored so far all share a crucial characteristic, which I call *positional equivalence*. Whether with the 'actor'-version, the 'undergoer'-version or the 'NMR'-version, the arguments in question have to be positionally equivalent. That is, they have to be able to occupy the relevant position in the LS individually and when conjoined. If there is positional equivalence, the comitative operation can take place: One of the two arguments is alternatively coded. With 'actor'-comitatives,

---

[7] Needless to say, initial x-argument positions of logical structures will require a higher actional status from their prospective referents than argument positions lower in the logical structure. In a way, Schlesinger (1989: 201) has a point when he states that the 'instrument' that is conjoined must have a similar degree of membership to the 'agent'.

there is an added complexity in that the actionality status of the arguments' referents must be similar enough. The driver behind alternative linking (if it is possible) is pragmatic in nature. Actors are default topics. By selecting only one of the arguments as the actor, it alone becomes the topic. Likewise, undergoers are more topical than NMRs. Therefore, selecting only one argument as undergoer is a strategy to modulate the pragmatics. The same logic can be extended to the NMR-version of the comitative.

7.2.4 Inanimate comitatives

There is also a second phenomenon where an inanimate component occurs in a seemingly comitative construction. I propose to call this subtype *inanimate comitatives*.[8] Consider:

(45) a. *John ran to the store with Mary.*
 b. *John ran to the store with his hammer.*
 c. *John and Mary ran to the store.*
 d. **John and the hammer ran the store.*
 e. **John acted on the hammer, causing it to run to the store.*
 f. **/?John ran to the store and simultaneously used the hammer.*
 g. **The hammer facilitated the running to the store.*

In (45b), the runner moves to the store and his hammer makes the same journey. Contrary to the type discussed above, these referents do not meet the structural criterion: The referent *hammer* cannot function in the same logical structure as *John*. This is exemplified in (45c) and (45d). In other words, it cannot be a comitative. The *hammer* is not embedded in a causal chain ((45e)) or under the scope of helping causation ((45f–45g)). Therefore, it cannot be an instrument, a causee or an implement. Then what are these?

---

[8] I use this terminology for the sake of simplicity and because in many cases the second argument is inanimate.

The referents in question cannot be part of a conjoined RP, despite the potentially confusing use of the preposition *with*: *Hammer* and *John* cannot be conjoined, contrary to *John* and *Mary* or *John* and *computer virus*. What is in fact being described is a situation where an individual performs an action (e.g. running to a certain location) and the inanimate accompanies the individual as a consequence of being carried or being stuffed in the individual's pocket. The inanimate is simply 'along for the ride' but otherwise uninvolved.

I propose to model this in a similar fashion to RRG's implements: A connective followed by a general predicate is added to the main logical structure. In case of implements, there is a general predicate of *usage*. I base my approach on Farrell's (2009) treatment of **be-with´**. Farrell argues in favor of a predicative use of *with* to account for a wide range of phenomena. Even though I reject much of his analysis, I do adopt the core concept of **be-with´** (in a modified way). I propose to treat **be-with´** as a general predicate of *accompaniment* that occurs in the LS if the arguments in question are nothing more than co-occurrents. That is, they are not co-authors, nor are they under the scope of one another.[9] **Be-with´** can also account for languages with so-called *with*-possessives (Stassen 2009: 54ff.). Thus, for sentences such as the one in (45b), I propose the structure below:

(46) [[**do´** (John, [**run´** (John)]) & INGR **be-at´** (store, John)] ∧ **be-with´** (hammer, John)]

The arguments of the accompaniment predicate can be considered *co-occurrents*. Such a predicate can also account for a wide range of sentences expressing some form of accompaniment, both literal and figurative. Consider the sentences in (47) and their corresponding logical structures.

(47) a. *John is with Mary.*
b. **be-with´** (Mary, John)
c. *He's with us.* (In the sense of *He belongs to our group/unit*)
d. **be-with´** (1PL, 3SG)

---

[9]   This is in contrast to Farrell (2009), who, in my view, greatly exaggerates the relevance of predicative *with*. Also see below.

e. *I'm with you.* (In the sense of *I am on your side, I share your opinion.* Van Valin, p.c.)
f. **be-with'** (2SG, 1SG)
g. *I put the CDs with the DVDs.* (Farrell 2009: 181)
h. [**do'** (1SG, Ø)] CAUSE [BECOME **be-with'** (DVDs, CDs)]

The sentences in (47c–47f) are figurative in nature, yet clearly metaphorically derived from the more primitive, basic local reading that (47a) exemplifies. This is similar to **be-at'** expressing possession in languages without a *have* predicate: Finnish, for instance, does not have a *have*-verb and thus, one cannot posit a **have'** predicate in its logical structures. RRG can solve this by positing (in the case of Finnish) **be-at'** with the possessive reading being a metaphorical extension (cf. Lakoff & Johnson 1980a & b). I follow this principle to capture the figurative uses of **be-with'** in English. Interestingly, in closely related languages like Dutch and German, **be-with'** has the literal local reading only. For instance, in Dutch, (47c) would have to be expressed with the phrasal verb *horen bij* (*belong to*) and (47e) would have to be expressed with the equivalent of *agree with* (*akkoord gaan/zijn met*).

This approach can also capture a perfectly possible reading of *Francis ran to the hospital with Mary* where *Mary* is not co-author, but rather is unconscious and being transported by *Francis*. This reading is made explicit in (48).

(48) a. *Francis ran to the hospital with his unconscious dog.*
b. [[**do'** (Francis, [**run'** (Francis)]) & INGR **be-at'** (hospital, Francis)] ∧ **be-with'** (his unconscious dog, Francis)]
c. *Marco ran to the hospital with his unconscious daughter.*
d. [[**do'** (Marco, [**run'** (Marco)]) & INGR **be-at'** (hospital, Marco)] ∧ **be-with'** (his unconscious daughter, Marco)]
e. **Marco and his unconscious daughter ran to the hospital.*

It would be difficult to account for (48c) with the standard RRG-approach to comitatives. On the telic quale, *daughter* would essentially have the same properties as *Marco*. This would predict that example (48e) is grammatical, whereas it is clearly not. The use of **be-with´** renders this problem moot. It would also be tricky to account for (49) with standard RRG.

(49)   **The unconscious construction worker ran to the hospital.*

Standard RRG captures selectional restrictions primarily in terms of qualia. The unconscious nature of the referent is what makes this sentence unacceptable. Yet, it would be very difficult to account for this induced feature with qualia. My actionality approach, however, allows for induced features. Introducing *unconscious* would lower the referent's autonomy to a level that is no longer compatible with the requirements of the argument position in the relevant LS.

The general nature of **be-with´** does not entail any specific information on the mode of transportation: The *dog* and the *daughter* can be carried, drawn in a cart, dragged etc. The only thing the predicate conveys is that during the action described by the first section of the LS, another entity occupies a point in space and time that is almost identical with that of the other. Farrell (2009: 193) points out that not only English has a linguistic expression similar to *be with*. Portuguese does too, as can be seen in ((50)).

(50)   Os   omens estão   com   as   mulheres.
       DEF men   be.PRS.3PL with DEF women
       'The men are with the women.' (Farrell 2009: 193, glossing mine)

It can be objected that **be-with´** only expresses a vague meaning. Yet, languages are full of mechanisms to express the vague and unspecific: Passives can be used as a strategy to make the actor unspecific, partitive constructions are cross-linguistically used to express unspecific amounts of something, ISA can be used to leave the instigator unspecified etc.

Farrell (2009: 196) argues in favor of treating (29a–29b, repeated in (51a–51b)) as involving different LSs. The latter would feature conjoined arguments, the former would add a **be-with´** predicate to include *Sonia* in the *with*-PP. Even though I also make a case for **be-with´**, I reject Farrell's assumptions regarding the difference between (51a) and (51b), due to the fact that the two referents are co-authors. The simple sentence alternations in (51) would require very different LSs, making it difficult to account for the co-authorhood of the two referents. I argue in favor of using **be-with´** more restrictively: It specifically codes cases where the two referents are not co-authors. In all of my examples of this phenomenon (e.g. (48)), the second referent is only passively involved in the event and cannot be considered co-author.

(51) a. *John walked with Sonia.*
b. *John and Sonia walked.*
c. *Sonia walked with John.*
d. *Sonia and John walked.*

The **be-with´** predicate is not yet included in contemporary RRG. Including it does not only explain the phenomenon above, but also complements the already existing **be-in´**, **be-on´** and **be-at´** predicates in a natural fashion. Furthermore, it is a natural instantiation of the underspecified **be-LOC´** (Farrell 2009: 193). Following Farrell (2009: 201), I propose to define the **be-with´** predicate as a predicate expressing a general spatio-temporal co-occurrence. This is distinct from location proper. Contrary to Farrell, I restrict the use of **be-with´** to cases where there is no co-authorhood. This includes *potential* comitatives ((52)).

(52) a. *Jack went to the store without Jill.* (Farrell 2009: 196)
b. ...∧ NOT **be-with´** (Jill, Jack)

Even though I agree with Farrell's treatment of (52), there is still no reason to assume **be-with´** for all comitatives. If an entity is not present, there cannot be co-authorhood and a representation in terms of conjoined arguments becomes moot. Therefore, recognizing (52b) does not contradict standard RRG's conception of comitatives. By way of conclusion to this section, I recognize a predicative *with*, contrary to standard RRG (Van Valin 2013: 102).

7.2.5 False inanimate comitatives

If *with*-phrases in inanimate comitatives are not extraposed, a reading of identity becomes possible and even likely, as illustrated in (53).

(53) a. *The woman ran into the store with the book.*
      b. *The woman with the book ran into the store.*
      c. *John ran into the store with the hammer.*
      d. *Jan met de hamer liep   de winkel*
          Jan with DEF hammer run\PST.3SG DEF store
          binnen.
          into (Dutch)

The *book* in (53b) is read as a defining feature of the woman. In Dutch, the *with*-PP can occur in adjacency to proper nouns, yielding an identity reading ((53d)). *Jan met de hamer* would attribute the hammer to *Jan* in that he often has a hammer with him. I propose to analyze such cases as an underlying possessive RP that obligatorily makes the possessor the head (at least in Dutch and English) to attain the attribute reading. Consider the analysis below (Van Valin & LaPolla 1997: 189–192, Van Valin 2005: 52).

(54) a. *The woman's book*
      b. **have´** (woman, <u>book</u>)
      c. *The woman with the book*
      d. **have´** (<u>woman</u>, book)
      e. *The man with the beard* (Farrell 2009: 194)
      f. **have-as-part´** (man, <u>beard</u>)

(54a–54b) represent the case where the possessed referent is selected as the head of the phrase, which is expressed by the underlining of *book*. If the possessor is chosen as head (as in (54d)), the corresponding result is (54c). The attribute reading is only possible with the possessor as the head:

(55) **The woman's book ran into the store.*

Extraposition, such as in the *hammer* example in (45b), is not possible because it is one single, complex RP. Put differently, extraposition is only a possible strategy if 1) there are conjoined RPs (in the case of comitatives) or 2) if there is an underlying **be-with´** predicate. With the latter, extraposition is obligatory. Otherwise, the attributive reading is triggered as (53b) showed. Bear in mind that this holds for common nouns as the actor in English. Proper nouns tend to complicate matters further. Following

Farrell (2009: 196), the absence of a property can be accounted for by including NOT.

(56) a. The man without a beard
b. NOT **have-as-part´** (man, beard)

7.3 Proper parts as instruments

Apart from the typical instrument referents such as *knife, cannon, brush* and the like, proper parts of an entity (such as body parts) can also be used as instruments. Luraghi (1995: 265) points out that humans can and will carry out activities with tools, including their own body parts. Some case grammarians have entertained the idea of a so-called 'body part instrument' as a case for almost every occurrence of a body part in an utterance (Bibović 1976: 313). From an RRG point of view, proper parts functioning as instruments must meet the very same criteria that more prototypical instruments meet. That is to say, the proper part in question must be causally embedded. A sentence like the one in (57a) does not feature a body part instrument but a simple undergoer that happens to be a body part. This verb patterns like a semelfactive and therefore correlates to the LS in (57b).

(57) a. *Ernesto nodded his head.* (adapted from Bibović 1976: 314)
b. SEML **do´** (Ernesto, [**nod´** (Ernesto, his head)])

However, consider sentences like (58) with their Dutch equivalents.

(58) a. *He untied the knot with his teeth.* (Nilsen 1973: 130)
b. *I bit him with my false teeth.* (Lyons 1968: 422)
c. Hij   deed   de   knoop los   met   zijn
3SG do\PST.3SG   DEF   knot   loose   with   POSS.3SG
tand-en.
tooth-PL
d. Ik   beet   hem met   mijn   valse tand-en.
1SG bite\PST.1SG   him   with   POSS.1SG   false   tooth-PL

Superficially, the relevant arguments seem to be instruments. This has to be put to the test using the appropriate paraphrase.

(59) a. ??He acted on his teeth, causing them to untie the knot.
     b. ??I acted on my false teeth, causing them to bite him.

The paraphrase test identifies *teeth/tanden* as something other than an instrument. The test shows that there is no causal embedding. This is not only the case for human body parts as instruments but also for proper parts of other referents. Consider:

(60) a. The digger dug a hole with its scoop.
     b. ??The digger acted on the scoop, causing it to dig a hole.
     c. The algorithm crippled the mainframe with its coding.
     d. ??The algorithm acted on the coding, causing it to the cripple the mainframe.
     e. The computer virus crippled the server with spam-mails.
     f. The computer virus acted on the spam-mails, causing them to cripple the server.

The paraphrase test reveals that proper parts of entities do not have the same status that 'normal' instruments have. Conceptually, this makes sense: A person does not act on the teeth, causing them to do something. Rather, body parts and proper parts are seen as extensions of the instigator rather than as separate entities. In (60c) and (60d), *coding* is what makes up an *algorithm*, rather than a separate entity that is impinged upon. Note that sentences like (60e–60f) are much more acceptable: A computer virus can use independent entities (such as files on the hard drive or *spam-mails*) to wreak havoc. Likewise, the digger does not really impinge on the scoop. Even though (60a) and (60c) can be expressed with a *with*-PP, they become more acceptable if *by means of* is used instead. Normal instruments normally disprefer such a linking, even though it is not entirely ruled out. Consider (61c–61d) and their Dutch and German equivalents in (61e–61f) and (61g–61h), respectively. The choice of *by means of* as marker primarily holds for inanimate proper parts ((61a–61b)), but much less for body parts of animates ((61i–61j)).

7.3 *Proper parts as instruments*

(61) a. *The digger dug a hole by means of its scoop.*
 b. *The algorithm crippled the mainframe by means of its coding.*
 c. *?The lumberjack cut down the tree by means of an axe.*
 d. *?John cut the cake by means of a knife.*
 e. *?De houthakker vel-de   de   boom*
    DEF lumberjack cut down-PST.3SG DEF tree
    door   middel van een   bijl.
    through means of   INDEF axe   (Dutch)
 f. *?Jan sneed   de   cake in stukk-en*
    Jan cut\PST.3SG DEF cake in piece-PL
    door   middel van een   mes.
    through means of   INDEF knife
 g. *?Der Holzfäller fäll-te   den Baum*
    DEF lumberjack cut down-PST.3SG DEF tree
    mittels   eine-r   Axt.
    by means of INDEF-GEN axe (German)

 h. *?Jan schnitt   den Kuchen in Stück-e*
    Jan cut\PST.3SG DEF cake   in piece-PL
    mittels   eine-s   Messer-s.
    by means of INDEF-GEN knife-GEN
 i. *?/*He untied the knot by means of his teeth.*
 j. *?/*The lion killed the gazelle by means of its teeth.*

Parallel to English, *door middel van* and *mittels* are the more marked linking options. In addition, German *mittels* was rated by an informant as written language as opposed to spoken language. However, even within written language, *mittels* was rated as better with proper parts than with true instruments. It seems then that there is a cross-linguistic preference for a different marker if proper parts of inanimates are concerned. In case of independent entities and proper parts of animates, *with/mit/met* are preferred. Note that these are only preferences rather than absolute rules. Having established this, the question remains what proper parts are, semantically speaking. As they fail the causal paraphrase, I propose to treat them as implements, as entities that *help* to cause something (cf. Koenig et al. 2008), but not cause something. The *teeth* arguably increase the chances of untying the knot, but they are not a causer. The larger entity that they are a part of is the true causer, as it passes the causal paraphrase. Therefore, I propose to incorporate proper parts as normal implements. The verbs *untie* and *bite* test as a causative accomplishment and an activity, respectively. As *teeth* is not an effector in the *untie* example, it has to be represented as an implement. The LSs in (62a–62d) correlate with the examples above:

(62) a. [[**do**′ (3SG, Ø)] CAUSE [BECOME **untied**′ (knot)] ∧ [**do**′ (3SG, [**use**′ (3SG, teeth)])]]
b. [**do**′ (1SG, [**bite**′ (1SG, 3SG) ∧ **use**′ (1SG, my false teeth)])]
c. [[**do**′ (3SG, Ø)] CAUSE [BECOME **untied**′ (knoop)] ∧ [**do**′ (3SG, [**use**′ (3SG, tanden)])]]
d. [**do**′ (1SG, [**bite**′ (1SG, 3SG) ∧ **use**′ (1SG, mijn valse tanden)])]

The main difference to normal implements is conceptual in nature: Proper parts are somewhat different than concrete objects like *stick* or *knife*, because the latter are independent entities.

7.4 Potential instruments, implements & comitatives

Farrell (2009) argues in favor of using **be-with**′ to account for all comitatives (amongst others). Although this completely ignores co-authorhood, I do believe a similar approach can account for potential instances of instruments, implements and comitatives. *Potential* refers to the absence of a referent from a certain state of affairs and the fact that the referent could *potentially* be used or involved in the action. This absence is largely conceptual, however, as the referents are still expressed in the morphosyntax. Following RRG's Completeness Constraint, these referents must be present in the LS. Comitatives are primarily defined over positional equivalence. If there is no positional equivalence, then positing co-authorhood

7.4 Potential instruments, implements & comitatives

and an LS with conjoined arguments would be paradoxical ((63c)). The typical comitative alternation in (63b) is inadmissible because it is not truth-conditionally equivalent to (63a). An LS where the second argument is left unspecified ((63d)) is problematic for two reasons: 1) it is unclear what it would link to and 2) it does not account for the occurrence of *Elena* thereby violating the completeness constraint. Following Farrell (2009: 196), I propose to capture *without* as NOT **be-with'**. This LS is given in (63e).

(63) a. Caroline ran to the store without Elena.
 b. *Elena ran to the store without Caroline.
 c. ?/*[[**do'** (Caroline ∧ ¬Elena, [**run'** (Caroline ∧ ¬Elena)]) & INGR **be-at'** (store, Caroline ∧ ¬Elena)]
 d. *[[**do'** (Caroline ∧ Ø, [**run'** (Caroline ∧ Ø)]) & INGR **be-at'** (store, Caroline ∧ Ø)]
 e. [[**do'** (Caroline, [**run'** (Caroline)]) & INGR **be-at'** (store, Caroline)] ∧ NOT **be-with'** (Elena, Caroline)]

Apart from potential comitatives, potential instruments and implements also exist. McKercher (2003: 173) gives an example of an implement where it is in fact, absent ((64a)).

(64) a. Kim ate pizza without a fork.
 b. Kim at pizza zonder vork.
  Kim eat\PST.3SG pizza without fork (Dutch, own data)
 c. Abdul ate soup without a spoon.
 d. Abdul at soep zonder lepel.
  Abdul eat\PST.3SG soup without spoon

To satisfy the completeness constraint, *spoon* must somehow be present in the LS. Similar to NOT **be-with'**, I propose to use a negated use-predicate. The LSs for (64a–64d) are given in (65).

(65) a. **do′** (Kim, [**eat′** (Kim, pizza) ∧ NOT **use′** (Kim, fork)])
b. **do′** (Kim, [**eat′** (Kim, pizza) ∧ NOT **use′** (Kim, vork)])
c. **do′** (Abdul, [**eat′** (Abdul, soup) ∧ NOT **use′** (Abdul, spoon)])
d. **do′** (Abdul, [**eat′** (Abdul, soep) ∧ NOT **use′** (Abdul, lepel)])

Not only comitatives and implements, but also instruments can be 'potential'. Consider the examples below:

(66) a. *Mara destroyed the barn with a wrecking ball.*
b. *Mara destroyed the barn without a wrecking ball.*
c. *Sonia melted the ice with a hair dryer.*
d. *Sonia melted the ice without a hair dryer.*
e. *The lumberjack cut down the tree with a chainsaw.*
f. *The lumberjack cut down the tree without a chainsaw.*

Here, too, the potential instruments need to be accounted for in the LS. Simply adding a ¬ sign or including NOT results in a paradox again. Consider such LSs in (67).

(67) a. *[**do′** (Mara, Ø)] CAUSE [[**do′** (¬wrecking ball, Ø)] CAUSE [BECOME **destroyed′** (barn)]]
b. *[**do′** (Sonia, Ø)] CAUSE [[**do′** (¬hair dryer, Ø)] CAUSE [BECOME **melted′** (ice)]]
c. *[**do′** (lumberjack, Ø)] CAUSE [[**do′** (¬chainsaw, Ø)] CAUSE [BECOME **cut down′** (tree)]]
d. *[**do′** (Mara, Ø)] CAUSE [[NOT **do′** (wrecking ball, Ø)] CAUSE [BECOME **destroyed′** (barn)]]
e. *[**do′** (Sonia, Ø)] CAUSE NOT [[**do′** (hair dryer, Ø)] CAUSE [BECOME **melted′** (ice)]]
f. *[**do′** (Sonia, Ø)] NOT CAUSE [[**do′** (hair dryer, Ø)] CAUSE [BECOME **melted′** (ice)]]
g. *Mara did not act on the wrecking ball, causing it to destroy the barn.*
h. *Mara acted on nothing, causing it to destroy the barn.*

7.4 Potential instruments, implements & comitatives

i. *Sonia did not act on the hair dryer, causing it to melt the ice.
g. *Sonia acted on nothing, causing it to melt the ice.
j. *The lumberjack did not act on the chainsaw causing it cut down the tree.
k. *The lumberjack acted on nothing, causing it to cut down the tree.

The LSs in (67a–67f) cannot be correct, as the causal paraphrases in (67g–67k) produce utterly bizarre results. The paraphrases above show that there can be no causal embedding. Yet, the potential instrument must be accounted for in the LS in order to satisfy the completeness constraint. Recall that instruments are only instruments if an implement is causally embedded. The examples in (65) illustrated that negating an implement is unproblematic. I propose to use the same approach for *potential* instruments. If an implement is not causally embedded, it is not an instrument. If the implement is not even manipulated at all, there certainly cannot be any kind of causal embedding. I therefore propose the LSs in (68):

(68) a. [[**do´** (Mara, Ø)] CAUSE [BECOME **destroyed´** (barn)] ∧ [**do´** (3SG, [NOT **use´** (Mara, wrecking ball)])]]
b. [[**do´** (Sonia, Ø)] CAUSE [BECOME **melted´** (ice)] ∧ [**do´** (3SG, [NOT **use´** (Sonia, hairdryer)])]]
c. [[**do´** (lumberjack, Ø)] CAUSE [BECOME **cut down´** (tree)] ∧ [**do´** (3SG, [NOT **use´** (lumberjack, chainsaw)])]]

In this section, I have adopted Farrell's **be-with´** approach to a modest degree. While I also treat potential comitatives with the predicate's negated version, I reject Farrell's proposal to use **be-with´** for all comitatives. Contrary to Farrell, I only use **be-with´** for strictly co-occurrent referents.

7.5 Problematic cases of instruments

A 'problematic case' I wish to address was introduced earlier in this chapter. Farrell (2009: 189–190) provides an example of a causative accomplishment that features an implement. This example, together with Farrell's proposed LS are given in (69a) and (69b), respectively.

(69) a. *The boy put together the bike with a manual.*
 b. [**do**′ (boy, Ø)] CAUSE [BECOME **together**′ (bike) ∧ **use**′ (boy, manual)]
 c. **The boy acted on the manual, causing it to put together the bike.*
 d. **The boy caused the manual to be used.*
 e. *The boy caused the bike to be put together/assembled.*

Using the causative paraphrase in (69c) shows that the *with*-PP is an implement and not an instrument. Farrell's proposed LS, however, is problematic. The way the LS in (69b) is written, the use of the *manual* is part of the caused event. This is wrong, as the contrast in acceptability of paraphrases in (69d) and (69e) shows. Rather, the *manual* is a tool that modifies the whole LS: The most likely interpretation for (69a) is that the boy assembled the bike while continuously using a manual. Therefore, it can only relate to the LS in (70a). The LS in (70b) implies that the boy's use of the manual caused the coming about of the event. If the context in (70c) is present, then the LS in (70b) is possible. The distinction between the two readings relates to the placement of the use-predicate in the LS.

(70) a. [[[**do**′ (boy, Ø)] CAUSE [BECOME **together**′ (bike)]] ∧ [**do**′ (boy, [**use**′ (boy, manual)])]]
 b. [**do**′ (boy, [**use**′ (boy, manual)])] CAUSE [BECOME **together**′ (bike)]
 c. *After having read the manual, the boy put together the bike.*

7.6 Conclusion

In this chapter, I explored the semantics of several concepts or phenomena that are superficially related to the typical instruments. Several varieties of comitative were discussed, revealing that the phenomenon is much wider than it is often assumed in the literature. Even though the most prototypical comitative is of the 'actor'-variety, undergoer and NMR-varieties also exist. Although there are some differences between them, they all share a crucial feature which I have called *positional equivalence*. That is, the two arguments in question must be able to occupy the same positions in the LS. For the actor-comitatives, the actionality levels of the argument's referents must be similar. Each of the arguments must be able to function in the relevant argument position in the LS and this depends on whether the actionality requirements of the slot are met. Whether or not it is possible to alternatively code one of the arguments varies. In the case of actor-comitatives, both arguments require a level of actionality that is almost identical. If the levels are too distinct, then alternatively coding the lower-ranking argument (in terms of the actionality level) would result in an instrument reading and thus link back to an instrument-LS.

Apart from comitatives, human referents in the typical instrument-effector position were also explored. I argued in favor of treating these as causees and proposed to include them as a distinct effector subtype. By contrast, pseudo-agents are not recognized as an effector subtype as they constitute a specific class of referent rather than a distinct reading of the effector role. That is, they can be conceptualized as instruments or instigators. It is also possible for causees to take instruments themselves. In this case, there is a very strong tendency for the causee to be higher in the LS, even though there are exceptions to this. I have formalized this strong tendency as the *Relative Power Principle*, which can be seen as a governing principle for causees and instruments when they occur in the same LS.

I also provided an updated version of predicative *with* (**be-with'**) to account for the expression of general spatio-temporal co-occurrence of two referents. This approach can account for sentences where a referent is not wielded by another and those where it cannot be co-author of a state of affairs. Typically, this includes cases where one referent is passively spatio-temporally present throughout the event as is *hammer* in *John ran to the store with his hammer.* **Be-with´** can also be used for figurative belonging to a group or unit. Potential instruments and implements were introduced as the expression of a non-use. Stating that an action was performed without a tool expresses that it was not used. However, as potentials occur in the morphosyntax, they must be present in the semantic representation so as not to violate the completeness constraint. To account for such cases, I proposed treating them as the negated versions of implements (i.e. NOT **use´**). Potential comitatives refer to non-accompaniment. It was illustrated that negating a normal comitative is overly simplistic and untenable. I therefore argued in favor of a predicative *without* (i.e. NOT **be-with´**).

Properties of individuals are often expressed with the preposition *with*, as in, for example, *the woman with the book.* To capture these, I adopted RRG's approach to the structure of RPs.

8 Linking semantics to syntax

In this chapter, I go into 1) linking the LS to the morphosyntax and the coding strategies, 2) the expansion of base logical structures to accommodate instruments, causees, comitatives and implements and 3) several constructions containing instruments. With respect to 3), recall from the introduction that instruments occur in a wide variety of morphosyntactic configurations. Consider:

(1) a. *Todd shattered the window with the rock.*
     b. *The rock shattered the window.* (ISA, see chapter 6)
     c. *The window was shattered by Todd with the rock.*
     d. *The window was shattered by the rock.*
     e. *The window shattered with the rock.*[1]
     f. *The window shatters easily with a rock.*

I refer to the typical examples featuring instruments that I have employed throughout this dissertation as the *standard instrument example*. It includes examples like the ones in (2).

(2) a. *John cut down the tree with an axe.*
     b. *Sarah opened the box with the knife.*

Parallel to the standard occurrence of instruments, there is a *standard implement example*. To date, no language has been found that morphologically distinguishes between implements and instruments. Both classes of tools do show syntactic differences in different languages, however. Implements can never undergo ISA and in languages where it is very productive, like English, this becomes immediately visible. The linking of

---

[1] This sentence is rejected by many native speakers and it does not fit naturally in RRG. Because it occurs in the relevant literature, sentences of this type have been included in this chapter.

both standard implements and standard instruments will be explored in the general linking sections (8.1 and 8.2). Special constructions featuring instruments and/or implements will be discussed in sections 8.3 onwards.

8.1 Three classes of prepositions

RRG makes a distinction between predicative and non-predicative prepositions (Van Valin 2005: 21ff.). In contrast to the former, the latter mark arguments in the core and have a flat syntactic structure. Predicative prepositions introduce new semantic content and license an argument. Jolly (1993: 286) argues in favor of recognizing a category in between, the semi-predicative prepositions (*class two-prepositions*). These prepositions are said to introduce a new argument to the larger LS. A crucial feature of class two-prepositions is argument-sharing: The added section of LS has to share an argument with the base LS. Van Valin & LaPolla 1997: 159–160) call these argument-adjunct prepositions. Syntactically, these PPs take the form of predicative PPs, but they occur in the core. Prime examples of this kind are PPs involved in the alternation between activities and active accomplishments. Consider (adapted from Van Valin & LaPolla 1997: 160):

(3) a. *Paul ran.*
    b. **do'** (Paul, [**run'** (Paul)])
    c. *Paul ran to the store.*
    d. **do'** (Paul, [**run'** (Paul)]) & INGR **be-at'** (store, Paul)[2]
    e. **do'** (x, [**run'** (x)]) → **do'** (x, [**run'** (x)]) & INGR **be-LOC'** (y, x)

In the examples above, *to* has its own logical structure that is added to the base LS by means of a lexical rule (Van Valin 2013: 85) given in (3e).

---

[2] The analysis of active accomplishments has changed over time due to updates in theory. In Van Valin & LaPolla (1997) BECOME is used in the LS, whereas in Van Valin (2005), INGR is used instead. The notation in (3) follows the theory as outlined in Van Valin (2005).

As this example involves argument sharing, it can be considered an argument-adjunct preposition.

Whenever a preposition is considered to be non-predicative, the corresponding PP in the syntax has the typical flat structure. If the preposition is considered to be class 2, then the PP will be predicative but occur in the core.

8.2 Argument linking in Role and Reference Grammar

Linking the logical structures to their morphosyntactic expression is handled in terms of the linking algorithm (see section 2.5.3) in RRG. In the following sections, I will primarily explore argument linking and marking in English, French, Dutch and German. The notions of macroroles are crucial in this regard as RRG does not use traditional notions like subject, object and indirect object to this end. The rules for assigning the macroroles to components of the LS were given in (2.5.1). Of these four languages, only German has a case system. The other three use prepositional marking to a large extent.[3] I use English as a preliminary reference point for the coming sections. In English, prepositions are used to mark some core arguments. The preposition *with* is particularly interesting for two reasons: 1) It is the main marker for instruments, and thus of the utmost importance for this study and 2) it has a wide array of functions beyond instrument marking (Van Valin & LaPolla 1997: 376ff., Jolly 1993). This last point is illustrated by the occurrence of multiple *with*-PPs in a sentence. Consider the English example in (5a) (Van Valin & LaPolla 1997: 377) and its direct Dutch equivalent in (5b).

(4) a. *The woman with strong arms loaded the truck with hay with a pitchfork with Bill with enthusiasm.*
 b. *De vrouw met sterke armen belaadde de vrachtwagen met hooi met een hooivork met Bill met enthousiasme.*

---

[3] It is important to point out that PP-internal cases, assigned by governing prepositions are not covered by these rules (Van Valin & LaPolla 1997: 359).

8 Linking semantics to syntax

RRG assumes that most uses of *with* can be captured with a single rule (Van Valin & LaPolla 1997: 381, 382), given in (5). There is a more recent version (Van Valin 2005: 113–114) version of the rule in (5), but it covers fewer cases than the 1997-version. I will therefore only use the version in (5) in this chapter.

(5) **Rule for assigning *with* in English**

Given two arguments, x and y, in a logical structure, with x lower than or equal to y on the Actor-Undergoer Hierarchy, and a specific grammatical status (macrorole, head of NP), assign *with* to the y-argument iff it is not selected for that status.

Essentially, this rule states that the non-selected y-argument of two candidates, x and y, is marked by *with*. They can also capture the attribute reading of *with*, explored in chapter 7. Attributive readings constitute a non-default realization of the RP and as such, the preposition *with* comes into play. In other words, *with* marks the default choice of two candidates for a specific status when the non-default choice is selected for it. As I will explore in the next section, this is how instrument marking is captured.

The status and the marking of causees are more complicated, as English causative constructions consist of multiple cores. Bolivian Quechua (see (7.15)), by contrast, has causative constructions that consist of a single core (nuclear-level juncture). As the examples in (7.15) showed, the causee can be marked by either the instrumental or the accusative. Thus for Bolivian Quechua, it would not suffice to draw up a single rule for causees as they do not only have *accusative* but also *instrumental* as a marking option. Furthermore, instruments and causees occupy the same position in the LS and are both core arguments in Bolivian Quechua, but are marked differently, meaning that a single rule does not suffice to account for their marking. A similar situation exists in Kannada

(Dravidian) with dative and instrumental[4] as marking options (Van Valin & LaPolla 1997: 588).

Even in English not all uses of *with* are captured by the rule in (5). In chapter 7, a predicative use of *with* was discussed (**be-with´** (z, x)). Furthermore, potential instruments, implements and comitatives are expressed by NOT **use´** (x, y) or NOT **be-with´** (x, y), meaning that the preposition is linked to a specific LS-configuration. This is contrasted by RRG's treatment of *with*, which is tied in with the linking process (Van Valin & LaPolla 1997: 380). In the following sections, I will explore the linking for the different notions with the rule in (5) as a starting point and go into the syntactic status of each.

8.2.1 Instrument and implement marking

Instruments are assigned on the basis of the *with*-rule in (5) and are linked to arguments in the core. In the LS in (6b), the instrument is outranked for actorhood as the instigator is to the left of it. Because actor selection is absolute, there is no direct way around this principle.[5] The instrument is also outranked for undergoerhood, leaving it as the NMR. Per rule (5), it is marked by *with*. A constituent projection of (6), together with its linking is given in figure 54.

(6) a. *Jacob broke the window with the rock.*
 b. [**do´** (Jacob, Ø)] CAUSE [[**do´** (rock, Ø)] CAUSE [BECOME **broken´** (window)]]

---

[4] In both Bolivian Quechua and Kannada, instrumental marking favors an agentive implicature on the causee, whereas the other marker disfavors the implicature (Van Valin & LaPolla 1997: 588).
[5] ISA is a strategy to assign actorhood to the instrument, by virtue of leaving the instigator position empty. This does not constitute a violation of actor assignment, however, as the highest overt argument is still assigned actorhood.

8 Linking semantics to syntax

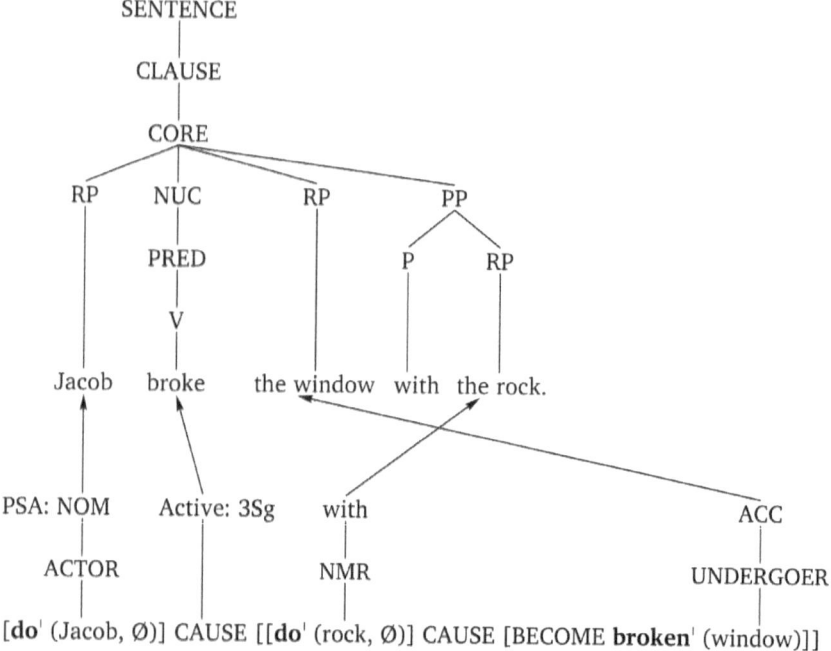

Figure 54: Linking to syntax of a clause containing an instrument.

In terms of valence in the LS, an instrument-slot is dependent on the presence of a causal chain. Causal chains can be considered to have a lexically unfilled instrument-slot by default. The causal structure of causative verbs can be 'expanded' in order to provide more specific information. By its very nature, a causal chain can accommodate additional arguments that such an expansion adds. Syntactic valence is language-dependent.

I generally follow standard RRG as far as the rule in (5) is concerned in accounting for implements. Van Valin (2013) argues that the telic quale of the implement-referent is what licenses the use-predicate. The information in the telic quale for *spoon* specifies that it can be used to facilitate eating. This information licenses the use-predicate, introducing a new argument. Implement arguments are, as it were, optional. As it is licensed by a quale, it is appended to the base LS and falls under the scope of the rule in (5). Consider the examples in (7).

(7) a. *Evie ate the soup with a spoon.*
b. **do**′ (Evie, [**eat**′ (Evie, soup) ∧ **use**′ (Evie, spoon)]) & INGR **consumed**′ (soup)
c. *Evie ate soup with a spoon.*
d. **do**′ (Evie, [**eat**′ (Evie, soup) ∧ **use**′ (Evie, spoon)])

In (7a–7b), *Evie* is selected as actor and *soup* is selected as undergoer as it is the lowest-ranking argument. *Spoon* is outranked for actorhood because there is a 'better' candidate (*Evie*). Furthermore, *spoon* is a very unlikely candidate for actorhood, as it the y-argument of a predicate instead of the x-argument. In (7c), *spoon* is outranked for actorhood by the same logic. However, it could be argued that *spoon* is as good a candidate for undergoer as *soup*: Both are y-arguments of a predicate under the scope of **do**′, that is, both are of equal rank. The left-most argument (*soup*) is selected as undergoer, leaving *spoon* to be marked by *with*, in accordance with the rule in (5). Syntactically, the implement is realized as an argument in the core. Contrary to LSs with instruments, those with implements do not have an argument slot available for the 'tool'. The telic quale creates an extra slot. Qualia are the driver behind the creation of an extra slot and the process can be captured with a lexical rule (Van Valin 2013: 90):

(8) **do**′ (x, [**pred**′ (x, (y))... → **do**′ (x, [**pred**′ (x, (y)) ∧ **use**′ (x, z)])...

In other words, the implement-PP is not the argument of a preposition, but rather the argument of a lexically augmented LS. This is the reason why it can be under the scope of the rule in (5). If it were the argument of a predicative *with*, then marking would follow from the preposition itself. In case of the full LS of instruments, it is clear then, why the instrument does not occur twice. If *with* were predicative here, it would occur twice. Once as a result of the rule in (5) and once as the result of the predicative preposition. Because it is part of a (derived) LS, it is an argument and not an argument-adjunct, as that would presuppose a predicative *with*.

Contrary to standard RRG, Jolly (1993: 298) proposes to treat the implement-*with* as a predicative preposition that has the semantic content of the use-predicate. This is problematic for several reasons. First, in chapter 7, I presented evidence in favor of a predicative *with* in the LS-form of **be-with'**. Recognizing **use'** as another predicative *with* would split the uses of *with*, ultimately leading to a treatment of all uses of *with* as separate entries. This is rejected by Van Valin & LaPolla (1997: 377) as a non-analysis. Second, the rule in (5) is a unified, simple rule that works without exception. There is no reason, then, to assume that it does not correctly explain implement-*with*. Third, assuming two predicative *with*s with very different corresponding LSs (**use'** vs. **be-with'**) is problematic from the point of view that predicative prepositions are more basic and historically precede non-predicative ones (Jolly 1993: 275–276). If this is so, then which predicative *with* is the basic, 'older' one and why do two predicative *with*s exist at the same time in language? How did one evolve from the other? Furthermore, why do their LSs take on such different forms? A representation of the linking to syntax of (7a) is given in figure 55.

8.2 Argument linking in Role and Reference Grammar

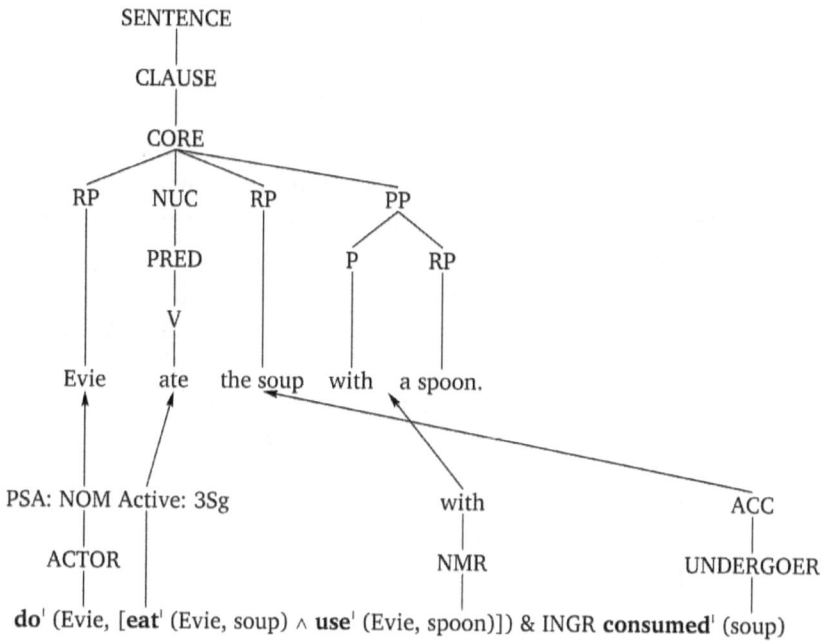

Figure 55: Linking to syntax of a clause containing an implement.

8.2.2 Causee marking

In chapter 7, a phenomenon where causees take instruments was explored. This dissertation is concerned with instruments, implements and their marking in simple cores. Because English causee constructions involve more than simple cores, I will use French as a language of illustration. In French, causatives expressing more direct causation involve nuclear junctures (for an overview of the complete theory of juncture-nexus relations in RRG, see Van Valin 2005, chapter 6), whereas weaker causation involves multiple cores. The coordination of *cores* means that both cores have their own set of arguments and one argument is shared. Consider the example from French in (9). In the example in (9), the argument *Jean* is semantically shared by the verbs. Syntactically, it is part of the first core.

(9) *Je   laisserai   Jean manger les   gateaux*
    1SG let.FUT.1SG Jean eat.INF DEF cake.PL
    'I will let Jean eat the cakes.' (Van Valin 2005: 189)

The example in (9) features permissive/enabling causation. More direct forms of causation are expressed (in French) as a combination of *nuclei*. An example of this is given in (10). The difference between the coordination of cores and the coordination of nuclei is visible (in French at least) in that with the former type the shared argument in (9) occurs in between the two verbs (cf. Van Valin 2005: 191). With nuclear cosubordination ((10a)), the two verbs occur directly next to each other. This situation also exists in Dutch and German ((10b-10c)). English, by contrast, expresses (10a) in terms of core coordination ((10d)).

(10) a. *Jean a   fait   courir Simon.*
        Jean AUX.3SG make.PTCP run   Simon
        'Jean made Simon run.' (French)
     b. *Jean heef-t   Simon doe-n   lop-en.*
        Jean AUX-3SG Simon do-INF run-INF
        'Jean made Simon run.' (Dutch)
     c. *Jean hat   Simon lauf-en   lass-en.*
        Jean AUX.3SG Simon run-INF let-INF
        'Jean made Simon run.' (German)
     d. *Jean made Simon run.*

The syntactic difference between (9) and (10a) is given in figures 56 (adapted from Van Valin 2005: 189) and 57, respectively.

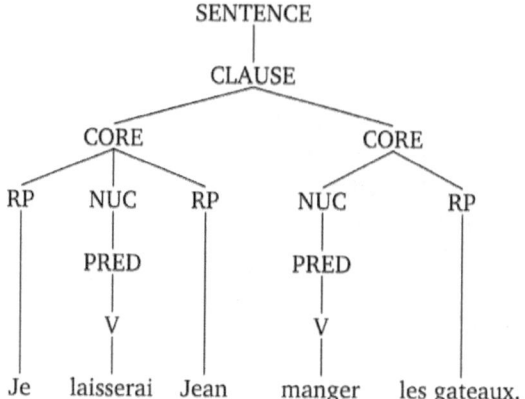

Figure 56: Syntactic structure of a French sentence expressing permissive causation.

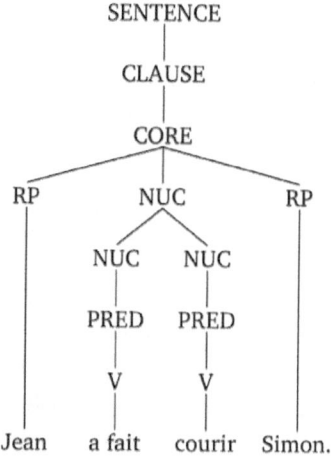

Figure 57: Syntactic structure of a French sentence expressing direct causation.

As far as linking is concerned, nuclear junctures behave the same way as simple, lexical verbs. In other words, the linking algorithm applies as it would with simple sentences. To ascertain the marking of causees taking

8 Linking semantics to syntax

instruments, I will explore several key examples, starting with the simplest structure.

(11) a. *Jean a   fait   manger Marie.*
        Jean AUX.3SG make.PTCP eat   Marie
        'Jean made Marie eat.'
    b. [**do**' (Jean, Ø)] CAUSE [**do**' (Marie, [**eat**' (Marie, Ø)])]
        A   U
    c. *Jean a   fait   manger la   soupe à*
        Jean AUX.3SG make.PTCP eat   DEF soup   to
        Marie.
        Marie
        'Jean made Marie eat the soup.'
    d. [[**do**' (Jean, Ø)] CAUSE [**do**' (Marie, [**eat**' (Marie,
            A   NMR
        soupe)])] & INGR **consumed**' (soupe)]
                                                        U

The difference between (11a–11b) and (11c–11d) in terms of marking follows from general principles and their application in French. In (11a–11b), *Jean* is the actor as it is the highest-ranking argument in the LS. Similarly, *Marie* is the undergoer as it is the lowest-ranking argument. French does not mark undergoers morphologically but positionally: It immediately follows the nucleus. In (11c–11d), the same principle is at work. The undergoer in (11c–11d) is *soupe* and is assigned the postnuclear position. *Marie* is NMR and is assigned the dative preposition *à* as it is the standard marker for NMRs, parallel to the rule governing English *to*. Parallel to the *with*-rule in English, there is the *avec*-rule marking instruments. In (12a–12b), this rule applies as *couteau* is a non-selected candidate for actorhood.

(12) a. *Marie a   coupé   le   pain   avec le   couteau.*
        Marie AUX.3SG cut.PTCP DEF bread with DEF knife
        'Marie cut the bread with the knife.'
    b. [**do**' (Marie, Ø)] CAUSE [[**do**' (couteau, Ø)] CAUSE
        [BECOME **cut**'(bread)]]

If causees take instruments, there are two NMRs. An example is given in (13a–13b). The first NMR is the causee and the second one is the instrument. The standard rule assigning *avec* would be problematic. For instance, *Marie* is a potential actor herself and, as *Marie* is not selected as actor, *avec* should be assigned. Yet, assigning *avec* would result in ungrammaticality. Furthermore, would the *avec*-rule be applied twice? Therefore, a rule capable of handling two NMRs and their relative ordering has to be established. If the instigator of (13a–13b) is left out, the result is the more basic structure in (13c). In (13c), *Marie* would be assigned actorhood and the instrument would be assigned *avec*. If the chain is expanded in such a way that an instigator is added, *Marie* loses its instigator status, leaving two intermediate effectors with both as potential actors. *Marie* is a better candidate for actorhood than *couteau*, as its referent ranks higher on the actionality scale. One could posit then, that the lower of the two arguments in terms of actionality is assigned *avec* and the higher is assigned *à*. It would not be correct to assume that the higher position in the LS correlates with *à*-marking and the lower LS-position correlates with *avec*-marking. In chapter 7, I explored a French example ((7.23a)) with two relevant interpretations. These interpretations are also available for (13a). The first is a typical causee-interpretation (LS in (13b)): *Jean* makes *Marie* do something and that is cutting the bread, using a knife to do this. The second is an interpretation where *Jean* uses a knife to make *Marie* do something and that is cutting bread. Parallel to the LS I proposed in (7.24b), the second reading has the instrument occupying a higher LS-slot than the causee (LS in (13d)). This LS shows that the LS-positions alone cannot account for the marking. If they did, then the instrument would be marked by *à* and the causee would be marked by *avec*. However, such marking is ungrammatical. It is therefore necessary – in case of two NMRs – to tie in the assignment rules with the referents' actionality status. *Couteau* ranks lower and is assigned *avec* and *Marie* ranks higher in terms of actionality and is assigned *à*. The rule I propose for this is given in (13e). Following the Paninian principle (cf. Kiparsky 1993) that more specific rules take priority over more general ones, the more specific rule in (13e) takes precedence over the more general rules assigning *avec* and *à*, respectively.

(13) a. *Jean a   fait   couper le   pain*
Jean AUX.3SG make.PTCP cut.INF DEF bread
à Marie avec un   couteau.
to Marie with INDEF knife
b. [**do´** (Jean, Ø)] CAUSE [[**do´** (Marie, Ø)] CAUSE [[**do´**
NMR₁
(couteau, Ø)] CAUSE [BECOME **cut´** (pain)]]]
NMR₂
c. [**do´** (Marie, Ø)] CAUSE [[**do´** (couteau, Ø)] CAUSE [BECOME **cut´** (pain)]]
d. [**do´** (Jean, Ø)] CAUSE [[**do´** (couteau, Ø)] CAUSE [[**do´** (Marie, Ø)] CAUSE [BECOME **cut´** (pain)]]]
e. **Rule for assigning *avec* and *à* in LS with two NMRs**
Given a logical structure with two non-macrorole arguments, α and β, with both as potential actors in terms of the AUH, assign *avec* to NMR α if its referent's actionality is lower than NMR β's referent's actionality. Assign à to NMR β.

8.2 Argument linking in Role and Reference Grammar

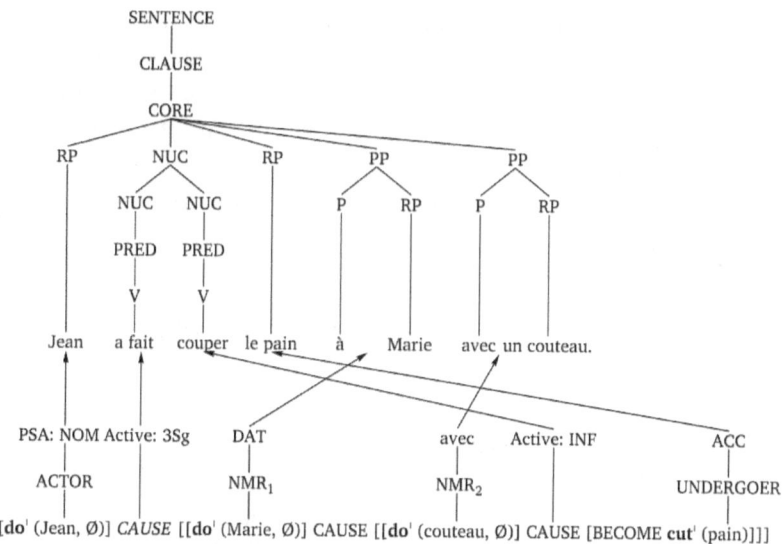

Figure 58: Causee under the scope of direct causation taking an instrument.

The example above is an example of direct causation. French has two causative auxiliaries (*faire* and *laisser*) whereas English has three (*make, have, let*). To express the difference between direct and indirect causation, for which English uses two different auxiliaries (*make* vs. *have*), French cannot use *laissser* because it expresses permissive and enabling causation. Rather than leaving the structure ambiguous like Dutch[6] or German, French has a linking option where the second, embedded LS-segment also takes two macroroles (Van Valin 2005: 236). This creates a problem as the compound LS would have three macroroles: An undergoer (contributed by the embedded LS), an actor (contributed by the first section of the LS) and a second actor (contributed by the embedded LS). This would create three macroroles for one core, which is not allowed. Because of this restriction, the actor of the matrix-level LS is selected as

---

[6] As I pointed out in chapter 5, Dutch has a disambiguation strategy but it is not open to all verbs. The French linking option is fairly productive, by contrast. Also recall that Netherlandic Dutch only has one causative auxiliary (*laten*).

8 Linking semantics to syntax

PSA and the second actor is realized in the periphery, marked as a passive agent so as not to violate the restriction. The main piece of evidence in favor of analyzing the second actor as being realized in the periphery is that it is optional. Contrary to the causee in (13a), it can be left out. The instrument-effector in (14) is an NMR, just as in (13a) and its marking is accounted for by the *avec*-rule. An example of this is given in (14a–14b) and the linking is given in figure 59.

(14) a. *Jean   a   fait   couper   le   pain   par*
       Jean AUX.3SG make.PTCP cut.INF   DEF bread   by
       Marie avec un   couteau.
       Marie with INDEF knife
       'Jean had Marie cut the cake with a knife.'
   b. [**do**´ (Jean, Ø)] *CAUSE* [[**do**´ (Marie, Ø)] *CAUSE* [[**do**´
       A_M   A_2
       (couteau, Ø)] *CAUSE* [*BECOME* **cut**´ (pain)]]]
       NMR_1   U

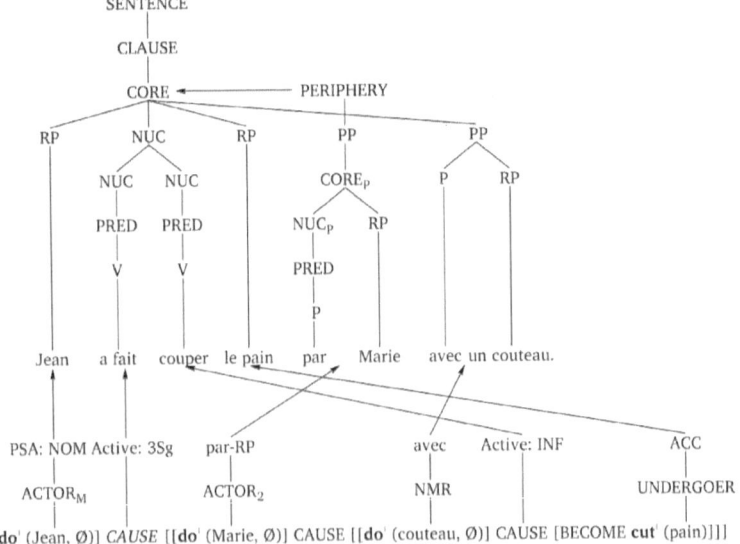

Figure 59: Causee under the scope of indirect causation taking an instrument.

As far as causation is concerned, the main difference is the strength of causation (direct and indirect causation, respectively). The initial causal operator is italicized (*CAUSE*) to indicate its underspecified nature. As I pointed out in chapter 7, the precise interpretation (CAUSE vs. IND) is supplied by Holisky's principle. In case of (13a), the *à*-marker serves as information to the contrary and the causee is interpreted as being under the scope of direct causation. *Par* allows for a volitional reading of the causee and the type of causation is considered to be *indirect*. In other words, I do not wish to posit two different versions of *faire* in the lexicon, but rather an underspecified one. This ties in to the discussion of the different types of causation: Languages allow for a degree of vagueness when it comes to expressing the strength of causation. French is no different here. The construction in (13) unambiguously expresses direct causation. The default interpretation for (14) is one of indirect causation, yet it can be interpreted as expressing direct causation given the right context (Simon Petitjean, p.c.). In this thesis, I assume the default reading for the sake of clarity. Both constructions can be summarized in terms of a unified constructional schema.[7] It is given in table 27.

Construction: French causative construction with instrument	
Syntax:	Juncture: Nuclear
	Nexus: Cosubordination
	Construction type: Serial verb
	[CL [CORE RP [NUC [NUC...] [NUC...]]] RP PP PP]...]
	PSA: Actor$_M$
	Linking: (1) Default (Direct causation)
	(2) Two Actors (Actor$_M$ and Actor$_2$) in case of indirect causation and transitive NUC$_2$. Link Actor$_2$ to CORE$_{PERIPHERY}$
Template:	Default Syntactic Template Selection Principle

---

[7] A$_M$ stands for actor on the matrix level.

8 Linking semantics to syntax

Morphology:	Verb: NUC₁: Default finite
	NUC₂: Non-finite
	Argument marking: Default (linking (1))
	Par (linking (2))
Semantics:	[PRED_NUC1] *CAUSE* [PRED_NUC2]
Pragmatics:	IF: unspecified
	Focus structure: unspecified

Table 27: Constructional schema for French causee construction with an instrument.

8.2.3 Comitative marking

As pointed out in chapter 7, comitatives are essentially conjoined arguments where only one is selected as actor or undergoer. The other is linked as an oblique core argument (in a *with*-PP). In terms of linking, comitative marking can be accounted for by the rule for NMRs in (5), as the object of *with* is still an argument of the main LS. This makes the comitative PP similar in status to an instrumental PP; both are non-predicative PPs functioning as arguments in the core. Consider:

(15) a. *Todd and Michael destroyed the ship.*
      b. *Todd destroyed the ship with Michael.*

In (15a), the conjoined RP *Todd and Michael* is selected as actor and becomes the PSA. In (15b) only *Todd* is selected as actor and PSA while *ship* is the undergoer. This leaves *Michael* as an intermediate argument. To use Jolly's (1993) terms, *Michael* is a potential macrorole candidate but not selected for a specific macrorole, leaving it as an NMR. The rule for non-predicative *with* applies and *Michael* is realized in a PP. The constituent projection for (15b) is given in figure 60.

8.2 Argument linking in Role and Reference Grammar

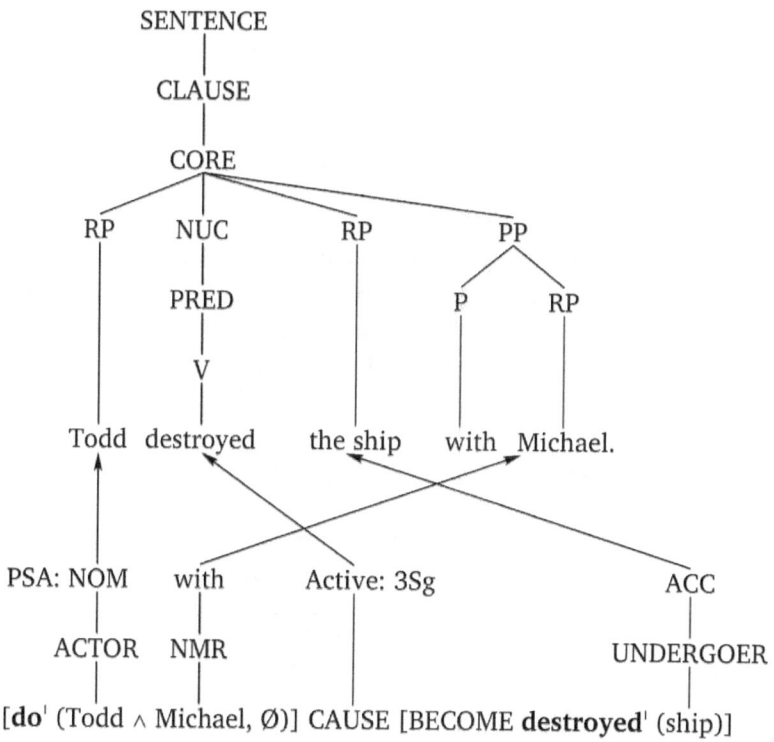

Figure 60: Linking to syntax for *Todd destroyed the ship with Michael.*

The NMR-marking rule is usually considered in the context of arguments that are not selected as actor, like instruments. Yet, it also applies to the lower section of the AUH. As undergoer selection is variable, the potential undergoer argument that is not selected as undergoer is (in English) canonically marked by *with*. In chapter 7, undergoer- and NMR-comitatives were discussed. Their marking is also accounted for by the rule in (5). In the example in (16b), only one argument is selected as undergoer, leaving the other as a non-macrorole argument. Because it is a potential candidate for a specific status (in this case undergoerhood) but not selected as such, it is marked by *with*. The other NMR, *Sam* is marked according to the default NMR-rule. The LS for (16a–16b) is given in (16c).

(16) a. *Jack served [cheese and wine] to Sam.*
        A   U   NMR
b. *Jack served cheese [with wine] [to Sam].*
        A   U   NMR$_2$ NMR$_1$
c. [**do′** (John, Ø)] CAUSE [BECOME **have′** (Sam, cheese ∧ wine)]

The marking of the NMR-comitative follows the same principles. The example from chapter 7 is repeated in (17). In (17a) the lowest-ranking argument is chosen as NMR and the intermediate argument is selected as undergoer. Similar to (16b), one of the arguments is not selected for a certain status (here: NMR) and is marked by *with* as a result ((17b–17c)). In chapter 7, I called this phenomenon *NMR-splitting*, as one NMR is split into two NMRs and the most topical one is unmarked.

(17) a. *John served his guests [the entree and the soup].*
        A   U   NMR
b. *John served his guests the entree with the soup.*
c. [**do′** (John, Ø)] CAUSE [BECOME **have′** (guests,
                                A   U
    entree ∧ soup)]
    NMR$_1$ NMR$_2$

There does seem to be a limitation to comitative phenomena. In the examples in (16) and (17) the verbs allowing variable undergoer selection are dative shift verbs. The main difference (in English) between dative shift verbs and the other class of verbs that allow variable undergoer selection (*transfer*-verbs) is that the former leave the shifted NMR unmarked (Van Valin 2005: 114), as is the case in (17a). Consider an example of a transfer-verb in (18).

8.2 Argument linking in Role and Reference Grammar

(18) a. Nicholas presented the notebook and the pad
              A   U
        [to Everett].
        NMR
    b. Nicholas presented Everett [with the notebook and the
              A   U   NMR
        pad].

In (18a), the default MR-assignment rules apply. In (18b), the intermediate argument is assigned the undergoer macrorole and the lowest-ranking argument is assigned NMR-hood. It is possible to apply comitative linking to (18a) but not to (18b):

(19) a. Nicholas presented the notebook with the pad to Everett.
    b. *Nicholas presented Everett [with the notebook]
              A   U   NMR1
        [with the pad].
        NMR2

With comitative marking and marked undergoer selection the arguments in question are eligible for a certain status but not selected as such. In the inadmissible (19b), the *with*-rule applies twice, once for the marked undergoer selection and once to split the NMR in two NMRs. Both linking procedures can individually apply, as illustrated by (18b) and (19a), but not together. It seems that the marked undergoer-*with* takes priority over comitative *with*. This is not a linking problem in itself, as applying marked undergoer selection and comitative linking together is possible in dative shift verbs ((20)). Rather, there is a constraint that prohibits two *with*s with essentially the same function and gives marked undergoer-*with* priority.

(20) Jack served Sam [cheese] [with wine].
      A   U   NMR$_1$ NMR$_2$

8 Linking semantics to syntax

8.2.4 Inanimate comitatives

In chapter 7, a type of 'comitative' was explored where no co-authorhood exists:

(21) a. *Edward ran to the hospital with the hammer.*
b. *Joan ran to the store with the goldfish.*

It was argued that in such cases, the LS-sequence **be-with′** (z, x) is appended to the main LS. This constitutes the prime predicative use of *with*. The sequence **be-with′** (z, x) introduces a new argument that cannot be licensed by the base LS and it crucially shares an argument with that same base LS, making this use of *with* an argument-adjunct preposition. Consider the LSs for (21a–21b):

(22) a. [[**do′** (Edward, [**run′** (Edward)]) & INGR **be-at′** (hospital, Edward)] ∧ **be-with′** (hammer, Edward)]
b. [[**do′** (Joan, [**run′** (Joan)]) & INGR **be-at′** (store, Joan)] ∧ **be-with′** (goldfish, Joan)]

The sentences in (21) contain two argument-adjuncts: The *with*-PPs and the goal PPs. The constituent projection and the linking for (21a) is given in figure 61.

8.2 Argument linking in Role and Reference Grammar

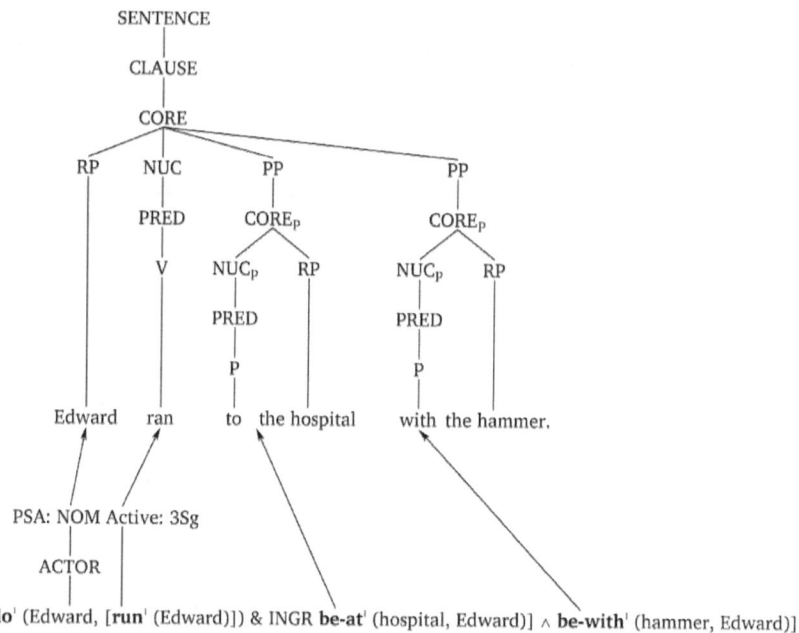

Figure 61: Linking to syntax for *Edward ran to the hospital with the hammer*.

8.2.5 Marking of proper part-implements

In chapter 7, it was pointed out that proper parts used as implements have a preference for a different marker. Consider the following examples with their LSs:

(23) a. *The digger dug a hole by means of its scoop.*
  b. *The computer virus crippled the mainframe by means of its coding.*
  c. *The digger dug a hole with its scoop.*
  d. *The computer virus crippled the mainframe with its coding.*
  e. [[**do´** (digger, Ø)] CAUSE [BECOME **dug´** (hole)] ∧ [**do´** (digger, [**use´** (digger, its scoop)])]]

f. [[**do′** (computer virus, Ø)] CAUSE [BECOME **crippled′** (mainframe)] ∧ [**do′** (computer virus, [**use′** (computer virus, its coding)])]]

The sentences in (23c–23d) are grammatical but less acceptable than their counterparts in (23a–23b). This means that as far as (23c) and (23d) are concerned, the normal *with*-rule that covers standard implements applies. The implement is eligible for undergoerhood but is not selected as such, leaving it to be marked by *with*. However, how can the linking with *by means of* be accounted for? The key feature here is that the implements in question are a proper-part relation to the effector. This information can be captured in terms of qualia. In qualia theory, the relation between parts of an entity and the whole are handled in terms of the *constitutive quale*. I propose the following (partial) qualia-annotation for *coding* and *computer virus*:

(24) a. **Coding** (a)
Constitutive: **programming subcomponent′** (b)
Formal: **digital sequence′** (a)
b. **Computer virus** (b)
Constitutive: **superordinate′** (a)
Formal: **Digital algorithm′** (b)
Telic: [**do′** (b, [...])] CAUSE [BECOME **pred′** (y)]

The crucial information here is located in in the constitutive quale and it can be integrated with a prepositional assignment rule.

(25) Assign *by means of* to non-MR argument *y* in LS segment **use′** (x, y_C).

The subscript with the y-argument refers to the constitutive quale in the sense that the slot filler must be listed in the lexicon as a proper part of the slot filler of the x-argument. The rule in (25) is a much more specific rule than the one in (5). Therefore, the Paninian principle regarding the order of rules applies here as well: The specific rule outranks the more general one. It is important to point out, however, that the rule in (25) applies primarily to inanimates and their proper parts. This is evidenced by examples (7.58a–b), repeated here in (26). In (26a–26b), the rule in (25) does not apply. Applying (25) to animates and their proper parts produces very odd, and to most informants, ungrammatical results ((26c–26d) and (7.61i–7.61j)). The preference surrounding *by means of* is very similar in Dutch ((26e–26f)).

(26)   a.   *He untied the knot with his teeth.* (Nilsen 1973: 130)
       b.   *I bit him with my false teeth.* (Lyons 1968: 422)
       c.   **He untied the knot by means of his teeth.*
       d.   **I bit him by means of my false teeth.*
       e.   Het   computer virus   leg-de   de   computer
           DEF   computer virus   cripple-PST.3SG   DEF   computer
           lam   met   zijn   code.
           VPR   with   POSS.3SG   code
       f.   Het   computer virus   leg-de   de   computer
           DEF   computer virus   cripple-PST.3SG   DEF   computer
           lam   met   door middel van   code.
           VPR   with   through means of   code

8.2.6 Marking of potential instruments, implements and comitatives

It is possible to use Van Valin's (2013) approach of co-composition to account for potential instruments and implements. In chapter 7, I argued that potential instruments and implements can be accounted for by including NOT in the typical implement LS. The preposition *without* is very specific and is restricted to three cases: NOT **have´**, NOT **be-with´** and NOT **use´**. NOT **be-with´** constitutes the predicative version of *without* and will be discussed below. As such, it does not need to be included the rule assigning the other cases of *without*.[8] I propose to treat the assignment of non-predicative *without* in terms of the rule in (27a). Matching examples are given in (27b–27e).

---

[8] I am aware that there are other uses of *without*, such as *without enthusiasm*. These uses fall outside the scope of this dissertation and will therefore not be explored here.

8 *Linking semantics to syntax*

(27) a. **Rule assigning *without* in English**
Assign *without* to non-macrorole y-argument in the logical structure segment:...NOT **pred′** (x, y)
b. *Evie ate the soup without a spoon.*
c. **do′** (Evie, [**eat′** (Evie, soup) ∧ NOT **use′** (Evie, spoon)]) & INGR **consumed′** (soup)
d. *The woman without the book*
e. NOT **have′** (<u>woman</u>, book)

The assignment of *without* is predicted by the rule in (27a): *Evie* and *soup* are selected as actor and undergoer, respectively leaving *spoon* as NMR. As the correct LS-segment is present, the NMR is marked by *without*. There is a close resemblance to the rule governing *from* in English (Van Valin & LaPolla 1997: 377). The crucial difference, however, is that the rule governing *from* includes either the BECOME or the INGR operator in the relevant LS-segment. In other words, despite the similarity, it and the rule in (27a) are quite distinct. The example in (27b) has a potential implement, but (27a) also captures potential instruments. Consider the example in (28a) below.

(28) a. *Jacob broke the window without a rock.*
b. [**do′** (Jacob, Ø)] CAUSE [BECOME **broken′** (window)] ∧ [**do′** (Jacob, [NOT **use′** (Jacob, rock)])]

Here, too, a similar linking presents itself: *Jacob* is the actor and *window* is the undergoer. *Rock* is outranked for both and becomes the NMR. As the segment NOT **pred′** (x, y) is present, both conditions of the rule are met and the argument is marked by *without*. Potential instruments have to be represented as in (28b), as any other configuration (e.g. negating the instrument in the causal chain) yields paradoxical results for the larger LS (see the examples in (7.67)). Essentially, I treat potential implements and instruments as the potential version of implements rather than of instruments. This has the consequence that the question of the source of the argument is raised once more. Van Valin (2013) assumes that implements are licensed by the telic quale of the referent. I propose to treat potential implements/instruments in virtually the same way. By explicitly stating that one is not using a certain tool, the assumption is that it *is* usually used in the state of affairs. This is illustrated by the lower acceptability of the second in each of the sentence pairs:

(29) a. Abdul ate the soup without a spoon.
 b. ?Abdul ate the soup without a telescope.
 c. Evie watched the birds without binoculars.
 d. ?Evie watched the birds without a hammer.

Telescopes and hammers are not readily used in eating or watching events and as a consequence, the examples in (29b) and (29d) sound odd. The telic quales of *spoon* and *binoculars* contain the information that they are used for eating and observing, respectively. Consider a partial qualia-entry for *spoon* and *binoculars*:

(30) a. **spoon** (a)
 Telic: **do´** (b, [**eat´** (b, c) ∧ **use´** (b, a)])...
 Agentive: **artifact´** (a)
 b. **binoculars** (a)
 Telic: **do´** (b, [**watch´** (b, c) ∧ **use´** (b, a)])...
 Agentive: **artifact´** (a)

This information creates the argument slot in the base LS, as explored in Van Valin (2013). Contextually supplied information then provides the *NOT* part of the LS-segment. Then, the rule in (27a) applies.[9] This can be captured with a lexical rule for negated instruments and implements:

(31) **do´** (x, [**pred´** (x, (y))... → **do´** (x, [**pred´** (x, (y)) ∧ NOT **use´** (x, z)])...

The constituent projection for (27b) is given in figure 62.

---

[9] It might be confusing that English *with* has some superficial similarity to *without*. However, in languages like Dutch (*met* vs. *zonder*), German (*mit* vs. *ohne*), French (*avec* vs. *sans*) and Bulgarian (*s* vs. *bez*) they are quite distinct.

8 Linking semantics to syntax

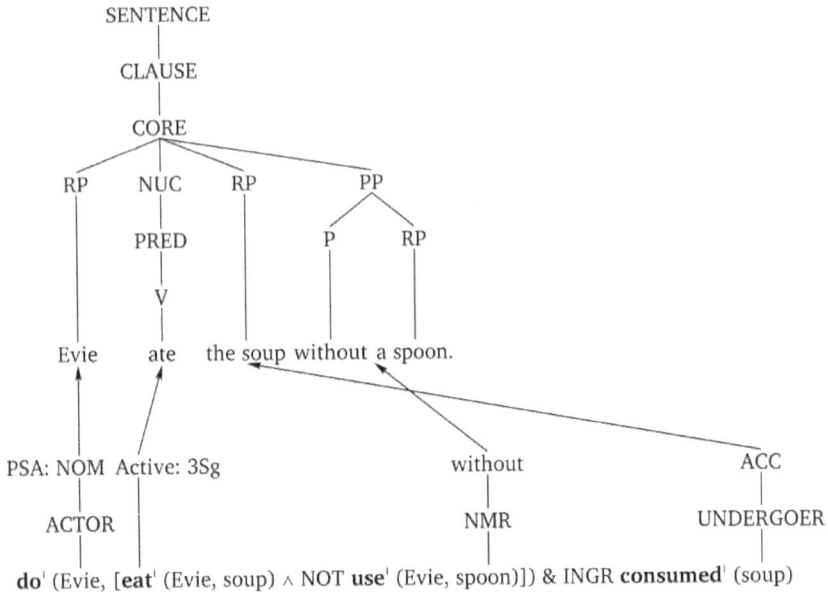

Figure 62: Linking to syntax for *Evie ate the soup without a spoon*.

As is the case with many prepositions, there is also a predicative version of *without*. This use was introduced in section 7.4 as the potential version of comitatives. It might seem counterintuitive to treat potential comitatives as involving a predicative preposition when normal comitatives are the result of argument marking options. Yet, as I explored in section 7.4, treating potential comitatives as a kind of linking option is implausible. Parallel to predicative *with* (**be-with´**), I propose NOT **be-with´**. I assume that predicative *without* is, similar to predicative *with*, a class 2-preposition (cf. Jolly 1993). That is to say, it introduces a new argument and shares an argument with the main LS. Consider:

(32) a. *Caroline ran to the store without Elena.*
      b. [[**do´** (Caroline, [**run´** (Caroline)]) & INGR **be-at´** (store, Caroline)] ∧ NOT **be-with´** (Elena, Caroline)]

In (32a), *without* is predicative, meaning that the preposition takes an argument, rather being the result of argument marking rules. This

340

8.2 Argument linking in Role and Reference Grammar

approach can also account for a variation to (17), as given in (33d). The PP *with the soup* in (17) is essentially the result of a linking option. As I have illustrated before, marking an argument negatively in the LS produces implausible results. As I argue for a difference in status, some behavioral difference must present itself. The examples in (33) show that the non-predicative *with*-PP and the non-predicative *without*-PP are positionally constrained: There is a clear preference for them to occur in direct adjacency to the RP *the soup* and after the undergoer-argument, respectively. The predicative *without*-PP does not show this tendency; it is positionally less constrained. This is illustrated in (33a–33b) and (33c–33d), respectively.

(33) a. *John served the entree with the soup to his guests.*
      b. *?John served the entree to his guests with the soup.*
      c. *John served the entree without the soup to his guests.*
      d. *John served the entree to his guests without the soup.*

As the predicative use of *without* introduces an argument to the LS and another is shared with that LS, syntactically, these PPs are argument-adjuncts. The linking for (32) is given in figure 63.

8 *Linking semantics to syntax*

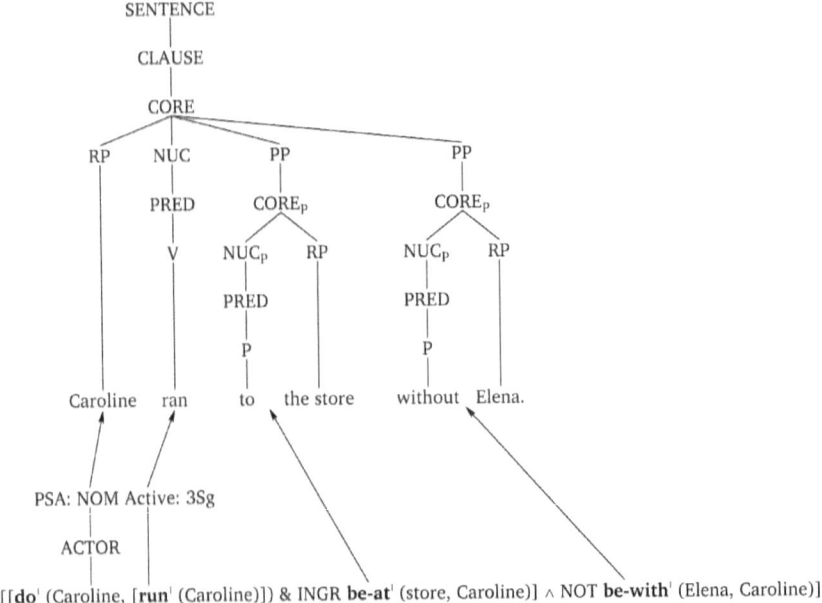

Figure 63: Linking to syntax for *Caroline ran to the store without Elena*.

8.2.7 Extending predicative *with* and *without*

Following Jolly, I assume that predicative uses of prepositions are more basic than non-predicative uses. Heine et al. (1991: 159) observed that there is a cross-linguistic pattern of grammaticalization where (for instance), the *location* case function serves a starting point with the expression of *companion* and *instrument* being often derived from it. Heine treats *instrument* as being more grammaticalized than *companion* but the essential insight is that both 'case functions' are derivative of the more basic *location* case function. What does this imply for my treatment of *with*?

In the previous sections, I argued in favor of recognizing a predicative *with* alongside its already recognized non-predicative version. Jolly's claim that the former function precedes the latter and are thus historically more basic, fits Heine's grammaticalization scale. The increasing grammaticalization in markers found by Heine has a direct reflection in the semantics (in terms of LS). These two claims can be combined with my treatment of *with*. This is schematized as in (34) below. The direction of the arrow indicates increasing grammaticalization, whereas the dashed line indicates the shift in corresponding LS-configuration.

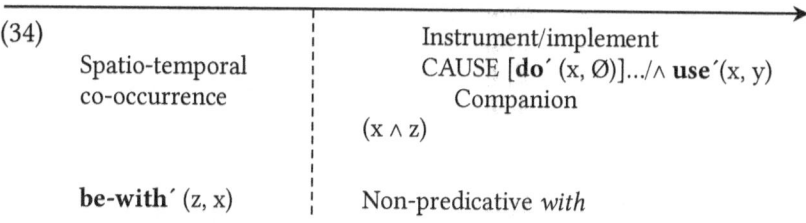

(34)
Spatio-temporal co-occurrence

(x ∧ z)

be-with' (z, x)

Instrument/implement
CAUSE [**do'** (x, ∅)].../∧ **use'**(x, y)
Companion

Non-predicative *with*

As far as *without* is concerned, I equally assume that the predicative use of *without* is more basic and that it can be modelled according to the same logic. This is given in (35).

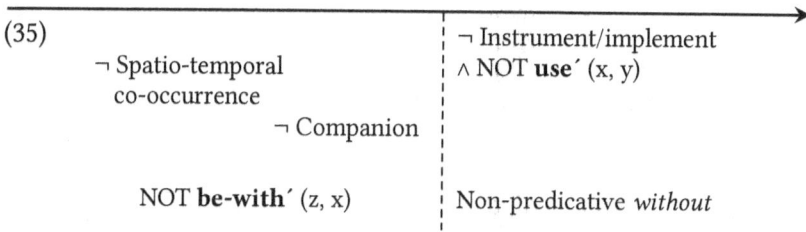

(35)
¬ Spatio-temporal co-occurrence

¬ Companion

NOT **be-with'** (z, x)

¬ Instrument/implement
∧ NOT **use'** (x, y)

Non-predicative *without*

The driver of these grammaticalization clines can be argued to be roughly of the same type of metaphoric extension I referred to earlier (cf. Luraghi 2014, Lakoff & Johnson 1980a & b, Stolz 1996): *Being* together with someone in the same location (more precisely: spatio-temporal co-occurrence) is considered as a prototypical prerequisite to *doing* something together. Prototypical instrumentality can be seen a wielder and a tool being together in the same location *and* doing something together (in a more general sense). This line of reasoning can be traced to Lakoff & Johnson's work on metaphors and more particularly on the metaphor where instruments are essentially treated as companions (Lakoff & Johnson 1980b: 135ff.). In the European languages, the historical shift from comitative to instrument is commonplace and well-documented (Narrog 2014: 76) and the extension from location to comitative is also a well-established fact (Ibid.: 74). Stolz (1996) provides evidence in favor of languages extending instrumental morphology to include comitative functions rather than the other way around. This presents many problems for the claimed universality of Lakoff & Johnson's instrument-as-companion metaphor. Yet, Heine (1991), amongst others, has found evidence in favor of grammaticalization clines from many different source domains extending to instrumentality. Be that as it may, the extension from companionship to instrumentality is well established for the Indo-European languages and especially for the SAE-languages (Stolz 1996: 120) which are the core of this dissertation.

8.3 Passive construction with an instrument

Instrument constructions can also be passivized. Consider the examples in (36).

(36) a. *Jack cut down the tree with the axe.*
b. *The tree was cut down by Jack with the axe.*
c. *The tree was cut down with the axe.*

The passive construction in (36b) is fairly straightforward from an RRG point of view. Passivization is treated in terms of PSA-modulation and argument modulation (Van Valin 2005: 116). That is to say, the PSA assignment is marked in that the lowest-ranking argument rather than the highest-ranking one is selected (in accusative systems). Argument modulation concerns the non-canonical realization of a macrorole argument. For English, this includes omitting it ((36c)), or realizing it in a *by*-PP as in (36b). In both (36b) and (36c), the actor (*Jack*) is modulated. Semantically, however, *Jack*, is still the instigator in the LS, meaning that the instrument does not change semantically or syntactically. Essentially, the same constructional schema can be posited as for ordinary passives, proposed by Van Valin (2005: 132). No reference is made to the instrument, resulting in the standard application of the linking algorithm. In other words, the occurrence of the instrument follows from general principles and does not need to be specified in any way. The schema for a plain English passive (in an adapted form) is given in table 28.

8.3 Passive construction with an instrument

Construction: English passive construction	
Syntax:	template: -1 core slots
	PSA: Undergoer arg. in terms of AUH
	Linking: (1) PSA modulation (voice)
	(2) Arg. modulation: Actor arg. omitted or in peripheral *by*-PP
Morphology:	Verb: Past participle
	AUX: *be*
Semantics:	PSA is not instigator of state of affairs but affected by it
Pragmatics:	IF: unspecified
	Focus structure: no restrictions; PSA = topic (default)

Table 28: English passive construction.

Sentences including implements can also be passivized:

(37) a. *Abdul ate soup with a spoon.*
 b. *Soup was eaten by Abdul with a spoon.*
 c. **do**′ (Abdul, [**eat**′ (Abdul, soup) ∧ **use**′ (Abdul, spoon)])
          A   U   NMR

Similar to instruments, the implement is not affected by any element in the constructional schema. As both instruments and implements are unaffected by passivization, the plain constructional schema suffices. Even though it bears a slightly different name, the schema in table 28 is the basic one for English. In Dutch, passivizing the sentence with an instrument is only really acceptable if the passive agent is not omitted ((38b)). This information can be stored in a schema, detailing that the passive agent *must* (or *should*) be present. The sentences in (38) are the Dutch versions of those in (36).

(38) a. Jan   vel-de   de   boom   met
        Jan   cut down-PST.3SG   DEF   tree   with
        een   bijl.
        INDEF axe

345

b. De   boom werd   ge-vel-d
   DEF   tree   AUX\PST.3SG   PTCP-cut down-PTCP
   door   Jan   met   een   bijl.
   through   Jan   with   INDEF   axe
c. */?De boom werd   ge-vel-d
   DEF   tree   AUX\PST.3SG   PTCP-cut down-PTCP
   met   een   bijl.
   with   INDEF   axe

8.4 Passive ISA construction

In chapter 6, an approach to ISA as a construction was explored. Following general construction grammar practice, I assume that constructions can be combined into more complex constructions that compound the characteristics of their components. A typical ISA example from chapter 6 has been repeated in (39).

(39) a. *Jack cut the bread with the knife.*
      b. [**do'** (Jack, Ø)] CAUSE [[**do'** (knife, Ø)] CAUSE
             A+PSA   NMR
          [BECOME **cut'** (bread)]]
                  U
      c. *The knife cut the bread.*
      d. [**do'** (Ø, Ø)] CAUSE [[**do'** (knife, Ø)] CAUSE [BECOME
          cut' (bread)]]   A+PSA
                  U

The passivized version of ISA is just that: It is essentially an ISA-construction (see table 22) combined with the passive construction as it was given in table 28. Rather than selecting the actor-argument, the undergoer is selected as the PSA. This is given in (40).

(40) a. *The bread was cut by the knife.*
      b. [**do'** (Ø, Ø)] CAUSE [[**do'** (knife, Ø)] CAUSE [BECOME
          cut' (bread)]]   A
                U+PSA

My informants are divided with respect to the acceptability of the passive ISA construction. Only slightly more than half the native speakers accept it. Assuming that the construction is possible, its constructional schema is given in table 29.

Construction: English passive instrument as actor construction	
Syntax:	template: -1 core slots
	PSA: Undergoer arg. in terms of AUH
	Linking: (1) PSA modulation (voice)
	(2) Arg. modulation: Actor arg. omitted or in peripheral *by*-PP
Morphology:	PSA: no explicit morphology
	Verb: Past participle
	AUX: *be*
Semantics:	(1) x-argument of initial **do´** is unspecified
	(2) Actor-macrorole is assigned to highest specified x-argument of **do´**
	(3) highest specified x-argument of **do´** must have minimum actional status as defined by the argument position
	(4) PSA is not instigator of state of affairs but affected by it
Pragmatics:	(1) Undergoer is topic, instrument-effector is backgrounded
	(2) Natural Event Condition must be met

Table 29: English passive instrument as actor construction.

8.5 Instrument unaccusative construction

Webb (2008: 71ff.) explores an instrument-like construction which he calls the *instrument unaccusative construction*, which has hardly been discussed in the literature at all. An example is given in (41a). It is necessary to point out that, by a large margin, more than half of the native speakers I consulted unambiguously reject this construction. This could

8 Linking semantics to syntax

account for the sporadic attention in the literature for it. Furthermore, it does not fit naturally with the theory of instruments in general and with RRG. Nevertheless, as the construction is discussed in the literature and considered grammatical by a not insignificant number of people, I will follow Webb's own native speaker judgments and provide an RRG-based account. As the name implies, it is essentially an unaccusative construction with an instrument. Consider:

(41) a. *The door opened with the key.* (Webb 2008: 71)
 b. *The door opened.*
 c. BECOME **open**′ (door)
 d. *John opened the door with the key.*
 e. *John acted on the key, causing it to open the door.*
 f. [**do**′ (John, Ø)] CAUSE [[**do**′ (key, Ø)] CAUSE [BECOME **open**′ (door)]]

I assume that the more basic (41b) is an intransitive accomplishment as it passes the relevant aktionsart-tests. The corresponding LS is given in (41c). In the sentence in (41d), *key* is clearly an instrument as it passes the relevant paraphrase ((41e)). The corresponding LS is given in (41f). The occurrence of an instrument in (41a) is somewhat confusing when contrasting it to (41e) and (41f). As RRG does not posit deletions or similar devices, the LSs and the linkings in (42) are inadmissible for (41a).

(42) a. [**do**′ (Ø, Ø)] CAUSE [[**do**′ (key, Ø)] CAUSE [BECOME
 open′ (door)]]   A+PSA
           U
 b. [**do**′ (John, Ø)] CAUSE [[**do**′ (key, Ø)] CAUSE
            A   NMR
 [BECOME **open**′ (door)]]
         U+PSA
 c. [**do**′ (Ø, Ø)] CAUSE [[**do**′ (key, Ø)] CAUSE [BECOME
 open′ (door)]]   A
 U + PSA
 d. *The key opened the door.*
 e. *The door was opened with the key by John.*
 f. *The door was opened by the key.*

8.5 Instrument unaccusative construction

g. *[**do**′ (Ø, Ø)] CAUSE [[**do**′ (key, Ø)] CAUSE [BECOME
   open′ (door)]]   NMR
   A

The LS in (42a) links to the ISA-sentence in (42d), (42b) links to the passive instrument construction in (42e) and the LS in (42c) links to the passive version of ISA in (42f). The LS in (42g) is incorrect because it violates the AUH. A reasonable solution for (41a) is to posit the base LS in (41c), but with *key* included. The only plausible way to do this is to include an implement, as the causal paraphrase cannot even be applied due to verb's intransitivity. Consider the LS for (41a) in (43a) and a second example and its LS ((43b–43c)).

(43) a. BECOME **open**′ (door) ∧ **do**′ (Ø, [**use**′ (Ø, key)])
     b. *The window broke with a hammer.* (Chomsky 1972: 170)
     c. BECOME **broken**′ (window) ∧ **do**′ (Ø, [**use**′ (Ø, hammer)])

The implement-section of the LS has to include an activity-component as implements can only be added to activity predicates. The x-argument of **do**′ and **use**′ is unspecified. The marking of the implement is captured by the rule in (5): In (43c), *hammer* cannot be assigned actorhood. From the point of view of the whole LS, that would violate the AUH as the 'actor' ranks lower than the undergoer. If one were to argue that the second **do**′ is sufficient to produce a 'new' actor, then the linking would assign it the PSA and link it to a plain transitive sentence with a causal chain. I assume, following the practice of the previous sections that MR-assignment concerns the whole chain including the *use*-predicate. In this case, the intransitive nature of (43b) prohibits an actor, leaving the x-argument of **do**′ unspecified. There are two potential candidates for undergoerhood (*window* and *hammer*). As *window* is selected, *hammer* is marked by *with* as the rule in (5) would predict. At this point, I wish to reiterate that many native speakers of English do not accept this construction. In Dutch ((44a–44b)) and German ((44c–44d)), this construction is utterly ungrammatical.

(44) a. *De   deur open-de   zich met de   sleutel.
         DEF   key   open-PST.3SG   REFL with DEF   key
         'The door opened with the key.'
    b. *Het raam   brak   met de   hamer.
         DEF window break\PST.3SG   with DEF hammer
         'The window broke with the hammer.'
    c. *Die   Tür öffne-te   (sich) mit dem
         DEF   door open-PST.3SG   (REFL) with DEF
         Schlüssel.
         key
         'The door opened with the key.'
    d. *Das Fenster   zerbrach   mit dem Hammer.
         DEF window   break\PST.3SG   with DEF hammer.
         'The window broke with the hammer.'

8.6 Middle construction with an instrument

In chapter 6, the difference between ability-readings and middle constructions was addressed. The middle construction I explored did not feature an instrument, yet it is sometimes possible to include one. I have given a more basic middle construction in (45a) with its LS in (45b). Due to RRG's inherent flexibility, including an instrument is unproblematic as the example in (45c) and its LS in (45d) illustrate.

(45) a. *This glass breaks easily.*
    b. **be'** ([[**do'** (Ø, Ø)] CAUSE [BECOME **broken'** (glass)]], [**easy'**])
    c. *This glass breaks easily with a hammer.*
       (Schäfer 2008: 2)
    d. **be'** ([[**do'** (Ø, Ø)] CAUSE [[**do'** (hammer, Ø)] CAUSE [BECOME **broken'** (glass)]]], [**easy'**])

The x-argument of **be'** has been expanded into a full causal chain, albeit with an unspecified instigator. Why do I posit a causal chain here but not in the LS for (41a)? There are two reasons for this: First, the 'unaccusative' construction does not imply an instigator, whereas the middle construction, by its very nature, does (Stalmaszczyk 1993: 135). This is also evidenced by Van Valin & LaPolla's (1997: 417) proposal to include an unspecified x-argument of the initial **do'**. Second, the aktionsart tests clearly identify the 'unaccusative' *open* as an accomplishment, whereas the transitive *break* tests as a causative accomplishment.

Middle constructions with implements are not as prevalent. Consider:

(46) a. ?*This book reads easily with glasses.*
 b. ?*This soup eats easily with a spoon.*
 c. ?*These birds are easily watched with binoculars.*

One reason for this is that base LSs of the verbs do not have the full causal structure that the ones in (45) have. As was explored in section 8.2.1, implements are licensed by the telic quale of the referent. It appears that this quale-based licensing is not readily compatible with middle constructions. It can be theorized that LSs functioning as arguments of middle constructions cannot take non-causal LS expansions like **use'** or **be-with'**. Attempts to include the latter also produces questionable results:

(47) a. **This glass breaks easily with the goldfish.*
 b. ??**be'** ([[**do'** (Ø, Ø)] CAUSE [BECOME **broken'** (glass)]], [**easy'**]) ∧ **be-with'** (goldfish, glass)
 c. ??**be'** ([[**do'** (Ø, Ø)] CAUSE [BECOME **broken'** (glass)]], [**easy'**]) ∧ **be-with'** (goldfish, [[**do'** (Ø, Ø)] CAUSE [BECOME **broken'** (glass)]])

Typical comitatives are obviously incompatible with middle constructions, as they are by definition without an instigator. Middle constructions are much less common (and acceptable) in Dutch than in English and the inclusion of an instrument is quite ungrammatical:

(48) a. *Dit glas breek-t makkelijk.*
 DEM glass break-PRS.3SG easily
 'This glass breaks easily.'

b. *Dit   glas   breek-t   makkelijk met
   DEM   glass   break-PRS.3SG easily   with
   een   hamer.
   INDEF hammer
   'This glass breaks easily with a hammer.'
c. ??Dit   boek   lees-t   makkelijk.
   DEM   book   read-PRS.3SG easily
   'This book reads easily.'
d. *Dit   boek   lees-t   makkelijk met
   DEM   book   read-PRS.3SG easily   with
   een   bril.
   INDEF glasses
   'This book reads easily with glasses.'

8.7 Impossible structures

In this section, I briefly discuss two impossible sentences featuring instruments. The reason for their impossibility is found in the logical structures, and more precisely, in violations of linking principles. Consider:

(49) a. *The key opened the door by Jack. (Webb 2008: 67)
     b. [**do**′ (Jack, Ø)] CAUSE [[**do**′ (key, Ø)] CAUSE
        [BECOME **open**′ (door)]]
     c. The door was opened by Jack with the key.

In (49a), PSA-assignment is violated. The PSA is assigned to the instrument argument. This is only possible if the highest-ranking argument (*Jack*) is omitted from the LS, which would constitute a case of ISA. By keeping the slot lexically filled, either it or the lowest-ranking argument can be assigned the PSA. The latter option is given in (49c). As *key* is neither the highest nor the lowest argument in (49a), it cannot be selected as PSA. In other words, English does not allow intermediate effectors to be selected as PSA if the instigator is lexically filled. It is true that English generally does not allow NMRs as PSA, but there are some varieties of English that do (Hudson 1992: 257). An example of this is given in (50e).

(50) a. *Todd gave the pad to Michael.*
A+PSA   U   NMR
b. *Todd gave Michael the pad.*
A + PSA   U   NMR
c. *The pad was given to Michael by Todd.*
U+PSA   NMR   A
d. *Michael was given the pad by Todd.*
U + PSA   NMR   A
e. *The pad was given Michael by Todd.*
NMR + PSA   U   A

In (50c), the undergoer is assigned PSA-hood as it is the passivized version of (50a). The example in (50d) has the added complexity that it has undergone dative shift. In other words, (50d) is the passivized version of (50b), rather than of (50a). The example in (50e) is also a passivized version of (50b), but with the NMR selected as PSA. This is only possible in a subset of English varieties (Hudson 1992: 257).

Examples like the one in (51a) are ungrammatical. There are two possible (but wrong) LSs for (51a). They are given in (51b–51c).

(51) a. **The key opened the door with Jack.*
b. **[**do**′ (Jack, Ø)] CAUSE [[**do**′ (key, Ø)] CAUSE
    NMR   A
[BECOME **open**′(door)]]
                U
c. **[**do**′ (key, Ø)] CAUSE [[**do**′ (Jack, Ø)] CAUSE
    A   NMR
[BECOME **open**′ (door)]]
                U

The LS in (51b) is inadmissible because the AUH is violated: The intermediate argument is selected as actor, which is not allowed. In (51c), the AUH is not violated, but actionality restrictions are violated: *Key* is simply too low on the actionality scale to occupy the initial x-argument position.

8.8 Conclusion

This chapter explored the linking of the concepts discussed in previous chapters. The central question of this chapter can therefore be stated in RRG-terms: How are the components in the LSs related to the constituent projection? I posited linking rules to account for instruments and causees in the same sentence. French was chosen as a language of illustration because 1) the relevant sentences are instances of nuclear cosubordination (i.e. they behave like simple sentences as far as linking is concerned) and 2) French has clear differential causee-marking, driven by differences in the strength of causation.

A proposal was also made to account for non-predicative *without*, which is assumed to be the marker for potential instruments, implements and the absence of an attribute. The rule governing non-predicative *without* is a very specific one and could potentially conflict with the more basic *with*-rule. To account for the ordering of both rules, I proposed to follow the Paninian principle which states that the more specific of two rules applies in case both are possible. Predicative *with* and *without*, on the other hand, are unproblematic as the occurrence of the prepositions in the morphosyntax is explained by their predicative nature.

Furthermore, I explored some of the less typical occurrences of instruments. It was shown that passives containing instruments are captured with the same constructional schema as a normal passive (at least in English) because the instrument-effector is unaffected by the construction. The passive version of ISA, on the other hand, was captured by combining the constructional schema for ISA with the basic schema for plain passives. Middle constructions with instruments are fairly straightforward as they obey the same principles as normal middle constructions. However, it was shown that middle constructions with implements are generally disfavored. An account for the instrument unaccusative construction was provided, even though this construction is

8.8 Conclusion

considered by many to be unnatural and ungrammatical. Because it receives some attention in the literature, it was investigated in this chapter.

9 Conclusion: A semantic-syntactic landscape for instruments and related concepts

In the introduction, I put forward three goals for this thesis: 1) To explore the status of instruments in linguistic theory and provide answers to problems connected to instruments, 2) to deepen RRG's approach to these concepts and 3) to contribute to the further development of RRG as a theory.

An overview of theories of instruments was presented in chapter 3 along with several problems that these analyses are confronted with. Theories of instruments are usually faced with two major problems: 1) The role is poorly defined and understudied, and, 2) ISA is an alternation that is difficult to account for in a systematic way. I have argued in favor of keeping RRG's distinction between the causally embedded *instruments* and the non-causally embedded *implements*. However, I have argued against using ISA as a diagnostic tool to distinguish between these types, as the universality of the LSs would be called into question. This makes ISA untenable as a diagnostic tool. Rather, a paraphrase was proposed (see section 9.3) that aims at making causal embedding (or the absence thereof) explicit. The exploration of instruments in chapter 3 revealed that there are several related concepts. These are either related semantically or superficially with causees as an example of the former and comitatives of the latter. In particular, the logical structures and RRG's linking algorithm (as explored in chapter 2) were used to capture these phenomena. In doing so, I deepened RRG's account of instruments and at the same time contributed to its ongoing development: I introduced the actionality scale as an addition to qualia theory, provided updated versions of predicative *with* and *without* (cf. Farrell 2009) and I drew up linking rules for causees taking instruments (in simple cores). In addition, variations to established phenomena, such as comitatives, were explored. In the introduction, it was established that instruments are intimately connected to the concept of causation. To explore the nature of causation in relation to instruments, a proposal was made to integrate Force Dynamics with RRG's logical structures. I attempted to merge these frameworks by treating the variables in the LSs as participants in a force dynamic-configuration. In turn, the subevents in the causal chain can feature as the participants in a higher-level configuration. This latter approach played a crucial role in my analysis of the semantics behind the non-causally embedded implement. In particular, a very specific type of causation called *helping* (cf. Wolff 2014, Talmy 2000) was posited.

The actionality scale was introduced primarily to analyze the behavior of instruments and implements in terms of a revised form of animacy, combined with *autonomy*. Simply put, *autonomy* refers to the degree of control a referent requires to perform an action. The actionality scale is an axis-system that uses the animacy and autonomy hierarchies as axes. This allows one to situate referents in *regions* of semantic space and allows for a characterization of the portions of semantic space that argument slots in the LS have access to. For instance, instigator argument slots in the causal chain typically require referents that rank higher on the actionality scale.

Actionality is central in the explanation of the instrument-subject alternation. In addition to causal embedding, ISA can only take place if the argument's referent is high enough on the actionality scale relative to the predicate's requirements. The occurrence of ISA is also contextually governed. I argued in favor of a new type of naturalness condition to rule out implausible instigators. If there is no plausible instigator, then the referent in question occupies the initial position in the LS and it is not under the scope of some kind of implicit instigator. It was also illustrated that ISA is strongly language-specific. Some languages disallow the construction completely (e.g. Japanese) whereas some allow for it fairly productively (e.g. English). Still others (e.g. German) allow for a phenomenon that is superficially similar to ISA, but in fact expresses the *ability* of a referent to perform an action. In addition to an account for

ISA in terms of a constructional schema, I proposed an ability-operator and a generic operator in the LS to capture phenomena superficially similar to ISA.

The nature of the argument's causal relationship with the other components of the LS plays an important role with respect to the distinction between instruments and implements. In addition to maintaining RRG's distinction between implements and instruments, I have argued that implements are arguments whose embedding subevent has a very specific causal relationship with another subevent. This relationship has been called *helping* and a very specific force dynamic configuration was proposed for it (figure 47). In addition, four generalized causative relations were posited as neutralizations of more basic causation types as proposed by Talmy (2000). These relations were introduced to replace the single causal operator CAUSE with four more specific operators, thereby providing a more detailed, practical account of causation that can directly be used in the logical structures. For example, instruments are always under the scope of the strongest type of causation, *direct causation*. Causees, by contrast, can be under the scope of both direct and indirect causation. A reason for this is the semantic status of their referents: Causees are typically human and anthropomorphic entities rank near the top of the actionality scale. Instruments, on the other hand, rank much lower on the actionality scale. Thus, certain portions of semantic space seem to correlate with the type of causation that such arguments are found under the scope of. Roughly speaking, higher-ranking referents will be under the scope of direct causation less often than lower-ranking ones.

9.1 Summary of instrument-like concepts

I have explored several related concepts: instruments, implements, causees, forces, pseudo-agents, comitatives, inanimate comitatives, false inanimate comitatives and potentials. These concepts were explored either because 1) they are semantically related or 2) their expressions consistently share marking cross-linguistically with each other. A summary of the concepts explored in this dissertation is given in table 30. It lists the concepts with a general classification, a typical actionality level

9 Conclusion: A semantic-syntactic landscape for instruments and related concepts

(if applicable) and the canonical LS-configuration the concept occurs in or with. Ranges of actionality levels are difficult to indicate precisely. Therefore, broad labels have been given.

	Classification	Actionality	Canonical LS-configuration
Instrument	Effector subtype	Low-Mid	CAUSE [**do**′ (x, Ø)] ...
Implement	y-argument of **use**′	Low-Mid	∧ **use**′ (x, y)
Causee	Effector subtype	High	CAUSE/IND [**do**′ (x, Ø)] ...
Force	Effector subtype	Para-autonomous	[**do**′ (x, Ø)] CAUSE...
Pseudo-agent	Class of referent	Mid-high	[**do**′ (x, Ø)] CAUSE... CAUSE [**do**′ (x, Ø)] ...
Comitative	Linking option	High	(x ∧ y)
Undergoer comitative	Linking option	Low-Mid	(x ∧ y)
NMR comitative	Linking option	Variable	(x ∧ y)
Inanimate comitative	Spatio-temporal co-occurrence	Low-Mid	∧ **be-with**′ (z, x)
False inanimate comitative	Phrasal extraposition	Variable	**have**′ (x̲, y)
Potential comitative	Non-occurrent	Variable	∧ NOT **be-with**′ (z, x)
Potential implement	Negated y-argument of **use**′	Low-Mid	∧ NOT **use**′ (x, y)

Potential instrument	Negated y-argument of use′	Low-Mid	∧ NOT **use**′ (x, y)
Potential false inanimate comitative	Phrasal extraposition	Variable	NOT **have**′ (x̠, y)
Conjoined instrument (symmetrical)	Double effector	Low-Mid	CAUSE [**do**′ (x ∧ y, Ø)] ...
Conjoined instrument (asymmetrical)	Double effector	Low-mid	CAUSE [**do**′ (x ∧ y, Ø)] ... + Qualia annotation
Conjoined implement	Double y-argument of use′	Low-mid	∧ **use**′ (x, y ∧ z)
ISA	Construction	Predicate dependent	Initial x-argument unspecified (see schema)
Ability reading	Construction	Irrelevant	Obligatory *ABIL*-operator in LS (see schema)
Generic reading	Construction	Irrelevant	Obligatory *GEN*-operator in LS (see schema)

Table 30: Overview of concepts explored in this dissertation.

9.2 Summary of expanded causation

Apart from the concepts summarized in table 30, I have explored causation from the point of view of Force Dynamics. More specifically, I have argued in favor of recognizing four types of causation, represented with different operators in the logical structures, defined over two independent features. A summary of this is given in table 31.

	[+direct]	[-direct]
[+impingement]	Direct (CAUSE)	Indirect (IND)
[-impingement]	Enabling (LET)	Permissive (ALLOW)

Table 31: Matrix table of causation types.

Table 31 summarizes the interaction between the two participants relevant in Force Dynamics: the *agonist* and *antagonist*. [±direct] refers to the nature of the interaction: Is the interaction direct or indirect? A prototypical example of the former would be direct physical manipulation of an antagonist with respect to an agonist (say, a lumberjack wielding an axe). Indirect forms of causation include verbal commands or psychosocial pressure. [+impingement] refers to whether the interaction between the two participants is permanent or begins, whereas [-impingement] refers to the absence or cessation of interaction. Each type of causation in table 31 has a characteristic, corresponding force dynamic configuration. These were given in figure 49. If the nature of causation is kept underspecified I proposed to use the italicized operator *CAUSE*. The type of causation called *helping* is not included in the matrix of causation types. Rather, it is considered much weaker than the types summarized in table 31. Figure 51 illustrated this graphically: *Helping* occupies one end of the scale whereas direct, indirect, enabling and permissive causation occupy the other (stronger) end of the scale.

9.3 Overview of tests

Throughout this dissertation, I have proposed and employed a number of diagnostics. Many tests (e.g. aktionsart-tests) are commonly used in the literature and in RRG. They will not be repeated here. The most prominent diagnostic in this thesis is the one that identifies instruments, setting them apart from implements. It is given in (1a). I have argued against using ISA as a test. Rather, the test in (1a) essentially makes the logical structure explicit in that it provides a direct translation of it. The assumed causal embedding of the target argument is explicitly tested for.

If the argument in question passes the test, then the target is meaningfully causally embedded and it is an instrument-effector. If it does not, there is no causal embedding and the target argument is an implement. That is, it is a y-argument of a **use**′-predicate and not an effector. The test in (1a) positively identifies instruments and negatively identifies implements. To positively identify implements, two tests can be used in conjunction. They are given in (1b–1c). The test in (1b) separates the use of the target argument from the other subevent(s). As the subevent containing instruments cannot be meaningfully separated from the rest, this generates bizarre results in the case of instruments, thereby negatively identifying them. The use of 'and simultaneously' can thus also be considered as a method to make the relevant section of the LS explicit. The test in (1c) isolates the more fundamental *helping*-type causation. The choice of verb is important in this respect as *facilitate* seems to be a purer reflection of the underlying force dynamic-configuration than, for example, *help*. Instruments fail this test, because they are not involved in helping causation. Rather, they are under the scope of direct causation.

(1) a. X acted on Y, causing it to V.
 b. X V-ed and simultaneously used Y.
 c. Y facilitated the V-ing.

The main tests to identify the prototypical comitatives test for what has been termed *co-authorhood*. Consider:

(2) a. X and Y V-ed.
 b. X V-ed with Y.
 c. Y V-ed with X.

The test in (2a) tests whether both components can occur as a conjoined actor. This is only possible if the actionality of both referents is similar enough. The ability to occur with alternative coding is tested for by (2b–2c), along with the interchangeability of the arguments. If the tests in (2) are passed, co-authorhood is present. The ability to occur with alternative coding ((2b–2c)) is only possible if the actionality status of the referents is almost identical (cf. chapter 4). In case of undergoer- and NMR-comitatives, the test in (2a) is irrelevant as it tests for the ability to occur as an actor. However, similar tests can be easily derived that follow the same line of thought: The arguments in question must be able to occupy the same position in the logical structures. In case of undergoer-comitatives, for example, both components must be able to receive the undergoer macrorole separately and when conjoined. In addition, they must be interchangeable without a difference in meaning.

As is the case with all linguistic tests, these tests have to be adapted to the language under investigation. For instance, English has a verb that very specifically conveys the *helping*-relation (*facilitate*). Dutch, by contrast, does not have a direct equivalent.

9.4 Future research

The primary goal of this dissertation has been the exploration of a set of concepts at the syntax-semantics interface. Throughout this dissertation, examples have been drawn from a modest set of languages. A logical extension of this work is to perform a comprehensive survey of these phenomena in a much larger selection of languages. Because most investigated languages are Indo-European, exploring the other macro-families is an interesting and necessary new perspective.

In section 4.5, I proposed a very preliminary multiple inheritance hierarchy analysis of the semantic range that the actionality scale captures. The tree-structure in figure 38 can serve as a starting point to translate the actionality scale into the CRC's frame model. Furthermore, the hierarchy is potentially well-suited for an optimality theoretical approach. Optimality theory could prove to be an invaluable method to determine which concepts and features take priority. Using optimality theory, it could be determined whether or not argument positions are more sensitive to particular features than to others. For example, can one feature be sufficient for the referent to fill the slot under investigation? If there are several defining features (e.g. [+sentient] and [+organization]), is one of them a sufficient criterion for the argument slot or are both required? In other words, do some features outrank others? A frame approach could then be used to discover *why* such priority relations exist. Are there further entailment relations? For instance, does [+organization] always entail that the referent is [+animate]?

A third interesting avenue for future research is the integration of the force dynamic configurations proposed in this dissertation into the frame semantic approach as developed in the CRC 991. As Löbner (2014, 2015) considers frames to be the universal format of human cognition, how can FD-configurations be translated into frames? Is each of the participants simply a node in the frame? If yes, how can the concept of open-ended generativity be accounted for? How can the features of [±impingement] and [±direct] be translated? Furthermore, as instruments and implements are distinguished over different types of causation and as there is cross-linguistic evidence to support the instrument-implement distinction, some difference in the frames must present itself.

The integration of Force Dynamics and RRG proposed in this dissertation is by no means exhaustive or final. It is a useful proposal to capture the behavior of instruments and implements but there is still a great deal of work to be done before the integration of these frameworks can be considered complete. For instance, the notions of permissive and enabling causation were not directly relevant for the topic of this dissertation. Apart from drawing up a configuration for them, they were only explored to a limited degree. Likewise, the neutralization of the subtypes of causation to the generalized causative relations (figure 50) is only a first step and needs to be explored in more detail. Are all the basic causative types Talmy proposes distinct from one another? Is there overlap between them? Furthermore, are there cross-linguistic correlations as far as juncture-nexus relations are concerned in connection to the four GCRs? For instance, are permissive and enabling causation always expressed with weaker linkage than direct and indirect causation? Do languages exhibit major marking differences between direct and indirect causation on the one hand and permissive and enabling causation on the other?

This dissertation set out to resolve some of the longstanding, but understudied issues concerning instruments, especially the instrument-subject alternation. Using RRG and Force Dynamics, I have provided a proposal that captures the behavior of instruments with respect to ISA.

9 Conclusion: A semantic-syntactic landscape for instruments and related concepts

Furthermore, the integration of FD and RRG has allowed for an alternative analysis of the weaker causal relation that the implement has with the rest of the logical structure.

Appendix: Figures

This appendix contains three figures that were too cumbersome and large to be integrated into the main text. The numbering of the figures has been kept in line with that of the others, so as to maintain text-internal consistency.

Figure 20 is Van Valin and Wilkins' (1996: 314–315) representation of the relation between agency and the referent's properties. It employs two interrelated, yet distinct hierarchies (Van Valin and Wilkins 1996: 313 & 316): 1) a *saliency hierarchy* which ranks entities according to the likelihood of them being interpreted as agent when placed in an actional event and 2) an *animacy hierarchy* with various degrees of animate entities (with prototypical animates near one end of the scale).

Figure 29 represents one of Grimm's (2005 & 2013) two proposed lattices. He posits a more basic agency lattice and an agency-animacy lattice, the latter being a combination of the former with a typical animacy hierarchy. The agency lattice is compiled from the features *instigation, motion, sentience, volition* and *persistence*, some of which are inspired by Dowty's proto-role properties (Grimm 2005: 20). The agency lattice is given in figure 29. Figure 30 is the combined *agency-animacy lattice*. For the construction of the animacy hierarchy, Grimm proposes a combination of features, compiled into a lattice-like structure (Grimm 2013: 5–6).

Appendix

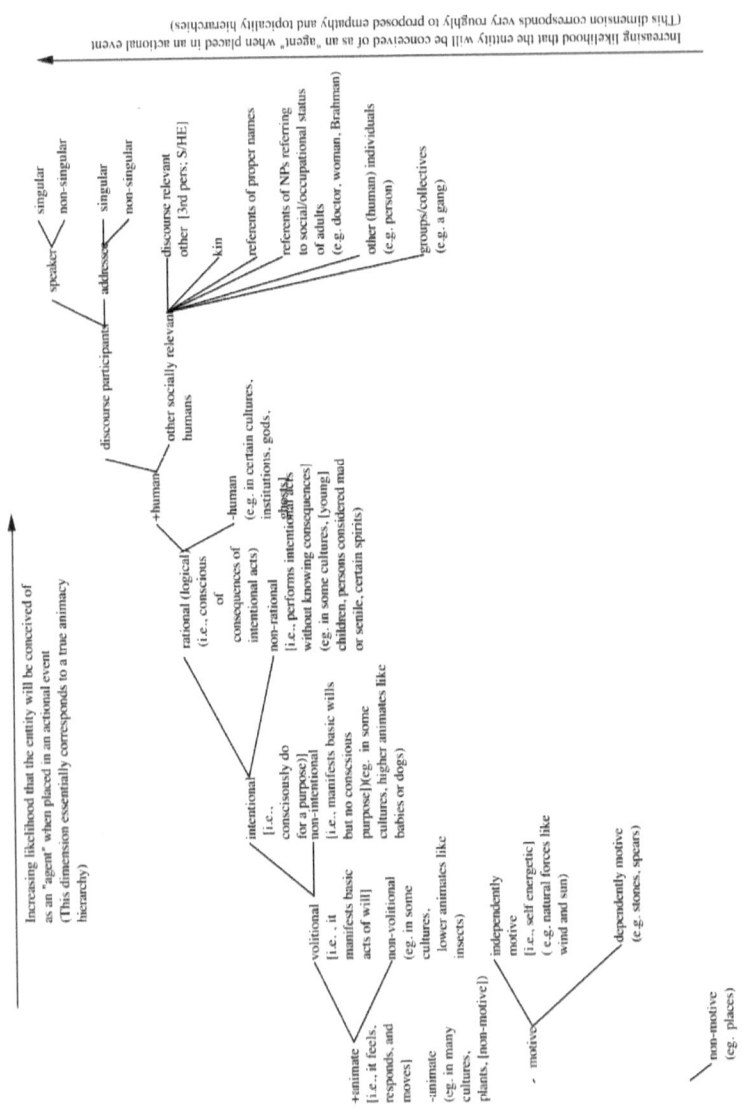

Figure 20: Top section of the saliency scale proposed by Van Valin & Wilkins (1996: 314-315).

Appendix

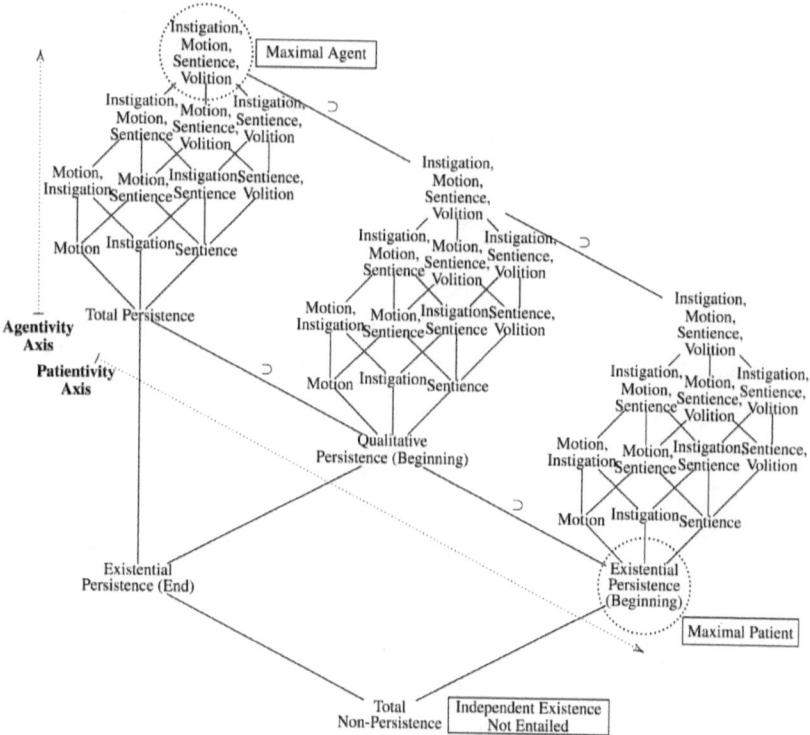

Figure 29: Grimm's (2013: 4) agency lattice.

Appendix

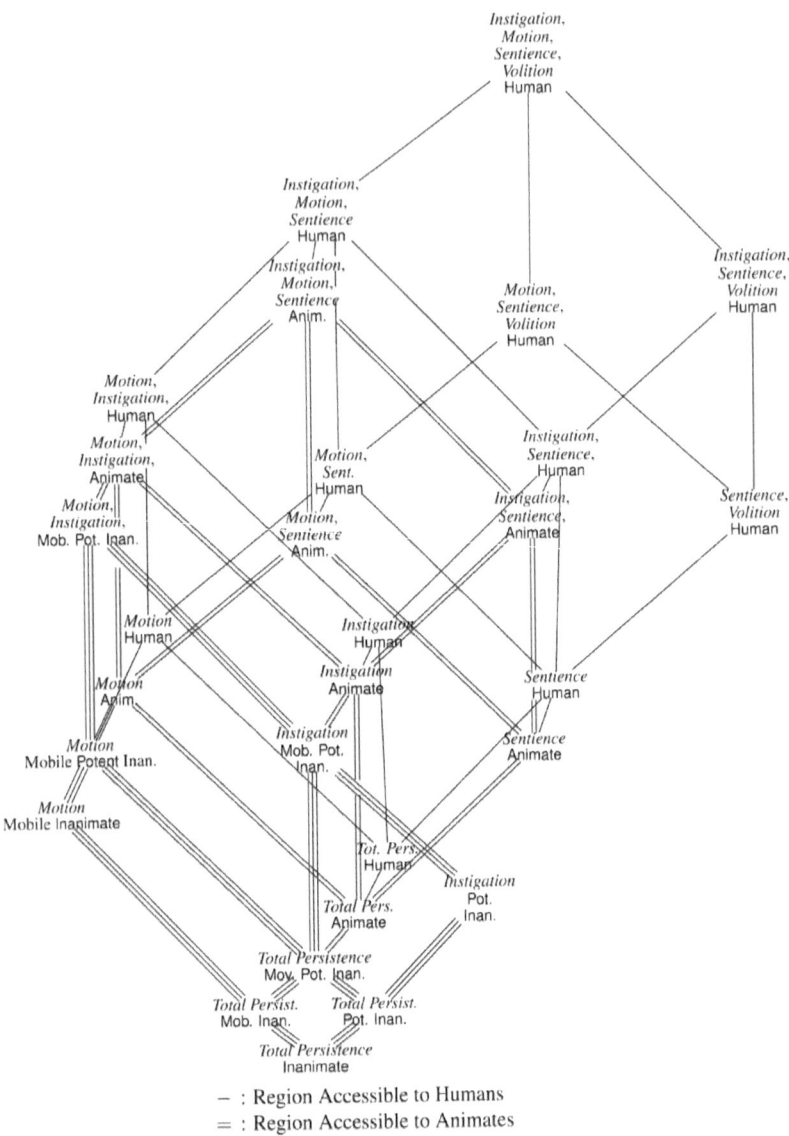

Figure 30: The combined agency-animacy lattice (Grimm 2013: 6).

References

Aissen, J. (2003). Differential Object Marking: Iconicity vs. Economy. *Natural Language & Linguistic Theory*, 21(3), pp. 435–483.

Alexiadou, A.; Schäfer, F. (2006). Instrument Subjects are Agents or Causers. In D. Baumer; D. Montero; M. Scanlon (Eds.), *Proceedings or the 25th West Coast Conference on Formal Linguistics* (pp. 40–48). Somerville, MA: Cascadilla Proceedings Project.

Anderson, J. M. (1977). On Case Grammar: Prolegomena to a Theory of Grammatical Relations. London: Croom Helm Humanities Press.

Anderson, J. M. (2006). Case grammar. In *Encyclopedia of language and linguistics. 2nd ed.* (pp. 220–233). Amsterdam: Elsevier.

Anderson, S. R. (1971). On the Role of Deep Structure in Semantic Interpretation. *Foundations of Language*, 6, pp. 197–219.

Asudeh, A.; Toivonen, I. (2012). Lexical-Functional Grammar. In B. Heine; H. Narrog (Eds.), *The Oxford Handbook of Linguistic Analysis* (pp. 1–26).

Barsalou, L. W. (1992). Frames, concepts, and conceptual fields. In A. Lehrer; E. F. Kittay (Eds.), *Frames, fields, and contrasts: New essays in semantic and lexical organization* (pp. 21–74). Hillsdale, NJ: Lawrence Erlbaum Associates.

Bibović, L. (1976). On the Notion of Body Part Instrument. *Folia Linguistica*, 9.1.4, pp. 311–324.

Bierwisch, M. (2006). Thematic roles - universal, particular, and idiosyncratic aspects. In I. Bornkessel; M. Schlesewsky; B. Comrie; A. D. Friederici (Eds.), *Semantic Role Universals and Argument Linking. Theoretical, Typological, and Psycholinguistic Perspectives* (pp. 89–126). Berlin: Mouton de Gruyter.

References

Bills, G.; Vallejo C. B.; Troike, R. C. (1969). *Introduction to Spoken Bolivian Quechua*. Austin: University of Texas Press.

Boas, F. (1911). Introduction. In F. Boas (Ed.), *Handbook of American Indian Languages* (pp. 1–83). Washington, D.C.: Smithsonian Institution.

Boersma, P.; Weenink, D. (2016). Praat: doing phonetics by computer [Computer program] (Version 6.0.17). Retrieved 21 April 2016 from http://www.praat.org/

Bossong, G. (2006). Meaning, form and function in basic case roles. In I. Bornkessel; M. Schlesewsky; B. Comrie; A. D. Friederici (Eds.), *Semantic Role Universals and Argument Linking. Theoretical, Typological, and Psycholinguistic Perspectives* (pp. 237–261). Berlin: Mouton de Gruyter.

Bresnan, J. (2001). *Lexical-Functional Syntax*. Oxford/Malden: Blackwell.

Bresnan, J.; Hay, J. (2008). Gradient grammar: An effect of animacy on the syntax of *give* in New Zealand and American English. *Lingua*, 118, 245–259.

Bresnan, J.; Kanerva, J. M. (1989). Locative inversion in Chichewa: a case study of factorization in grammar. *Linguistic Inquiry*, 20, pp. 1–50.

Bresnan, J.; Zaenen, A. (1990). Deep unaccusativity in LFG. In K. Dziwirek; P. Farrell; E. Meijas-Bikandi (Eds.), *Grammatical relations: A cross-theoretical perspective* (pp. 45–57). Stanford, CA: CSLI Publications.

Butt, M.; Dalrymple, M.; Frank, A. (1997). An architecture of linking theory in LFG. In M. Butt; T. H. King (Eds.), *Proceedings of the LFG97 Conference* (p. 16). Stanford: CSLI Publications.

Carlson, G. N. (1984). Thematic roles and their role in semantic interpretation. *Linguistics*, 22, pp. 259–279.

Chafe, W. (1970). *Meaning and the Structure of Language*. Chicago: University of Chicago Press.

Chierchia, G. (1984). *Topics in the Syntax and Semantics of Infinitives and Gerunds*. University of Massachusetts, Amherst, MA.

Chomsky, N. (1972). Some Empirical Issues in the Theory of Transformational Grammar. In *Studies on Semantics in Generative Grammar* (pp. 120–202). The Hague: Mouton.

Comrie, B. (1981). *Language Universals and Linguistic Typology.* Oxford: Basil Blackwell Publisher Limited.

Comrie, B. (2008). *Conventions for interlinear morphme-by-morpheme glosses.* Leipzig: Max Planck Institute for Evolutionary Anthropology. Department of Linguistics. Retrieved from http://www.eva.mpg.de/lingua/resources/glossing-rules.php. (accessed on 30.5.2016)

Copley, B.; Harley, H. (2014). Eliminating causative entailments with the force-theoretic framework. *The case of the Tohono O'odham frustrative cem.* In *Causation in Grammatical Structures* (pp. 120–151). Oxford: Oxford University Press.

Copley, B.; Wolff, P. (2014). Theories of causation should inform linguistic theory and vice versa. In *Causation in Grammatical Structures* (pp. 11–57). Oxford: Oxford University Press.

Croft, W. (1991). *Syntactic Categories and Grammatical Relations: The Cognitive Organization of Information.* Chicago and London: The University of Chicago Press.

Croft, W. (2012). *Verbs: Aspect and Causal Structure.* Oxford: Oxford University Press.

Croft, W. (2015). Force Dynamics and Directed Change in Event Lexicalization and Argument Realization. In R. G. de Almeida; C. Manouilidou (Eds.), *Cognitive Science Perspectives on Verb Representation and Processing* (pp. 103–129). New York: Springer.

Cruse, D. A. (1973). Some Thoughts on Agentivity. *Journal of Linguistics*, 9(1), pp. 11–23.

Dabrowska, E. (1998). How metaphor affects grammatical coding: the Saxon genitive in computer manuals. *English Language and Linguistics*, (2(1)), pp. 121–127.

Dahl, Ö. (2008). Animacy and egophoricity: Grammar, ontology and phylogeny. *Lingua, 118*, pp. 141–150.

Dahl, Ö.; Fraurud, K. (1996). Animacy in Grammar and Discourse. In T. Fretheim; J. K. Gundel (Eds.), *Reference and Referent Accessibility* (pp. 47–64). Amsterdam/Philadelphia: John Benjamins Publishing Company.

Dahm-Draksic, T. (1997). *A Role and Reference Grammar Analysis of Case-Marking in Croatian.* State University of New York at Buffalo. Retrieved from http://www.acsu.buffalo.edu/~rrgpage/rrg/dahm-draksic/dahmdraksicmasters.pdf

Dalrymple, M. (2001). *Lexical Functional Grammar.* New York: Academic Press.

Dalrymple, M. (2006). Lexical Functional Grammar. In K. Brown (Ed.), *Encyclopedia of language and linguistics, 2nd edition* (pp. 82–94). Oxford: Elsevier.

Davis, A. R. (2011). Thematic roles. In C. Maienborn; K. von Heusinger; P. Portner (Eds.), *Semantics* (Vol. 33.1, pp. 399–420). Berlin/Boston: Mouton de Gruyter.

DeLancey, S. (1984). Notes on Agentivity and Causation. *Studies in Language, 8(2),* pp. 181–213.

DeLancey, S. (1991). Event Construal and Case Role Assignment. *Proceedings of the Seventeenth Annual Meeting of the Berkeley Linguistics Society: General Session and Parasession on The Grammar of Event Structure,* pp. 338–353.

De Mulder, W. (2012). Force Dynamics. In D. Geeraerts; H. Cuykens (Eds.), *The Oxford Handbook of Cognitive Linguistics* (pp. 1–18). Oxford University Press. Retrieved from www.oxfordhandbooks.com

De Swart, P.; Lamers, M.; Lestrade, S. (2008). Animacy, argument structure, and argument encoding. *Lingua, 118,* pp. 131–140.

Dowty, D. R. (1979). *Word Meaning and Montague Grammar: The Semantics of Verbs and Times in Generative Semantics and in Montague's PTQ.* Dordrecht/Boston/London: Kluwer Academic Publishers.

Dowty, D. R. (1989). On the Semantic Content of the Notion of "Thematic Role." In G. Chierchia; B. H. Partee; R. Turner (Eds.), *Properties, Types, and Meaning II* (pp. 69–129). Dordrecht: Kluwer.

Dowty, D. R. (1991). Thematic proto-roles and argument selection. *Language*, 67, pp. 547–619.

Engelberg, S. (2011a). Frameworks of lexical decomposition of verbs. In *Semantics* (Vol. 33.1, pp. 358–399). Berlin/Boston: Mouton de Gruyter.

Engelberg, S. (2011b). Lexical decomposition: Foundational issues. In *Semantics* (Vol. 33.1, pp. 124–144). Berlin/Boston: Mouton de Gruyter.

Falk, Y. N. (2001). *Lexical-Functional Grammar: An Introduction to Parallel Constraint-Based Syntax*. Stanford, CA: CSLI Publications.

Farrell, P. (2009). The Preposition *with* in Role and Reference Grammar. In L. Guerrero; S. Ibáñez Cerda; V. A. Belloro (Eds.), *Studies in Role and Reference Grammar* (pp. 179–202). México: Universidad Nacional Autónoma de México.

Fauconnier, S. (2011). Differential Agent Marking and animacy. *Lingua*, 121, pp. 533–547.

Fillmore, C. J. (1968). The Case for Case. In E. Bach; R. T. Harms (Eds.), *Universals in linguistic theory* (pp. 1–88). New York: Holt, Rinehart & Winston.

Fillmore, C. J. (1969). Toward a modern theory of case. In D. A. Reibel; S. A. Schane (Eds.), *Modern studies in English* (pp. 361–375) [Reprint from: Toward a modern theory of case, Project on Linguistic Analysis, Ohio State University 13, pp. 1–24]. Englewood Cliffs, NJ: Prentice-Hall.

Fillmore, C. J. (1971a). Some problems for case grammar. In *22nd Annual Round Table. Linguistics: Developments of the Sixties - Viewpoints for the Seventies* (pp. 35–56). Washington, D.C.: Georgetown University Press.

Fillmore, C. J. (1971b). Types of Lexical Information. In D. D. Steinberg; L. A. Jakobovits (Eds.), *Semantics: An Interdisciplinary Reader in Philosophy, Linguistics and Psychology* (pp. 370–393). Cambridge, UK: Cambridge University Press.

Fillmore, C. J. (1971c). Verbs of judging. In C. J. Fillmore; D. T. Langendoen (Eds.), *Studies in linguistic semantics* (pp. 273–289). New York: Holt, Rinehart & Winston.

Fillmore, C. J. (1972). Subjects, speakers and roles. In D. Davidson; G. H. Harman (Eds.), *Semantics of natural language* (pp. 273–289). Dordrecht: Reidel.

Fillmore, C. J. (1977a). The Case for Case Reopened. *Syntax and Semantics*, pp. 59–81.

Fillmore, C. J. (1977b). Topics in lexical semantics. In R. W. Cole (Ed.), *Current issues in linguistic theory* (pp. 76–138). Bloomington: Indiana University Press.

Foley, W. A.; Van Valin, Jr., R. D. (1984). *Functional Syntax and Universal Grammar*. Cambridge: Cambridge University Press.

Foley, W. A.; Van Valin, Jr., R. D. (1985). Information packaging in the clause. *Language Typology and Syntactic Description*, pp. 282–364.

Geurts, B. (1985). Generics. *Journal of Semantics, 4(3)*, pp. 247–255.

Goldberg, A. E. (1995). *Constructions. A Construction Grammar Approach to Argument Structure.* Chicago and London: The University of Chicago Press.

Goldberg, A. E. (2003). Constructions: a new theoretical approach to language. *Trends in Cognitive Sciences, 7(5)*, pp. 219–224. Retrieved from http://doi.org/10.1016/S1364-6613(03)00080-9 (accessed on 30.5.2016)

Grewe, T.; Bornkessel, I.; Zysset, S.; Wiese, R.; von Cramon, D. Y.; Schlesewsky, M. (2006). Linguistic prominence and Broca's area: the influence of animacy as a linearization principle. *NeuroImage, 32*, pp. 1395–1402.

Grimm, S. (2005). *The Lattice of Case and Agentivity.* Universiteit van Amsterdam, Amsterdam, The Netherlands.

Grimm, S. (2013). The Bounds of Subjecthood: Evidence from Instruments. *Proceedings of the 33rd Meeting of the Berkeley Linguistic Society,* pp. 1–12.

Gruber, J. S. (1965). *Studies in lexical relations.* Massachussetts Institute of Technology, Cambridge, MA.

Guerrero, L.; Van Valin, Jr., R. D. (2004). Yaqui and the analysis of primary object languages. *International Journal of American Linguistics, 70,* pp. 290–319.

Hasagawa, Y. (1996). *A Study of Japanese Clause Linkage. The Connective TE in Japanese.* Stanford/Tokyo: CSLI Publications & Kurosio Publishers.

Heine, B.; Claudi, U.; Hünnemeyer, F. (1991). *Grammaticalization. A Conceptual Framework.* Chicago: Chicago University Press.

Heine, B.; Kuteva, T. (2006). *The Changing Languages of Europe.* Oxford/New York: Oxford University Press.

Holisky, D. A. (1987). The case of the intransitive subject in Tsova-Tush (Batsbi). *Lingua, 71,* pp. 103–132.

Hudson, R. (1992). So-Called "Double Objects" and Grammatical Relations. *Language, 68(2),* pp. 251–276.

Hyman, L. M.; Zimmer, K. (1976). Embedded Topic in French. In C. N. Li (Ed.), *Subject and Topic* (pp. 189–211). New York: Academic Press.

Jackendoff, R. (1972). *Semantic interpretation in generative grammar* (Vol. 2). Cambridge, MA: MIT Press.

Jackendoff, R. (1983). *Semantics and Cognition.* Cambridge, MA: MIT Press.

Jackendoff, R. (1987). The Status of Thematic Relations in Linguistic Theory. *Linguistic Inquiry, 18(3),* pp. 369–411.

Jackendoff, R. (1990). *Semantic Structures.* Cambridge, MA: MIT Press.

Jackendoff, R. (1991). Parts and boundaries. *Cognition, 41,* pp. 9–45.

Jackendoff, R. (2002). *Foundations of Language*. Oxford/New York: Oxford University Press.

Jackendoff, R. (2011). Conceptual Semantics. In C. Maienborn; K. von Heusinger; P. Portner (Eds.), *Semantics* (Vol. 33.1, pp. 688–709). Berlin/Boston: Mouton de Gruyter.

Jackendoff, R. (2014). Genesis of a theory of language: From thematic roles (source) to the Parallel Architecture (goal) (Sort of an intellectual memoir). Personal Website. Retrieved from http://ase.tufts.edu/cogstud/jackendoff/papers/GenesisofPA.pdf (accessed on 30.5.2016)

Jolly, J. A. (1993). Preposition Assignment in English. In R. D. Van Valin, Jr. (Ed.), *Advances in Role and Reference Grammar* (Vol. 82, pp. 275–310). Amsterdam/Philadelphia: John Benjamins Publishing Company.

Kallmeyer, L.; Osswald, R. (2013). Syntax-driven semantic frame composition in Lexicalized Tree Adjoining Grammars. *Journal of Language Modelling 1, (2)*, pp. 267–330.

Kamp, H.; Rossdeutscher, A. (1994). Remarks on Lexical Structure and DRS Construction. *Theoretical Linguistics, 20 (2/3)*, pp. 97–164.

Karlsson, F. (2004). *Finnische Grammatik*. (K.-H. Rabe, Trans.) (4th ed.). Hamburg: Helmut Buske Verlag.

Kearns, K. (2000). *Semantics*. London: Macmillan.

Kemmer, S.; Verhagen, A. (1994). The grammar of causatives and the conceptual structure of events. *Cognitive Linguistics, 5*, pp. 115–156.

Kiparsky, P. (1993). Pāṇinian Linguistics. In R. E. Asher; J. M. Y. Simpson (Eds.), *The Encyclopedia of Language and Linguistics* (pp. 1918–1923). Oxford: Pergamon.

Koenig, J.-P.; Mauner, G.; Bienvenue, B.; Conklin, K. (2008). What with? The Anatomy of a (Proto)-Role. *Journal of Semantics, 25*(2), pp. 175–220.

Krifka, M. (1995). Focus and the Interpretation of Generic Sentences. In G. N. Carlson; F. J. Pelletier (Eds.), *The Generic Book* (pp. 238–264). Chicago: The University of Chicago Press.

Kuno, S. (1973). *The Structure of the Japanese Language*. Cambridge, MA: MIT Press.

Lakoff, G. (1968). Instrumental adverbs and the concept of deep structure. *Foundations of Language*, 4(1), pp. 4–29.

Lakoff, G.; Johnson, M. (1980a). Conceptual Metaphor in Everyday Language. *The Jounal of Philosophy*, 77(8), pp. 453–486.

Lakoff, G.; Johnson, M. (1980b). *Metaphors We Live By*. Chicago, London: The University of Chicago Press.

Lakoff, G. (1987). *Women, Fire, and Dangerous Things*. Chicago: The University of Chicago Press.

Langacker, R. W. (1991). *Foundations of Cognitive Grammar. Vol II: Descriptive Application*. Stanford: Stanford University Press.

Levin, B.; Rappaport Hovav, M. (2005). *Argument Realization*. Cambridge/New York: Cambridge University Press.

Löbner, S. (2014). Evidence for Frames from Human Language. In T. Gamerschlag; D. Gerland; R. Osswald; W. Petersen (Eds.), *Frames and Concept Types* (pp. 23–67). Cham/Heidelberg: Springer.

Löbner, S. (2015). Functional Concepts and Frames. In T. Gamerschlag; D. Gerland; R. Osswald; W. Petersen (Eds.), *Meanings, Frames, and Conceptual Representation* (pp. 15–42). Düsseldorf: Düsseldorf University Press.

Luraghi, S. (1995). Prototypicality and Agenthood in Indo-European. In H. Andersen (Ed.), *Historical Linguistics 1993* (pp. 259–268). Amsterdam: John Benjamins.

Luraghi, S. (2014). Plotting diachronic semantic maps: The role of metaphors. In *Perspectives on Semantic Roles* (pp. 99–150). Amsterdam/Philadelphia: John Benjamins B.V.

Lyons, J. (1968). *Introduction to Theoretical Linguistics*. London: Cambridge University Press.

Marantz, A. P. (1981). *On the Nature of Grammatical Relations*. Massachussetts Institute of Technology, Massachussetts.

Martín Arista, J. (2008). Unification and Separation in a Functional Theory of Morphology. In R. D. Van Valin, Jr. (Ed.), *Investigations of the Syntax-Semantics-Pragmatics Interface* (pp. 119–145). Amsterdam: John Benjamins.

Martín Arista, J. (2009). A Typology of Morphological Constructions. In C. S. Butler; J. Martín Arista (Eds.), *Deconstructing Constructions* (pp. 85–115). Amsterdam: John Benjamins.

Martín Arista, J. (2011). Projections and Constructions in Functional Morphology. The Case of Old English HRĒOW. *Language and Linguistics, 12(2)*, pp. 393–425.

Martín Arista, J. (2012). La morfología flexiva. In R. Mairal; L. Guerrero; C. González Vergara (Eds.), *El functionalismo en la teoría lingüística. La Gramática der Papel y la Referencia: Introduccíon, avances y aplicaciones*. Madrid: Akal.

Martin, F.; Schäfer, F. (2014). Causation at the syntax-semantics interface. In *Causation in Grammatical Structures* (pp. 209–244). Oxford: Oxford University Press.

Matasović, R. (2004). Infixed Pronouns and Case Marking in Old Irish. *RRG2004. Book of Proceedings*, pp. 181–188.

McKercher, D. A. (2003). Possessive *with* and Locative *with* in Event Semantics. *Proceedings of the Thirty-First Western Conference on Linguistics (WECOL 2002), 14*, pp. 173–179.

Miller, G. A.; Johnson-Laird, P. N. (1976). *Language and Perception*. Cambridge: Cambridge University Press.

Narrog, H. (2014). The grammaticalization chain of case functions: Extension and reanalysis of case marking vs. universals of grammaticalization. In *Perspectives on Semantic Roles* (pp. 69–97). Amsterdam/Philadelphia: John Benjamins B.V.

Nikanne, U. (1995). Action tier formation and argument linking. *Studia Linguistica, 49(1)*, pp. 1–31.

Nilsen, D. L. F. (1973). *The Instrumental Case in English: Syntactic and semantic considerations*. The Hague. Paris.: Mouton.

Nolan, B. (2010). The Layered Structure of the Modern Irish Word: An RRG Account of Derivational Morphology Based on Lexeme Constructional Schemata. *Proceedings of the 10th International Conference on Role and Reference Grammar (RRG 2009)*, pp. 228–242.

Nolan, B. (2011). Meaning Construction and Grammatical Inflection in the Layered Structure of the Irish Word: An RRG Account of Morphological Constructions. In W. Nakamura (Ed.), *New Perspectives in Role and Reference Grammar* (pp. 64–103). Newcastle upon Tyne: Cambridge Scholars Publishing.

Ono, N. (1992). Instruments: A Case Study of the Interface between Syntax and Lexical Semantics. *English Linguistics*, 9, pp. 196–222.

Osswald, R. (2002). *A Logic of Classification with Applications to Linguistic Theory*. FernUniversität Hagen.

Ostler, N.D. (1979). *Case Linking: a theory of case and verb diathesis, applied to classical Sanskrit*. Massachussetts Institute of Technology, Massachussetts.

Øvrelid, L. (2006). Towards robust animacy classification using morphosyntactic distributional features. *EACL '06 Proceedings of the Eleventh Conference of the European Chapter of the Association for Computational Linguistics: Student Research Workshop*, pp. 47–54.

Pensalfini, R. (2003). *A Grammar of Jingulu. An Aboriginal Language of the Northern Territory*. Canberra: Pacific Linguistics.

Petersen, W. (2015). Representation of Concepts as Frames. In T. Gamerschlag; D. Gerland; R. Osswald; W. Petersen (Eds.), *Meanings, Frames, and Conceptual Representation* (pp. 39–63). Düsseldorf: Düsseldorf University Press. [Reprint from: J. Skilters; F. Toccafondi; G. Stemberger (Eds.), *Complex cognition and qualitative science* (pp. 151–170). Riga: University of Latvia.]

Piñango, M. M. (2006). Thematic roles as event structure relations. In I. Bornkessel; M. Schlesewsky; B. Comrie; A. D. Friederici (Eds.), *Semantic Role Universals and Argument Linking. Theoretical, Typological, and Psycholinguistic Perspectives* (pp. 303–326). Berlin: Mouton de Gruyter.

Primus, B. (1999). *Cases and thematic roles: Ergative, accusative and active.* Tübingen: Niemeyer.

Quirk, R.; Greenbaum, S.; Leech, G.; Svartvik, J. (1972). *A grammar of contemporary English.* London: Longman.

Rosenbach, A. (2008). Animacy and grammatical variation - Findings from English genitive variation. *Lingua, 118*, pp. 151–171.

Rozwadowska, B. (1988). Thematic restrictions on derived nominals. In W. Wilkins (Ed.), *Syntax and Semantics 21: Thematic Relations* (pp. 147–165). New York: Academic Press.

Schlesinger, I. M. (1989). Instruments as agents: on the nature of semantic relations. *Journal of Linguistics, 25(1)*, pp. 189–210.

Silverstein, M. (1976). Hierarchy of features and ergativity. In R. M. W. Dixon (Ed.), *Grammatical categories in Australian languages* (pp. 112–171). Canberra: Australian National University.

Silverstein, M. (1981). Case marking and the nature of language. *Australian Journal of Linguistics, 1(2)*, pp. 227–244.

Stalmaszczyk, P. (1993). The English Middle Construction and Lexical Semantics. *Papers and Studies in Cognitive Linguistics, XXVII*, pp. 133–147.

Stassen, L. (2009). *Predicative Possession.* New York: Oxford University Press.

Stolz, T. (1996). Some Instruments are really good companions - some are not. *Theoretical Linguistics, 23*, pp. 113–200.

Stolz, T.; Stroh, C.; Urdze, A. (2013). Comitatives and Instrumentals. In M. S. Dryer & M. Haspelmath (Eds.), *The World Atlas of Language Structures Online*. Leipzig: Max Planck Institute for Evolutionary Anthropology. Retrieved from http://wals.info/chapter/52 (accessed on 22.2.2016)

Taeldeman, J. (1978). Französisch-Flämische Sprachinterferenz in Flandern. In *Ureland* (pp. 43–66).

Talmy, L. (1976). Semantic Causative Types. In M. Shibatani (Ed.), *Syntax and Semantics 6: The Grammar of Causative Constructions* (pp. 43–116). New York/San Francisco/London: Academic Press.

Talmy, L. (1988). Force dynamics in language and cognition. *Cognitive Science, 12*, pp. 49–100.

Talmy, L. (2000). *Toward a Cognitive Semantics* (Vol. 1: Concept Structuring Systems (Language, Speech and Communication)). MIT Press.

Tomasello, M. (2003). *Constructing a Language. A Usage-Based Theory of Language Acquisition*. Cambridge, Massachussetts, and London, England: Harvard University Press.

Van Valin, Jr., R. D. (1977). *Aspects of Lakhota Syntax*. University of California at Berkeley, Berkeley.

Van Valin, Jr., R. D. (1991). Another Look at Icelandic Case Marking and Grammatical Relations. *Natural Language and Linguistic Theory, 9*, pp. 145–194.

Van Valin, Jr., R. D. (1999). Generalized Semantic Roles and the Syntax-Semantics Interface. *Empirical Issues in Formal Syntax and Semantics, 2*, pp. 373–389.

Van Valin, Jr., R. D. (2001). *An Introduction to Syntax*. Cambridge: Cambridge University Press.

Van Valin, Jr., R. D. (2004). Semantic Macroroles in Role and Reference Grammar. In R. Kailuweit; M. Hummel (Eds.), *Semantische rollen* (pp. 62–82). Tübingen: Gunter Narr Verlag.

Van Valin, Jr., R. D. (2005). *Exploring the Syntax-Semantics Interface*. Cambridge: Cambridge University Press.

Van Valin, Jr., R. D. (2008). RPs and the Nature of Lexical and Syntactic Categories in RRG. In R. D. Van Valin, Jr. (Ed.), *Investigations of the Syntax–Semantics–Pragmatics Interface* (pp. 161–178). Amsterdam/Philadelphia: John Benjamins Publishing Company.

Van Valin, Jr., R. D. (2009a). Case in Role and Reference Grammar. In A. Malchukov; A. Spencer (Eds.), *The Oxford Handbook of Case* (pp. 102–120). Oxford: Oxford University Press.

Van Valin, Jr., R. D. (2009b). Privileged Syntactic Arguments, Pivots, and Controllers. In L. Guerrero; S. Ibáñez Cerda; V. A. Belloro (Eds.), *Studies in role and reference grammar* (pp. 45–68). Universidad Nacional Autónoma de México.

Van Valin, Jr., R. D. (2013). Lexical Representation, Co-composition, and Linking Syntax and Semantics. In J. Pustejovsky; P. Bouillon, H. Isahara; K. Kanzaki; C. Lee (Eds.), *Advances in Generative Lexicon Theory* (pp. 67–107). Dordrecht: Springer.

Van Valin, Jr., R. D.; LaPolla, R. (1997). *Syntax: Structure, meaning and function*. (S. R. Anderson; J. Bresnan; B. Comrie; W. Dressler; C. Ewen; R. Huddleston; ... H. Vincent, Eds.). Cambridge: Cambridge University Press.

Van Valin, Jr., R. D.; Wilkins, D. P. (1993). Predicting Syntactic Structure from Semantic Representations: *Remember* in English and its Equivalents in Mparntwe Arrernte. In *Advances in Role and Reference Grammar* (Vol. 82, pp. 499–534). Amsterdam/Philadelphia: John Benjamins Publishing Company.

Van Valin, Jr., R. D.; Wilkins, D. P. (1996). The case for "Effector": Case roles, agents and agency revisited. In M. Shibatani; S. A. Thompson (Eds.), *Grammatical Constructions: Their Form and Meaning* (pp. 289–322). Oxford University Press.

Vendler, Z. (1957). Verbs and Times. *The Philosophical Review, (66)2*, pp. 143–160.

Vendler, Z. (1967). Verbs and Times. In Z. Vendler (Ed.), *Linguistics in Philosophy* (pp. 97–121). Ithaca: Cornell University Press.

Verhagen, A.; Kemmer, S. (1997). Interaction and causation: Causative constructions in modern standard Dutch. *Journal of Pragmatics*, *27*, pp. 61–82.

Vogels, J.; Maes, A.; Krahmer, E. (2014). Choosing referring expressions in Belgian and Netherlandic Dutch: Effects of animacy. *Lingua*, *145*, pp. 104–121.

Webb, J. (2008). *Instruments in LFG's Argument-structure*. University of Oxford.

Wechsler, S. (2006). Thematic Structure. In *The Encyclopedia of Language and Linguistics* (2nd ed., pp. 645–653). Amsterdam: Elsevier.

Wojcik, R. (1976). Where Do Instrumental NPs Come From? In M. Shibatani (Ed.), *Syntax and Semantics 6: the Grammar of Causative Constructions* (pp. 165–180). New York: Academic Press.

Wolff, P. (2007). Representing Causation. *Journal of Experimental Psychology: General*, *136(1)*, pp. 82–111.

Wolff, P. (2014). Causal pluralism and force dynamics. In *Causation in Grammatical Structures* (pp. 100–119). Oxford: Oxford University Press.

Wunderlich, D. (1997). Cause and Structure of Verbs. *Linguistic Inquiry*, *28*, pp. 27–68.

Yamamoto, M. (1999). *Animacy and Reference. A cognitive approach to corpus linguistics (SLCS)*. (W. Abraham & M. Noonan, Eds.) (Vol. 46). Amsterdam/Philadelphia: John Benjamins Publishing Company.

Zaenen, A.; Carletta, J.; Garretson, G.; Bresnan, J.; Koontz-Garboden, A.; Nikitina, T.; ... Wasow, T. (2004). Animacy encoding in English: why and how. *DiscAnnotation '04 Proceedings of the 2004 ACL Workshop on Discourse Annotation*, pp. 118–125.

www.ingramcontent.com/pod-product-compliance
Lightning Source LLC
Chambersburg PA
CBHW021114300426
44113CB00006B/147